Peace making

Practicing at the Intersection of Law and Human Conflict

Peacemaking

Practicing at the Intersection of Law and Human Conflict

Douglas Noll

Foreword by Howard Zehr

Cascadia
Publishing House
the new name of Pandora Press U.S.
Telford, Pennsylvania

copublished with
Herald Press
Scottdale, Pennsylvania

Cascadia Publishing House orders, information, reprint permissions:
contact@CascadiaPublishingHouse.com
1-215-723-9125
126 Klingerman Road, Telford PA 18969
www.CascadiaPublishingHouse.com

The paper used in this publication is recycled and meets the
minimum requirements of American National Standard for Information Sciences—Permanence of Paper for Printed Library Materials, ANSI Z39.48-1984.

Where credit is not provided by context or actual credit line, charts and tables
are by Douglas Noll and are to be reproduced only by permission of the publisher. In addition, grateful acknowledgment is made to the following for materials included in this volume, used by permission, all rights reserved: pp. 49-50,
113 from *Peace Tales* (North Haven, Conn.: Linnet Press, an imprint of the Shoe
String Press, 1992); pp. 50-51, the X-Cross model and p. 77 the L. Angle model,
from E. Van De Vliert, *Complex Interpersonal Conflict Behavior: Theoretical Frontiers* (East Sussex, UK: Psychology Press, 2000); p. 172, Configuration of States
During Conflict by Noll but adapted from M. J. Horowitz, *Cognitive Psychodynamics: From Conflict to Character* (New York: John Wiley and Sons, 1998); pp.
209-210, 13 headlines from the *Fresno Bee* (1990); pp. 66ff., Ron Claasen, the
Four-Way Model of Conflict Resolution.

Library of Congress Cataloguing-in-Publication Data
Noll, Douglas, 1950-
    Peacemaking : practicing at the intersection of law and human
    conflict / Douglas Noll
      p. cm.
    Includes bibliographical references.
    ISBN 1-931038-11-2 (alk. paper)
    1. Dispute resolution (Law)--United States. 2. Reconciliation (Law)--
United States. 3. Preventive law. 4. Mediation. 5. Conflict management.
I. Title.

KF9084 .N65 2003
347.73'9--dc21

                               2002041143

12 11 10 09 08 07 06 05   10 9 8 7 6 5 4

To
my wife Jan

CONTENTS

PART FIVE: PEACEMAKING

Foreword

A LAWYER FRIEND TELLS ME ABOUT THE MALAISE affecting many in his field—a spiritual crisis, he calls it.

The daughter of a friend graduates from a prestigious law school with high marks, practices for several years, then decides that law is not for her.

A note from a judge says he is finding his work meaningless. A zealous death penalty attorney says he feels isolated from the rest of humanity.

Then there are all the nasty lawyer jokes we all hear.

What is going on?

As a practicing attorney, Douglas Noll knows what is wrong and, in this book, has part of the answer. The problem is in how we have come to conceive law, justice, and especially the lawyer's task. The solution requires us to understand not only how the legal system works but also how people work. Above all, the answer lies in a reconception of the lawyer's task and self-image.

Because the problem begins in law school, in how law students are trained, the place to start is in law school. Thus this book, designed as a text but of obvious relevance to anyone interested in the law or in conflict.

One of the primary origins and functions of law is to provide a means of managing conflict. Yet lawyers receive little training in understanding conflict, and they rarely conceive their responsibility as helping to find a peaceful resolution to conflict. It is no surprise, then, that the process of the law often actually increases conflict and creates more wounds.

Key to the problem is in how attorneys' primary task has come to be defined: as zealous advocates for their clients. Noll does not ask them to give up the role of advocate but to balance it with another role, another way of serving clients' interests: that of *peacemaker*. Someday, if we listen to him, it will be normal for lawyers to prepare not just one brief but two: a legal brief, but also a "conflict map:" an analysis of the underlying conflict and possible processes for resolving it.

This is not pie-in-the sky. I know lawyers who work in this way, and I have seen the results. New Zealand is an example of a country where lawyers' work is beginning to be reconceived like this. Here, lawyers ("youth advocates") are specially selected to be part of the restorative conferences that take the place of the courtroom for most juvenile cases. I have sat through screening interviews for attorneys who want to do this, and the interviews are tough—the bar is higher than for death penalty lawyers in this country! These youth advocates are being asked to be not only highly competent but compassionate; their task is not only to watch out for the interests of their clients, but to help the whole process of resolving the situation, for victim as well as offender. Although it would be a surprise in an American legal setting, in New Zealand it seems normal to hear a conference facilitator specifically thank a lawyer for being present "to help us through."

Another example is the pioneering work in death penalty cases called "defense-based victim outreach." While the specific work must be carried out by an independent "victim-liaison" worker, rather than by a lawyer, it grew out of the concern of death penalty lawyers to go beyond their role as advocate. To function effectively, this work requires cooperation and support from attorneys who have a vision for peacemaking.

Defense-based victim outreach has emerged as an effort to incorporate survivor's needs and concerns in the trial and outcome by giving them access to the defense as well as the prosecution. Reflecting a restorative justice perspective, this approach also seeks to encourage defendants to take appropriate responsibility in these cases. A number of plea agreements have been reached that were based on victims' needs and allowed offenders to accept responsibility. While there can be no fully happy ending in such cases, the process can reduce harm and assist victims as well as offenders on their difficult journeys.

Among lawyers today there is a movement in the legal profession today to reframe their profession to incorporate a more humanistic vision. It is still a minority movement, to be sure, but it is growing and reflects a larger concern. Various terms have been used:

wholistic law, restorative lawyering, the lawyer as healer. Noll has given us a very concrete and practical image: the lawyer as peacemaker. As I think of each of the people I mentioned above, I believe they will welcome this. I believe you will as well.

—*Howard Zehr, Harrisonburg, Virginia, is Professor of Restorative Justice in Eastern Mennonite University's graduate Conflict Transformation Program, which he co-directs. Zehr's book,* Changing Lenses: A New Focus for Crime and Justice, *has been a foundational work in the restorative justice field. Other recent publications include* Doing Life: Reflections of Men and Women Serving Life Sentences *(1996),* Transcending: Reflections of Crime Victims *(2001); and* The Little Book of Restorative Justice *(2002).*

AUTHOR'S PREFACE

*T*HIS PROJECT BEGAN with two related questions. The first question was one I posed to myself. I asked, "What material would I need and want to teach law students and lawyers how to become peacemakers?" The second question was posed to me by a number of lawyers and judges attending my mediation training courses: "What do you recommend for further reading on all of this?"

The answers to these questions could not be found in the existing literature. From my perspective, the literature was fragmented between practice and theory. The law literature focused on process, but not on technique and underlying human conflict. The negotiation and social psychology literature developed some theoretical perspectives, but did not attend to practice or process. The conflict resolution literature was either theoretical, but not practical, or practical, but not theoretical. In short, no single, integrated source of information was available for teaching principles of peacemaking to law students and lawyers. Thus, I developed the idea of an integrated textbook on peacemaking.

I take some pains to distinguish peacemaking from mediation because I believe that the reconciliation of relationships implicit in peacemaking is a higher value than the settlement of disputes. Many mediators probably should be called peacemakers, while many others should not. Peacemakers should have the knowledge, skill, and experience to reconcile relationships and settle disputes. Mediators generally have the more limited skill of settling disputes.

My view of the future of the legal profession is from the perspective of a twenty-three-year trial court veteran who has won and lost large cases before judges, juries, arbitrators, and administrative law tribunals. I believe lawyers must learn to be peacemakers. I do not advocate abandonment of the judicial system. I do urge abandon-

19

ment of the adversary ideology, an ideology not grounded in legal ethics, common sense, or fairness. In my view, litigation should be the resolution model of last resort. Lawsuits should be filed only after all other means of resolution have been exhausted.

Unfortunately, legal education perpetuates the myth that litigation is the only true, legitimate model of dispute resolution. This project is my attempt to nudge legal education off that traditional course. This is not a book about alternative dispute resolution, a term I dislike, but about primary dispute resolution or PDR. This book is designed to educate students about human conflict in a multidisciplinary approach. It then takes on conflict analysis to demonstrate that human conflict follows predictable patterns and lends itself to the same analysis as legal problems. Finally, the book considers some of the theoretical and practical issues of peacemaking.

Pedagogically, this book may be used as a principal text in a two- or three-unit law school, graduate psychology, and graduate level or upper division undergraduate conflict resolution course. In some ways it is introductory, but in others it is quite advanced.

I also wish to note the dilemma inherent in a multidisciplinary approach such as this. On the one hand, I have aimed to weave together strands of intellectual, scientific, and academic thought from a vast range of disciplines. On the other hand, I have explicitly generalized in ways with which experts in any given field might take issue. My purpose is not to explain nuances and details of each academic discipline but to provide more of a gestalt about human conflict, its relationship to law and legal disputing, and my view of the knowledge necessary to engage in peacemaking. I would lose an academic debate on fine points and distinctions in any of the disciplines I borrow from (except perhaps my own field of law). I therefore do not pretend this book is the final word in any of the disciplines I have brought together. At best, it is a summary and overview of human conflict from the perspective of a lawyer and law professor interpreting the academic disciplines that have considered it.

I have also attempted to make the text of interest and useful for the general reader curious about peacemaking. I hope that this book begins a trend toward peacemaking by providing a foundation for law students, lawyers, and all other conflict resolution professionals to understand, analyze, and transform human conflict rather than merely to settle disputes.

—*Douglas Noll*
  Fresno, California

INTRODUCTION

*T*HE LAW SCHOOL curriculum teaches critical thinking and analysis within the discipline of the American legal system. Consequently, conflicts are resolved through decision-making at the factual or evidentiary level and at the rule or legal level. Law students are taught to sort through the facts of a conflict and decide what is relevant, then decide which rules of law are applicable. By applying the rules to the facts, students are able to reach conclusions about the decisions a court might reach.

In practice, business, corporate, tax, and transactional lawyers focus on the future. They ask, How can we prevent adverse situations from arising? Or, How can we comply with the law? Trial lawyers focus on the past and the future. They ask, What happened and why? Then, How can we present our best, most persuasive case to the court? How can we prevent or hinder the other side from presenting its best case? These are important and vital questions, but do not speak to the issues of conflict resolution except through an adversarial, third party, decision-making process.

Peacemakers look at conflicts from a different perspective. In addition to considering what facts might be chosen or what rule of law may apply to formulate a decision, peacemakers consider underlying dynamics of a conflict. They might ask, What factors have caused the parties not to want to cooperate? How must party perceptions change or expand to enable seeing possibilities of collaborative problem solving? How can the parties be empowered to transform their conflict back into a profitable and rewarding relationship? Such questions are subtle and difficult because they require inferential reasoning about what is going on inside hearts and minds. Peacemaking thus requires a significantly broader view of human nature and human conflict than is afforded by traditional legal training.

Human conflict is full of paradoxes. It is simple and complex, repetitious and unique, and predictable and surprising. These paradoxes mean that technique is not sufficient without a strong theoretical background. Attending mediation classes will permit a certain level of competence in helping people settle disputes. Without a fundamental understanding of human conflict, however, these practitioners will be technicians, not peacemakers.

This book's purpose, therefore, is to introduce law students, lawyers, and other interested persons to peacemaking concepts through a multidisciplinary treatment of the field of human conflict. The book follows the classical approach to education. Classical learning is based on a particular pattern called the *Trivium* consisting of grammar, dialectic, and rhetoric. The grammar of each subject is the information within that subject and is what the subject is about. After mastering grammar, students learn dialectic, or the relationships of these particulars to one another. Finally, students learn rhetoric. That is, they learn how to practice what they have learned in an effective and coherent fashion. This pattern is not to teach everything there is to know, but rather to establish a habit of mind that instinctively knows how to recognize and deal with problems when the formal schooling process is only a faint memory.

Part One, "Lawyers as Peacemakers," starts with what is familiar to lawyers and law students. Conflict resolution systems and mediation orientations are described and analyzed. This is the grammar of process.

Part Two, "Conflict Resolution Processes," concerns the grammar of conflict by starting with the question, What is human nature? Philosophic and psychological perspectives show how scholars have debated the questions of capacity and inherency for thousands of years. Capacity means that humans have the ability or capacity to perform acts of good and acts of evil, but are not automatically predestined to either. Inherency means that humans have intrinsic attributes that, depending on one's beliefs, make for inherent goodness or inherent evilness. The debate has circled endlessly with each succeeding wave of scholars recapitulating the work of the previous wave.

With the advent of advanced brain scanning technology such as functional magnetic resonance imaging and positron emission tomography, the neurosciences have finally began to understand in detail, how human brains function. While much remains to be learned, neuropsychology has provided fascinating explanations for how the human brain perceives and processes conflict. Thus, another aspect of the grammar of conflict entails some understanding of how human brains operate. Without becoming too technical, but without losing essential accuracy, students learn about cognitive operators, the basis and purpose of emotions, and the functions of neurotransmitters and neuromodulators. From the more psychological perspective, the concepts of automaticity and schemas show how conflict behaviors are largely preconscious. One of the many conclusions drawn from the neurosciences is that humans are hard-wired identically across cultures, nations, and ethnic origins because their brains are genetically created to be the same. Consequently, core conflict behaviors are remarkably similar across humanity. For example, anger is a universal conflict emotion that can be recognized regardless of language differences. What differs between groups are the things that people disagree over and how they express their disagreement. Thus, the emergence and expression of conflict is culturally based, while the experience of conflict is similar. Understanding brain processes consequently unravels some of the mystery of conflict and shows how people are quite alike in their objective experiences.

Identity is a key psychological concept in conflict because self-esteem and self-confidence is essential to human well-being and survival. Conflict often arises because of threats to identity. Therefore, the grammar of identity is explored in personal identity theory and social identity theory. Religion is a key component of identity and the source of many conflicts. Understanding the nature of religion and formation of religious beliefs, especially through the concept of neurotheology, provides useful tools for deciphering intractable conflicts. Likewise, conflict and culture are closely linked concepts. Culture is about how people interpret information. We call something cultural when it arises from an interpretation of events, history, or experiences shared by a group of people. Different cultures imply different interpretations, and different interpretations cause conflict because of disagreement over what appears from each perspective to be truth.

In peacemaking, justice is an important consideration. But what is justice? The grammar of justice is examined through the three classical theories of justice: positivism, social good, and natural rights. Some dialectical work is also achieved from examining the relationship between justice, identity, and cooperation. Finally, the critics of informal justice are given their time to discuss the dangers of peacemaking.

The last part of the grammar of conflict concerns conflict behaviors and conflict escalation. Conflict behaviors are plotted on a grid based on the relative concern for one's own goals versus one's concerns for the other person's goals. This yields the five basic conflict behaviors of competing, avoiding, accommodating, compromising, and problem solving. Schema theory, from psychoanalysis, shows how people interpret their own and other's conflict behaviors through the use of preprogrammed scripts or schemas. Finally, escalation theories are developed to show how conflicts move dynamically from minor disagreements to violent fights.

Part Three, "Understanding Conflict," is the dialectical training of peacemaking, and concerns conflict theories and analysis. Scholars have long sought a basic theory of human conflict. While no single theory has dominated the field, several theories provide ways of understanding the causes of conflict. Another approach to conflict analysis is through game theory and the mathematical analysis of noncooperative situations. Game theory points out that, when faced with the potential for exploitation, if one guesses wrong about the other's motives, the least damaging choice will be selected rather than the most profitable choice. In addition, game theory illustrates the importance of information and describes various information conditions found in conflict. Finally, game theory, through the work of Robert Axelrod, reveals some interesting strategies of cooperation.

Part Three concludes with a logical process for performing conflict analysis through conflict mapping.

Part Four, "Conflict Analysis," concerns practice and may therefore be considered the rhetorical training in peacemaking. Peacemaking as a value-laden practice must consider the behaviors of peacemakers. Therefore, ethics and ethical problems of peacemaking are shown to be quite different from legal ethics. In addition, apology and forgiveness become important peacemaking processes. The basic concepts and the many structural, psychological, and cultural barriers to apology and forgiveness are discussed.

Without going into great practical detail, the final chapter takes up principles of peacemaking. Peacemaking can be understood as a leadership model in which the peacemaker provides important psychological services to the parties that they cannot provide themselves. Concepts such as momentum of agreement and commitments to cooperation help people to reach out to one another when their emotions are crying out for them to defend and attack. Empathic communication is described as a basic peacemaking process in terms of automatic and intentional empathy and empathic accuracy. Finally, the relationship between process choice and conflict de-escalation is discussed.

This book is an ambitious undertaking for anyone interested in peacemaking. Despite its broad scope, it cannot cover everything. However, its classical approach intends to provide a foundation for further understanding of conflict and peacemaking. By itself, this book will not turn law students or lawyers into peacemakers. Coupled with a sound mediation process class, however, this book and any course built upon it, will provide the basis for a thoroughly grounded professional practice. In addition, as an introductory text to conflict studies, this book prepares students to explore the various disciplines touching on conflict.

We move then to the grammar of human nature as the starting point on the journey into peacemaking.

Part One

The Law and Peacemaking

CHAPTER ONE

LAWYERS
AS PEACEMAKERS

*T*HE CONCEPT OF LAWYERS as peacemakers strikes many as an oxymoron. Yet even in these litigious times, lawyers do act as peacemakers in preventative law and dispute resolution. These roles, however, do not begin to realize the full potential of lawyers to transform conflicts into positive personal and social outcomes. The adversary ideology is perhaps the greatest barrier to lawyers viewing themselves as peacemakers. Until we fully understand the adversary ideology and the myths that support it, we cannot transform lawyers into peacemakers.

The Current Narrow View
of Lawyers as Peacemakers

Preventing disputes in the first place contributes to peace in society by reducing conflict (Esau, 1988). The vast bulk of lawyering involves prevention of disputes, and, in this sense, the law is both facilitative and protective. Laws protect personal and social interests that may conflict because of social interaction. For example, in a home purchase, the law protects the buyer's interests. First, the law establishes a land title system that registers whether a bank owns an interest in the property that must be paid off, whether there is a lien on the house that needs to be discharged, whether the seller actually owns the property, and so forth. Without that system, the buyer might find herself a victim of fraud, paying for a house from which she will be evicted because she did not know someone else owned an interest with a priority. Thus, the law prevents a dispute between the seller and the buyer by clarifying interests before the property is transferred and money changes hands.

To say that lawyers are involved in peacemaking by preventing disputes through legal advice and channeling activities is, however, a narrow conception of peacemaking. The majority of preventative lawyers work for the more powerful interests in society. Many people cannot afford lawyers for advice about their transactions. In addition, the law is not a simple system of preexisting rules, but a system that can be manipulated on behalf of the powerful. Thus, there is room for substantial improvement in the role of preventative and transactional lawyers as peacemakers.

In addition to preventing disputes, the law offers an institution for resolving disputes—the court system. We live in a liberal society that is itself a political structure of negative peacekeeping (Esau, 1988). Negative peacekeeping means that violence is prohibited as a means of conflict resolution. Thus, peace is defined by the absence of violence, rather than by the presence of harmonious relationships between people.

For centuries, the Western world was characterized by one bloody war after another. These wars were most often religious civil wars. Liberalism arose as an alternative theory of society based on tolerance and peaceful coexistence instead of never-ending warfare based on mutually exclusive claims of truth. In liberal theory, people are allowed to have different beliefs about what constitutes the good life. To allow groups and people to exist within the same state with contradictory beliefs about morality means, however, that society cannot be unified in a fundamental wholistic sense. Individualism must take priority over communitarianism. Liberal society is consequently based on the fundamental agreement to tolerate pluralism as a way of keeping the peace.

Society accepts the absence of bloody conflict as better than the coercive establishment of the good and the true. People and groups have rights against each other and rights against the government. These rights are given priority over some overarching conception of the public good. Liberal theory gives freedom to individuals and groups to exist and act as much as possible within their own conceptions of moral truth. However, it must find ways for different groups and individuals to engage in joint activities. It must also define the minimum legal standards necessary to hold pluralism together within a framework of order. The liberal system of law must also provide conditions of justice for all (Esau, 1988). Some argue that a liberal social structure is not the best structure for a society because no particular set of beliefs or values guides society. Critics of political liberalism argue that the lack of values lead to moral decline, crime, and social disintegration. Nevertheless, a liberal, pluralistic society is the best we can expect given the reality of fundamental moral and religious conflict that would erupt into armed violence if not accommodated within structures of law.

Imagine a society in which the government did not provide a system of dispute resolution paid for by all the taxpayers and backed by the state's power. The great strength of the formal legal system is that one party can compel another to participate in the formal system or face penalties for not participating. Eventually, a party's case will be heard whether the other side likes it or not. Without some final and official way to resolve disputes that are not voluntarily resolved, there would not only be gross violations of law without remedy, but there would also be more physical violence. For all of its flaws, the legal system is better than the violence of self-help. Consequently, the argument might be made that when lawyers represent clients within the adversary system, they are in fact paradoxically engaging in peacemaking. This function exists in the narrow sense of ensuring that the client's legal interests and perspectives are placed in front of a court for decision (Esau, 1988).

The courts play another important role beyond being the ultimate forum for dispute resolution. In Western common law tradition, *stare decisis*, the doctrine of precedent, applies. Like cases should be treated alike. Consequently, the courts make law for all of society when they decide a particular dispute. In a theoretical sense, this actually contributes to peacemaking. Not only is the dispute between the parties resolved, but a rule of law is established so that in similar cases the same result applies. But when the court is making law, it must look at the dispute with reference to the law that already exists in past precedents and legislation. Courts must also consider what the law should be if there is ambiguity and openness in the preexisting law. The focus of justice is not solely on the parties before the court, but for all others in similar circumstances. The stakes are high. We expect courts, particularly appellate courts, to give elaborate written reasons for their decisions. We expect the law to be argued for (Esau, 1988).

The problem is that the competitive, adversarial nature of the judicial system has perverted the essential role of lawyers as peacemakers. There are historical and structural reasons for this evolution.

The American Legal Profession—A Short History

At the beginning of the twentieth century, law in the United States covered the purchase of real property and the problems of real people. Wills and estates were the foundation of most large practices, and lawyers that designed intricate trusts were considered the most highly skilled of the profession (Linowitz, 1994).

Litigation was uncommon. Lawyers brought suit to compel the execution of contracts that businesses had made with each other. Contracts were usually enforced by the customs of the trade rather than specific clauses drawn by counsel for specific purposes. The business lawyer's expertise was most heavily solicited to secure injunctions against labor unions seeking individual bargaining for a company's workers, against competitors infringing on trademarks or patents, or against retailers selling in ways the company did not like.

Because the law limited an injured person's right to compensation, companies did not need lawyers to defend them against personal injury lawsuits. Thus, the law was regarded as a way the powerful kept the weak in their place. As a consequence, the lack of legal services for ordinary people strengthened the political machines in the cities. Political patronage was the method of redress and protection, not litigation.

In addition, companies rarely needed a lawyer when dealing with the government because there was little business regulation. At the turn of the century, the most time-consuming cases in the "large" seven and eight men metropolitan offices were customs cases and the occasional antitrust case. For example, in 1901 J.P. Morgan put together U.S. Steel in a four-hour meeting in his grand library in New York. The participants were steelmaker Charles Schwab, banker Robert Bacon, and stockmarket operator John Gates. No lawyers were present.

Times changed with the Great Depression. Roosevelt's New Deal created government regulation unprecedented in history. Huge programs were created and new tax laws were enacted to pay for them. Regulation and taxation meant that for the first time companies of any size could not be effectively managed without the advice of lawyers. Enterprises had to change their orientation, now calculating the government's action along with market competition. New generations of managers passed through business schools and learned that disclosures to stockholders and the public, labor relations, marketing practices, and financing plans were matters now scrutinized by government bureaucrats.

Business lawsuits also changed as the government became an adversary. Losing a contract case to a private opponent meant money out of pocket to a company. Losing an antitrust case, a rate case, or a labor relations case might well make a permanent change in how the company would be organized or would do its business. In traditional lawsuits, the lawyer's function was to reach a settlement that allowed both parties to go about their business. In the large majority of cases, once the dispute had passed, the companies would resume their business relationship.

With the government, compromise seemed impossible. Since complex defenses had to be mounted, large law firms developed litigation departments. Corporate clients expected no-holds-barred advocacy when the government was, from their point of view, at their throats, and the law firms met that demand. Nevertheless, most major law firms regarded litigation departments as a necessary evil and kept them small.

Before World War II, the best lawyers counseled their clients to avoid litigation wherever possible. The lawyer's self-interest was to avoid litigation because few clients could afford to pay for the time that would be consumed by a trial. After World War II, the large law firms grew rapidly and steadily on ever increasing government intervention. Partners in large firms enjoyed a confident sense of control over their working conditions and their destinies. This hubris lasted less than two decades.

In the post-war years, a new legal trend developed as consumerism rose to cultural prominence. State court appellate judges such as California Supreme Court Chief Justice Roger Traynor saw that the injuries from products and negligent conduct could be best regulated through the insurance market. Consequently, personal injury liability rules began to liberalize, and injured people began to win cases against corporate and business interests.

At the same time, Earl Warren, leading the United States Supreme Court, construed the United States Constitution in criminal cases to provide basic protections against confessions and searches and seizures. Until the 1950s, constitutional law under the United

States Supreme Court had generally concerned itself with federalism and the Commerce Clause, neglecting the Bill of Rights and the Fourteenth Amendment. In the 1950s, the Supreme Court, in a new focus of constitutional doctrine, expanded the jurisprudence of individual and minority rights. Thus, while the 1950s were profitable for business, the foundation was laid for the social upheaval to come in the 1960s and 1970s.

Another unheralded, but significant trend started in the postwar years. For centuries, lawyers had to prepare for trial without the benefit of discovering the other side's case. In many cases, the lawyers engaged in trial-by-ambush, seeking victory through surprise. To help settlements and make trials more efficient, the courts began to allow pretrial discovery. The basic idea was that all parties would benefit from advance disclosure of testimony. Thus, pretrial discovery rules were adopted. These rules permitted each party in a civil lawsuit to pose written questions to the other parties, to inspect documents in the other's possession, and to take a formal statement under oath from parties and potential witnesses. Considered radical by most lawyers of the era, the new procedures were to level the playing field so that the small guy had a chance to uncover facts to prove his or her case.

In the 1960s, the world as most knew it seemed to go crazy. Civil rights, free speech, women's liberation, sexual revolution, and the war in Vietnam ignited fervor for the enforcement of personal rights. Since the legislative and executive branches of government had failed to respond to the new demands for justice, lawyers began to take on social cases. In addition, while the government imposed more rules and regulations on the populace, the people had less direct involvement in politics. Frustration with normal politics fueled resort to a poor alternative: litigation aimed at social change. To the chagrin of the government and corporate America, people began to win rights in court that had been systematically repudiated by the other branches of government.

By the mid-1970s, a new breed of litigator was becoming prominent. Lawyers began to see negotiation and settlement not as peacemaking activity but as war by other means. Corporate litigation focused on victory by intimidating, outspending, or otherwise grinding down an opponent. The goal of fair dispute resolution by impartial trial was abandoned. Large firm litigators were sought as much for their ingenuity in wearing out their adversaries through expensive delaying tactics as for their courtroom skills (Linowitz, 1994).

LAWYERS AS PEACEMAKERS / 35

This state of affairs was brought about partly by realization that pretrial discovery rules adopted in the late 1950s could be used to harass opponents. Court officers and academics who designed these discovery rules did not foresee the abuses. Nevertheless, attorneys representing economically powerful clients regularly used pretrial discovery devices to outwait and outspend opponents as well as to gain pertinent information. A financially weaker party would often be brought to his knees under a barrage of discovery spewed out by an army of young associates, lengthy and intrusive depositions, and voluminous demands for production of documents (Kanner, 1991).

The financial growth of the early 1980s created more business for the litigation departments of major law firms. By now, the corporate litigators commanded the highest salaries and respect within corporate law firms. Merger and acquisition specialists, especially, developed highly aggressive litigation tactics designed to give clients strategic advantage in hostile corporate takeovers. The legal system was not used for resolving disputes, but to force the other side to capitulate as quickly as possible. The term "scorched earth tactics," borrowed from the Vietnam experience, arose during the late 1970s and early 1980s to describe the pressure placed on parties through litigation in hostile takeover situations. From this scorched earth practice emerged the Rambo lawyer, a term taken from the title character of John Morrell's novel, *First Blood* (Morrell, 1972). Professor Cary (Cary, 1996) has identified the six traits of a Rambo lawyer as follows:

- a mindset that litigation is war and that describes trial practice in military terms;
- a conviction that making life miserable for opponents is in one's best interest;
- a disdain for common courtesy and civility, assuming that they ill befit the true warrior;
- a wondrous facility for manipulating facts and engaging in revisionist history;
- a hair-trigger willingness to fire off unnecessary motions and to use discovery for intimidation rather than fact-finding;
- an urge to put the trial lawyer on center stage rather than the client or his cause.

At first, these litigation tactics were confined to corporate litigation practices in the larger cities. Two factors caused the spread of these tactics across the country. First, they seemed to work. Lawyers used to the traditional, more genteel way of litigation, with the ultimate aim of making peace, were steamrolled by aggressive tactics. The Rambo lawyers could care less about a just result or a fair settlement. Their objective was to make life as miserable and expensive as possible for the opponent. Their motto was "Crush the enemy." Victory resulted not when a judge or jury gave a final decision on the merits, but when the opponent crumbled under the enormous burden imposed by litigation.

Rambo tactics also spread because lawyers are great imitators. A lawyer in a mid-sized city might read about the aggressive tactics of corporate lawyers in New York City. Wanting to make a good impression for a new corporate client, the lawyer would crank out reams of unnecessary discovery, and a new Rambo lawyer would be born. This repeated itself thousands of times across the country in a matter of a few years.

Rambo lawyers consequently became a fact of life. They asserted themselves in the plush offices of corporate law firms and in multiparty federal court cases. Not surprising, government lawyers adopted these tactics too.

The Adversary Ideology

In an article in *Dispute Resolution Magazine*, W. Reece Bader, a partner in a large northern California law firm, summed up the adversary ideology as follows (Bader, 2000):

> The trial lawyer is trained as a warrior, not a peacemaker. We approach each new case with an 'I win, you lose' philosophy. The concept of 'win-win' is anathema to the trial advocate. Far too many of us need to be retooled if we are to effectively represent clients in seeking alternatives to the courtroom. (p. 21)

Aggressive lawyers claim that the ethical obligation of zealous advocacy justifies their behavior. Unfortunately, this rationalization misreads the Model Rules of Professional Conduct.

The duty of zealousness was expressed in Canon 7, ABA Model Code of Professional Responsibility, and its predecessor. However, the current Model Rules do not expressly impose an obligation of zealousness. The old standard has been abandoned in favor of the commentary to Model Rule 1.1 (American Bar Association, 1999):

> Having accepted employment, a lawyer should act with competence, commitment and dedication to the interests of the client and with zeal in advocacy upon the client's behalf.

Zeal in advocacy does not justify threats, racial slurs, gender discrimination, intimidation tactics, or uncivil behavior. Thus, the ethical standards do not rationalize the violently aggressive behavior of modern lawyers. What then is the cause of the problem?

One part of the problem originates with the adversarial ideology inherent in the United States legal system. Adversarial ideology is more than a structural or institutional characteristic. The adversary system encourages an ethical viewpoint that motivates and guides American lawyers away from peaceful behavior.

In theory, the adversarial system is designed to (1) determine the truth, (2) safeguard individual legal rights, and (3) provide a check against the government's misuse of power. The elements of the adversary system are composed of a neutral, passive decision maker and partisan presentation of evidence and argument. Partisanship, the central premise of the adversarial ideology, asserts that a lawyer, within the bounds of the law, must maximize his or her client's interests. Thus, partisanship requires loyalty, fiduciary responsibility, and candor to the client. It also requires diligent attention to the client's needs and zeal in enforcing those interests within the system. Partisanship thus represents a preference for individualistic values, rather than communitarian values. Individualism and property rights are more important than relationships (Croft, 1992).

The decision-maker, the judge, enforces procedural safeguards and acts as a neutral umpire. This role helps an authoritative decision in a system otherwise dominated by client-centered advocacy. The neutral decision-maker also insulates the advocate from responsibility to maintain systemic integrity. The advocate is left to partisanship, and adjudicative integrity is left to the judge, jury, or professional bar. Thus, the neutral, passive decision-maker is critical to the system's legitimacy.

Untethered from these systemic responsibilities, the advocate is easily led into the second dominant premise of the adversary ideology: nonaccountability. So long as partisanship and nonaccountability are exercised within the minimum requirements of the law, the lawyer is neither legally, professionally, nor morally accountable for the means used or ends achieved.

An unwritten code of behavior has emerged from these premises. This unwritten code states that the trial lawyer is a "hired gun, a "warrior' who sells his or her mercenary services to those who are willing to retain and pay for them. Furthermore, the code states that this mind-set is what clients want. Trial lawyers assume that when clients retain an aggressive lawyer, they want aggressive behavior. In fact, this is all a myth perpetuated by cultural beliefs, one that has been identified as the "Myth of Redemptive Violence."

The Myth of Redemptive Violence

Walter Wink, a professor of theology, has developed a thesis of culture that he calls the "Myth of Redemptive Violence" (Wink, 1993). The myth states that our society is based on a view of good versus evil in which a violent savior or redeemer overcomes evil. Hence, we are saved from violence, through violence.

The myth is based on the Enuma Elis, dating from around 1250 BCE and found in traditions considerably older. This ancient story provides the mythic foundation of modern civilization. It is the myth that violence redeems.

In the beginning, according to this myth, the first gods, Apsu and Tiamat, give birth to a succession of younger gods. Their frolicking makes so much noise that the elder gods resolve to kill them so they can sleep. When the younger gods discover this plot, they kill Apsu. Tiamat pledges to revenge Apsu's death. Terrified, the rebel gods turn for salvation to their youngest, Marduk. He exacts a steep price: if he succeeds, he will be given absolute power in the assembly of the gods. Having extorted this promise, he catches Tiamat in a net, drives an evil wind down her throat, and shoots an arrow that bursts her distended belly and pierces her heart. He splits her skull with a club, stretches out her corpse full length, and from it creates the cosmos.

According to this story, creation was an act of violence: Tiamat was murdered and dismembered, and from her cadaver the universe was formed. Order was established out of chaos through violence. Violence was thus redemptive. Chaos (symbolized by Tiamat) is before order (represented by Marduk, god of Babylon); hence, evil is before good. Evil is an ineradicable constituent of ultimate reality and possesses ontological priority over good.

By way of contrast, the Judeo-Christian biblical myth of Creation is diametrically opposed to the Babylonian myth. In the biblical Creation story, a good God creates a good creation. Chaos does not resist order. Good is ontologically before evil. Evil and violence enter as a result of the first couple's sin and the machinations of the serpent. A basically good reality is thus corrupted by free decisions made by creatures. In this far more complex and subtle cosmology, evil emerges for the first time as a problem requiring solution.

In the Babylonian myth, however, there is no "problem" of evil. Evil is simply a primordial fact. Typically, a male war god—Wotan, Zeus, or Indra, for example—fights a decisive battle with a female god, usually depicted as a monster or dragon residing in the sea or abyss (representing chaos). Having vanquished the enemy by murder, the male victor fashions a cosmos from the female monster's corpse. Cosmic order is thus derived from the violent suppression of the feminine and is mirrored in the social order by the subjugation of women to men.

According to this myth, humanity is created from the blood of a murdered god. Humanity does not originate evil, but always finds evil present. Humanity consequently perpetuates evil and is incapable of peaceful coexistence. Therefore, order must continually be imposed through violence. The myth reflects a highly centralized state in which the king rules as Marduk's representative on earth. Resistance to the king or the flag is treason against the gods. Unquestioning obedience is the highest virtue, and order the highest religious value.

The ultimate outcome of this myth is a theology that identifies the enemy with the powers vanquished during the creation. Every coherent theology of holy war ultimately reverts to this basic mythology. Unlike the biblical myth, which sees evil as an intrusion into a good creation and war as a consequence of the Fall, this myth regards war as older than the created world. War, or the metaphor of war in conflict, is therefore a constituent element of reality.

According to the myth, any form of order is preferable to chaos. Thus, the modern American worldview is a world of perpetual conflict in which the prize goes to the strong. "Peace through war" and "security through strength" are core convictions arising from the myth of redemptive violence.

This primordial myth is as universally present today as at any time in its long and bloody history. It is the contemporary world's dominant myth. It undergirds popular culture (video games, comics, cartoons, Westerns, spy thrillers, cop shows, combat movies), foreign policy, militarism, televangelism, and nationalism. It enshrines a cult of violence at the very heart of the state (Wink, 1993). It is the underlying myth that supports the incivility, expense, and contentiousness of the legal system. This myth explains the existence of the Rambo lawyer. It also explains why judicial hand wringing, commissions, rules, and sanctions will not deter overly aggressive lawyer behavior. Finally, it explains why lawyers must become peacemakers.

The myth of redemptive violence in its simplest form is found in children's entertainment. An indestructible good guy opposes an irreformable and equally indestructible bad guy. Nothing can kill the good guy, though for most of the (comic book, television episode, movie, or novel) he suffers grievously. Somehow, the hero breaks free, vanquishes the villain, and restores order. Nothing finally destroys the bad guy or prevents his reappearance.

In Popeye the Sailor, for example, Bluto abducts a screaming and kicking Olive Oyl. When Popeye attempts to rescue her, the massive Bluto beats Popeye to a pulp, while Olive Oyl hopelessly stands by. At the last moment, as the hero oozes to the floor, a can of spinach pops from Popeye's pocket and spills into his mouth. Transformed by this infusion of power, Popeye easily defeats Bluto and rescues his beloved Olive Oyl. The format never varies. Neither party ever gains insight nor learns from these encounters. Violence does not teach Bluto to honor Olive Oyl's humanity, and repeated beatings do not teach Popeye to swallow his spinach before the fight.

Only the names have changed. Marduk subdues Tiamat through violence. Though he defeats Tiamat, chaos incessantly reasserts itself. Chaos is kept at bay only by repeated battles. The structure of the combat myth is thus faithfully repeated on television week after week. A superior force representing chaos attacks aggressively; the champion fights back, defensively, only to be humiliated in apparent defeat; the evil power satisfies its lust while the hero is incapacitated; the hero escapes, defeats the evil power decisively, and reaffirms order over chaos.

This structure cannot be altered. Bluto does not simply lose more often; he must always lose. Otherwise this entire view of reality would collapse. The good guys must always win. To suppress the fear of erupting chaos, the same mythic pattern must be endlessly repeated.

No premium is placed on reasoning, persuasion, negotiation, or diplomacy. Confession and repentance are alien concepts in this myth. Villains are never redeemed from their bondage to evil or restored to true humanity. The law is viewed as too weak to deal with pure evil. Hence the gunslinger in the Wild West or Dirty Harry of the inner city takes the law into his own hands. In the movies, John Rambo acts outside the law to achieve justice. The heroic results he achieves justify the illegal acts he employs. And, the Rambo lawyer does not see the procedural niceties of the law as anything but constraints on the ability to annihilate the opponent.

The story carries easily into the legal system, because lawyers are seen as "hired guns" or "mouthpieces." They are the representatives sent out to resolve human conflict through legal battle (Wink and Wink, 1993). Peacemaking and ethical negotiation are considered weak, passive, and ineffective. Even the concept of Alternative Dispute Resolution is marginalized as an alternative to the primary resolution process of litigation. Consequently, violence begets violence.

Not surprisingly, the myth finds its way into the popular portrayal of the legal system. Good versus evil is fought out in the television and movie courtrooms. Good always prevails. Evil always loses. As a result, the public has become acculturated to the legal system as good vs. evil. One's own lawyers are good. Opponents are evil and their lawyers are worse. To crush the opponent and its lawyers with overwhelming and superior legal force is therefore a great virtue. The Rambo lawyer is born.

This cultural ideology is reflected in television programs such as "L.A. Law." In one show, summarized by Professor Gillers (Gillers, 1989), Arnie Becker, the firm's divorce lawyer, meets with Lydia, a woman nearing forty who has decided to accept her husband's settlement offer. Lydia has come to Arnie because her original lawyer, Julia, had qualms about the settlement and urged Lydia to talk to Arnie about it. Lydia tells Arnie she does not want a fight. "I just do not want it to get into an ugly, pitched battle with name calling and recriminations," she insists. Here is a client seeking a peaceful resolution to her marital dissolution, recognizing that she might not be getting the best deal possible under the law.

On the day Arnie meets Lydia, a gun-carrying former client threatens him because he has not stopped her from accepting a settlement she now realizes was too low. Arnie is subjected to a violent act and learns that violence is always a solution. With the memory of that assault, Arnie tells Lydia that her husband surely has another woman. He urges Lydia to be more aggressive in protecting her economic interests. Violence is now begetting more violence. Lydia does not believe there is another woman or doesn't want to believe it." My husband and I are not statistics," she declares, "We're individuals." Arnie responds: "For your husband, divorce is a fiscal inconvenience. But for you, this can be the most important financial decision that you'll ever make in your life."

At the conclusion of their meeting, Lydia is wavering. Citing "friendship to Julia" and "admiration for your principles," Arnie offers to review the proposed settlement agreement and tell Lydia his conclusions over lunch at a fancy restaurant the following Thursday. Meanwhile, without Lydia's knowledge or consent, Arnie has his private detective follow the husband. She obtains photographs of Lydia's husband and the inevitable other woman in compromising positions.

Arnie takes the glossies to the fancy lunch, where Lydia informs him that she has decided to accept the settlement offer. "In the long run, there are more important things than money," she insists. Tapping the envelope containing the glossies, Arnie muses that he will just put the "investigation" of her "husband's affairs, financial, and otherwise," on hold. Predictably curious, Lydia asks if it will obligate her financially to look in the envelope. "In no way," Arnie assures, but then in a rare burst of compassion, he warns Lydia "it may be painful." Of course she looks, then quickly escapes to the lady's room to give up her lunch, as nonchalant Arnie had previously told the investigator she would. Arnie summons the waiter for dessert.

In the next scene, a retributive Lydia, in a conference with her husband and counsel, can hardly contain her anger. She hurls insults and her pocketbook across the conference table. Arnie uses other financial information the investigator obtained to force the husband to increase his offer considerably. The not-so-veiled threat is that otherwise the information will get the husband into trouble with the law ("lots of cash transactions"). The extortion issue is not addressed.

Afterwards, Arnie is pleased with himself ("We really socked it to them"), but Lydia is crying uncontrollably. She tells Arnie: "I think what you did was despicable. I'll never be able to look at him again with any kind of respect or affection." For Arnie, she says, it was "all so easy . . . Just sock it to him and get the money. I lost my life; my children lost a family. And there's no amount of money that would compensate for that." Arnie asks Lydia if she wants to return the money. She does not. Having thereby proved his point to his own satisfaction, Arnie predicts that in two weeks Lydia will be recommending him to a friend.

Let's review this case critically. Without his client's permission, Arnie Becker used an investigator to obtain a legally irrelevant but inflammatory fact—in California the husband's affair has no bearing on the grant of a divorce or support obligations. Furthermore, the investigator probably violated the husband's right to privacy by surreptitiously obtaining the compromising photographs. Arnie then used that fact to get his client angry enough to fight for a larger settlement. He knowingly employed weapons that would inevitably destroy the modicum of civility the couple still enjoyed and that Lydia had declared at the outset that she wanted to retain. Arnie's investigator violates other privacy rights by obtaining private financial information detrimental to the husband's interests. By implication, Arnie threatens criminal sanctions (extortion based on questionable cash transactions) during negotiations of a civil matter—a clear breach of ethical responsibilities. All of this is done under the justification of zealous advocacy.

This episode, while dramatically far from normal law practice, shows how the myth of redemptive violence portrays lawyers in modern culture. Arnie is the armed-redeemer, using questionable conduct to "save" Lydia from a "bad settlement." Arnie, of course, was the sole judge of whether the settlement was good for Lydia or not. Arnie and his agent invaded the privacy of another person for personal gain. Arnie destroyed the essential emotional tranquility of his client. And Arnie, on his own initiative, escalated the conflict between the parties. Was the outcome better? Were the violent means used to force Lydia to demand a higher settlement and her husband to accept it justified? These are difficult questions without easy answers. However, the fact that a lawyer is portrayed as engaging in this conduct without an underlying examination of the problems typifies the recurrence of the myth in modern culture.

The problem in the legal system is that the myth of redemptive violence has corrupted the adversary ideology. Partisanship is practiced to an extreme and is considered normal. Adversary ideology thus corrupted by redemptive violence has permeated society. In workplaces, schools, shops, streets, playgrounds, and homes, men, women, and children caricature the behavior of the Rambo lawyer. Harvard Law professor Mary Ann Glendon (Glendon, 1994) reports an instance in an elementary school when a principal required all members of the third grade to write apologies for participating in a "riot." Those eight-year-olds that had not participated were understandably offended. Their language reveals the problem: "Should we sue her?" asked one child. "Isn't it illegal for her to punish those of us who did nothing?" demanded another. Glendon asks rhetorically where eight-year-olds learn to talk this way. The answer is clear: The myth of redemptive violence has already been inculcated in these children.

Lawsuits over the disappointments of everyday life have become more common. The law is civilization's attempt to provide a substitute for violence. When it is used to threaten, harass, or extort settlements or is used to vindicate personal affronts not normally amounting to a legal offense, it no longer is a substitute, it is violence itself. The myth of redemptive violence predicts that the law will change into a violent means of conflict resolution. Customs, courtesy, conventions, etiquette, and manners likewise fall to the myth because violence is seen as the ultimate solution to human conflict.

Legal Training and Law Students

One final concept requires examination in the light of the myth of redemptive violence: Legal training, law professors, and law students. The myth perpetuates in part because of the nature of legal education. Who is attracted to law school, how testing screens aptitudes, the isolation of law professors from practice, the case method of legal education, and the lack of true ethical training all reinforce the myth of redemptive violence. Other than practice-oriented, continuing legal education classes, post-graduate education for new lawyers is non-existent. Instead, competitive pressures force them to bill hours.

By and large, undergraduates entering law school are ambivalent toward lawyering and the practice of law. Law schools became, in the 1970s, the place for bright, upper middle-class liberal arts majors with no idea what to do in life. Others have been drawn to law for idealistic reasons or to advance careers in politics. Still others attend with the idea that law is a financially lucrative profession. Law students generally do not have strong ideologies, but if they do, the ideologies are subsumed under the intense academic pressures of the law curriculum (Glendon, 1994).

Application to law school requires most students to take the Law School Admission Test (LSAT). The LSAT does not identify those well suited for law practice. Instead, it tests aptitude for studying law, particularly in the first year. The LSAT was once an all-around test of knowledge and critical thinking skills. It tested verbal and logical-analytical skills, as well as spatial and mathematical problems. In addition, it tested applicants for general cultural literacy. In the late 1960s, the spatial relations and cultural questions were eliminated (Glendon, 1994). Then the math questions were abandoned. Finally, the number of logical-analytical questions was reduced. Currently, the LSAT does not test for creativity, right-brain cognition, or problem solving. The test, which makes no pretense of identifying talents relevant to the practice of law, coupled with undergraduate grades, significantly affects the ultimate composition of the nation's lawyers.

Law professors come from those in the law student ranks who like the job of student. Many law professors, but not all, have little or no experience as practicing private lawyers. As a group, law professors have lost touch with the law practiced as a craft. Many professors look down on careers that do not meet their standards of social awareness. As a result, academia and professional practice have separated. Few academic publications interest practitioners and little in the practice excites law professors (Glendon, 1994).

The law curriculum is based on the case method invented by Dean Langdell at the Harvard Law School. Langdell saw law as a science. The raw data for this science was to be found in the reported decisions of appellate courts, called cases. Textbooks compiled difficult, unusual cases for students to study. By definition, casebooks are a collection of pathological situations where things went spectacularly wrong (Glendon, 1994). Fed on a three- or four-year diet of borderline cases, law students learn that litigation is the only way to solve human conflict. Thus, law students are trained for conflict making, not for peacemaking. Nothing in law school trains lawyers to notice, measure, explain, temper, or adjust to the increase in demand for judicial services. Instead, law students are taught that the court system is the only legitimate institution for resolving disputes. Human conflict is abstracted into rights, remedies, and procedures so that a decision by a court can be obtained. Law students are not trained to consider whether the parties themselves are best equipped to resolve their conflict, given a proper working environment. Finally, alternative dispute resolution is taught as just that: an alternative, marginalized process from the litigation paradigm.

In addition, law schools do not consider morals or values as important guideposts. Ethical training is relegated to memorization of the rules of professional ethics necessary to pass the professional responsibility examination. Ethical issues are not part of the core legal curriculum.

Legal training is not multidisciplinary. Law students are presumed to have some general knowledge of the world from undergraduate training. Hence, the core curriculum does not examine human conflict in a broad wholistic picture. Rather, the curriculum focuses on the tight boundaries of law and rights and remedies, without often questioning whether this method is the best or most appropriate for the situation at hand. Human conflict from the disciplines of psychology, sociology, anthropology, and theology are ignored. This curriculum is supported by accrediting agencies such as the American Bar Association and the various state agencies governing the admission to and practice of law. Nevertheless, young lawyers are expected to understand and appropriately deal with human conflict upon entering the legal profession.

New lawyers in big firms have little client contact and are relegated to extraordinarily tedious tasks handed down from senior partner to junior partner to senior associate to new associate. Billable hours are the measure of worth, not client outcomes. Apprenticeships under experienced lawyers are rare. Thus, competitive pressures become the normative context for professional behavior. When new lawyers gain responsibility of their own, the billing mentality and competition are the values that tend to drive their practices and professional conduct (Glendon, 1994).

In summary, little in law school inoculates new lawyers from the myth of redemptive violence. Similarly, the first five years or so of practice reinforce the delusional assumptions underlying the myth. Consequently, the shift to aggressive, uncivil, violent professional behavior is predictable and almost inevitable.

A New Paradigm

Our definitions of reality in a particular culture and era are models or paradigms. Paradigms shape our approach not only to the physical but also to the social, psychological, and philosophical world. To quote Howard Zehr, "they provide the lens through which we understand phenomena (Zehr, 1990, p. 86)." They determine how we solve problems. They shape what we know to be possible and impossible. Our paradigms form our common sense. The adversarial ideology is an example of a paradigm. The myth of redemptive violence is another paradigm.

Our understandings of what is possible and impossible are based on our constructions of reality, which can and do change. Thomas Kuhn, in *The Structure of Scientific Revolutions* (Kuhn, 1970), suggested that changes in outlook come about through paradigm shifts. One model or paradigm replaces another, thus causing a revolution in the way we view and understand the world. Kuhn suggests that a particular model, a particular paradigm, governs how we understand phenomena. This governing paradigm seems to fit, and various exceptions are made for those phenomena that do not fit.

Over time, dysfunction begins to develop as more and more phenomena do not fit the paradigm. However, we keep trying to rescue the model by inventing reforms that piece it together. Eventually, though, the dysfunction becomes so great that another replaces the model. This cannot happen, however, before a new "physics" is developed. That is, a variety of building blocks must be in place before a new synthesis is possible and a new common sense emerges.

The adversary ideology is a paradigm now so dysfunctional as to be mostly useless for resolving many human conflicts. The ideology, coupled with the myth of redemptive violence, has created what it was designed to prevent: violence. Admittedly, the violence is not physical. However, the emotional violence is probably worse because it cannot be avoided and it is equally stressful. When our legal system has evolved to such an extreme culture of individualism and competitiveness that respectful norms of behavior are considered weak, the system is dreadfully, if not mortally, sick.

Are the building blocks required for a new synthesis in place? What might they be in the law? Alternative dispute resolution, as a movement and ideology holds some promise. However, ADR is too often a simple substitute for the courtroom. Thus, ADR simply changes the nature of the forum without changing the underlying ideology or myths. Worse, in ADR, courts do not control uncivil, disruptive, or unduly competitive behavior of counsel because courts are cut out of the process. If mediation is the process of choice, possibilities again exist. But mediation is most often experienced as a coercive, evaluative process in which competitive, adversarial bargaining is the dominant model. Again, mediation does not promote nonviolent behavior. In fact, mediation as a simple mode of competitive negotiation may encourage the type of behavior most would consider violent. However, ADR, including mediation, contains the seeds of change. If lawyers could be trained in processes and ideologies other than the adversary ideology, ADR and mediation could be transformed into positive, transformative, nonviolent processes for resolving human conflict.

Thus, the argument to train lawyers as peacemakers is made. When faced with disputes and conflicts where relationships are at issue, lawyers should be problem-solvers, not conflict escalators. In many types of cases, lawyers should consider whether to counter their clients' natural inclination to fight. Litigation should be reserved for cases of severe power imbalance, and where relationships are not at issue. Even in these cases, the litigation process should be viewed as a means to bring people to the table to work out their differences. Only those small numbers of cases truly requiring decision should go to trial. This book then is about lawyering as peacemaking. Its goal is to provide a multidisciplinary understanding about human conflict to those students and professionals wishing to explore an expanded understanding of lawyering.

Reflections on Chapter One

Freddie Green was a general building contractor in the small rural town of Kingston He built custom homes and had developed a reputation as an honest businessman. At church one Wednesday evening, one of his customers approached him and said, "Freddie, I have to cancel my contract with you."

Freddie, astounded, asked, "Why John? What's happened?"

John said, "The city manager told me that anyone who does business with you is no friend of the city. Since I do a lot of work for the city, I can't afford to get on the city manager's bad side. I'm really sorry."

Freddie released John from the contract and refunded the $15,000 deposit. That evening, he called his longtime friend and lawyer. An emergency meeting was set for the next morning.

Imagine you are the lawyer. Work through the following questions:

What do you think Freddie's goals are?

What is the very best result that Freddie could hope for?

Can litigation achieve that result?

If litigation cannot achieve the result, what will you do?

Describe how the myth of redemptive violence might lead a lawyer to file a lawsuit against the city manager and the city.

CHAPTER TWO

CONCEPTS OF PEACEMAKING

O LD JOE LIVED OUT IN THE COUNTRY and had one good neighbor. They'd been best friends from childhood and had grown old together. And now that their wives were dead and their children grown and moved away, they only had their farms and each other.

But for the first time in their relationship, they'd had an argument. It seems that a stray calf had been found on Joe's neighbor's land so the neighbor claimed it as his own. But Old Joe said, "No, no, now that calf has the same markings as my favorite cow, and I recognize it as being mine."

Well, they were both a bit stubborn, so they stopped talking to each other. About a week later, a young man knocked at Old Joe's door. Old Joe wasn't expecting anyone, and as he opened the door, he saw before him a man with a carpenter's tool box. "I'm just a carpenter looking for work," the man said. "Maybe you have some odd jobs for me around your place?"

Joe invited the man in and, after chatting for a few minutes, pointed out the window across his pastures to his neighbor's farmland. "I do have a job for you. See that farm over there across the way? That's my neighbor's place. And see that crick running right down there between our property lines? That crick wasn't there last week. My neighbor did that to me to spite me, dadburn it. He took his plow and just dug a big old furrow from the upper pond and then flooded it."

"Well, I want you to do one better. I want you to build me a big, strong fence so I don't have to see his place no more . . . Goldurn him anyhow!"

The carpenter said, "If you have the lumber and the nails, I got the tools, and I'll be able to do a job like that for you." So Old Joe gathered up the lumber and nails and set the carpenter to work.

And, oh how fast and smooth that carpenter worked as he measured and sawed and began his construction.

About sunset, Old Joe came down to look at the progress. As Old Joe pulled up his wagon, his jaw dropped in surprise because . . . there wasn't a fence there at all!

It was a bridge going from one side of the crick to the other! It had handrails and was a fine piece of work. Just as Old Joe drove up; his neighbor was midway across the bridge with his hand stuck out. "Joe, you've got quite a fellow to build this bridge. I'd never have been able to do it, and I'm glad we're friends again."

"And Joe," as he put his arms around Old Joe, "That calf is yours. I've known it all the time. I just want to be your friend too."

About that time, the young man finished putting his tools away and started to walk away. Joe said, "No, hold it. Wait! I've got more jobs for you."

And the carpenter just smiled and said, "I'd like to stay on Joe, but you see, I can't. I got more bridges to build."

—From Peace Tales (*Macdonald, 1992*)

What Is Peacemaking?

This allegory provides an interesting question for lawyers as they consider peacemaking. Do we take on the task of creating more barriers between our clients and those with whom they dispute? Or, do we look beyond the immediate anger, frustration, and emotion our clients are expressing and consider whether we might help achieve our clients' true goals in different ways. This is the thinking of a peacemaker.

Peacemaking is a complicated concept because peace can be defined in so many different ways. For our purposes, peacemaking is not a process of passive acceptance of mistreatment, a turning of the other cheek in the face of clear injustice or abuse, or other weak images of meekness or nonresistance. Instead, peacemaking is a vibrant, powerful concept. At its best, peacemaking creates relational and structural justice that allows for social and personal well-being.

This is an ideal objective, perhaps not attainable in many conflicts. Nevertheless, peacemaking implies the use of cooperative, constructive processes to resolve human conflicts, while restoring relationships. Peacemaking does not deny the essential need for adversary process, but peacemaking places adversary process into a larger perspective. Litigating disputes is not seen as a primary dispute resolution mechanism, but as a tertiary, last-resort process.

When we speak of peace, we understand it in two ways. First, there is negative peace. Negative peace means the absence of violence, typically through coercion rather than cooperation. When Mom tells Sally to stop beating up on Sarah, she is imposing a negative peace in the household. Sally's conflict with Sarah is not resolved, but merely suppressed. The concept of negative peace extends not only from our mundane example in the home, but also to international peace. International peace is said to exist at a cessation of violence and hostility. This form of peace is often imposed by U.N. peacekeepers. Again, peace is defined as an absence of war and is imposed coercively or through balances of power or terror, as in the Cold War.

Our law enforcement mechanisms, euphemistically called criminal justice, create another form of negative peace. The bad guys are taken off the street so that crimes are reduced. Thus, law enforcement officials are called "peace" officers even though they use extremely coercive and sometimes violent means to achieve their ends. Finally, the civil justice system perpetuates a form of negative peace. At best, the civil justice system renders a fair and impartial decision. However, the result is a decision, not a resolution or transformation of the conflict. When the opposing sides have learned who won and who lost, a negative peace has occurred. The legal conflict is finished and people are expected to get on with their lives. Generally speaking, however, the underlying causes of the conflict are left unresolved.

The second way of understanding peace is as positive peace. Positive peace implies reconciliation and restoration through creative transformation of conflict. In positive peace, Mom sits Sally and Sarah down and invites them to exchange stories about what led to the fight. Mom and Sarah learn for the first time that Sally feels angry at the way Sarah ignores her. In five minutes, they work out a plan that allows Sally the safety and security to speak out about what she is feeling. Sarah promises to listen more carefully to Sally. Sally promises not to hit Sarah when she, Sally, becomes frustrated. The fighting has stopped, but more importantly the relationship has been reconciled and restored. In the process, Sally and Sarah have grown morally just a little. In the same way, a lawyer as peacemaker looks at conflict not just as an abstract, intellectual exercise in analysis and persuasion, but as an opportunity to help people reconcile. When reconciliation is not possible, separation and resolution is possible with a minimum of hostility and acrimony.

Peace, negative or positive, is not in most lawyers' professional vocabulary. Especially trial lawyers say they are hired guns, implying that they will use whatever coercive methods are allowed by the legal process to achieve the best result for their clients. This implies that the conflict can be decided on the basis of rights, obligations, and remedies. If a conflict is not open to legal process because no rights have been violated, these lawyers do not have a remedy for their clients. Even when a remedy exists, many lawyers do not look beyond what the law provides to consider if other options or processes might work. This narrow view of conflict misses many opportunities to help people in difficult situations without resort to litigation.

Ten Principles of Peacemaking

For many people, including lawyers, the term *peacemaking* conjures up either various aspects of international efforts to stop war or points to aspects of religious beliefs. If used in interpersonal relationships, peacemaking may connote some informal talking and meetings conducted by elders to restore harmony in a community. Peacemaking, the word, seems largely irrelevant in the twenty-first century. Nevertheless, the term peacemaking is used here consciously to describe the values and processes involved in transforming difficult and intractable conflicts grounded in relationships between individuals or groups. Ten principles of peacemaking guide practitioners as they work in day-to-day-conflicts that challenge the patience of every affected person.

Peacemaking works through problems and conflicts by seeking sustainable solutions rather than superficially polite behavior or uneasy and fragile truces. Unlike many other forms of conflict resolution, peacemaking seeks long-term solutions to difficult conflicts. Often people avoid the difficult work of conflict by layering over the problem with a superficial, nice fix. They sidestep the true issues for one reason or another. The conflict does not cease, but continues to fester away in the relationships. Peacemaking takes on the painful, difficult, and sometimes frightening aspects of conflict directly.

In peacemaking, truth telling and truth seeking are honored, integrity is valued, and trust is given because it is earned. People learn in the peacemaking process to speak from their hearts and minds what they have personally experienced. They are honored for revealing difficult truths when they could brush over them. The peacemaker instills this value in the process and insists on a commitment to truth telling from everyone participating in the process.

Peacemaking offers an opportunity to explore and discover that which is as yet unimagined. In many conflicts, the conflict issues are forbidden subjects to talk about. Implicitly, people agree not to address the true issues because the anxiety of dealing with them is too uncomfortable. Peacemaking allows that anxiety, which is very normal, to be contained and managed. As a result, people begin to feel a sense of relief at being able to talk about issues that have irked them, sometimes for years. Furthermore, peacemaking allows new visions and ideas about relationships to be explored and perhaps created. The process permits discovery of ideas and solutions that before seemed unimaginable.

Peacemaking techniques are creative, exploratory, and filled with the risk, fear, and excitement of discovery. Peacemaking is a fearful undertaking because no one, not even the peacemaker, knows where people will end up. Once the process is underway, however, the fear generated from the anxiety is transformed into a different fear. This is the fear of discovery, which creates a certain excitement in people. Thus, debilitating anxiety is converted to positive fear and excitement that energizes people into action.

Peacemaking is a refuge—a safe haven from the incivility and outright nastiness of conflict. Conflict can be brutal. Few people enjoy the emotions invoked by conflict situations. The processes involved in peacemaking create an environment of safety and security where the conflict issues can be dealt with carefully and respectfully.

The peacemaker is charged with the sacred duty of creating a refuge where people from different backgrounds know they will be heard and understood, where their needs and ideas will be respected, and where they can safely do the difficult work of reconciling their differences. This is a primary value difference between peacemaking and other forms of conflict resolution. The peacemaker takes on the obligation of protecting everyone, seeing that all are given equally high respect and dignity, that all may fully express themselves or not, as they wish— all in a place where there will be no personal attacks, insults, or other emotional or physical violence.

The peacemaker must create a place where people are able to approach, rather than freeze, flee, or fight. Peacemakers, knowledgeable in the neuropsychology of fear, always recognize the importance of the environment on preconscious brain processes. Peacemakers are therefore charged with the duty of controlling environments that allow people to approach one another, rather than to defend against one another.

Peacemaking seeks to disenfranchise, or confront in a process of controlled escalation, those who seek unfair advantage, who exploit racial or class or gender differences, and who prefer to maintain disparities that favor themselves. Justice is a core value of peacemaking. Resolution without justice does not resolve conflict; it is simply a demonstration of which party holds greater power. A peacemaker's values and integrity may require that the process be shut down. Some conflicts are such that they must be escalated before peacemaking will be possible. The peacemaker recognizes this and therefore does not sacrifice justice for expediency.

Peacemaking involves risks, not the least of which is failure. No guarantees can ever be made that peace will be restored between parties. Every conflict contains the seeds of further escalation that may take root despite the best efforts of everyone. However, the risk of failure is never a deterrent to the attempt at peace, especially when peace seems hopeless.

Peacemaking requires tremendous courage by those faced with difficult conflict. Conflict causes people to fear others as well as themselves. What people detest in others is what is inside of them. Thus, to confront others is to confront the same thing within. People know this intuitively, but cannot articulate it. This fear is why so many people avoid peacemaking—they do not have the courage to face themselves, their secret inadequacies, and their deepest fears. Peacemaking is not easy nor is it soft.

Relationship Between Peace and Conflict

Peace and conflict are related to each other such that without one the other cannot exist. One way of examining the relationship between peace and conflict is as true dichotomy. Here violence equates to "not peace" and peace equates to "no conflict." Peace and conflict are opposite states, mostly defined by the absence of the opposite.

In this dichotomous relationship, peace and conflict are equated to good and evil. No process guarantees that peace will prevail over conflict. The uncertain outcome reduces anxiety, which is controlled by taking some action. The action is usually coercive because it is easy, fast, and gives a quick, but temporary, relief from anxiety. This is the basis for the Myth of Redemptive Violence developed in chapter 1.

As a variation on this dichotomous expression of relationship, either peace or evil is believed to ultimately triumph. This is expressed in some Christian teachings, for example, as the Second Coming (peace over conflict) and Armageddon (conflict of evil over good). When this dichotomous relationship prevails, social relationships are often managed crisis to crisis to stop the conflict. The peacemaking work is usually not completed because the issues driving the conflict are not exposed and transformed. Thus, people seem to become stuck in conflict cycles.

 Another way of expressing the relationship between peace and conflict is as a dynamic interchange. In peace, the potential for conflict exists. In conflict, the potential for peace exists. In this dynamic state, peace and conflict coexist, are absorbed by one another, and in turn, absorb each other. Peace and conflict are in harmony with each other, each moving with the other. The ancient tai chi symbol expresses this dynamic relationship.

In the dynamic, paradoxical relationship, peace and conflict are complementary opposites. One cannot exist without the other, and a little of one is within the other. Moreover, peace and conflict are in dynamic equilibrium. This means that peace and conflict push against each other to create balance. Sometimes, the balance shifts one way or the other and an extreme of the one (e.g., too peaceful so as to create lethargy and complacency) leads to the ability of the other to dominate. Thus, unlike the traditional, dichotomous relationship, the dynamic, paradoxical relationship is cyclical and never-ending.

The dynamic relationship between peace and conflict suggests that conflict is not always destructive. Some conflict is necessary to promote peace. In addition, the dynamic relationship suggested in the tai chi diagram indicates that conflict represents danger and opportunity. In fact, the Chinese ideograph for conflict is "danger + opportunity."

Peacemaking is attuned to the *dynamic relationship* of peace and conflict more than to the *dichotomous relationship* of peace and conflict. Thus, the peacemaker's orientation to conflict is not that conflict is always negative or destructive, but that it is an essential part of human existence. Like most other things in life, too much conflict is not healthy, but too little conflict leads to apathy and stagnation. The peacemakers work in environments where too much conflict exists, but keep in mind the need for balance.

Reconciliation or Therapy?

In the medical metaphor, healing occurs through a process of diagnosis, prognosis, and therapy. Healing assumes that the patient is ill and should be restored to health. In the mental health fields, healing involves therapies to help a patient function normally in day-to-day living. Peacemaking, however, is considerably different than therapy. The ideal goal of peacemaking is reconciliation and restoration of relationships. The focus is on conflicts that rupture relationships between two or more people. Peacemakers do not think about how to help dysfunctional people manage day-to-day living, although an astute peacemaker may suggest that a party consider counseling. Peacemakers create safe environments and manage fair processes that allow parties to learn about, understand, and creatively transform serious conflicts on their own.

Although peacemaking involves social processes that appear to be like therapeutic counseling, the similarities are superficial. The dynamics of the peacemaking process involve convening all necessary parties, educating parties about processes, establishing ground rules, securing commitments to process and cooperation, providing for time to share perspectives, clarifying goals, injustices, and interests, generating options, negotiating agreements, reducing the agreements to writing, and seeing that the agreements are kept.

In the diagnosis-prognosis-therapy metaphor, the peacemaker may make a diagnosis but will often keep it to herself. Prognosis is always difficult because the people in the conflict will choose the path of transformation best for them. Finally, the peacemaker provides no therapeutic solution to the conflict. She may offer opinions, suggest ways of breaking through barriers, or change processes, but leaves the final decision-making to the parties. Nevertheless, if peacemaking is successful, it can be therapeutic to the parties as it allows reconciliation and healing to occur.

Peacemaking and Mediation

Mediation encompasses a broad array of processes that typically involves a third party working with the disputants. The third party may or may not be neutral or impartial. For example, in communal societies, elders may mediate disputes between families. They know all the parties and may have an interest in the outcome. Because of age, station, and experience, and particularly because the elder is not impartial and neutral, the elder is sought out by the parties.

Mediation in modern culture has taken on a more formal process. Mediators may be called in to work with labor disputes and, in the last generation, broker settlements of litigated disputes. In addition, mediation has gained increasing popularity in community and church disputes and in international disputes.

Peacemaking, in the sense that a third party is involved in a dispute, is similar to mediation. The difference between mediation and peacemaking has to do with value. Peacemaking seeks positive peace—restored relationships, personal responsibility, and apology and forgiveness when appropriate. Mediation tends to be more value-neutral and may be satisfied with negative peace. That is, mediation concentrates on the cessation of conflict and resolution of disputes without necessarily regarding the relationships involved. As will be discussed in chapter 4, North American mediation orientations range from evaluative to narrative practices. To the degree that a particular orientation examines and opens the deeper, underlying causes of the conflict, it engages in a form of peacemaking.

More significantly, peacemaking actively looks for ways to help people in conflict relate to each other in respectful ways. Obviously, peacemaking is not suitable for all conflicts, but should be a consideration when relationships are at issue. Furthermore, peacemaking may demand more of the practitioner in terms of knowledge and experience than other forms of mediation.

Peacemaking also differs from mediation in what the parties are asked to do. In peacemaking, people are asked, often against their current feelings, to activate their capacity for good. This requires peacemakers to support, hold, and encourage the parties as they struggle to overcome the negativity of their conflict. In mainstream mediation, the process is not so demanding. People are asked to come to the process in good faith, but they are not always asked to activate their capacity for good.

Asking people to activate their capacity for good is not a normal lawyering skill. In fact, many lawyers in adversary mode discourage people from activating their capacity for good. Lawyers like to be viewed as confident, competent, can-do problem-solvers. Some think that they lose a reputational (read "marketing") advantage by advising clients to make things as rights as possible.

In peacemaking, apology and forgiveness are often powerful tools for restoring relationships and dealing with injustices. In mediation, apology and forgiveness is occasionally considered, but usually as a side issue. Lawyers, while in adversary mode, see forgiveness and generosity as surrendering legal rights. The underlying fear is that Other may exploit Party because Other sees Party's expression of capacity for good as weakness. Furthermore, most lawyers wish to avoid the implication of apology as an admission against interest. Lawyers therefore may advise clients in mediation to say nothing and get out of the dispute with the best possible financial terms.

Finally, peacemaking involves much more than clarifying issues and managing an auction (the exchange of offers and counteroffers) for the purchase and sale of settlement. Peacemaking involves the strategic questions of knowing what to do, why and how, when and where, by whom and to or with whom, and sometimes, against whom. In contrast, the mediator of litigated disputes sees conflict as an object or problem to be solved. Using tools of legal and business analysis, the problem is defined, likely outcomes are explored, and competitive negotiations lead toward an agreed result or impasse.

Peacemaking is quite different. Peacemaking is resolution-as-process instead of resolution-as-object. The peacemaking processes do their own work. The peacemaker's task is to provide the parties what they need to do their work. In peacemaking, people do for themselves most of what has been done for them in the past. That is to say, instead of being unconscious and unaware of the dynamics of the conflict relationship, the peacemaking process makes those dynamics explicit and available for examination. In this way, people can agree on behaviors and relationships that make sense to them. In this way too, peacemakers give up the idea that they make peace or stop conflict. Instead, they simply put the pieces in play in a proper environment, control the energy, and let the parties work.

This orientation challenges lawyers in traditional roles. Lawyers often see themselves as professionals, with technical knowledge of how to do the job. They know best, otherwise why would clients seek their services? The idea of letting the parties do the hard lifting in transforming conflicts into peace also cuts against the economic grain. If clients can solve their own problems, why do they need lawyers? The answer is that clients need the wisdom, experience, knowledge, and advice lawyers can offer, but do not always need to be the silent participant. In peacemaking, the roles of lawyer and client are often reversed.

Unlike legal disputes, which are often viewed as one-shot problems to be litigated or settled, peacemaking sees disputes and conflicts and peace as all temporary conditions. Peacemakers expect conflict to emerge and recede as needed to draw attention to issues needing consideration. Thus, peacemakers are not concerned as much with specifics as they are with the conditions that will support the emergence of peace.

The Lawyer as Counselor and Representative

Clearly the current ethical standards do not require a lawyer to be an advocate when engaged in peacemaking practices. What does this mean? First, peacemaking is explicitly based on constructive, cooperative, mutual, and non-adversarial processes for resolving human conflict. As we have seen, zealous advocacy, to have any relevance at all, must be limited to the inside of a courtroom or arbitration hearing. Advocacy only is relevant in a procedure designed for partisanship, refereed by a judge or arbitrator, with rules of procedure and substantive law governing process and decision-making. None of these elements are present in any peacemaking process. Therefore, abandoning zealous advocacy in peacemaking processes violates no ethical norm.

What then is the role of a lawyer in the peacemaking process? I perceive it as the role of counselor and advisor. The following tasks are appropriate for lawyers entering with their clients into peacemaking processes:

Lawyers should understand and analyze the underlying conflict dynamics from a broader multidisciplinary perspective than narrow rights and obligations. Using conflict mapping principles, lawyers should understand the conflict styles in play, the context of the conflict, the conflict goals, the power issues, the escalation stages, and who the primary, secondary, and tertiary parties are. Just as a case memorandum may be prepared concerning the legal orientation of the conflict, a conflict analysis memorandum should be prepared based on conflict mapping principles.

Lawyers must be able to educate clients about the process, necessary orientation, and benefits and risks of peacemaking. The proposed revisions to the ABA Model Rules of Professional Responsibility suggest that a lawyer has an ethical duty to advise clients of various processes and options other than litigation for dispute resolution. To discharge this duty, lawyers must be broadly trained in conflict theory, mediation theory, and dispute resolution practices.

Many conflicts involve dignitary offenses, which means that they result in relationship and identity conflicts. Apology and forgiveness are deep processes for resolving aspects of conflicts for which judicial remedies do not exist. Lawyers as peacemakers should therefore be sensitive to the socio-psychological processes of apology and forgiveness, consider the legal implications (which do not necessarily lead to admissions against interest), consider the prospects for apology and forgiveness in a given conflict and, finally, decide how best to bring it about.

Rather than limit the conflict analysis to an abstraction of rights and remedies or reformulating a conflict into monetary terms, lawyers should take a broader, multidisciplinary approach to conflict analysis. Lawyers as peacemakers should explore the client's needs and interests, including financial issues and injustices that need reconciliation. Only with a thorough understanding of the total picture should a lawyer consider what processes might be appropriate. Furthermore, although lawyers should take great care to educate their clients about their legal rights, they should be equally resistant to coercing clients into litigation simply because the lawyer loathes the idea of waiving rights.

Lawyers as peacemakers should also use recent knowledge gained about human decision-making processes. In particular, lawyers should reframe issues and potential outcomes for clients to avoid the problems of valence framing and prospect theory. How an issue is verbalized or framed has an enormous effect on decisions concerning choice. Lawyers today may often aggravate a conflict by unknowingly presenting choices in a language form that unwittingly leads to conflict escalation.

Lawyers should, of course, advise clients on the alternatives if peacemaking is unsuccessful. This advice should include the range of outcomes, the cost, and the time frame for a final decision. Many experienced lawyers incorporate this into practice. Younger, inexperienced lawyers need specific training in this counseling.

Lawyers as peacemakers will play a wide range of roles in the peacemaking process. Most of the time, lawyers will counsel, but not necessarily be active participants. The attorney's role in a peacemaking session may be quite different than in a brokered negotiation. In a peacemaking session, attorneys should generally expect to help the parties toward resolution and reconciliation. In a brokered negotiation, the attorneys may more actively speak on behalf of the client and counsel on the strategies of the bargaining auction.

What must an attorney acting as a peacemaker be careful about? First, deciding for the client what is fair, versus what the law might say is equitable or right. The concept of peacemaking places personal responsibility and accountability on the client. There are times and cases when the client cannot accept full accountability. Nevertheless, most people most of the time can make informed decisions about conflicts. Lawyers as peacemakers must resist the temptation, a la Arnie Becker, to decide what is best or fair for the parties.

Lawyers are trained to be active. The concept of advocacy means getting up and arguing or persuading others to a point of view. Lawyers must therefore overcome a natural feeling that inactivity or nonaggressive behavior signifies incompetence or weakness. With experience, lawyers will learn that representing clients in peacemaking processes is a far more subtle and sophisticated process than the usual adversarial advocacy. We can teach new lawyers to be effective courtroom lawyers in a short period of time. Learning peacemaking skills is, however, far more difficult and sophisticated.

Reflections on Chapter Two

Georgia Jones is your client. She owns a residential real estate brokerage firm in town and is well known in the community. Georgia is in a partnership that owns a local shopping center. The center has been profitable, but she is tired of dealing with what she considers to be the arrogance of the managing partner. He refuses to return her telephone calls and treats her disrespectfully, calling her "Honey" and "Dear." She wants some advice on what she should do about the situation.

What might be your advice if acting in the Jones situation in a traditional role of advocate?

What might be your advice if acting as a peacemaker?

If your advice is different, depending on the role you assume, why might that be?

Part Two

CONFLICT RESOLUTION PROCESSES

CHAPTER THREE

CONFLICT RESOLUTION MODELS AND PROCESSES

Introduction

CONFLICT RESOLUTION PROCESSES can be categorized into decision processes and agreement processes. An agreement process occurs when the parties themselves decide how to resolve the conflict. Thus, decisions imply unilateral action, while agreements imply bilateral action.

One party may impose a decision upon another. In this situation, the deciding party is said to have power over the other. Examples include commands by parents over children or supervisors over employees. Outside parties may also impose decisions on the parties to conflict. Litigation and arbitration are examples of third party decision-making because judges, juries, or arbitrators are charged with deciding the conflict. In this case, neither of the parties in the conflict holds power to decide the outcome. Their task is to persuade the decision-maker to resolve the conflict in their respective favor. Oftentimes in third party decision-making, conflict settlement centers on the range of possible decisions and the likelihood of each.

In contrast to decision-making, agreements reflect retention of power by the parties. Agreements may approach unilateral decisions if the power balance is skewed toward one party. Or, agreements may be relatively well balanced. Parties may reach agreement through face-to-face bargaining and negotiation or through the use of an intermediary, such as a mediator.

Two models of conflict resolution are useful for understanding how peacemaking works. The first model is the Four-Way Model of Conflict Resolution developed by Ron Claassen of the Center for Peacemaking and Conflict Studies at Fresno Pacific University. Claassen proposes four ways to resolve human conflict, based on how the power of decision-making is shared between the parties. The second useful model is a power, rights and interests model developed by Ury, Brett and Goldberg (Ury, Brett, and Goldberg, 1988). They look more to the substantive ways conflicts are resolved rather than to the power of the decision-makers. A synthesis of these models leads to a peacemaking model of conflict resolution.

The Four-Way Model of Conflict Resolution

Claassen's Four-Way model consists of coercion, outside authority, mediation (mutual agreement-making with outside assistance), and negotiation (mutual agreement-making).

Coercion

The first model of conflict resolution involves coercion or power over others. Examples of this model include employer-employee relationships, teachers over students, and parents over children. The line with the circle around it designates who has the power.

Resolving conflict through power is the first lesson learned about conflict. From the earliest age, children are coerced into wanted behaviors by their parents. Coercion consequently becomes the conflict resolution model of first choice for many people.

Coercion is a way that power is exercised over others. The word derives from the Latin words *arca* (box or coffin) and *arcere* (to shut in). Thus, coercion comes from Latin words meaning "restraint exercised by outside forces."

Reactions to coercion are generally negative. Coercion limits freedom and is therefore perceived as a threat to survival. If I am coerced, I am not free to choose for myself who I am. If another controls me, then I am unable to control my ability to meet my needs. Response to coercion may be to accede to it or to resist. Counter-coercion leads to conflict spirals.

Destructive coercive power based on naked force is the answer large numbers of people find to the problems of social inequality, dissatisfaction, protest, deep alienation, and bitter cries for justice. Constructive coercion reaches the same goal, but through nonviolence. Gandhi, Martin Luther King Jr., and Saul Alinsky illustrate constructive coercive power in the form of nonviolent civil disobedience.

Using coercive tactics is risky. People with the strongest incentive to be coercive face greater loss. Thus, people using coercion not only risk a punitive retaliation, but the loss of the relationship itself. Coercion is often perceived as unjust, and the perception of injustice increases resistance to submit to the coercion.

Structural conditions also decrease coercive effectiveness. Risk is reduced when a relation is so unrewarding that a person has little to lose from the partner's withdrawal from the exchange. This means that coercion becomes probable only when dependence is so low, and the power imbalance so high, that a pattern of cooperation cannot be sustained. However, the lower the dependence, the more difficult it becomes to coerce another.

Coercion, moreover, depends on motivation, skill, and persistence. Consequently, in everyday application, coercion is generally ineffective. Successful coercion requires diligent monitoring of behavior, skillful application of punishment, and a willingness to accept short-term losses in return for uncertain long-term gains. Most coercive power users fall short of this model. The primary problem seems to be not that people punish, but that they punish poorly (Molm, 1997). People may express displeasure and annoyance, but not follow through with any real costs and without risking more serious confrontation. Unfortunately, low-level coercion actually extends an unsatisfactory relationship and prolongs conflict.

Controlled Escalation

In some conflicts, however, the only sensible conflict resolution process is controlled escalation. The danger is that parties will resort to controlled escalation when it is unnecessary or inappropriate. Since exercising power is an exercise of self-sovereignty, however, escalation is very tempting. Furthermore, as an expression of self-assertion and personal autonomy, escalation temporarily reduces the anxiety of the conflict. These temptations lead people to escalate when escalation is inappropriate.

There are, however, several situations that call for controlled escalation before peacemaking should be attempted.

The first situation occurs when one party fails to recognize the conflict. Usually, avoidance, denial, or rigidity of a party manifests this. Escalation is used to coerce a party into recognizing the existence of a conflict and take some action toward resolution.

The second situation arises when one party fails to legitimize another party. In this case, someone has been excluded from resources, power, or respect. Escalating the conflict compels the dominant party to pay attention to the subordinate party. The goal of escalation is to reach a resolution in which the disputed resources or power are shared on a legitimate basis.

Escalation may also be justified when one party fails to acknowledge the existence of another party. This is often the basis for an identity-based conflict and leads to the most intractable disputes. When Afro-Americans were simply not acknowledged in the Deep South during the first half of the twentieth century, they were forced into civil disobedience.

Finally, escalation can be necessary when the parties fail to be sufficiently clear on conflict issues. First, parties can be ambivalent toward issues. They may hold two or more conflicting feelings or attitudes toward the issues, neither one predominating. Ambivalence tends to freeze action such that no progress can be made toward resolution. Escalation forces examination of one's beliefs and attitudes with the goal of reducing ambivalence. Second, the issues might be ambiguous. Ambiguous issues are those that are susceptible of two or more interpretations, meanings, or even resolutions. Escalation may sharpen the parties' focus on the issues, causing the issues to be clarified through redefinition.

Oftentimes, the conditions that justify controlled escalation arise from power imbalances. Power imbalance gives one party the luxury of dictating conflict resolution by suppression, repression, denial, or benevolent command. In the case of power imbalance, escalation alternatives are therefore only feasible when they can rebalance power.

Escalation in the context of social action, such as civil disobedience, must shake up the prevailing patterns of lives. It must agitate, create disenchantment and discontent with the current values, to produce a passive, affirmative, non-challenging climate. In this climate, the social activist can mobilize a small force of committed followers to challenge the status quo.

Escalation in the context of personal conflict may require litigation. However, the legal system is severely limited by the civil remedies it can provide. Thus, the cost, time, and outcomes of the system often frustrate parties. To its credit, the legal system requires parties to respond to the conflict with formal appearances, clarify their issues, and present their evidence and arguments to the judge or jury.

When the escalation has awakened the dominant party or has sufficiently rebalanced the power, a transition into peacemaking is possible. However, the parties may be in such an advanced stage of escalation that immediate peacemaking will not be useful. Instead, the parties must begin de-escalating toward a stage of conflict where they can begin to recognize each other's interests and concerns.

What conditions are necessary to make escalation successful? The party seeking it must be motivated toward a specific articulated, measurable, and attainable goal. Next, the party seeking to escalate must have the resolve to see action through hard times, setbacks, and failures. Third, the party seeking escalation must have the courage to face the possibility of failure, to accept adverse personal consequences, and to live with the anxiety implicit in the conflict process. Many lawyers do not go through these costs with client's before filing lawsuits or asserting expensive defenses. As a result, people are sometimes naively led to believe that the litigation process is like what they see on television: a flashy, entertaining, fast process. The opposite is true. Litigation is a slow, tedious, mind-numbing process.

Outside Authority

The second way to resolve conflict is to give a third person power to decide the conflict. This might typically involve a parent deciding a conflict between children, a teacher resolving a conflict between students, or a supervisor deciding a conflict between employees. This model also describes the litigation and arbitration processes. The parties give up all control over the outcome of the conflict, but hope that, at some point in time, a third party will resolve the conflict.

Typically, delegating conflict resolution to outside authorities requires a distributive orientation to conflict. The problem for the decision-maker is to sort out competing claims to resources. Ideally, resources are allocated to the party holding the superior claim, according to principles of rights and procedural fairness. Practically, resources are often allocated on the basis of privilege, position, and power. When the allocation becomes grossly unfair, a rights-based system may redistribute the resources more equitably. However, decision-based systems of conflict resolution are generally criticized as costly and destructive of relationships.

Decision-based conflict resolution requires a third party to decide which rights are involved, whether injury has occurred, and whether excuses or justifications mitigate liability. Generally, the final decision is in the form of a judgment awarding damages, imposing a coercive order, or declaring rights. The third party may be a judge, a judge and jury working together, or an arbitrator.

Decision-based conflict resolution emphasizes the importance of the individual. Generally, larger social issues are only important to the degree they affect individual rights. In rights-based conflict resolution, communitarian ideals are largely abandoned. Thus, resolving a dispute over resources between individuals takes precedence over maintaining long-term relationships.

Decision-based conflict resolution is generally adversarial. The premise of adversary ideology is that the fairest decision comes from each side pressing a case and challenging the other's case. Out of this tug-of-war comes some semblance of truth.

Decision-based conflict resolution often creates unwarranted expectancies in parties. Because they hold a theoretical right or claim, they often believe they have a vested, immutable right. Furthermore, releasing the expectancy of a right for settlement is difficult for people to accept. Nevertheless, the civil trial process is well suited for resolving questions of competing legal rights. The judge and ultimately the appellate court can decide issues of law. These decisions have binding effect on future cases through the doctrine of *stare decisis*. Conflicts based on competing claims to resources can be resolved based on legal principles, which reflect political and social values. In addition, the civil trial process helps to establish the community conscience. Juries tell the community what is fair and what is not. Juries in unusual cases will even ignore unjust laws.

In terms of conflict resolution, the civil trial process has considerable strength. First, the process is well understood by practitioners and by repeat users. Although it seems arcane to the uninformed, trials do follow a very predictable path to a final decision. Second, procedural due process is usually followed. Thus, the civil trial process is viewed as a legitimate form of government because all parties have the right to be heard.

Finally, the greatest strength of the civil trial is that ultimately, decisions are reached. Civil trials provide for finality by providing a binding decision. A review process, called an appeal, affords protection against gross abuse. The decision can be affirmed, modified, or reversed based on fairly narrow and specific legal standards.

Civil trials also have significant weaknesses. First, the parties lose complete control over the decision-making process. They must delegate authority to their professional representatives. Because the process is complex and intangible, the parties have difficulty evaluating the performance of their lawyers. In addition, the parties give up all control for deciding the case. The power is given to the court or arbitrator, who has the ultimate word.

Furthermore, the civil trial process can be very expensive. A typical five day jury trial might cost a party as much as $100,000. The process also does not care about substantive justice, only about making a decision. Civil trials are about assuring some procedural fairness, not about the quality of the decision.

The trial process may not consider all evidence. The rules of evidence may exclude important information from the decision-maker on public policy or reliability grounds. Thus, the decision can be directly affected by limiting the available information.

Despite the emphasis on procedural fairness, civil trial decisions are subject to the biases and prejudices of the judge and jury. Some safeguards are built in to protect against obvious prejudice, but lawyers will agree that the preferences and worldviews of the trial judge and jury are wild cards in the trial process.

Finally, three significant weaknesses challenge the civil trial process as a conflict resolution system. First, the process, by design and intent, is adversarial and therefore extremely disruptive to relationships. Second, the civil trial remedies are limited a judgment for damages, a coercive order (injunction or contempt), or a declaration of rights. These remedies are always insufficient in relationship or identity based conflicts. Finally, the civil trial process does not guarantee that decision will result in satisfaction (e.g., unenforceable judgments, bankruptcy, etc.). Thus, there is uncertainty in the decision and uncertainty in the final outcome.

This model is useful when there are severe power imbalances. Nevertheless, it is costly, and the outcome is always uncertain. Competitors and contenders, who seek control and dominance in conflict are attracted to litigation. Ironically, they give up the very thing they seek because they often confuse the metaphor of sports competition with this model.

Litigation and arbitration are not same as football, golf, or tennis. In team or individual sports, the winner is determined by some objective score—touchdowns, strokes, or sets. Competitors engaged in sport compete directly against each other, and the better player wins by amassing more points. In litigation and arbitration, however, the decision is made by a presumably impartial decision-maker that can only be influenced by the parties, but not controlled. Thus, a party may put on an excellent case, but still lose because the decision-maker was not sufficiently influenced. Since the mental processes of the decision-maker can never be known, the outcome is always unpredictable. At least in games there will be clear winner and loser (or a tie) after the allotted time for play has expired.

Agreement-Based Processes

Agreement-based processes of conflict resolution are characterized by the decision-making power retained by the parties. Unlike Model One, based on one party having the unilateral power to coerce a resolution, or Model Two that delegated the resolution to a third party for decision, agreement-based processes rely on the parties to keep the power to resolve the conflict to themselves. The two principle agreement-based processes are cooperative decision-making with outside help and pure cooperative decision-making.

Cooperative decision-making with outside help. In cooperative decision-making with outside help, parties bring in a third party to help them. Mediation falls within this model as do other forms of conflict resolution. Notice in the diagram that the third party is outside of the power circle. The parties retain the power to decide how the conflict should be managed, resolved, and transformed. This model therefore includes mediation and peacemaking processes. Mediation will be explored in chapter 4.

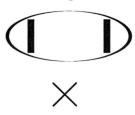

Pure cooperative decision-making. The fourth model of conflict resolution is pure cooperative decision-making, and this is the way most conflicts are resolved. This model includes negotiation and problem solving without the assistance of an outsider. We learn to negotiate from the days we begin to communicate as children and spend a considerable amount of time and effort developing our negotiation skills and using them in day-to-day interactions with others.

Process Choice

When faced with conflict, most people tend to start with Model Four. If the conflict is not quickly resolved, one or both parties will move to Model One, the power model. Particularly if one person's dominant conflict style is contentious, she will attempt to coerce the other party. This often occurs in small businesses or work groups when the owner or supervisor uses power to dictate how a conflict will be resolved. Sometimes Model One is used from fear of exploitation. Many business people believe that if they show too much cooperation, they will be perceived as soft. They tend to believe that being tough and tenacious is in their long-term financial interests. However, a significant number of research studies have established that cooperative behavior provides higher long-term profits than competitive behavior (Johnson and Johnson, 1989).

The contentious person also fails to account for the response to power. Typically, he might say, "I'm the boss and this is the way it's going to be. Period!" Aside from the lack of respect, failure to listen, and the self-centeredness implicit in this approach, it challenges colleagues to a nonproductive response. They may counterattack, yield, or avoid the conflict. Since the boss has sent a signal that cooperative problem solving is not an option, the others will see no choice but to escalate.

If Model One fails to resolve the conflict, as it usually does, either party will resort to Model Two. In business disputes, this often means litigation. Litigation is an appropriate, useful, and highly effective process, but only in a limited class of conflicts.

After the parties have spent considerable time and money in litigation, they finally move to Model 3 and bring in an outsider.

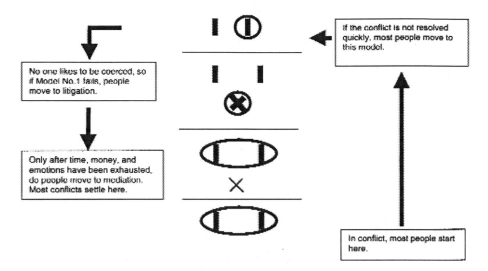

Power, Rights, and Interests

The Claassen model focuses on how the power to resolve the conflict is distributed or shared between parties. Another way of looking at conflict resolution is through power, rights, and interests. In *Getting Disputes Resolved*, William Ury, Jeanne Brett, and Stephen Goldberg (1988) analyze conflict resolution processes as belonging to power-based, rights-based, or interest-based processes.

Power-based processes involve the idea that one party has the power to dictate the resolution of the conflict over another. Power is determined by dependency such that the more dependency one party has or is perceived to have on another, the more power the other may hold. Power processes may be either power contests or power negotiations. Thus, power-based processes may be found in any of Claassen's four models. For example, a power negotiation could occur in mediation or in a pure negotiation. Similarly, a pow-contest could be found in Models One or Two, with the outcome being determined by which party was more powerful or a determination of power by an outside authority.

Rights-based processes involve some standard of fairness or legitimacy. Some rights are formalized by laws and contracts while others are more informal social or cultural expectations. When conflicts are resolved through a rights-based process, the parties must decide and agree what rights apply, what the facts are, and whether the facts give rise to enforcement of the rights. Obviously, much conflict can arise just trying to answer these issues. Similar to power-based processes, rights-based processes may be found in each of Claassen's models. In Model One, for example, a party may decide to resolve a conflict based on that person's understanding of the rights of all of the parties to the dispute. In Model Two a judge or arbitrator may choose which rights apply to the facts presented. In Model Three, the parties, helped by a mediator or peacemaker, may explore whether rights have been violated. Finally, in Model Four, the parties may agree themselves what rights are implicated by the conflict.

Interest-based processes are generally deeper than power or rights-based ones. Interests are needs, desires, concerns, fears. They are what people want or care about. Interests underlie positions, which are the tangible things people say they want. For example, in a personal injury case, an injured plaintiff might demand $75,000 to settle. This demand is a position. The interests that support the position might include compensation for lost earnings, medical expenses, lost earning capacity, future medical expenses, pain and suffering, attorney's fees, costs, and so forth. The defendant in the case may say, "I'm not paying you anything because you contributed to the accident by not wearing your seatbelt!" The interests underlying this position might be a desire not to have insurance rates affected, a desire not to pay out more money than is absolutely necessary to settle the case (stated another way, a desire to preserve wealth), and a desire not to accept partial or full responsibility for the accident.

Positions are often difficult to reconcile. The parties must probe for the true interests behind the positions, which is in itself difficult due to the fear of exploitation if too much of one's real needs are divulged. Reconciling interests requires reaching out for creative problem solving and through give and take and offer and counteroffer exchanges of proposals.

Comparing the Models

Claassen's Four-Way Model of conflict resolution differs from Ury, Brett, and Goldberg in several important ways. First, Claassen's model focuses on the power and choices of the parties to define the type of resolution process. Under Claassen's model, the power to choose the process in large part determines what the process will be. In Model One, one person retains the power to decide the conflict to the exclusion of another. In Model Two, both parties give up their power to agree on a resolution and give the power to an outside authority. In Models Three and Four, the parties keep the power to resolve the conflict to themselves. If an outsider is brought in, as in Model Three, the outsider has no power to decide the outcome.

In contrast, Ury, Brett, and Goldberg's model focuses on the substance of the conflict, giving less weight to the processes involved. In a power-based conflict resolution system, for example, the issue is over a power contest determined by who ultimately can coerce the other. In a rights-based system, the issue largely concerns defining and ordering rights between disputants. Finally, an interest-based system concerns itself with the needs, desires, wants, and aspirations underlying the parties' positions.

These differences also suggest different views of power within conflict resolution systems. In Claassen's model, the relevant power from a systems perspective is the power to decide how the conflict will be resolved. In Ury, Brett, and Goldberg's model, power relates to a dispute's ultimate outcome. This leads to a consideration of how one determines whether a conflict resolution system is good or not.

Under Claassen's model, Models Three and Four would be preferred in most disputes over Models One and Two. Even when Models One and Two are necessary to maintain order and public safety or to decide disputes that cannot be resolved between the parties themselves, they are still to incorporate elements of Models Three and Four. Thus, Claassen sees coercive and outside authority as necessary back ups in case collaborative approaches fail. However, coercion and outside authority should be used respectfully, always giving the parties the option to move to more collaborative processes.

Ury, Brett, and Goldberg measure the health of a conflict resolution system by their triangles. They note that an unhealthy conflict resolution system would order power, rights, and interests:

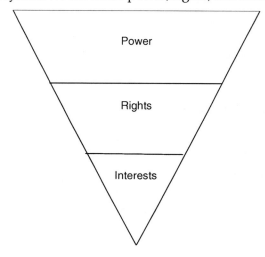

In contrast, they argue that a healthy conflict resolution system would look like this:

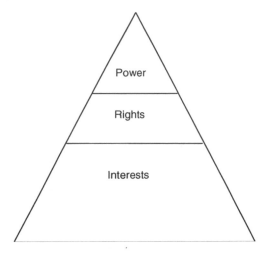

From Ury, Brett, and Goldberg, 1988

Their emphasis is on interest-based conflict resolutions systems, with much less reliance on rights-based or power-based methods of resolving disputes.

Peacemaking—A Synthesis of Models

Claassen has developed a peacemaking model of conflict resolution by synthesizing his Four-Way Model with Ury, Brett, and Goldberg's power, rights, and interests model. Claassen's peacemaking model seeks to move parties to Model Three, or better, Model Four. When the parties have committed to either of these processes, the actual resolution of the conflict follows an interest-based approach, as opposed to a power-based or rights-based approach. Claassen divides the interests defined by Ury, Brett, and Goldberg in the reconciliation of injustices and the reconciliation of all other interests.

Briefly stated, Claassen has defined the reconciliation of injustices in a three-step process. The first step is perspective sharing, except that the parties describe the injustices they have experienced, and the listening party summarizes back the injustices. This step repeats until all parties have expressed all of their injustices and feel that they have been adequately heard. The second step, restoring equity, requires the parties to consider how the injustices might be made as right as possible. Because injustices cannot be undone and cannot by their nature be remedied entirely by compensation, some process of apology and forgiveness is considered. In addition, the idea of "letting go" is part of the process. The third step involves future intentions as the parties consider how to prevent these injustices from occurring in the future. When these three steps are successfully completed, forgiveness is discovered.

Reconciliation of interests is an integrative problem solving process again taking three steps. The first step requires the parties to identify and list all the interests that must be satisfied for the dispute to be resolved. The second step requires each party to develop at least three options that satisfy all the interests, including the interests of the other party. The third step develops, from the options, proposals for satisfying the interests. Each party commits that he or she will consider the interests of the other to the same degree that his or her interests are personally important. Only if interests are truly irreconcilable, such that the satisfaction of one party's interest necessarily excludes the satisfaction of another party's interest, do the parties discuss rights-based solutions to the dispute.

Conclusion

Lawyers by training focus on power and rights-based methods of conflict resolution. The law school curriculum immerses students in legal rights and remedies involving the many subjects of law. New lawyers learn quickly that while rights-based resolution is theoretically nice, the true ability to help clients comes with understanding power. As we saw in chapter 1, Arnie Becker was not interested in his client's rights as much as he was in coercing the husband through inflammatory information to accede to the wife's financial demands.

Lawyers as peacemakers have a different orientation. In addition to considering rights-based solutions to disputes, lawyers as peacemakers will consider peacemaking models that strive to reconcile injustices and interests between the parties. This leads us naturally to understanding orientations to mediation, which is the subject of chapter 4.

Reflections on Chapter Three

You have been retained by the Republic of the Ukraine to give advice on a national justice system. Outline what considerations will be important in this engagement.

Why has litigation been considered the primary system for resolving rights-based disputes?

The State of Northern Siskiyou is considering a new statute requiring mediation of all disputes as a jurisdictional requirement before filing a civil lawsuit. What do you think about this idea? Should all cases be subjected to this rule? If not, what kinds of cases should be exempt?

CHAPTER FOUR

MEDIATION ORIENTATION

*T*WO FARMERS EACH CLAIMED to own a certain cow. While one farmer pulled on the cow's head and the other farmer pulled on her tail, the cow was milked simultaneously by the farmers' lawyers.

Another pair of farmers each claimed to own another cow. One farmer pulled on the cow's head and the other pulled on her tail. When they realized that their efforts were accomplishing nothing and that the cow's milk was going to waste, they decided to find a neutral third party to help mediate their dispute.

With the mediator's assistance, the farmers agreed to milk the cow on alternating days and split the meat when it came time to butcher her. These farmers' dispute was resolved quickly and it cost them each less milk and (more importantly) time. Meanwhile, the first pair of farmers eventually agreed to sell the cow to pay their legal fees.

Introduction

The concept of resolving disputes, especially legal disputes, without the civil trial process, has evolved quickly. In the 1970s, mediation and facilitation of litigated disputes was rare. Most lawyers had never heard of mediation and barely understood the concept of arbitration.

In states like California, a new process was introduced called the mandatory settlement conference. This process formalized a judicial practice that had been informally used for years. A trial court judge was assigned the task of meeting with counsel and parties to help agree on a settlement. Over the years, the mandatory settlement conference became a standard, expected process. It worked in enough cases that both court administrators and the bar supported it.

The mandatory settlement conference was a form of mediation insofar as an impartial third party worked with counsel to broker a resolution of the case. Typical settlement conference tactics involved evaluations and opinions by the judge on the likely outcome of the case and strong-arming concessions from counsel. Although the judge could not compel settlement, the power of the office coupled with a strong personality led to a fairly coercive process.

In the mid-1980s, as mediation began to emerge as a process for resolving litigated disputes, judges who had conducted settlement conferences successfully retired from public service and opened private mediation practices. They carried their settlement conference techniques with them and from this emerged a style of mediation now known as evaluative mediation.

Since that time, the dispute resolution community has split over the meaning of mediation. Is an evaluative style of intervention true mediation or not? Many argue that mediation is party empowering. Thus, the mediator's role is facilitative, not evaluative, and evaluative processes simply do not fall within mediation. Others contend that the market calls for evaluative mediators; therefore, the practice is accepted by the bar and is a legitimate form of mediation. This debate has been picked up in the law academy and, typical of many disputes, has generated some strong feelings on both sides.

One way to examine this debate is to explore orientations to processes and outcomes. Orientation to process draws us into the evaluative versus facilitative debate. Orientations to outcome, based on Folger and Bush's classic, *The Promise of Mediation* (Bush and Folger, 1994), consists of a continuum from a problem solving model to a transformative model. The recent work of Winslade and Monk and their narrative mediation concepts is also treated here (Winslade and Monk, 2000).

Taking all of these ideas into account, a theory of mediation develops to integrate and reconcile the various orientations based on the nature of the conflict. The theory proposes that the outcome will depend upon the nature of the conflict.

A Brief History

While mediation has existed throughout history, it did not come into practical use in America until the late 1900s. Beginning in the late nineteenth century, mediation emerged in response to disruptive conflicts between labor and management. Congress created special mediation agencies, such as the Board of Mediation and Conciliation for railroad labor (renamed the National Mediation Board in 1934) and the Federal Mediation and Conciliation Service to mediate collective bargaining disputes (Rogers and McEwen, 1994). This legislation reflected the belief that stable industrial peace could be achieved through the settlement of collective bargaining disputes. Settlement, in turn, could be advanced through conciliation, mediation, and voluntary arbitration. Mediation was not seen as an alternative to litigation. Instead, it was an alternative to strikes and the economic disruption that occurred when assisted settlement negotiations failed (Rogers and McEwen, 1994).

At about the same time, and for different reasons, various forms of mediation for nonlabor matters were introduced into courts. A group of lawyers and judges spoke on the topic to an American Bar Association meeting in 1923 (ABA Address, 1923). They advocated conciliation based on its cost-effectiveness for the courts and parties. They compared conciliation with litigation using traditional values from the legal system—speed, cost for the parties and the system, excess ability, repose, and fairness. In addition, they believed that conciliation taught honorable compromise and produced greater satisfaction among parties and witnesses. Thus, in contrast to the focus on interests of society-at-large that spurred the use of mediation in collective bargaining, supporters of conciliation focused on the needs of the parties and the courts (Rogers and McEwen, 1994).

Conciliation also appeared in domestic relations courts. An outgrowth of concern over rising divorce rates in the postwar years, these programs were intended to reduce the number divorces by requiring efforts at reconciliation, not to help divorces through less adversarial proceedings. While considered unsuccessful, they provided the structure for child custody mediation that emerged much later for other reasons.

After privately funded mediation efforts by the American Arbitration Association and others in the late 1960s, the Community Relations Service (CRS) of the United States Department of Justice in 1972 initiated mediation for civil rights disputes. The CRS staff mediated standards of prison, school, police-community, and other civil rights conflicts. Settlements became possible because the statutes also created new rights and remedies for persons subjected to discrimination thus increasing their bargaining power. Community-wide civil rights mediation was based on a policy of reducing discriminatory practices and promoting racial harmony rather than achieving less expensive dispositions of lawsuits (Rogers and McEwen, 1994).

Despite steady growth in labor, civil rights, and court mediation, conflict resolution and dispute resolution did not receive widespread attention until the 1970s. Although the 1970s were not a particularly litigious period, the federal appellate judges perceived substantial increases in their caseloads. Thus, these judges became interested in the greater efficiency of consensual dispute resolution compared to traditional litigation. Chief Justice Warren E. Burger called for a "fresh, hard look" at court procedures and alternative methods of dispute resolution. He warned that we had "reached the point where our system of justice—both state and federal—may literally break down before the end of this century, notwithstanding the great increase in the number of judges and a large infusion of court administrators." (Burger, 1982).

Many judges believed that informal alternatives would save the parties time and expense, divert cases from the courts, and reduce delay. Nevertheless, few courts seemed to support consensual dispute resolution programs that contributed to court efficiency. For example, nonbinding arbitration programs designed to make courts more efficient proliferated despite indications that the parties did not benefit. These programs remained even after some studies showed that the average cost of litigation increased.

Some people expressed a rising concern with impediments to "access to justice." The high costs, confusing and overly complex procedures, delay, and intimidation kept people with real grievances from pursuing them through the formal legal system. Informal alternatives such as mediation were advocated not only to streamline case processing and provide quicker and less expensive resolutions, but also to increase access to dispute resolution among parties who previously might have let their conflicts fester (Rogers and McEwen, 1994).

Others suggested that the growth of alternatives might provide more appropriate remedies and standards of decision than litigation, particularly for parties whose long-term relationships and disputes involved complex trade-offs. In addition, alternative methods would let parties control the resolution of their disputes instead of delegating them to lawyers and judges for decision. This meant altering the role of attorneys as representatives and principal actors in the dispute resolution process (Rogers and McEwen, 1994).

During this period, there were divergent assessments of the existing legal system and ADR. Those critiquing the legal system focused on how disputes were transformed when lawyers and judges translated the conflict into legal terms for litigation. They were also concerned about the exaggeration of conflict created by the litigation process, the court procedures that advantage parties with greater legal resources, especially the repeat players (Galanter, 1974), and the perceived "win/lose" results in litigation.

Those attacking settlement processes claimed that the use of individual rather than legal values in defining and reaching outcomes resulted in inequities for those groups already disadvantaged. Others predicted that ADR processes would lead to diminished protection of parties not at the table, frustration of laws designed to create social change, and the loss of the court's voice on public values through precedent. These critiques are considered at greater length in chapter 10.

In the 1990s, mediation and other dispute resolution procedures exploded in civil cases and administrative agency matters. Private dispute resolution and mediation grew into thriving professional practices. Mediation was perceived as a more efficient and powerful process than negotiation in settling cases. By the early 1990s, the problem of mediation specifically and dispute resolution generally was redefined from second-class justice to lack of access for the economically disadvantaged (Rogers and McEwen, 1994). The growth of civil case mediation and dispute resolution has been spurred by concerns about delay and the cost to parties and to the courts of traditional litigation. Increasingly, mediation has been viewed as an alternative to negotiation, not to trial.

In addition, conflicting visions of "true mediation" have been based on different views of mediation outcomes. Different outcomes are being translated into debates about what mediators should do and mediation should be. Thus, distinctions are made between rights-based and interest-based mediation and between the settlement-oriented and transformative approaches. Dean James Alfini has described differing mediation styles as the "bashers" who pressure for settlement, the "trashers" who evaluate case merits and values, and the "hashers" who play a role as negotiation facilitators (Alfini, 1991).

Orientation to Process

Some Terminology Issues

In *Preparing for Peace* (Lederach, 1995), John Paul Lederach points out how the evolution of terminology in conflict resolution illustrates social and cultural attitudes toward conflict and its outcomes. This is especially true in the emerging profession of mediation. A raging debate exists about the language of mediation and conflict resolution. This debate is so heated that those who use a particular nomenclature, description, or meaning have difficulty accepting how critics characterize their language. A full appreciation of peacemaking processes requires us to understand and accept this diversity of opinion.

Conflict resolution, as a description of conflict outcome, is an early and still dominant concept describing the more academic field of study and its practical application. The term "conflict resolution" indicates a need to understand the nature and cause of conflict. It encourages strategies and skills for dealing with the too often destructive outcomes of conflict. However, it subtly promotes the idea that conflict is undesirable and should be eliminated or reduced.

Conflict resolution as a term has another, deeper problem. As Nader has pointed out, it has too often meant seeking to stop the conflict and create harmony at the expense of justice (Nader, 1993). If justice has not occurred because the root cause of conflict remains untouched, reducing the overt expression of conflict may be an exercise of co-optation. Thus, conflict resolution may not be the best concept for describing conflict ebb and flow or the role of conflict in peacemaking.

"Conflict management" was another term that first came into vogue in the late 1970s. Conflict management views conflict as highly predictable, with understood patterns and dynamics that can be regulated. Conflict management did not seek to eliminate conflict, which was viewed as normal, but to prevent the destructive consequences of conflict. The problem with the term is that it does not describe our experiences with conflict. Everyday life tells us we do not really manage conflict in the way we manage other physical things in the world. Thus, like conflict resolution, conflict management has become a euphemism for avoiding the root causes of conflict and too often describes a superficial process.

Conflict management implies a primary interest in reducing or controlling volatility. While useful in defining and developing professionalism, conflict management does not capture the broader sense of peacemaking. Instead, conflict management narrows its focus to the technical and practical side of the effort.

A third term in common use is "conflict transformation." The concept of conflict transformation emerged in the 1990s as thinking about the potential of mediation evolved from reduction of hostility to engendering moral growth. Transformation does not suggest elimination or control of conflict, but takes a more wholistic view. Transformation views conflict as a necessary element in reconstructing and restructuring social organizations and realities. It may also be seen in descriptive terms. For example, conflict is seen to move through certain predictable phases, transforming relationships and social organization. Furthermore, expressions of conflict can be transformed from verbal disagreement, to antagonism, to overt mutually destructive hostility. Conflict may also transform perceptions of self, others, and issues, which raises the matter of self-identity and self-esteem.

Transformation may be seen in prescriptive terms. For example, in a transformational perspective, conflict can be seen as destructive energy needing to be channeled constructively. Likewise, conflict can be seen as a transforming agent for systemic change.

Riskin's Grid

Over the past decade, a debate has raged about orientation to mediation process. In 1994, Leonard Riskin proposed a system for classifying mediator orientations (Riskin, 1994, 1996). His classification system asked two principle questions. First, does the mediator tend to define problems narrowly or broadly? Second, does the mediator think she should evaluate—make assessments or predictions or proposals for agreements—or help the parties' negotiation without evaluating? According to Riskin, answers to these questions reflect mediator beliefs about the nature and scope of mediation and assumptions about the parties' expectations.

In Riskin's system, mediators with a narrow focus assume that the parties have come to them for help in solving a technical problem. This problem has been defined by the positions the parties have asserted in negotiations or pleadings. Typically, the parties have a distributive orientation. They ask questions such as "Who pays how much to whom?" Or, "Who can use the property?" The parties see the problem as a division of a resource in which one person gains and the other loses. Outcomes at trial, uncertainty, delay, and expense drive the mediation process. Parties, through their lawyers, will bargain as adversaries, emphasizing positions over interests. For example, an attorney might say "Our position is that the defendant is liable for his or her dishonest and fraudulent acts." An interest-based statement might be phrased instead as "My client relied on promises made by the defendant. As a result of this reliance, my client incurred relocation costs, lost earnings, and also lost other opportunities."

Mediators with a broad focus assume that the parties can benefit if the problem is defined beyond the narrow legal issues. Interests often lie beneath positions, and the mediator should help the parties satisfy those interests when possible.

The evaluative mediator assumes the parties need some direction for settlement. The direction might be based on law, industry standards, or technology. The mediator also assumes that she is qualified to give such direction based on experience, education, training, and objectivity. In contrast, the facilitative mediator assumes that the parties are intelligent, capable of solving their own problems, and understand their situation better than the lawyers and the mediator. Thus, the facilitative mediator sees her mission as enhancing and clarifying communications between the parties. Unlike an evaluative mediator, the facilitative mediator will not give an opinion concerning possible outcomes or settlements. First, the facilitative mediator believes that an opinion might impair her impartiality. Second, the facilitative mediator does not believe that she has enough information to render an informed opinion.

Based on these formulations, Riskin's grid looks as follows:

Evaluative

	Evaluative Narrow	evaluative broad	
Narrow			Broad
	Facilitative Narrow	facilitative broad	

Facilitative

From Riskin, 1994, 1996

According to Riskin, this grid implies that each type of mediator will use certain strategies to resolve conflict. The evaluative-narrow mediator defines the conflict in terms of strengths and weaknesses of positions and likely outcome at trial. This mediator will study carefully pertinent documents and pleadings before the mediation. During the mediation, this mediator employs evaluative techniques such as urging parties to settle or accept a settlement proposal; proposing position-based compromise agreements; predicting court outcomes; persuading parties to accept mediator assessments; and assessing strengths and weaknesses of each side, usually in private caucuses.

The facilitative-narrow mediator, like the evaluative-narrow mediator, provides reality checks for the parties. However, this mediator uses different techniques. The facilitative-narrow mediator will not assess or predict outcomes, study relevant documents, or apply pressure to settle. Instead, usually in private caucuses, the facilitative-narrow mediator will help the parties understand each side's position and the consequences of not settling. In addition, in private caucuses, the facilitative-narrow mediator will help the parties assess proposals and formulate alternatives. The facilitative-narrow mediator might ask what are the strengths and weaknesses of your case? Of the other side's case? What are the best, worst, and most likely outcomes of litigation? How did you make these assessments? Have you thought about other issues? How long will it take to get to trial? How long will the trial last? What will be the associated costs in money, emotions, or reputation?

The evaluative-broad mediator emphasizes interests over positions and proposes solutions to accommodate those interests. Because the evaluative-broad mediator constructs the agreement, she emphasizes her own understanding of the conflict as much as the parties. The evaluative-broad mediator will study relevant documents, pleadings, and briefs, but will also uncover underlying interests. Typical techniques include explaining that the goal of mediation can include addressing underlying interests; encouraging the real parties or decision-makers to attend and participate; asking about situations, plans, needs, and interests; and speculating about underlying interests and asking for confirmation.

The evaluative-broad mediator provides predictions, assessments, and recommendations, emphasizing options that satisfy broader interests rather than narrow positions.

The facilitative-broad mediator encourages parties to consider underlying interests rather than positions. She helps parties generate and assess proposals designed to accommodate those interests. Techniques might include encouraging the parties to discuss underlying interests in joint sessions and encouraging and helping the parties develop their own proposals.

The facilitative-broad mediator does not provide predictions, assessments, or recommendations. In facilitative-broad mediation, legal argument occupies a lesser position. The facilitative-broad mediator does not need to understand fully the legal posture of the case, but must be able to grasp quickly the legal and substantive issues to respond to the dynamics of the situation. In addition, this mediator must be able to help the parties realistically evaluate proposals.

Kovach and Love's Model

Riskin's Grid has made a substantial contribution by clarifying the state of mediation practice and stimulating debate about ways to improve it. But the grid has been criticized as tending to legitimize evaluative mediation. Many scholars and practitioners believe evaluative processes do not belong in the definition of mediation. Mediation, in their view, is a process that fosters party autonomy and party decision-making. This understanding of mediation corresponds to Claassen's Models Three and Four insofar as the processes involve a reconciliation of injustices and interests.

Kimberlee K. Kovach and Lela P. Love offer a model slightly different than Riskin's Grid (Kovach and Love, 1998). Their model emphasizes what they see as profound differences between adjudicative-evaluative dispute processing and facilitative dispute processing. In this model, a "Great Divide" separates processes that require evaluation from those that require facilitation. In processes where the mediator renders a judgment, decision, or opinion, the neutral has an evaluative role. In consensus-building processes, the mediator has a facilitative role.

They point out certain implications of their model. First, they recognize that some evaluations require substantial qualifications. They believe that evaluators in legal contexts must be lawyers. This is because lawyers are constrained by rules of professional conduct, liable for malpractice, and educated in norms of credible evidence, fact-finding procedures, burdens of proof, and appropriate legal research and analysis. In nonlegal disputes, similarly high standards for evaluators should apply.

Second, they believe that tactics and strategies should be appropriate to the orientation of the mediator. Evaluators should not use caucuses because of due process concerns. Furthermore, mediators should not be evaluators because mediation training normally does not include instruction on assessing credibility, weighing evidence, assigning the proper burden of proof, or conducting appropriate research. When mediators offer opinions on likely judicial outcomes, questions are raised about the duty to research before evaluating, the liability for erroneous conclusions, and the possible unauthorized practice of law.

On the other hand, facilitators may elicit information about assumptions, feelings, and perspectives that would be inadmissible in a fact-finding or evaluative process. In an evaluative process, hearsay evidence would normally not be considered or would be discounted substantially. In a facilitative process, rules of evidence simply would not apply.

Strategic Choice Model

While Riskin's Grid and the Kovach and Love model describe orientations to processes, the strategic choice model of mediation (Carnevale, 1986) was designed to predict mediator strategies and orientations based on circumstances. The model considers four basic mediator strategies: compensation, pressure, integration, and inaction. Compensation occurs when the mediator provides some outside incentive to the parties (such as building an airport in the Gaza Strip). Pressure includes tactics such as threats and promises and other forms of coercion and heavy persuasion. Integration is a form of informational power that involves efforts to find a solution satisfying both parties' major aspirations. Inaction involves letting the disputants handle the controversy by themselves.

The model assumes that mediator strategy is determined by the mediator's assessment of the costs and benefits associated with a strategy, the perceived feasibility of a strategy, and mediator incentives. According to the model, two factors determine the mediator's choice of strategy. The first factor is the value the mediator places on having disputants achieve their aspirations. This value may be based on a genuine concern for the disputants' welfare or from a strategic concern when the mediator has interests in the outcome of the dispute. The second factor is the mediator's assessment of the probability that a mutually acceptable solution will be found, or "perceived common ground." Perceived common ground implies that the parties have low aspirations or that they are being cooperative with one another.

According to the model, mediators integrate when they want the parties to achieve their aspirations and there is common ground. In this case, an integrating strategy is worth the time and effort and is feasible because there is a good chance of finding a mutually acceptable solution.

Mediators press when they do not care whether the parties achieve their aspirations and when there is little common ground. In this case, pressure is feasible because the mediator is not afraid to alienate the parties.

Mediators compensate when they want the parties to achieve their aspirations, but there is little common ground. In this case, compensation is worth the costs. Mediators become inactive when they do not care if the parties achieve their aspirations and when there is much common ground. Inaction becomes feasible because there is a good chance that the parties will reach agreement on their own.

The model assumes that mediators not only consider reasons to use a strategy, but also reasons not to use a strategy. When there is little perceived common ground, for example, mediators may decide not to integrate because there is little chance that an integrative agreement will be found. When perceived common ground is high, mediators may decide not to compensate or press because the strategies are not necessary. When mediators do not value the parties' aspirations, they may decide not to compensate or integrate because the strategies are not worth the cost and effort. When the parties' aspirations are valued, mediators decide not to press or be inactive because the strategies are not likely to lead to the parties' aspirations being met.

Carnevale's model describes mediator behavior (e.g., facilitative or evaluative) as contingent on the perceived common ground between the parties. Carnevale's model assumes that mediators have the skills and abilities to engage in the four strategies. In addition, his model assumes that a mediator can correctly assess the conflict and choose an appropriate strategy.

Evaluative Mediation

A mediator is being "evaluative" when she has an evaluative orientation and identity, when she asserts an opinion on the likely court outcome, or when she advocates a "fair" or correct resolution of an issue in dispute. In the mediation of litigated disputes, mediators are usually lawyers or retired judges (Love, 1997). They tend to revert to their default adversarial mode, analyzing the legal merits of the case to move toward settlement. Although many of these mediators are trained in facilitative techniques, case evaluation dominates their practice. This "legalized" approach often resembles nonbinding arbitration more than pure mediation. It neither reorients parties toward each other nor fosters collaborative problem solving, but instead provides a forum for third-party evaluation of the situation.

This practice is defended on the theory that the parties want it. In the court-connected context, lawyers are the consumers of mediation services. Studies indicate that lawyers prefer mediators who give evaluations, who have experience as litigators, and who have expertise in the subject matter of the dispute. These lawyer preferences are not surprising. Lawyers, like most people, feel more comfortable with what they know best. Lawyers customarily speak for their clients and present adversarial arguments about the merits of the case. Accordingly, they attempt to draw mediation back into the adversarial paradigm and look for mediators who accommodate this.

Arguments Supporting Evaluative Mediation

Evaluative mediation can unfold in a variety of ways. The stereotypical evaluative mediator is the retired judge turned mediator. The judge, focusing narrowly on the issues at hand, listens to both sides. Drawing upon years of judicial experience, she suggests to the parties what they ought to do to settle the case in explicit and specific terms. She is not reluctant to address, from expertise, the strengths and weaknesses of the case. She is extremely confident about her understanding and ability to predict the likely outcome in an adjudicatory forum. She believes her role is to be honest and direct and, drawing on years of experience, to get the case settled (Kovach and Love, 1996).

Evaluative mediation poses some risk to the settlement of a particular case; some risk to the process of mediation, including its reputation; and some risk to the particular mediators and parties involved in a specific case. The fact that there may be risk, however, may not be justification for ignoring a technique that might aid settlement.

Those who support evaluative mediation observe that there is risk in not evaluating a dispute that could be settled but then turns into protracted, expensive, and harmful litigation. There is risk in allowing parties to settle a case in such a way that it does not comply with an outcome the court will require. There is risk in allowing inexperience to prevail over experience. The response is not to try to eliminate the risk of evaluation, but to manage it intelligently, thoughtfully, and strategically (Lowery, 2000).

In addition, evaluative supporters say that the mediation community must accept the reality of the marketplace. For a large number of lawyers and clients, evaluation is exactly what they expect from mediation. Retired judges and experienced litigators who offer specific evaluation as a normal and important part of the process are professionally and financially successful. They are regularly chosen voluntarily, and many of their practices are booming, because disputants and lawyers desire their understanding of the settlement context of a particular case. The Judicial and Meditation Service (JAMS), a for-profit organization that supplies private judges and mediators for lawyers and their clients, one of the largest dispute resolution providers in the nation, is composed primarily of retired judges who lean toward the evaluative side of the continuum. The approach of those mediators might be offensive to some. While their technique might not be included as a separate chapter in most mediation textbooks, the tens of thousands who are their clients endorse and embrace the evaluative process.

Thus, the question to evaluate or to not evaluate is not the question for many practitioners. The question is when and how a mediator should evaluate. The answer: Evaluation ought to take place at a time when its influence will be greatest. Evaluation is neither a tool for the mediator to demonstrate the mediator's own competence, nor a challenge for the mediator to manipulate a case so it comes out as he or she designates. Rather, evaluation is a technique to move parties from impasse to a mutually agreeable settlement. Evaluation ought to be saved for those moments when movement from clear impasse is essential to resolution. That time might be during caucus when the evaluation is used to frame what is relevant to a settlement, or it might be very late in the process as parties are trying to decide who gets how much of the last relatively small amount of value. An evaluation can help the parties move sufficiently so a settlement can occur. The exact time for evaluation is never the same, but timing is an important, perhaps critical, consideration.

The evaluation style may also be critical. Some evaluators, in a self-effacing way, suggest an extremely tentative perspective on a particular issue or outcome. Others, with a great deal of self-confidence and egocentric focus, express in a dogmatic and perhaps abrasive way their evaluation on how a particular issue should be resolved.

The nature of the evaluation will also be affected by the relationship the mediator wants to establish with participants. Some mediators want to be liked and want to be perceived as a colleague in the grand problem solving process. This mediator, having established excellent relationships with the parties, will draw upon the great sense of trust and regard to provide an evaluative perspective. Alternatively, some individuals could care less about their personal relationship with the parties at the table. They are more interested in putting a notch on their mediation success belt, and cannot believe that parties would not call them back for another successful mediation session. Obviously, the kind of relationship one would want with the parties might influence the nature and approach to evaluation.

Oftentimes, the nature of the conflict calls for evaluation. For instance, a claim relating to something for which the alternative is extraordinarily clear may allow the mediator greater confidence and promote more willingness to be evaluative. In the family area, mediators suggest that there are relatively few questions as to the preferences of the court on a number of items in a marriage dissolution case. If that is true, the mediator may be more willing to evaluate with a great deal of confidence. On the other hand, there are cases for which there are no clear external alternatives— for instance, a management dispute between an employer and an employee. Thus, in that context, the predictability of an outcome in another forum is uncertain. In essence, the basis for evaluation may simply not exist.

The focus of evaluation should also be considered carefully. Sometimes evaluation on the merits of a party's case will move people from their position. Sometimes the focus of evaluation is a numerical settlement value of the case at hand. Sometimes the actions, attitudes, and behavior of the parties need to be evaluated by a neutral third party. Sometimes, the evaluation is of the state of the negotiation and what it might take to move from impasse to resolution. Consequently, the focus of what is evaluated should be the subject of careful analysis and planning.

The method of evaluation may make a difference as well. For instance, if the issue is the amount of appropriate damages in a simple personal injury case, the mediator might simply state what the damages appear to be. Such a mediator might say, "I have seen these before. I know what this kind of case will be worth in court. I urge you to settle it in the range of $18,000 to $20,000. This means you, plaintiff, need to lower your demand by $5,000." There is a simplicity that is attractive in this statement. There is a sense of expertise. There is an expression of confidence that such expertise is right. This confidence may well influence a party's negotiating position.

Alternatively, the mediator could lead the parties to the same place through a series of questions. These questions reflect evaluation, but may be less onerous. For instance, in the same personal injury case, the mediator might ask plaintiff's counsel, "What is the jury verdict range for these kinds of cases?" "What is the settlement range for these types of injuries?" "Does the existence of this particular fact increase or decrease the likelihood of being at the top of that settlement range?" "If that fact puts this case at the bottom of the settlement range, does it not seem reasonable to lower your demand so that you are within an accepted range and therefore are attracting the insurance company to meet you there and settle the case?"

The questions lead to a conclusion, based upon the mediator's understanding or, if you will, evaluation of the case. Such questioning can be expressed in an indicting spirit, or it can be expressed in the spirit of one who is seeking to understand a way that the parties can come together. In any event, the mediator has never made a statement of his or her opinion, but has reflected it in his questions.

Thus, although evaluative mediation has been heavily criticized, it forms a substantial portion of the market, at least in the mediation of litigated disputes. Supporters of evaluative mediation insist on its appropriateness when used correctly by experienced neutrals.

Critiques of Evaluative Mediation

There are many reactions to the picture of the retired judge-mediator throwing her weight around in the mediation conference room. Critics first suggest that the evaluative approach reduces the parties' ability to resolve their case independently. The parties may be influenced by the power of the mediator's position. When encouraged to settle based upon the evaluation of the neutral, the parties may be dissatisfied with both the result and the process.

The evaluation could be wrong. Studies of evaluators suggest that, giving ten case files to ten experts, will probably result in not a consensus evaluation, but a range of the "right" outcome. To be more specific, the evaluative mediator may simply be wrong in the substantive evaluation. Erroneous evaluations are a risk to the parties, a risk to the mediator's personal reputation, and a risk to the ultimate success of the process.

Evaluation may close the mediation process too quickly. Even if the result is right, an early evaluation may deprive the parties of the chance to share their story or describe their case. People need to be listened to, and mediation provides that opportunity. A hasty evaluation may result in a sense of injustice and may decrease, in the parties' eyes, the uniqueness and value of the mediation moment. People's perception of justice depends heavily on whether they have been heard.

Evaluation may irreparably damage the negotiation. If the core of the mediation is negotiation—a communication process used to put deals together or resolve conflicts—then activities inhibiting communication may adversely affect the negotiation. An evaluation that encourages one side and discourages the other side could result in less willingness to negotiate.

The evaluation may define the conflict too narrowly. Although some cases involve a simple, single money issue, most cases reflect highly complex, deeply layered conflicts. Gravitation to the purely legal issues and evaluating what is likely to occur in a court room may miss other more important, but less legalistic, issues. The mindset of litigation defines what is "relevant" in that forum, but not what is necessarily relevant in mediation.

Evaluation necessitates that the mediator be trained for evaluation, which may limit mediation to lawyers and judges. If an opinion on a likely jury verdict or the merits of a particular legal case must be given, only those who have substantive legal expertise will be able to do so. This could decrease the talent and diversity in the pool of mediators, and push mediation into a more adversarial process.

The evaluation confuses the role of the mediator. Although some make substantial effort to clarify and seek specific permission from the parties to carry out the role of facilitator, if any evaluation occurs, the participants may become confused. This is more likely with inexperienced parties. They hear the introductory comments about the facilitative nature of mediation and allowing parties to control process and the outcome. Sometime later, the mediator suggests a predicted outcome if the case is resolved in another forum. If the groundwork for such activity is not painstakingly laid, parties are likely to be offended by the mediator's evaluation.

If the mediator assumes an evaluative orientation, the parties concentrate on influencing the mediator instead of crafting outcomes for themselves. Most evaluative mediators do not cultivate opportunities for self-determination or enhanced understanding among parties. They seek presentation of evidence and arguments, typically by lawyers. Expert advocates—not parties—become the central players. The mediator's evaluation—not the parties' decision-making—becomes the main focus of the process. This "lawyerization" of mediation not only minimizes party participation but also requires that the mediator be, first and foremost, a capable evaluator. This changes the mediator's role and de-emphasizes the skills necessary to promote constructive party participation and self-determination.

Evaluative mediation is based on threats and rewards. The threats are usually implied, but are based on fear of losing. Evaluative mediation can be controlling and coercive when parties are forced to come to settlement or face an unpleasant future. Thus, evaluative mediation builds settlements on negative emotions: Fear of the unknown; fear of losing, fear of unbounded costs; and anxiety arising from uncertainty.

Evaluative mediation cannot deal with injustice. Ultimately, evaluative mediation is limited to an assessment of what judicial remedies might be possible. Since courts are limited to three remedies (compensation, coercive orders, and declarations of rights), evaluative mediation, to the extent it purports to be predictive of judicial outcome, is likewise limited. Thus, apology and forgiveness, acknowledgement and recognition of others' perspectives, and creative problem solving are not possible within the evaluative model.

Evaluative mediation is useless against people immune to fear. Since it is predicated on describing dire outcomes, evaluative mediation will not work against those parties or counsel with a high tolerance for risk. Generally, immunity to fear is caused by psychological rigidity, training, gross power imbalance, or experience and sophistication. Evaluative mediation is helpless against parties with these characteristics.

Evaluative mediation makes a huge assumption that parties are rationally self-interested decision-makers. Evaluative mediation does not consider two fundamentally different views of rational self-interest—maximizing utility versus minimizing the maximum loss the other can impose (the minimax solution). Furthermore, evaluative orientations ignore the dominating effects of human emotional processing on higher cognitive processes. Evaluative mediators are most likely to face impasse when the conflict is driven by relationship or identity goals.

Evaluative orientations also raise ethical issues for lawyers acting as mediators. At the national level, the American Bar Association Sections of Dispute Resolution and Litigation (ABA), the Society of

Professionals in Dispute Resolution (SPIDR), and the American Arbitration Association (AAA) developed and adopted the "Standards of Conduct for Mediators" in 1994.[1] These standards seem to reject evaluative orientation, recognizing self-determination as "the fundamental principle of mediation." In reference to the evaluative-facilitative debate, the Joint Standards state that mediators should not advise the parties. The drafting committee asserts that mediator conduct should focus primarily on assisting the parties so they might reach their own solution. Furthermore, the "Comments to the Joint Standards" notes that when mediators give advice, they engage in an activity other than mediation and accordingly should so advise the disputing parties. These issues are taken up in chapter 15 on ethics.

The evaluative orientation also raises professional liability issues for mediators. Lawyer-mediators who accept the parties' invitation to evaluate the merits of the dispute after having received confidential information, without having invested the same degree of research and factual exploration as would be required to support a formal legal opinion, risk being sued for malpractice. Lawyer-mediators are often asked for their opinions because parties tend to perceive lawyer-mediators as experts in the law. This is especially true if a lawyer-mediator is a trial lawyer, a specialist in a particular substantive area of law, or a former judge.

An attorney's legal opinion must be based on adequate research and sufficient factual inquiry to support an intelligent assessment of the problem. Oftentimes, lawyer-mediators will offer opinions about trial outcomes without being grounded in the necessary research and factual investigation. Thus, even though lawyer-mediators attempt to distance themselves from an attorney-client relationship, they are still subject to ethical rules. Under these rules, an attorney-client relationship may be implied from giving advice and expecting the parties to rely upon it. Thus, a lawyer-mediator may inadvertently create an attorney-client relationship by engaging in evaluative mediation processes (Hoffman and Affolder, 2000).

Facilitative Mediation

A facilitative orientation is marked by consensus-building processes that support party decision-making and reflect the parties' priorities and sense of justice. The facilitative mediator assumes the parties are intelligent, able to work with their counterparts, and capable of understanding their situations better than either their lawyers or the mediator. Consequently, the facilitative mediator understands that the parties may develop better solutions. For these reasons, the facilitative mediator sees her principal mission as enhancing and clarifying communication between the parties to help them decide how the resolve their conflict (Kovach and Love, 1998).

The facilitative mediator believes her opinion or evaluation is inappropriate because she might be compromising her impartiality. She also recognizes that she does not have enough information to give an informed opinion. Typically, the facilitative mediator will help the parties to find, understand, and resolve the problems they wished to address. The parties are encouraged to consider underlying interests rather than positions. The facilitative mediator helps the parties generate and assess proposals designed to accommodate those interests. Finally, the facilitative mediator does not provide assessments, predictions, or proposals. Instead, the facilitative mediator prods the parties to generate and consider options for satisfying all the interests raised in the conflict.

Facilitative mediators have difficulty in purely distributive bargaining situations. These disputes typically involve a transfer of resources from one party to another, such as from an insurance company to an automobile accident victim. The discussion centers on factors that either raise or lower the effective "market" value of the case. The assumptions underlying facilitative mediation simply do not apply in pure distributive bargaining conflicts. First, the parties may not necessarily be equally intelligent or equally educated. A first generation immigrant from Southeast Asia is not at the same level as an experienced insurance adjuster or defense attorney

Second, in distributive bargaining situations, the parties may not be able to work together simply because their interests are so divergent. Finally, in common personal injury cases, the parties, at least the victims, do not understand their situation better than the lawyers. Since the court system provides, through jury verdicts, a valuation system, the lawyers and insurance adjusters have exclusive access to relevant information about settlement.

Facilitative mediation is most effective when existing relationships are in place, the parties have some motivation to settle, even if they are highly escalated, and the parties are relatively equal in social power. Facilitative mediation is also effective when the parties have the time and desire to engage in integrative problem solving as opposed to distributive bargaining.

Orientation to Outcome

Another way to look at orientation is to consider outcomes. Based on outcomes, three orientations have developed: problem solving, transformation, and narrative. Each of these orientations measures the successful outcome of conflict differently. Problem solving asks if the conflict was settled to the parties' satisfaction. Transformation asks if through empowerment and recognition, the parties experienced some moral growth. Narrative mediation asks if a new reality has been constructed to replace the conflict-laden reality of the past. Each of these orientations has advantages to peacemakers.

Problem-Solving Orientation

The dominant approach to mediation practice focuses on solving problems and achieving settlement (Bush and Folger, 1994). This approach is based on the premise that meeting the needs of the parties produces the highest satisfaction. Thus, the orientation to conflict is that conflict is caused by incompatible or clashing needs. The problem posed by mediation is how to satisfy all of the needs collaboratively. This orientation emphasizes reframing conflict as mutual problems to be solved jointly by the parties. Mediation is therefore viewed as a technology for problem solving.

Fisher, Ury, and Patton (1981) epitomize the problem-solving orientation to outcome. They introduced the idea of principled negotiation, focusing on interests not positions, on problems as problems, and on people as people. Their concepts, such as BATNA (Best Alternative to a Negotiated Agreement) and ACBD (Always Consult Before Deciding) have become entrenched in the conflict resolution lexicon. Ultimately, they see effective conflict resolution as collaborative problem solving. Outcomes are best when the interests of all parties have been satisfied.

The problem-solving orientation to conflict has largely been accepted because the dominant alternative, a distributive orientation, has been too destructive. The adversary ideology implicit in civil trials reflects a strong distributive orientation in that a decision ends the conflict by declaring one party right and the other wrong. Ideally, in a distributive orientation, the party with the superior claim on limited resources should prevail. The determination of the superior claim is based on fairness embodied in rules of law. Thus, a contest is held to determine the winner. Unfortunately, the contest becomes the focus of effort, leading to a costly, inefficient, unsatisfactory process. Mediation, having a problem-solving orientation, provides a necessary corrective to that process.

In a classic study of mediator style differences, Silbey and Merry described the two different problem-solving styles as the bargaining mode and the therapeutic mode (Silbey and Merry, 1986). In the bargaining mode, the mediator claims professional expertise in law and adjudication. This mediator criticizes the legal system as costly, inefficient, and unpredictable. Mediation is intended to reach settlement through private caucuses, looking for bottom lines, narrowing issues, managing auctions (the cycle of offers and counteroffers), and avoiding intractable differences. In the therapeutic mode, the mediator claims professional expertise in managing interpersonal relationships. Mediation is intended to improve communication and reach mutual understanding through collective agreements. The therapeutic mediator focuses on emotional concerns, criticizing the legal system for its tendency to ignore emotions and destroy relationships.

Although different in process, both styles are strongly oriented to problem solving. The bargaining mode is a no-nonsense, get to the bottom line approach to resolving conflict. It emphasizes rational self-interest, business efficiency, and nonemotional detachment from what are usually seen ultimately as financial decisions. Emotions are avoided because they tend to divert people off the problem-solving course and, worse, are viewed as unpredictable, uncontrollable, and dangerous. The therapeutic mode is viewed condescendingly by the bargaining school as too subjective and is therefore discounted as an effective way of dealing with hardheaded business and legal problems. However, the therapeutic school sees the circuitous and time-consuming process of rebuilding communication as more likely to deal realistically with the root causes of conflict. Even therapeutic mediators, however, must return to the narrow focus of the conflict, which, in litigation, is almost always about money.

Most studies of mediation measure rates of settlement, levels of party satisfaction, and the quality of substantive outcomes. The focus of these studies is to find strategies that will help mediators settle cases. Not surprisingly, many mediators tout their abilities on their success rate measured by percentage of settled cases. In fact, a certain degree of competition between some problem-solving mediators exists concerning settlement rates.

In the problem-solving orientation, many mediators believe their job is to find the optimal solution to the conflict. Thus, they are willing to be directive and influential over the outcome of the case. The difficulty arises because mediator bias or professional prejudice leads the mediator to control the process to achieve what the mediator believes to be the best outcome. Through global assessments of the conflict, reframing issues, and discarding intangible issues, the problem-solving mediator focuses the parties on optimal, from the mediator's perspective, outcomes.

Transformative Orientation

Folger and Bush have a different view of proper orientation to outcome. In their classic, *The Promise of Mediation* (Bush and Folger, 1994), they propose a Transformative Model of conflict resolution. In this model, the mediator's primary goal is not to reach settlement, but to allow the parties to experience moral growth. In the Transformative Model, moral growth is engendered through self-empowerment and recognition of the other. Folger and Bush argue that only this type of mediation has the power to transform conflicts and the people within them.

The transformative orientation to conflict sees conflict as an opportunity for moral growth and transformation by reflecting on choices and actions. Through the transformative process, the individual is allowed to reach self and relate to others, strengthening his capacity for experiencing concern and consideration for others. According to Folger and Bush, full moral development involves an integration of individual autonomy and concern for others.

The transformational view of conflict is different than the problem-solving orientation. A conflict confronts each party with a challenge because there is some difficulty or adversity to be grappled with. Conflict also affords people the opportunity to develop self-determination and self-reliance, to acknowledge the perspectives of others, and to feel and express some degree of understanding and concern for another. All of these opportunities exist despite diversity and disagreement. In short, the transformational orientation sees the response to conflict as transforming people from fearful, defensive, or self-centered beings into confident, responsive, and caring beings.

Mediator behavior under a transformative orientation is likewise different from problem-solving mediation. First, the transformative mediator is focused on the parties' contributions to the process. He enters the session looking for and expecting to find myriad opportunities for empowerment and recognition. He encourages the parties' deliberation and choice making. He clarifies available

MEDIATION ORIENTATION / 103

choice at all key junctures. He encourages parties to reflect and deliberate with full awareness of their options, goals, and resources. He looks for openings that allow one party to consider the other's situation or point of view. He reinterprets, translates, and reframes parties' statements to make the parties more intelligible to each other. He asks the parties to consider the significance of reformulation, pointing out opportunities for recognition without forcing them.

Hallmarks of Transformative Mediation. The book, *The Promise of Mediation,* was largely conceptual and theoretical. Following its publication, mediators wondered how a transformative practice differed from problem solving. Folger and Bush answered this in a 1996 article concerning the hallmarks of transformative practice (Bush and Folger, 1996). They described 10 habits of a transformative mediator. Each of the ten habits describes what the transformative mediation process is about. In addition, these habits illustrate the attitudes of the transformative mediator. As characterized by Folger and Bush, the ten hallmarks of transformative practice are as follows:

- The opening statement describes the mediator's role and objectives in terms based on empowerment and recognition.
- The mediator leaves the responsibility for outcome with the parties.
- The mediator consciously refuses to be judgmental about the parties' views and decisions.
- The mediator holds an optimistic view of the parties' competence and motives.
- The mediator allows for and responds to the parties' expression of emotion.
- The mediator allows for and explores the parties' uncertainty.
- The mediator remains focused on the here and now of the conflict interaction.
- The mediator is responsive to the parties' statements about past events.
- The mediator views an intervention as one point in a larger sequence of conflict interaction.
- The mediator feels a sense of success when empowerment and recognition occur, even in small degrees.

The transformative orientation to outcome defines success based on the parties' perceptions, growth in knowledge, and improved ability to choose. A transformative mediation is successful if the parties saw opportunities during the process for empowerment and recognition; the parties clarified their goals, options, and resources;

the parties made free, well-informed decisions at every decision point; and the parties gave recognition to the other whenever it was their decision to do so.

Narrative Orientation

Australian mediators Winslade and Monk have developed a third orientation to outcome based on their process of narrative mediation (Winslade and Monk, 2000). Their thesis is based on post-modernist thought, which states that reality is constructed from people's conversations or discourses with each other. The narrative orientation sees conflict as normal and expected. Under the narrative mediation model, the parties, with the assistance of the mediator, construct a new narrative story. This story reframes the parties' perceptions to permit the conflict to be resolved cooperatively.

According to the narrative orientation, problem- solving approaches emphasize the individual as an independent, stable, unitary, self-motivating, and self-regulating entity. This definition relies on internal unmet or unsatisfied needs as the cause of conflict. More often that not, a person's perceptions of unmet needs is culturally created. Thus, conflict, when viewed as clash of unmet needs, is a creature of culture.

Narrative mediation consequently looks for the narrow cultural and social prescriptions that create unmet needs and constrain the ability to view other options. Problems are seen as constructed within a pattern of relationships, and social context is the key to understanding self and identity. Identity is not fixed, but is constantly changing under the effects of cultural arrangements present in day-to-day interactions with people. In each interaction, people re-create or reconstruct themselves anew. Thus, people take on multiple identities. In narrative mediation, the context in which alternatives are created is itself changed, and new choices then become possible.

The narrative orientation believes that when a conflict story takes root, it generates a momentum that does not reflect the facts or realities of the situation. In narrative mediation, success is dependent on the extent to which the mediator can work with the parties to create an alternative story. The story needs to be plausible and to include significant events of the conflict story in a way that makes sense to the participants.

The narrative mediation process has three phases: engagement, deconstructing the conflict-saturated story, and constructing the alternate story.

In the engagement, the narrative mediator is interested in learning the story from which the person is operating, not what the person is telling. Narrative engagement validates people's perspectives as a preliminary step toward expanding the possibilities available in the stories beyond what the complex story might predict. The narrative orientation might be described as an effort to join the parties in an alliance against the effects of the conflict.

After the participants have told their stories, the narrative mediator begins to separate the parties from the conflict-saturated story. This work is deconstructive because it undermines the certainties on which the conflict feeds. It invites the parties to view the story of the dispute from a different perspective.

The heart of the deconstructive phase of narrative mediation involves the mediator asking questions that will open up space for reconsideration of the conflict-saturated story. Careful inquiry into the meanings of the elements of the stories that parties tell avoids taking any particular meaning for granted. It also conveys the idea that meanings are not fixed, but are instead negotiable in conversation. Oftentimes, the narrative mediator might take up a curious, naive posture to understand how the conflict began.

In a narrative conversation the problem is objectified and the people are approached as subjects. The spirit of narrative mediation is embodied as always speaking to people as if they are subjects, or are active rather than passive. In contrast, the conflict is treated as an object, with a separate identity from the parties.

The parties are invited to make a judgment about whether they wish the conflict to continue or not. Since social constructionism states that we speak ourselves into existence, speaking out loud the desire to end an argument opens the door for that to happen. Both parties hear themselves state that they wish the argument to end and they know that they have been heard to say it. They both have also heard the other person say it. This gives them the chance to make meaning about the other person that may not have been possible under the influence of the conflict story.

The narrative mediator does not just allow such meaning to happen, but actually solicits it by asking direct questions. These questions are kept small so as not to require too big a step toward change. The process is closely analogous to managing the process of adaptive change.

Comparison of Orientations

The following table compares the three orientations to outcome.

	Problem-Solving	Transformative	Narrative
Assumption	People want their problems solved	People are best able to choose their outcomes.	Reality is socially constructed through discourses.
Conflict orientation	Clash of unmet needs	Conflict is an opportunity	Conflict is normal and necessary
Process	Bargaining Mode Therapeutic Mode	Empowerment and recognition	Perspective, deconstruction, new construction
Outcome	Case settled, problem solved	Moral growth	New reality without conflict-laden story

All of these orientations are valid. All have their strengths and weaknesses. How then do we reconcile their various sharp differences? The answer is in what is missing from each orientation—an understanding and assessment of the nature of the conflict. This turns us to consideration of a theory of mediation reconciling these three orientations.

A Theory of Mediation

A theory of mediation should provide a descriptive prediction of what orientations, processes, and outcomes might be expected in a given conflict or dispute. Considering these criteria, a theory of mediation can be stated as follows:

The nature of the conflict dictates the mediation process to be used and the conflict's likely outcome.

Theorem 1: As long as the conflict remains centered on content goals and has not escalated beyond Stage 3[2], brokered distributive bargaining, interest-based negotiation, and evaluative mediation with an outcome orientation directed to problem solving are effective and efficient processes for gaining conflict resolution.

Corollary to Theorem 1: Brokered bargaining, interest-based negotiation, and evaluative mediation processes are not efficient or effective at high levels of conflict escalation or when identity or relationship goals[3] are in play.

Rationale: Evaluative mediation and problem solving implicitly assumes that the disputants are rationally self interested in maximizing their utility. Thus, evaluative mediators expect that disputants will attempt to avoid losses and seek economic gains. At low levels of conflict escalation and when content goals are solely in play, these assumptions are generally valid. When the conflict has escalated to Stage 4 or Stage 5, the disputants are no longer acting in their rational self-interest. Similarly, when relationship or identity goals are in play, rational self-interest is not operative. Thus, in these cases evaluative mediation will probably not be effective.

Theorem 2: As long as the conflict remains centered on identity or relationship goals or has escalated to Stage 4 or 5, transformative or narrative mediation processes are effective and efficient processes for achieving appropriate conflict resolution.

Corollary to No. 2: Transformative and narrative processes are not efficient or effective at low levels of escalation or in purely distributive bargaining conflict situations.

Rationale: Transformative and narrative mediation processes do not assume that disputants are rationally self-interested. Consequently, these processes are effective in nonrational conditions (e.g., relationship and identity conflicts). In particular, narrative mediation assumes only that conflict is one reality constructed by the disputants, that it can be deconstructed, and that a new reality can replace the old, conflict-laden reality. Transformative mediation likewise does not rely on rational self-interest. Instead, it seeks a reordering of internal perception (empowerment) and external perceptions (acknowledgement and recognition of the other).

If the disputants' internal and external perceptions are sufficiently changed to permit empowerment and recognition, transformative mediation declares itself successful. Transformative and narrative processes tend to be ineffective in purely distributive bargaining conflicts at low levels of escalation because the disputants' are acting from positions of rational self-interest. They do not need the interpersonal processes designed to change perceptions or create new realities.

Theorem 3: Parties will be satisfied with their outcomes based on the nature of their conflict.

Corollary 1 to Theorem 3: Outcomes based on settlements or mutual agreements will be satisfactory to parties when their conflict is Stage 3 or below and is not driven by relationship or identity goals.

Corollary 2 to Theorem 3: Outcomes based on the transformative principles of empowerment and recognition or narrative principles of reconstructing reality will be satisfactory to parties when their conflict escalated above Stage 3 or was driven by relationship or identity goals.

Corollary 3 to Theorem 3: Outcomes based on reconciliation will be satisfactory to the parties when the conflict is predominately driven by relationship and identity goals.

Rationale: The obviousness of Theorem 3 and its corollaries is based on the observation that conflicts have different sources and accelerators. A plaintiff injured in an automobile accident is not as likely to be interested in reconciliation as in compensation. Of course, an apology by the negligent driver would be appropriate, but the real issue concerns the economic losses and general damages the insurance company will pay the plaintiff on behalf of the defendant. Most plaintiffs will be satisfied with a mediation that results in fair compensation for their losses. On the other hand, if dignitary interests are involved, such that identity and relationship goals are in play, no amount of money will truly satisfy the victim. In these conflicts, parties will usually be satisfied only when the offender acknowledges and accepts responsibility for the offense. Transformative or narrative processes are more likely to achieve this outcome because they rely on interpersonal relationship building.

Conclusion

This theory approaches mediation from a conflict dynamics perspective, rather than from a process perspective. The debates over process and outcome seem to have ignored the fact that conflicts are as diverse as human society. Thus, this theory anchors the process and outcome debate to the nature of the conflict. When this occurs, the differences between evaluative and facilitative processes can be reconciled and justified.

This theory has a further significant implication for practitioners. A competent mediator must be able to assess the conflict goals in play (including the fact that goals are dynamic during a conflict) and the conflict escalation level (which may not be the same for each disputant). Based on this assessment, the mediator must choose the process most appropriate to the situation, with the goal of moving the parties from high to low levels of escalation. As the parties move backward through the escalatory stages and reintegrate their personalities to adult levels of development, the mediator must change processes. Thus, a mediator capable of handling all types of conflicts must be well educated in conflict theory, conflict dynamics, and process theory. Otherwise, the mediator will face too many conflicts without the skills necessary to produce effective outcomes.

Finally, this model provides a way of explaining the different processes and outcomes to parties and their representatives. Many lawyers and business people are resistant to the transformative and narrative approaches to mediation. Likewise, many people from the therapeutic and counseling professions are antagonistic to evaluative mediation. This theory explains when a process is appropriate and why it is appropriate. The logic of the theory should appeal to a broad array of potential clients.

Reflections on Chapter Four

Many lawyers do not like transformative or narrative mediation and prefer mediators to act as evaluators. List some of the reasons that might account for this.

Many mediators argue that evaluative mediation is not mediation at all, but some other process. What are your views on this question?

Retired judges tend toward evaluative processes. List some of the reasons that might account for this.

In a complicated litigation, how much power should the parties be given to resolve the case themselves? How much power should the lawyers have? Describe what you think the role of a lawyer should be in the mediation of a complicated case? What are the variables that might change the lawyer's role?

Part Three

UNDER-
STANDING
CONFLICT

CHAPTER FIVE

HUMAN NATURE

A FARMER ONCE LOST his axe. He felt certain that his neighbor had stolen the axe and so he watched his neighbor with suspicion. He noticed that the neighbor's son seemed as shifty as his father. That boy looked just like a thief, and the farmer knew he could never trust either of them.One day when he visited a distant field where he sometimes worked, the farmer discovered his axe. He had left it behind the last time he worked in that field. When the farmer returned home, he noticed his neighbor's son at play. The boy looked absolutely normal now. There seemed nothing shifty or suspicious about him at all.
—From *Peace Tales* (MacDonald, 1992)

Philosophical Views of Humankind

Introduction
Human conflict is a complex, exceedingly difficult area of study. Unlike other bodies of knowledge, human conflict cannot be classified into a single discipline. Instead, it crosses the lines of every aspect of human experience and knowledge. For the lawyer-peacemaker, this presents a daunting task. How do we go about understanding the conflict presented to us? What tools might we derive from the wisdom of the academy?

We start with a philosophic study of human nature. What is it, if anything, about human nature that causes people to be in conflict

113

with each other? Why do some conflicts resolve easily while other conflicts escalate into violence? Why do some people choose a cooperative, peaceful approach to conflict, while many others choose to be adversarial? And why, as the story of the farmer and his axe shows, do our perceptions of human nature seem to change depending on our personal experiences and states of mind. In essence, are humans simply adversarial by nature? Or are they forced into adversary situations by circumstances?

The arguments for each position, although numerous and varied, can be integrated along three philosophic ideas. The first idea concerns free choice. Some thinkers say that humans have free choice either to act on personal desires or to act on moral principle. Conflict arises when the choice is self-interest or gratification rather than toward a higher ethical good.

For these thinkers, the key issue is, given free choice, How do we induce humans to act morally? In the peacemaking vocabulary, the issue is framed as, How do we induce people to engage in cooperative rather than adversarial processes. Some philosophers believe that outside authority must compel people to choose correctly. Coercion, in their view, is the only sure way of maintaining order and cooperative conduct. Others believe that true happiness or self-actualization can come only from voluntarily choosing cooperative conduct over contentious conduct. Human history provides plenty of examples to justify each of these streams of thought, but is either of them correct?

The second idea involves capacity versus inherency. If humans are perceived as essentially evil or aggressive, human nature is inherent. Instances of benevolence, cooperation, or charity would be seen as deviant mutations from the fundamental depravity of humanity. On of the other hand, human aggression, for example, may be claimed as a learned behavior. This view sees humankind as possessing a capacity for both peace and violence. How the capacity expresses itself depends on personal experience, knowledge, and culture. The inherency vs. capacity distinction separates and clarifies much philosophic thought on human nature.

The third idea concerns the tension between physical needs, emotions, and rationality. Philosophers expend considerable effort to describe the relationship between these attributes of humanness. Physical needs include the three components of physical survival: food, shelter, and sex, as well as other needs. Emotions encompass a broad array of reactions to environmental and social events, both actually experienced and recalled through memory. Rationality is the intellectual, problem-solving, forward-predicting process that allows for planning and solutions. Within this idea, conflict arises when physical needs or emotions dominate rationality. Under this view, restoring rationality will resolve conflict.

The following pages present summaries of some of these ideas. The choice of ideas, of course incomplete and somewhat arbitrary, illustrate the thrust of historical thinking on the nature of humanity. The presentation is chronological, starting in ancient China and finishing with postmodernism. Think of this as a short course in the history of civilization as it pertains to what it means to be human.

Early Views

Confucius. Confucius lived in the declining years of the late Chou Dynasty, which was marked by an extremely wealthy upper class and a vast underclass living in desperate poverty. The ruling class's indifference to the plight of the peasantry created social extremes set against a backdrop of political decadence and corruption (Stevenson and Haberman, 1998).

Generally speaking, Confucius saw five causes for this discord. First, people are attached to profit. The opposition between rightness and profit is a central theme in Confucianism, and illustrates the basic choice between self-interest and ethical behavior. While people usually act to increase wealth or power, Confucius believed that only morality should guide action. Action guided by profit leads to social disharmony because people look out for their selfish interests to the exclusion of others. Thus, in the tension between needs, emotions, and rationality, Confucius saw excessive fulfillment of needs as a cause of conflict.

Second, people lack filial piety, in the form of disrespect for elders. Selfish conduct motivated by personal profit implies a lack of true respect for others. This lack of respect reveals itself in poor family relationships, which in turn reveals a lack of self-discipline. In this sense, Confucius advocated family values. Corrupt individuals who have not learned proper family relationships spread conflict throughout society.

Third, people live in hypocrisy, with a difference between what they say and what they do. Without a direct connection between word and deed there is no basis for trust. Without basic trust, individuals lose the ability to represent themselves sincerely and to rely on others with any degree of confidence.

Fourth, people are ignorant of the past. Confucius meant by ignorance unfamiliarity with the Way of the Sages. Without an understanding of the past, the wisdom of the ages cannot be applied to the problems of the present.

Finally, people lack benevolence. Benevolence, the most important of Confucian virtues, is expressed as two people standing in harmony with one another, much like the Old Testament concept of shalom.

The Confucian solution is self-discipline through self-cultivation. Thus, knowledge and education temper people's choice to favor morality over desire. The practice of benevolence consists of balanced consideration of others and oneself. One measure of the consideration for others is determined by the treatment one desires for oneself. In his analects, Confucius said:

> Tzu-kung asked, saying "Is there one word which may serve as a rule of practice for all one's life?" The Master said, "Is not reciprocity such a word? What you do not want done to yourself, do not do to others." (Lau, 1979, chap. XV. 23)

Even if a person's heart is in the right place, Confucius saw how others could be offended because of a lack of knowledge about what is appropriate conduct in a particular situation. Consequently, Confucius taught that knowledge is the key to ethical action. Knowledge, for Confucius, was not the knowledge of things as we understand it today. By knowledge, Confucius meant knowing ritual behavior in every aspect of life. Rituals, according to Confucius, teach individuals how to act well, and by observing these rituals, a person transcends self-interest. In effect, Confucius substitutes rituals for outside, coercive authority. Rituals, as accepted, repetitive, and predictable behaviors, establish powerful norms of social control to inhibit self-interest. Thus, developing and imposing ritual behaviors instills in people the way to act morally.

Later Developments. After Confucius died, his followers engaged in a major debate, asking the question: Is human nature originally good or evil? They were, of course, raising the capacity versus inherency argument. Mencius argued that human nature was originally good. Mencius's opponent, Hsun-tzu, argued that human nature was originally evil. Both asserted inherency, but from diametrical positions.

Mencius believed that the thinking, compassionate heart is a gift from heaven that sets humans apart from animals. The heart contains the four tendencies of compassion, shame, courtesy, and sense of right and wrong, which, if nurtured, sprout into the four virtues of benevolence, dutifulness, observance of rights, and wisdom.

Hsun-tzu believed that humans are dominated by dynamic impulses of desire, a concept recapitulated by Freud 2,500 years later. According to Hsun-tzu, human urges have no clear limit. Nature gives humans unlimited desires in a world with limited resources. Hence, conflict arises among necessarily competitive human beings.

Thus, in Hsun-tzu's view, human nature is evil: good is the result of conscious activity. Hsun-tzu replaced Mencius' four tendencies with his own: profit, envy, hatred, and desire. These tendencies if left in their natural state give rise to the four evils of strife, violence, crime, and wantonness. Hsun-tzu believed that everything good is a product of conscious human effort. In other words, he saw choice as a dominant theme in human nature. He asserted that humans can override their inherent characteristics through choice. However, like a warped board that must be steamed and pressed into shape, humans need to subject themselves to rites and rituals to achieve perfection.

Lao Tzu. Taoism and Confucianism were two responses to the social, political, and philosophical conditions of life two and a half millennia ago in China. While Confucianism was concerned with social relations, conduct, and human society, Taoism was individualistic and mystical. The philosophy of Taoism began with the Sixth Century BCE philosopher Lao Tzu (Old Sage).

The Tao Te Ching is an anthology of brief passages of wisdom. The Tao Te Ching does not constitute a single, systematic scheme of thought, but does present a view of human nature that profoundly influenced Buddhism.

According to the Tao Te Ching, Tao is the inexpressible source of being which provides a Way for men to follow. The Tao is the Principle that underlies and controls the world. The Tao may be analogous to the Logos of the biblical Gospel of John. While the Tao Te Ching is elliptical in meaning, several principles are clear.

Contemplating the natural world, Lao Tzu felt that human activities disrupt the otherwise perfect order of things. Thus, Lao Tzu counseled people to turn away from human pursuits and to return to one's essential nature. Lao Tzu saw humankind as having a choice in resolving the tensions between needs, emotions, and rationality. In addition, Lao Tzu saw a capacity for growth, rather than being bound by inherent characteristics.

The central vehicle of achieving tranquility was the *Tao*, a term which has been translated as "the way" or "the path." *Te* in this context refers to virtue and *Ching* refers to laws. Thus the Tao Te Ching could be translated as The Law (or Canon) of Virtue and Its Way. The *Tao* was the formless, unfathomable source of all things.

Lao Tzu taught that all striving is counterproductive. One should endeavor to do nothing (*wu-wei*). But what does this mean? It means not to literally do nothing, but to discern and follow the natural forces—to follow and shape the flow of events and not to pit oneself against the natural order of things. First and foremost, doing nothing means to be spontaneous in one's actions. In the idea of choice, Lao Tzu advocated that choices be made to conform to the circumstances of the moment.

The wise person seeks harmony with the Tao. The ideal person, through the naturalness of his existence, becomes self-sufficient and not dependent upon wealth and prestige. By desiring the conditions in which one desires nothing and by managing to gain such a condition spontaneously and without strain, the wise person fulfills all possible desires. By losing the world, she gains it.

In this sense, the Taoist doctrine of wu-wei is a way of mastering circumstances by understanding their nature or principle, then shaping one's actions accordingly. This understanding underlies the ancient martial art, Tai Chi Chuan. It is also one approach to peacemaking. Understanding this, Taoist philosophy followed a circle. On the one hand, the Taoists rejected the Confucian attempts to regulate life and society through ritual. They counseled instead to turn to a solitary contemplation of nature. By doing so, one could ultimately harness the powers of the universe. By "doing nothing" one could "accomplish everything."

The Tao Te Ching also has a prescription for conflict:

Therefore, one who is good at being a warrior
doesn't make a show of his might;
One who is good in battle doesn't get angry;
One who is good at defeating the enemy doesn't engage him.
And one who is good at using men places himself below them.
This is called the virtue of not competing;
This is called correctly using men;
This is called matching Heaven.
It's the high point of the past. (Henricks, 1989)

Lao Tzu would therefore say that humans seek gratification from possession of things, but these things not being the Tao, cannot satisfy. Nevertheless, as people strive for possession or dominance, conflict arises.

To reduce conflict, people must turn to the Tao and become empty. Interestingly, a Christian parallel exists in Philippians 2:5-7, NRSV, which says,

> Let the same mind be in you that was in Christ Jesus, who, though he was in the form of God, did not regard equality with God as something to be exploited, but emptied himself, taking the form of a slave, being born in human likeness.

To summarize, Lao Tzu saw conflict as arising from the tensions between needs, emotions, and rationality. He advocated the choice of *wu-wei,* or acting naturally and harmoniously with nature, as the way to conflict transformation.

Plato. Plato was born in the city-state of Athens, which had for some time enjoyed economic prosperity through its trade, democratic government, and advances in intellectual inquiry culminating in the great ethical philosopher Socrates. Plato grew up during a period of war, which ended in defeat for Athens and a brief period of tyranny. When democracy was restored, Socrates was condemned to death on a charge of impiety. Socrates' main concern was with knowing the right way to live. Plato, greatly influenced by his teacher, was shocked that Socrates would be killed for questioning conventional opinions. Disillusioned, Plato sought knowledge of the universe and the cures to social ills.

Plato's concept of the universe was based on his theory of Forms. Forms, he said, have four aspects: logical, metaphysical, epistemological, and moral. The metaphysical aspect of a Form does not change or decay, is not in space or time, and is not perceivable by any of the senses. The things seen and touched are only very distantly related to these ultimate realities. Humans are only shadows of Forms and are, therefore, not inherently good or evil. Thus, Plato solved the problem of inherency by moving it outside and beyond human nature through his abstract construction of the Forms.

Plato also believed in a dualist view of humanity in which the soul is a nonmaterial entity existing apart from the body. Plato maintained that the human soul is indestructible, that it exists eternally before birth and will exist externally after death. This concept was picked up by Augustine and others a thousand years later and incorporated into Christian theology.

Plato described three parts of the soul. Appetite includes the physical desires, such as hunger, thirst, and sex. Reason is the ability to solve problems and conflicts through logic. Spirit consists of the emotional characteristics of humans, including anger and joy. Reason ought to control spirit and appetite because rationality is superior to needs and emotions. In this description, we see again the tension between needs, emotions, and rationality. The problem for Plato was how to establish harmony between these elements.

If the soul were out of balance such that reason did not control appetite and spirit, conflict would arise. Plato, like Confucius, believed a defined social structure provides the best means for obtaining balance within the soul. Consequently, Plato's vision of a utopian society is hierarchical, with individuals finding harmony within their designated stations in life. External control is a final solution to resolving the tension between needs, emotions, and rationality.

St. Augustine. St. Augustine, Bishop of Hippo, had a profound effect on medieval Christian theology and on modern views of the nature of humans. Augustine (354CE-430CE) lived in the Late Antiquity Era. Augustine was one of the founders of Western philosophical thought as he linked Greco-Roman ideas to concepts of Christianity. Augustine's life is recorded in his *Confessions*, the first autobiography in the Western tradition.

Augustine was born in North Africa, the son of a devout Christian mother and a pagan father. After schooling in his home city and in Carthage, he became a wandering professor, teaching in Carthage, Rome, and Milan. At the same time, he began a spiritual wandering among the philosophies and faiths of the time. He converted to Catholic Christianity in 386 CE and withdrew into seclusion for meditation. Then he traveled back to North Africa with his mother, where he started a monastery. Augustine spent the remainder of his life in the church, first as a monastic leader, then a priest, then as Bishop of Hippo. His writings constitute the first great synthesis of Christian philosophy and thought.

One of Augustine's roles was as spokesman for church orthodoxy, especially when competing ideologies threatened the supremacy of church ideas. Whereas Catholic Christianity accepted Augustine's view of the church and rejected his view of humankind, Reformation Protestantism took the opposite position. Protestants rejected Augustine's view of the church but embraced his grim view of the nature of humans. Augustine's ideas on the nature of humankind were developed in the church's conflict with the Pelagians.

Pelagius, a British monk, was appalled by the moral laxity of the church leadership, particularly among the monks. He sought to achieve higher moral standards by teaching human freedom and responsibility. Pelagius argued that a loving God would not have commanded people to obey moral laws if they were unable to do so. The power to be good is given to humans in creation and remains with them still, usually lying dormant. But it is capable of being awakened and strengthened through instruction and moral effort. Pelagius focused on sinful acts that can be repented of and forgiven, thus cleansing the soul and restoring it to an original righteousness. Pelagius therefore saw human nature as having capacity for good and not inherently evil.

Augustine repudiated Pelagius by devising the doctrine of original sin, which argues that humans are totally depraved. He asserted that ever since the Fall of Adam, humans have sunk so far into evil that, except for God's grace, perdition will be their just and inevitable end. Augustine therefore saw humans as inherently evil, without capacity for good, except through grace.

Augustine's logical argument began with the assertion that God created all things and made them good. Evil is a corruption of being, like a hole in a shirt, and originates from free will. Will is the power of choice. For Augustine, every act of the will is an act of love. Love seeks to unite with some good. Sin, on the other hand, is the perversity of the will, a turning away from God, the Supreme Good. For Augustine, free will means freedom from external coercion, not autonomy or freedom from God. Thus, he believed that sin stems from a defect in free will, as blindness stems from a defect in one's eyes.

According to Augustine, because of Adam's sin humans are born with a corrupted nature. Because of this corrupted nature, people find it impossible not to sin. Men and women still have free will, but it is too weak to be free from sin. Original sin means also that all people share in the guilt of Adam's sin. In addition to original sin, each person is guilty of committing his or her own sins. Because every human being after Adam is born in original sin, even infants are not innocent and suffer damnation if not baptized. The only way out of this horrible fate is through faith and obedience to the church.

Thus, for Augustine the nature of humanity is inherently evil. Only through God's grace can men and women be redeemed from their sinful nature.

Modern Views
Hobbes. Thomas Hobbes, an Enlightenment philosopher, maintained that infants are born with neither moral sense nor a con-

cern for anyone but themselves. Thus, education and training can make them act in a wide variety of ways from many different motives. Hobbes subscribed to a theory of psychological egoism—the view that all people care about is their own welfare. However, Hobbes also realized that people act the way they do not because of inherent qualities, but because of the way they are trained. Hobbes consequently argued that human nature has inherency and capacity.

Hobbes' believed that human dispositions come from six sources: the constitution of the body, experience, habit, goods of fortune, the opinion one has of oneself, and from authorities. Emotions are not irrational by themselves, but only become irrational when they conflict with reason. Hobbes reflected the Platonic view that placed reason over needs and emotion.

Perhaps the most quoted phrase of Hobbes is his observation that human life in the state of nature is "solitary, poore, nasty, brutish and short." This phrase has been misinterpreted to mean that Hobbes held this view of human nature. Actually, Hobbes was commenting on the state of humans in nature, without civilization. As Hobbes put it, if humans were to arise on earth like mushrooms, this is what they would be like. By state of nature, Hobbes meant a condition in which humans are not inferior to some higher authority that can create and enforce rules to govern behavior. Hobbes did not believe in some natural attraction to good. At best, humans have an aversion to death and unpleasantness. Thus, humans allow themselves to be socialized into cooperative behavior.

In the natural state (no government), humans appear to each other as a threat and therefore are actual threats. Threats arise from three causes. The first is scarce resources, which create competition. If resources are scarce, I must worry about you taking from me what I need to survive. Similarly, you must worry about me attempting to take what you have and need to survive.

The second cause of threat is fear. The logic, according to Hobbes, is that I look at you and know that you can kill me if you have to. I also know that you must have asked the question, Do you have to? The answer is not clear but possibly you will have looked at me and have understood that I have every reason to be afraid of you because you might need to attack me. But if that's true, you do need to attack me, and if I know that about you, I can see that I must attack you. If I let you strike me first, my loss is complete. So, however little I am inclined to attack you, I have a strong incentive to do so. Thus, aggression flows from the logical necessity of survival.

Interestingly, Hobbes' account of the way we are forced into conflict explains conflict, not as a desire for aggression, but as the result of a wish for a quiet life. We are only forced to aggression to protect our way of life. Hobbes, therefore, did not see humans as inherently aggressive. Rather, aggression was learned as a response to threat. With respect to choice, however, Hobbes saw no way for most humans to act altruistically. He perceived the human condition to preclude choosing a moral course because of fear of being exploited.

The third cause of threat is glory, which is related to anxiety. Not only do humans constantly change their ideas about what they want, they are chronically unsure whether what they want is worth having. One crude test of value, however, is envy of others. Thus, glory is only possible when at the top of the hierarchy. Since there cannot be only one person at the top, the conflict between the top person and all subordinates is absolute. The combined pressure of competition, fear, and glory leads to a war of all against all and thus to a life that is poor, solitary, nasty, brutish, and short.

According to Hobbes, knowledge of moral law does not affect inherent anxiety, or the human propensity for conflict. In this way, Hobbes differed from Plato. However, like Confucius and Plato, Hobbes prescribed a secure system of law to protect people from each other. In the Hobbesian world, deterrence through fear of punishment secures peace. In this sense, Hobbes' vision was limited to negative peace—the absence of violence—as opposed to positive peace—right relations among people.

Hobbes' solution is for each human to give up as many of his or her natural rights as others will allow. Thus, rights are ceded to a sovereign authority so large its power cannot be challenged by any individual. Hence, Hobbes used the term Leviathan to describe government. The motivation for giving up these rights is the fear of disaster if one does not give them up. The fear of anarchy keeps people obedient to their agreements.

According to Hobbes, once humans agree to cooperate, they cooperate unless it threatens their lives. This is in stark contrast to the economic view of humans that see humans as utility maximizers. Utility maximizers may agree to a cooperative plan, but will violate the agreement when the penalty for violation is less than the gains made from the violation. Thus, utility maximizers have no incentive to cooperate when cooperation cannot be enforced by external means. Even then, if net gains can be made from noncooperation, cooperative behavior will be rejected.

The difference between Hobbes and the economic view of humankind can be stated this way: the Economic Person seeks opportunities to take advantage of other's compliance with laws of nature. The Hobbesian Person watches out for those who would take advantage of compliance with the laws of nature and seeks to punish them for violations. In other words, the Economic Person looks for exploitation as opportunity; the Hobbesian Person looks for exploitation as a violation of the social contract and therefore punishable.

Kant. Immanuel Kant is generally recognized as the greatest Western philosopher since Plato and Aristotle. Kant was born in 1724 and spent his life in the Prussian city of Konigsberg. Kant had a well-rounded humanistic education in classical philosophy, literature, theology, and political theory. Kant's major works of critical philosophy were published in the final decades of the eighteenth century, and he died in 1804.

Because of the Enlightenment, philosophers began to question the scientific validity of church dogma. Kant's project was to reconcile the claims of morality and religion with the new scientific knowledge. To Kant, knowledge depended on the interaction of two factors: perception of objects by the senses (sensibility) and cognition that actively organizes perception (understanding). The mental process used to organize perception into understanding Kant called synthesis, an unconscious process he attributed to imagination. Kant saw reason as the process of integrating many pieces of information into a unified system. Reason led toward a unification of knowledge based on the observation that any one fact must cohere with all others (Stevenson and Haberman, 1998).

Kant said that humans not only perceive, judge, and theorize, but also act. Humans are agents—they do things and affect the world by their actions. Unlike animals, which cannot explain what they do and therefore lack reason, humans have concepts of what they are trying to achieve. In this sense, animals do not act; they behave.

Kant also distinguished among reasons for human action. Some appeal only to the agent's own desires. "I am doing A because I want to achieve B, and I believe in the present circumstances A will be the most effective way to bring about B." Kant called this a hypothetical imperative. Sometimes humans accept an obligation, a moral "ought" that may actually go against personal desires. Kant called this a categorical imperative.

Kant, like others before him, recognized that humans have physical needs and drives for love, approval, status, and power. Humans are also rational beings. For Kant, rationality allows humans to recognize moral obligations. The conflict between needs and moral obligations create a tension within each person because fulfilling one aspect of human nature denies the other. This internal conflict, in Kant's view leads to external conflict and unhappiness. In this way, Kant synthesized the idea of free choice with the tension between needs, emotions, and rationality.

Kant wondered how people are motivated to fulfill a moral obligation when it goes against their own desires. In other words, how do people acquire the motivation to do the right thing? One response (e.g., Hobbes) is to threaten punishment. Kant recognized that a system of rewards and punishments amounts to putting new self-interested reasons in place. An external system cannot create a truly virtuous inner self—the will to do the right action just because it is right. No ethical duties can be enforced without violating the rights of free beings. Kant therefore rejected the Hobbesian solution of the Leviathan, but in the end could not find a better solution.

Existentialism—Kierkegaard and Sartre. Existentialism is centered on three concerns. First, individuals are important. General theories of human nature leave out the uniqueness of each individual and his or her life situation. Second, the meaning of individual life is important, as opposed to a scientific or metaphysical truth. Third, existentialism emphasizes human freedom—the ability to choose attitudes, purposes, values, and actions. Existentialists faced a tension between a relativist thesis of ethics, that there is no objective basis for valuing one way of life over another, against recommendations of a particular choice. Nietszche, for example, rejected religion-based values for a "will to power" (Stevenson and Haberman, 1998).

Soren Kierkegaard is considered the first modern existentialist. Kierkegaard maintained the importance of the individual and his or her way of life. Kierkegaard said that most people are merely spectators in life in that they are not involved and do not make decisions.

This occurs, according to Kierkegaard, because humans are free to choose what they want to be and do. Since the freedom of choice is unlimited, it creates anxiety. If a person chooses one possibility, she excludes others. Facing choice, people are afraid of losing what they have. Thus, anxiety arises in the insecurity of one's freedom. For Kierkegaard, conflict arises from free choice, as people struggle to avoid decisions and fail to take responsibility for their lives.

To allay their insecurity, people seek security. They may look to themselves, relying on their intelligence, health, and strength. Or they may look to someone else or an institution—someone that will tell them what to do. Or they may take up a life of sensuous indulgence, trying to obliterate from consciousness the anxiety of choice.

Kierkegaard distinguished three ways of life: the aesthetic, the ethical, and the religious. Most people live in the aesthetic stage, enjoying what they sense and taking meaning from the material world around them. Consequently, they do not live life seriously. To move from the aesthetic to the ethical requires a higher degree of freedom through the free act of decision. Those at the ethical level have realized that life is serious. They take responsibility for making choices that affect them and others. They have some ideals in life and try to live by those ideals. The highest level is a religious life with a relationship to the Absolute. The implication of this level is that people must give up attachments to all things. Kierkegaard's thinking in this regard seems to parallel some of the concepts of Taoism.

Jean-Paul Sartre, the most famous French existentialist, was born in 1905 and died in 1980. Sartre's most important metaphysical assertion was his denial of the existence of God. Sartre held the view that if God does not exist, then everything is permitted. There are no transcendent values, either in the laws of God or the Forms of Plato. Furthermore, life has no ultimate meaning or purpose. Thus, people are left to make their own choices with their inherent freedom (Stevenson and Haberman, 1998).

Sartre asserted that existence precedes essence. Thus, each person has the responsibility of developing his or her own essence. Essence is not something inherent in humans at birth. While Sartre does not deny the existence of certain universals—the necessity to eat, the physiology of metabolism, and the strength of human sexual impulses, there are no general truths about what human beings want to be or ought to be. Sartre thus rejects Plato's dualistic view of humanity. Sartre saw humankind as having no inherency and believed in a complete capacity to grow and control life.

Sartre's central statement was that humans are condemned to freedom. To be a conscious being is to continually face choices about what to believe and what to do. To be conscious is to be free.

Sartre believed that people choose every aspect of their emotional lives. If I am sad, I am sad because I choose to make myself sad. Emotions are not moods that come over people, but are ways in which people perceive the world. Emotions are ways in which people chose to react to the world. Humans suffer from their awareness of the unpredictability of their own behavior.[4]

Anguish, the consciousness of freedom, is painful. Consequently, people avoid it. However, escape is illusory because humans are conscious beings. Sartre concluded most people deceive themselves by thinking that their attitudes and actions are determined by one's situation, character, relationship to others or social role—by anything other than one's own choices. Sartre emphatically rejected any explanation of self-deception in terms of unconscious states.

Sartre held that the relationship between two conscious beings is necessarily one of conflict. Each must want to possess the other, to make the other into a mere object. This is because consciousness depends on an object outside of consciousness to attend to. He suggested that genuine respect for the freedom of others, for non-possessive love, is an impossible ideal.

Buber. Martin Buber was a great Jewish theologian and philosopher living in the first half of the twentieth century. Born in Germany in 1878, Buber eventually studied at the Universities of Vienna and Berlin. He was appointed to a chair of Jewish philosophy at the University of Frankfurt, but lost his position as the Nazis came to power. Buber immigrated to Israel where he became professor of social philosophy at Hebrew University. He retired in 1951 and lectured extensively in the United States and Europe. Buber died in 1965 (LeFevre, 1966).

Buber's classic work was *I and Thou* (Buber, 1958). In this book, Buber said that humans are oriented to others in two ways: I-Thou or I-It. A person may regard another as a Thou or as an It. Buber analyzed human relationships along these two dimensions and considered how people treated each other. The I-It relationship is a subject-object relationship. Buber said that such a relationship is created out of a desire for control. In a subject-object relationship, the object can be ignored fully or partly and can be used as one pleases. Furthermore, such a relationship is a monologue, not a dialogue.

In an I-Thou relationship, people are related as subject to subject. What happens in the relationship is not what happens inside of people, but what happens between them. The relationship is not one way, but is mutual. The experience is not just "mine," it is "ours."

Depending on which orientation is dominant, a person may live life as a monologue or as a dialogue. In monologue, one is interested in impressions and images created. She therefore contrives speech and looks to create the image she wants others to have. Sociologist Erving Goffman identified this as impression management. Interaction is one of appearances, and true communication between people does not exist.

In dialogue, on the other hand, a person tries to overcome the inadequacy of his or her perceptions of the other. A person in dialogue seeks awareness of the other as different and by doing so accepts that difference despite thinking that the other is wrong. A person in dialogue accepts the other for what she is and affirms her freedom to become what she would become.

Thus, a person in dialogue does not try to reduce another to abstractions or stereotypes. Instead, a person in dialogue looks for the uniqueness of the other. This can only be done by cultivating sensitivity to others and by using imagination to see things from the other's perspective.

To Buber, being in dialogue with another requires a unity within self. If a person is divided inside, dialogue becomes impossible. Buber characterizes evil as the condition of inner division. Evil is not something built into the nature of humans, but is eradicable. Thus, Buber sees human drives and impulses not as inherently evil, but as forces to be drawn into unity to serve the good. They cannot be controlled by suppression or repression, but must be channeled through decision into a unified life. Buber saw free choice as a means of resolving the tension between needs, emotions, and rationality. Buber said that true happiness can only be achieved by freely choosing to unify and balance needs and emotions. Living a unified life will therefore motivate moral choice.

René Girard. Girard asks, "Why is reciprocity fundamental to human existence (Girard, 1977)?" Why do we think retributively: tit for tat, giving and getting, always exchanging? What's in it for me? One good turn deserves another? One hand washes the other? Give and you shall receive?

All of these sayings point to a fundamental principle of retribution that underlies much of human wisdom. Girard's answer is in terms of mimesis, rivalry, and collective violence.

The individual is wrongly thought to desire spontaneously, that is, in a direct and immediate relation to the objects of desire. Girard therefore rejects the needs, emotions, and rationality tension, claiming that human desire is mediated, or "mimetic." This means that people desire "according to others," not in terms of his or her intrinsic preferences. Mimesis implies copying/imitating with the attribute of acquisitiveness—a desire to copy and acquire. Mimesis is consequently a mechanism that generates patterns of action and interaction, personality formations, beliefs, attitudes, symbolic forms, and cultural practices. In Girard's opinion, not to focus on the mimetic structure of human motivation misses the fundamental basis of human experience.

Girard claims that mimetic capacity developed as a survival mechanism. Essential needs had to be met in some way, but how to meet them was learned through imitation of others. Over time, a realm of symbols instructed participants in a given culture how and what they are to desire.

As brain and mimetic capacity developed, rivalry arose from mimetic desire. One person, the model, would do or have something. Another person would desire what the model had or represented. From this desire, a rivalry would begin. The model was loath to give up what he had, while the other wanted it. The rivalry created conflict that threatened to move the parties into violence.

In Girard's mimetic model, rivalry stemming from mimetic desire can reach a point where the difference between the subject and the rival break down. At that point, the rival becomes the double of the subject. Because they are now undifferentiated, they lose their sense of separate identities. Social order is threatened because roles and hierarchies become confused. The rivals become anxious and fearful of losing their separate identities. For Girard, this moment of mimetic crisis can only be resolved by one rival killing the other or by some act that restores differentiation.

Oftentimes the rival cannot slay the model, and the model cannot slay the rival. To alleviate the crisis, they join together to act against an innocent victim. This differentiates the model and rival from the victim and thereby restores a sense of social order.

Girard points out that the children's game of tag is a form of sacrificial violence. The child tagged as "it" becomes the "victim" and is outcast from the group. The others are now differentiated as "not it" and are able to enjoy social solidarity at the expense of "it."

In summary, Girard's view of human nature is psychological. Humans are imitative and acquisitive. As societies form, rivalries based on mimetic desires erupt. The rivalries cannot be dissipated by internal violence, so the group looks outward for victims to outcast or kill. Collective violence against a victim restores internal social order by creating a differentiation between the rival and model on the one hand and the sacrificial victim on the other. This violence may not be physical, but includes stereotyping, discrimination, and outcasting.

Aggression—Lorenz vs. Montagu. Perhaps the fundamental question in beginning to understand conflict is whether humans are inherently aggressive or not. In 1963, Nobel Laureate Konrad Lorenz published *On Aggression* in German. It was republished in English in 1966. Lorenz argued that humans, like all vertebrates, are inherently aggressive. Anthropologist Ashley Montagu, finding Lorenz's arguments incorrect and misleading, compiled a book of essays and commentaries critical of Lorenz entitled *Man and Aggression*, published in 1973. Thus, the debate was joined. In this section, we will examine a little of the life of both men and look at their respective views on human nature.

Konrad Lorenz grew up in Altenberg, Austria, and at an early age was strongly attracted to animals. From a neighbor, he obtained a one-day-old duckling and found, to his intense joy, that it transferred its following response to him. He became irreversibly fixated on waterfowl, and an expert on their behavior even as a child. Upon finishing high school, Lorenz wanted to study zoology and paleontology. However, he obeyed his father and studied medicine.

In medical school, Lorenz discovered that comparative anatomy and embryology offered better solutions to the problems of evolution than did paleontology. He also learned that the comparative method was as applicable to behavior patterns as it was to anatomical structure. Thus, he began to apply comparative methods to the study of animal behavior. Working as an assistant at the anatomical institute, Lorenz continued keeping birds and animals in Altenberg. Among them the jackdaws (related to but smaller than common crows) soon became most important. Lorenz began to regarded the comparative study of behavior as his chief task in life. Gradually, he concentrated on the problems of aggressiveness, its survival function, and on the mechanisms counteracting its dangerous effects. Fighting behavior in fish and bonding behavior in wild geese were the main objects of Lorenz's research, for which he was awarded a Nobel Prize.

Lorenz assumed the validity of the theory of evolution. Thus, when examining behavior patterns, Lorenz looked for its adaptive value to the species. According to Lorenz, intra-species aggression had a strong survival value to a species. First, aggression was a mechanism to assure territorial diversity. The danger of population density was a scarcity of resources that might threaten the species. Consequently, intra-specific aggression caused an even distribution of animals over a given inhabitable area.

Intra-species aggression also assured selection of the strongest by rival fights. The strongest members of a species were best able to defend the family and herd. Hence, they were the fittest to reproduce, as their offspring were more likely to survive. Finally, intra-species aggression established rankings and pecking order. This hierarchy was beneficial in that the older, mature animals led the group and passed on what they knew. In addition, rankings or pecking order limited fighting between members of a society, leading to protection against outside aggressors, and to the protection of weaker members.

Typically, age was directly proportional to the position in the ranking order of society. Lorenz used his jackdaws to illustrate this point. The movements of an older, high-ranking jackdaw were given much more attention than the movements of a younger bird. According to Lorenz, the "opinion" of a surviving "old" bird was more valuable than that of a younger bird. Lorenz also noted how a baboon troop upon encountering a sleeping lion allowed the eldest to lead the group around the lion. All the other baboons followed without question.

Despite the presence of aggression among vertebrates, Lorenz noted that animals were rarely killed or even seriously injured by members of their own species. Much aggression was in the form of threats or pursuits rather than actual combat. According to Lorenz, aggression in many animals became ritualized to produce evolutionary advantages without injury. Thus, appeasing behavior by the loser seemed to inhibit further aggression by the winner.

Lorenz viewed humans as subject to the same laws of evolution as all other living things. He therefore presumed that human behaviors developed for their survival value just as had behaviors of other animals. Lorenz thus saw inherency dominating capacity. Lorenz postulated that similarities in social behavior between animals and humans were not derived from a common ancestor, but from convergent adaptation. The similarity of behavior patterns of geese, for example, such as falling in love, strife for ranking order, jealousy, and grieving, as with humans, meant that these behaviors had a very special survival value.

From this, Lorenz concluded that humans had an innate drive to aggressive behavior toward each other. However, humans did not develop the inhibitory responses existing in lower animals, because without claws, fangs, or horns, humans could not kill each other easily. Thus, there was no survival advantage to inhibiting aggression among humans. As humans developed culture and technology, the ability to kill became easier, and the evolutionary balance between inhibition and killing potential was upset.

Lorenz argued that human aggression can be brought under control if humans know themselves. True knowledge of and acceptance of innate human aggression is difficult because of human pride; humans simply cannot accept their inherent aggressiveness. Until this fact is recognized, he believed that violence will continue to torment human civilization.

Born in 1905 in London, **Ashley Montagu** decided in childhood to learn everything he could to understand how some people can grow up to be so injurious to others. His interests gradually centered on the manifestations and human significance of love, which was the focus of much of his later work. In 1922, at the University of London (and later at the University of Florence) Montagu studied psychology and anthropology. In 1936 at Columbia University he earned a Ph.D. in anthropology under Professors Franz Boas and Ruth Benedict.

Montagu challenged the Lorenzian thesis that humans are inherently aggressive. He believed that Lorenz's theory of aggression posed two major questions: First, was Lorenz's evidence reliable? Did it include all the available and relevant knowledge about behavior in lower animals? Second, how well did the evidence and theory of aggression in lower animals apply to humans (Montagu, 1973)?

Montagu did not believe that Lorenz had demonstrated that lower animals were innately aggressive. But even if Lorenz had made a case, Montagu did not believe that lower animal behavior and human behavior could be cogently compared. Montagu said flatly that Lorenz's theory of human aggression was naïve. Montagu pointed out that, unlike many other animals, human behavior was learned, and he rejected inherency, arguing that humans had capacity for cooperation as well as aggression.

Montagu attacked Lorenz's inherency argument on several levels. First, behavior is not phylogenetic; that is, behaviors cannot be traced from lower animals to higher animals. The aggressive behavior of a mouse cannot lead one to the conclusion that the same behavior exists in humans. While lower order animals may have "instincts," no evidence suggests that humans have "instincts." As Montagu stated, "The human being is entirely instinctless."

Second, Montagu argued that behavioral evidence derived from primates shows them to be generally very amiable toward one another. Primates simply do not kill each other. Thus, Lorenz could not possibly extrapolate from primates the conclusion that humans were innately aggressive.

Third, Lorenz failed to present any evidence that human aggressive behavior occurs spontaneously. In fact, said Montagu, Lorenz ignored the considerable body of evidence concluding that human aggression arises from frustration and thus is situational. Further, Lorenz ignored the abundant evidence concluding that aggression is a learned, not an innate, behavior in humans.

In Montagu's mind, Lorenz fundamentally ignored human evolutionary history. The human brain, far from containing any phylogenetic programming, is a highly plastic, supremely developed device designed for learning. Thus, humans must learn human nature from the environment, from experience, and from culture.

Finally, Montagu argued that through human evolution the highest premium has been placed on cooperation, both within and between groups. Without this high level of cooperation, human society would not have evolved to its current complex and high level. Innate aggression would have endangered the existence of small groups and would have prevented complex societies from forming.

Postmodernism. Postmodernism describes a set of themes developed initially by French humanities scholars. The term "postmodernism" arose during the 1970s to describe a new style of architecture that asserted abandonment of pure form in favor of local idiosyncrasy leading to playfulness and individuality. The concept expanded to encompass a broad critique of culture. Modernism, dating from the Enlightenment, was the consensus of educated Western people about history, identity, art, and other core cultural values. High culture, in Modernism, was the repository for moral and spiritual wisdom. Individualism, rationalism, and empiricism characterized Modernist philosophy as it developed in reaction to the coercive order of medieval church and state.

Postmodernism rejects the philosophy of ideas embodied in Modernism. Postmodernism makes a number of assertions. Modernism states that objectivity is the aspiration to eliminate beliefs based on bias, personal idiosyncrasy, or careless investigation. Postmodernism says that reality is socially created and therefore subjective. Objective reality is really a form of subjective reality created by the elite to perpetuate hegemony over the oppressed. Objective reality discovered through empirical investigation does not exist. Therefore, postmodernists reject empiricism. Instead, the postmodernist attempts to deconstruct the Modernist view of objective reality and knowledge to demonstrate how it is based on illusions. Postmodernist thought believes that exposing the illusory basis of history, culture, and identity is crucial, even at the cost of no longer saying anything.

The second assertion is that, since reality is subjective, no meaning has preference or priority over any other meaning. Postmodernist nomenclature has taken the noun "privilege" and turned into a verb. Thus, postmodernists would say that no idea is privileged over another idea. Thus, postmodernism rejects rationality in that no argument can prevail over any other argument.

The third assertion is that meaning is created by discourse between people. Without discourse, meaning cannot exist. Furthermore, identity is created by and embedded within community. Therefore, postmodernism rejects individualism.

Postmodern historians and philosophers question how history and cultural identities have been represented. Rather than seeing history as "what really happened," postmodernists see history as a narrative of what happened from the point of view of those in power, either culturally or ideologically. In essence, postmodernists view history as the story told by the victors. Consequently, the story of the vanquished is not told. From this perspective, postmodernists question the legitimacy of traditional views and values. They see history as local and contingent, asking who can write history. For whom can history be written and from what standpoint? In short, postmodernists seek to demystify authority.

Postmodern philosophy uses the concept of deconstruction as a principal tool of critique and exposure. Championed by Jacques Derrida, deconstruction sees language as a constantly moving, independent force. Because language is so dynamic, it does not provide stable meanings or definite communication. Derrida insisted that language is metaphorical and cannot therefore directly convey truth. Thus, deconstruction subverts any system's claim to transcendent truth. This contrasts with the modernist theory of representation that holds that meaning or truth precedes and prescribes the representations that communicate it. Deconstruction undercuts the epistemological claims of representation, showing, for example, that language is not up to the task of representation of truth.

As to human nature, at least some streams of postmodernism tend to be critical and negative. Often in postmodernism humans as individual agents are absent. The skeptical vein of postmodernism calls for communities that do not impose collective choices or democratic decisions on its members. The affirmative vein of postmodernism leaves room for a socially sensitive, active human being, groping for a new postmodern politics, religion, and life. Hence, New Age, New Wave, and new postmodern social movements animate the affirmative postmodern view of humans (Rosenau, 1992).

Within the academic legal community, a postmodern strand of thought has emerged through the radical multiculturalists. Radical multiculturalism rejects the determinacy of law. Applying postmodern thought to law, the radical multiculturalists say that law is not objective, but is completely subjective. Therefore, it cannot be known. Radical multiculturalism also rejects meritocracy, claiming that standards, evaluations, and rankings are subjectively created by those in power to oppress those not in power. Finally, radical multiculturalism rejects truth. The heart of the radical multicultural philosophy is that below the deceptive surface of things, social institutions are universally designed to keep the oppressed at the bottom and the powerful at the top (Farber and Sherry, 1997).

Some Recurring Philosophical Themes

This short overview of 3,000 years of philosophical thinking on human nature reveals several recurring questions. First, are humans inherently good or evil? Proponents exist for both sides of this question and a few straddle the question. The inherency-capacity argument is an attempt to explain abominable cruelty as well as examples of selflessness that seem to transcend everyday existence. Humans are capable of both extremes, so no final answer will ever satisfy everyone. The question, however, illustrates a common conflict situation called polarization. As a conflict intensifies, each side begins to see the other as evil, wrong, and irredeemable. Likewise, each side sees itself as righteous, virtuous, just, and good. This polarization occurs in many situations, from neighborhood disputes to complex business conflicts to international terrorism. It is very common in litigation as each side views the other with enmity and distrust. The irony is that as each side reviles the other as inherently evil, they all fail to recognize their common humanity. Furthermore, they fail to see the paradox of their behavior. If the other side is inherently evil, then so we must be also because we are human. On the other hand, if we are just and righteous, then the other side must have that capacity as well because they are human. These mirror images are very common in conflicts.

How does altruism transcend self-interest? Nearly all philosophers agree that altruism is a virtue itself and a necessary behavior if humans are to survive together. However, altruism is easily forgotten in the effort to satisfy personal desires, ambitions, and goals. The altruism-self-interest question finds expression in distributive and integrative conflict behaviors. While this will be taken up in more detail later, the basic idea is that distributive behaviors view a conflict as a fixed pie. What you get, I lose; therefore, I will fight for as much of the pie as I can, because if I don't you will take it all. Integrative behaviors are motivated from a view that the pie can be expanded. What I lose, you lose too. Therefore, we have a common interest to expand the resources for both of us to share. This is a form of enlightened self-interest, but is altruistic in the sense that I must be concerned about your goals to satisfy my own goals. The problem is to move people from a distributive orientation to an integrative orientation. Thus, the altruism-self-interest problem is a core issue in thinking about conflict and its transformation.

By the end of the nineteenth century, philosophy had been overtaken by science. Thus, scientists, particularly psychiatrists and psychologists, began to consider human nature. The next section traces some of the major threads of scientific thinking on human nature up to the 1970s.

Psychological Views of Human Nature—Freud to Rogers

Freud

Freud's life, from 1856 to 1939, spans one of the most creative periods in the history of science. The same year Freud was taken by his family to Vienna, Darwin published *Origin of Species*. This book revolutionized the human conception of humanity. Before Darwin, humans were set apart from the rest of the animal kingdom by virtue of their having souls. The evolutionary doctrine made humans a part of nature. The acceptance of this radical view meant that the study of humans could proceed along naturalistic lines. Humans became an object of scientific study, no different, save in complexity, than other forms of life (Gay, 1998).

The year following the publication of the *Origin of Species*, Gustav Fechner founded the science of psychology. Fechner demonstrated that mind could be studied scientifically and measured quantitatively. As a consequence, psychology took its place among the other natural sciences. Darwin and Fechner deeply influenced Freud's intellectual development.

Freud was also profoundly influenced by developments in physics. In the middle of the nineteenth century, Hermann von Helmholtz formulated the principle of the conservation of energy. This principle stated, in effect, that energy is a quantity just as mass is a quantity. Energy can be transformed but not destroyed. When energy disappears from one part of the system, it has to appear elsewhere. For example, as one object becomes cooler, an adjacent object becomes warmer. Energy and dynamics were seeping into every laboratory, making possible an even more radical view of humanity. Humans could be viewed as an energy system such that they obeyed the same physical laws regulating the movement of the planets.

From the insights of the physical sciences, Freud created his constancy principle, which stated that the nervous system sought to rid itself of all tension. The constancy principle was influenced by the energy metaphor dominant in scientific circles—the mind was constructed like a machine driven by the flow of energetic forces. According to Freud, tensions built up that must be discharged. If one channel of discharge was dammed up, another outlet must be found.

Freud also theorized that the unconscious mind sought expression of drives that the conscious mind fought to repress. Freud believed that most of the unconscious therefore consisted of repressed materials. The desire to recall was strongly countered by the desire to forget. Consequently, the conscious and unconscious minds were in constant conflict. Human conflict, according to Freud, was caused by the clash of unexpressed unconscious desires.

Freud thus developed a drive/structure theory of human nature. Humans had innate drives bubbling from instinctual urges destructive to self and society if not contained through social training and conditioning. Thus, personality structure developed to manage the drives. That structure, composed of id, ego, and super ego, had to remain in relative balance for normal behavior. Imbalances in the personality structure led to maladjusted human behavior and conflict. Freud saw mental life as more or less continual warfare. Consequently, conflict was an inevitable part of the human condition.

Harry Stack Sullivan—Interpersonal Psychoanalysis

For the first forty years, psychoanalysis was relatively homogenous. However, during the 1930s, an alternative tradition broke away from Freud's drive/structure model. The comprehensive framework developed within this alternative tradition has come to be known as interpersonal psychoanalysis.

Interpersonal psychoanalysis is not a unified theory. It is a set of different approaches to theory and clinical practice held together by a relational/structure model. According to this second generation of psychoanalysts, classical Freudian theory was fundamentally wrong concerning human motivation, the nature of experience, and difficulties in living. Therefore, drive/structure theory provided an inadequate and misleading foundation for psychoanalytic theory. Freudian theory under-emphasized the larger social and cultural context necessary for the origins, development, and workings of personality. This emphasis on cultural contributions set the interpersonal psychoanalysis theorists apart from the other major source of the relational/structure model-the British school of object relations theory.

Harry Stack Sullivan (1892-1949) exemplified interpersonal psychoanalysis. Sullivan, not yet affected by Freud, developed many of his insights from his own observations. For Sullivan, personality was not within a person, but was the continual unfolding of a person's interactions and relationships with others. Sullivan's therapeutic process was to make the patient aware of interpersonal processes occurring between the client and others. From these premises, Sullivan derived advanced theories of anxiety, motivation, and self-system (Greenberg and Mitchell, 1998).

According to Sullivan, a personality could never be isolated from his or her set of interpersonal relations. All knowledge of another person was mediated through interaction. We come to know another by observing what she does, by observing ourselves in interaction with her, and by listening to her reports of these interactions and experiences.

Persons were motivated by "needs," separable, in Sullivan's system, into two broad categories: needs for satisfaction and needs for security. The relative balance between these needs was the key factor in determining emotional richness and health versus difficulties in living. Both sets of needs operated in an interpersonal field and concerned relations between the self and others.

Needs or satisfactions included a broad range of physical and emotional tensions and desires. Many of these, such as needs for food, warmth, and oxygen concerned the survival of the organism. Other needs pertained to the necessity for emotional contact with other human beings. These needs began with a simple "need for contact" in the infant and developed to needs for complex and intimate relations with others. Needs for satisfaction also included the simple and joyful exercise of capacities and functions. Infants find satisfaction in "playing with their abilities," which extends later to adult forms of play and self-expression. In the tension between needs, emotions and rationality, Sullivan saw needs and emotions as primary to rationality.

Within Sullivan's system, anxiety was at the core of all psychopathology. Anxiety constituted the organizational principle of the self. Original experience with anxiety, because it entailed such intense helplessness and passivity, left behind a residue of terror. It generated a phobic attitude toward even mild degrees of anxiety. The self operated solely on the need for security, based on the principle that anxiety was to be avoided at all costs. Thus, power, status, and prestige in one's own eyes and in the eyes of others were the broadest and surest route to safety. The self, in Sullivan's use of the term, served a negative and preservative function. The self protected the rest of the personality from the threat of anxiety and preserved a sense of security in which satisfactions and pleasures could be enjoyed.

Life was lived in a broad dialectic between needs for satisfaction and security. Needs for satisfaction were essentially "selfless" and required no particular self-reflexiveness, self-aggrandizement, or self-organization. Life based on the satisfaction of needs simply flowed. Anxiety constantly interrupted this flow, and because of the phobic terror of anxiety, a legacy from early childhood, anxiety aroused the need for security. The pursuit of security was carried out and pervaded by the operations of the self. The self steered attention away from anxiety emerging in the flow of life by creating an illusory sense of power and control over life. All security behaviors started out with this sense of "I" and the "power of "I" imparts a sense of false domination (Greenberg and Mitchell, 1998).

Sullivan described the self as having narcissistic, fantastic qualities that makes anxiety reduction possible (Sullivan, 1964).

> Each of us comes to be possessed of a self which he esteems and cherishes, shelters from questioning and criticism, and expands by commendation, all without much regard to his objectively observable performances, which include contradictions and gross inconsistencies. The central aim in the pursuit of security is to bolster and protect this "cherished self." (p. 35)

Sullivan thus postulated a theory of face and self-esteem that becomes critically important in understanding conflict.

The pursuit of satisfactions and security causes continual internal tension. Pursuing satisfaction leads toward simple, constructive integration with others and the joyful exercise of life. Pursuing security leads toward disintegration, non-constructive integration with others, and self-absorbed fantasy: "Any interpersonal situation is thus prone to stir conflict between the drive to reaffirm the importance of the self, and some other drive for satisfaction by way of cooperation" (Sullivan, 1972, p. 72).

The pursuit of security, if unchecked and unattended, crowds out the joyful pursuit of satisfactions:

> The content of consciousness pertaining to the pursuit of satisfaction and the enjoyment of life is at best marginal. It is one's prestige, one's status, the importance which people feel one is entitled to that dominate awareness. (Sullivan, 1964, p. 219)

Thus, Sullivan felt the pursuit of security in its various forms and through its various operations motivated most people. Security behaviors usurped and warped interpersonal situations; making needs satisfaction peripheral at best.

Sullivan's theories offer insights into origins of human conflict. His ideas suggest that anxiety avoidance is the cause of human conflict. To avoid anxiety, people engage in an inflated sense of self that creates an illusion of control. People act to reduce or eliminate anxiety through expression of their self, thereby causing others to feel increased anxiety as their selves are threatened. Under Sullivan's theories, anxiety is the driving force behind a person's need for security. Until security is assured, anxiety will continue to escalate conflict.

Object Relations

Melanie Klein is the first therapist associated with object relations theory. Born in Vienna in 1882, Klein was a pioneer of child analysis. Klein saw that play could be the basis of analysis of the child, and she used child's play along with verbal communications as a more or less equivalent to adult free association.

Klein's analysis gave her insight to the unconscious fantasies dominating the child's mind. The child's mind was a complex internal world of internal objects formed by both projection and introjection. This insight enabled her to recognize the inner world existing in the adult (Greenberg and Mitchell, 1998).

Object relations represent a fundamental shift of vision concerning human motivation and mental processes. Freud's view of drives required a layered vision of the psychic apparatus. At the base is the "seething cauldron" of the drives, directionless and isolated from the outside world, operating through loose and fluid primary process thinking. The ego, operating through more organized, reality-oriented, secondary process thinking, gives direction, structure, and continuity. The ego's functions are thus superimposed upon the primary energy of the drives, organizing mental events and orienting toward reality.

For Klein, the drives possess, through their inherent objective-relatedness, many of the features that in Freud's theory were the province of the ego and the secondary process. The drives are oriented toward others, toward reality, and contain information concerning the objects from which they seek gratification.

This primary relationship to others contrasts with Freud's view that the child turns to reality, and so to his mother, only because his original drive demands are frustrated. For Klein, however, the basic units of mental processes are not packets of objectless energy, but relational units. All psychic energy is inherently directional and structured.

A Kleinian view of the origins of human conflict arises from the unacceptable bad objects within. These elements exist in adults, who under normal circumstances have successfully navigated past them to maturity in the depressive position. The bad object within is combined with the perception of evil in the opponent. In fear, people move backward through their depressive capacities, splitting good and bad apart. The split-off bad portion threatens to appear and destroy our fragile good-self image. Then, to our relief, an enemy appears who embodies all of the cruelty, hatred, greed, hostility, duplicity or sadism we feared and felt within ourselves. As we see these traits in our opponent, they disappear within us, reducing our anxiety and guilt.

In this condition, a person cannot experience equality, commonality, or mutuality with the opponent. Blame produces blame in a bond of hate that creates an adversarial symbiosis.

Behaviorism

Behaviorism attempts to answer the question: What are the relationships between an organism and its environment that will predict what the organism will do at any given time? In answering this question, a behaviorist analysis rests on the following assumptions. First, a person is an organism, a member of a species and a subspecies, possessing a genetic endowment of anatomical and physiological characteristics. These characteristics have been produced by the contingencies of survival during evolutionary process. Second, the organism becomes a person as it acquires a repertoire of behavior. This repertoire is developed as a person is exposed to contingencies of reinforcement. Finally, the behavior a person exhibits at any moment is under the control of a current setting. A person acquires a repertoire under such control because of genetically endowed conditioning processes (Skinner, 1974).

In the traditional psychoanalytic view, on the other hand, a person is a member of the human species whose behavior is shaped by internal drives that create emotions and behaviors. Internal drives do not exist in the behaviorist's view of the world. Behaviorism rejects the unconscious and the conscious mind as an agent. By turning to the facts on which expressions of consciousness or unconsciousness are based, the contingencies of reinforcement that account for intra-psychic activities can usually be identified. For example, while Freud would trace frustration back to drives, Skinner argues that frustration is generated by the extinction of a positive reinforcer.

According to Skinner, personality is a repertoire of behavior created by an organized set of contingencies. People develop and exhibit different personalities, depending on contingencies they encounter. Different contingencies create different persons in the same skin, of which so-called multiple personalities are an extreme manifestation. The behavior acquired from family composes one self. The behavior acquired in the armed services composes another self. The two selves may exist in the same person without conflict until the contingencies conflict. Conflicting contingencies lead to conflicting repertoires of behavior, but they are all exhibited by one person.

Skinner does not deny the complexity of human behavior. Complex contingencies of reinforcement create complex repertoires. However, Skinner does not view a person as an originating agent. A person is a point at which many genetic and environmental conditions come together in a joint effect. As such, each person remains unquestionably unique. No one else has her generic endowment and, without exception, no one else has her personal history. Hence, no one else will behave in precisely the same way.

In behaviorist analysis, knowing a person is simply knowing what he does, has done, or will do and the genetic endowment and past and present environments that explain why he does it. Skinner acknowledged that because many relevant facts are unknown this is not an easy assignment.

One aspect of conflict, under the behaviorist view, arises from power imbalances. In the simplest case, one person controls reinforcing contingencies that affect another. These can be positive contingencies, in the nature of rewards, or negative contingencies, in the nature of punishments. According to behaviorists, by modifying the environment in which the behavior occurs, conflict behavior is controlled. This assumes (1) that one knows which environmental variables to change, (2) how these environmental variables intersect with the particular repertoires of the people involved, and (3) that one has the power to modify the environment appropriately. Skinner clearly distinguished between punishment and aversive control. Aversive control is designed to promote expected behaviors. Punishment is designed to suppress unwanted behaviors. Skinner argued vigorously against punishment and considered punishment evil. Punishment in his view did not weaken the tendency to respond; it merely temporarily suppressed behavior.

Another aspect of conflict arises from the presence of reinforcers. A behavior that removes a negative reinforcer tends to increase in frequency. Therefore, if a person is employed in a tedious, boring job, he may be conditioned to escape the job (a negative reinforcer) by becoming injured, being absent, or quitting. A representative to a negotiation settlement is positively reinforced by her group's admiration for her toughness and tenacity, even if her style exacerbates a conflict. Conflict therefore arises from how people respond with their unique repertoires of behaviors to specific environmental situations.

Conflict, in behaviorist terms, is not caused by conscious states. For example, behavior is often attributed to feelings as when a person feels angry or insulted or offended. In Skinner's analysis, both feelings and overt behaviors are the result of environmental conditions. According to Skinner, feelings do not cause behavior. Lack of reinforcement may cause depression, discouragement, or anger, but the feelings are collateral products of environmental factors.

Humanistic Psychology

Certain ideas that Carl Rogers championed have become so widely accepted that we forget how fresh, even revolutionary, they were in their time. Freudian psychoanalysis held that human drives-sex and aggression-were inherently selfish, constrained at a price and with difficulty by the forces of culture. Rogers, in contrast, believed that people needed relationships in which they are accepted. Rogers marshaled a substantial intellectual effort in the service of a simple belief: Humans require acceptance, and given acceptance, they move toward "self-actualization" (Rogers, 1980).

Rogers' view of humanity is generally referred to as a "self theory, a "phenomenological theory," or an "actualization theory." Rogers assumes that basic human nature is positive-that there is nothing inherently negative or evil about humanity. He suggests that if individuals are not forced into socially constructed molds, but are accepted for what they are, they will turn out "good." They will live in ways that enhance both themselves and society. According to Rogers, humans need both personal fulfillment and close, intimate relationships with others.

Phenomenology stresses the individual's immediate conscious experiences in determining reality. Rogers maintained that knowledge of these individual perceptions of reality was required for the understanding of human behavior. He suggested that people behave in accordance with their subjective awareness of selves and their world.[5] Objective reality was not the important determinant of action. Rather, people react on the basis of how they view that reality.

According to Rogers, the actualizing tendency is the single, common basic human motive. When the self develops, the individual wants love and acceptance. This creates a need for positive regard from others. Rogers suggested that this need for love and affection is innate. Because of this need, significant other persons in a child's life assume great importance. The significant others (for example, parents) can strongly influence the individual by giving and withholding love and acceptance. Their influence may overcome a self-valuing process. In other words, to be accepted and to gain needed love and affection, the child may be forced to please parents and other significant persons while ignoring her own inner experience. The child may gradually become less and less "tuned in" to herself and more and more a product of social influence.

Early in life, then, children learn to view themselves as others view them. They come to like or dislike their total configuration of self-experiences independently of the presence of their parents or other significant others. In other words, they incorporate within themselves a set of values that initially was applied externally. The internalization of these values of significant others results in alienation from their own valuing process.

The introjected values of others generally tend to be rigid and unchanging, in contrast to the flexible and changing values of the organismic valuing process operating in early infancy. Rogers suggests a number of introjected values that are often learned in the home, at school, in church, from the government, and so on. These values may be out of line with organismic experiencing, but they are often accepted to have the positive regard of a significant other person. For example, sexuality is bad; questioning obedience to authority is good; making money is crucial; scholarly learning is good; and unstructured, aimless learning is a waste of time.

A person's self-regard is determined by these introjected values. The thoughts, feelings, and actions approved by significant others may be so different from the experiences approved by the person's own organismic valuing process that an almost complete dissociation develops between self-concept and fundamental inner experiences. This situation is very unhealthy, causing the person to function in a restricted and inefficient way.

Unconditional positive regard is received when a person perceives that her self-experiences are worthy of positive regard from significant others. Unconditional positive regard is given when another person's self-experiences are valued equally; in other words, no conditions of worth are imposed on that individual.

Synthesizing Perspectives on Human Nature

Philosophers engaged in free-ranging speculation and argument over human nature, generally addressing three questions: How do we induce humans to act morally? Do humans have capacity for good and evil or are they inherently good or evil? How does an account of human nature balance physical needs, emotions, and rationality? As this survey shows, no philosopher established a complete theory of human nature. At best, some aspects of human nature were described, and from observations, some inferences about human nature were made. These descriptions and inferences were incomplete and at times, simply wrong.

As the scientific revolution established itself in Western culture, speculation gave way to more systematic, albeit still speculative, analysis of human nature and behavior. Early psychoanalytic theories were based upon four fundamental issues.

The first issue concerned the basic unit of analysis. What were the basic building blocks of experience: Drives, wishes, values, goals, relations with others, identifications, choices, or action? In other words, what was personality?

The second issue concerned motivation: What did people want? What were the goals of human activity?

The third issue concerned development. What were the crucial events in the transformation from a relatively uninformed infant to the relatively patterned adult?

Finally, psychoanalytic theory concerned structure. What gave an individual his or her distinctive shape, governing the regularity of behavior, events, and relationships within individual life? What mediated between past events, present experience, and behavior?

The development of psychology in the twentieth century started with Freud's revolutionary theories of mind. According to Freud, humans had innate, powerful drives that constantly bubbled forth and demanded satisfaction. Humans learned to channel, constrain, and repress their drives so they could live together. Recapitulating Hobbes, Freud believed that without out rigid social structures, humans were naturally aggressive. Thus, conflict arose when drives went out of control or were not adequately repressed. Freud saw no possibility for self-fulfillment or self-actualization, and psychoanalysis could only take a miserable person and make her more normally unhappy. Consequently, without rigid external controls, people could not be induced to act morally. Freud's theories placed him with those philosophers believing that human nature was inherently evil. Furthermore, unlike Plato, Freud believed that physical needs and emotions dominated rationality. Only through the super ego, could humans control their basic drives manifested through the id.

A group in the second generation of psychoanalysts rejected Freud's drive/structure theory, emphasizing instead the importance of the mother-infant dyad in human development. Object relations theory provided a theory of personality based on human relationships rather than innate drives. For these theorists, humans, if raised in a nurturing environment, would be well-adjusted, moral adults. They saw humans having capacity for good or evil based largely on early personality development.

B. F. Skinner rejected Freudian and object relations theory altogether. For Skinner, anything that could not be observed, i.e., was empirically provable, did not exist. He therefore constructed a theory of psychology based on cause and effect. An environmental stimulus caused a response. If repeated sufficiently, the response became conditioned or habituated to the stimulus. All human behavior, according to Skinner, was composed of conditioned responses to environmental stimuli. Conflict arose when people with control over resources that acted as positive reinforcers withheld the reinforcers from others. For Skinner, the answer to the question of moral choice was simply one of finding the right stimuli. Similarly, because humans were nothing more than a complex array of conditioned responses, they had capacity for good and evil, and were not inherent. Finally, Skinner believed that the consideration of the relationship between physical needs, emotions, and rationality was irrelevant because all three attributes were outcomes of reinforcers.

Carl Rogers, a contemporary of Skinner, rejected both classical psychoanalytic theory and behaviorism. Rogers looked at the positive side of human nature and discovered how people responded well to empathic communication. Rogers did not engage in the vast theoretical constructions, as did Freud, or spend time in empirical research, as did Skinner. Consequently, Rogers had no organizing theory of personality or human nature. However, his orientation and practices were successful when psychotherapy failed. Furthermore, much of the current practice in peacemaking has its roots in Rogers' thinking. Rogers believed that humans were inherently good, turning to evil only when deprived of an accepting, empathic relationship. Once embedded in an empathic relationship, Rogers believed that people could be easily induced to act morally. Finally, in considering the relationship between physical needs, emotions, and rationality, Rogers gave primacy to emotions.

Orientations to conflict stem largely from beliefs about human nature. Some people may believe, for example, that humans are inherently evil. Thus, human behavior in conflict may be explained in terms of Augustine's original sin or Freud's drive-structure theory. If one views human nature as inherently evil, one may incline toward viewing conflict as both unavoidable and not transformable. Then coercion, power over, strength, and violence become the conflict resolution tools. Peace, in this orientation, is not only weak but ineffective. Many lawyers unconsciously adopt this orientation when taking on engagements for clients. Insurance defense lawyers may stereotype plaintiffs as malingers, evildoers seeking free rides on the insurance industry. Ironically, plaintiffs' lawyers will have the mirror image, characterizing insurance companies as large, malevolent corporations interested only in profit and having no care for the injured.

Thus, one essential challenge for lawyers as peacemakers is to become aware of orientations to human nature. Instead of falling into a routine pattern of thinking, lawyers trained as peacemakers should recognize the fundamental issues concerning human nature, be slow to draw conclusions, and be willing to listen. Then they should guide those clients, parties, and representatives who are so locked into a singular orientation, that they have lost all perspective. Understanding the orientations and beliefs of the parties to broad issues such as human nature provides insights into the immediate conflict, its history and the possible routes to constructive, positive resolution.

Another theme important to lawyers is the relationship between rationality and emotionality? Law students are trained to be "objective." They detach from the emotionality of cases to focus only on the relevant legal principles and their application to the facts. The priority given by lawyers to rational thinking comes from Plato, who advocated that our rational ability must have priority over our senses. His solution to the obvious difficulty of this task was to create philosopher kings. Plato thought that at least a few humans could be trained in philosophic thinking and ethics so that they would be rational rather than emotional. Modern law does not support an institution of philosopher kings, but does idealize rational analysis through inductive and deductive argument.

Unfortunately, rationality does not guarantee the end of conflict. In a later chapter, we will see how rational thinking, whether inductive or deductive, actually leads to intractable conflicts. Furthermore, we will see that humans are 98 percent emotional and about 2 percent rational. Worse, emotions are outside of conscious control, are triggered by events and memories, and occur preconsciously long before they filter into awareness as feelings. Conflict is emotional, not rational. Therefore, understanding conflict means understanding something about emotions. To the extent that lawyers dealing in conflict are not versed in the theories of emotion, they become limited in their ability to analyze and help clients.

The early philosophers and theorists struggled to interpret the nature of man, understand a theory of mind, both conscious and unconscious, and prescribe therapies for healing dysfunction. They were limited by their cultural milieu and by the relative lack of scientific advancement in neurophysiology. In recent years, empirical investigations have provided us with new insights into thoughts and emotions. We turn to these insights next.

Reflections on Chapter Five

During Hitler's extermination of the Jews, the churches in Germany, in large part, remained silent and uncritical of the Nazi atrocities. Some historians believe that Hitler would have never begun the pogroms had the German faith communities challenged him. Using some of the material from this chapter, provide an analysis of the character of the German churches during this period and give some thought as to why a Christian faith would do such a thing as passively accept genocide within its country's boundaries.

The pro-life/pro-choice debate has resulted in heated debate and violence. Using the material in this chapter, provide an analysis of how representatives of each side of the issue view the human nature of themselves and their opponents.

Describe what assumptions about human nature seem implied by each of Claassen's four models of conflict resolution. Review chapter 3 for help on this.

How would you characterize the human nature of the people involved in the terrorist attack on the World Trade Center and the Pentagon on September 11, 2001?

CHAPTER SIX

THE NEURO-PSYCHOLOGY OF CONFLICT

WHILE GREAT ADVANCES HAVE BEEN MADE by social psychologists in de-scribing conflict behaviors, very little work has been done on under-standing why these behaviors exist. Instead, the work that has been done has relied largely upon psychological explanations for conflict behavior. Hence, we still see explanations for certain types of conflict behavior couched in Freudian or behaviorist terms. These explana-tions are misleading in that they assume too much intentionality within a conflict situation. In other words, researchers now under-stand that rationality does not have priority over emotions, but, in fact, the opposite is true. Thus, human beings may act from precon-scious brain processes of which there is no conscious awareness.

Advances in the neurosciences now provide better explanations for conflict behaviors than older theories of human nature. In rcent decades, a small group of neuroscientists in the fields of neurology, neuroanatomy, neurophysiology, and neuropsychology have begun to piece together the brain's actual functions. Although incomplete, the current knowledge points away from many of the older theories of mind. More importantly, the research provides us with insight into conflict behavior. Certain myths and conventional wisdom need to be discarded. This chapter looks at some of the findings of the neuro-sciences and develops some new ideas about human conflict.

Orientation to Brain Function and Anatomy

An in-depth discussion of neuroanatomy is well beyond the scope of this book. Nevertheless, a general introduction to brain function and anatomy should be useful in understanding some of the discussion that follows.

Brains are not, as is commonly imagined, aggregations of gray matter. Brains are built from a large number of specialized substructures, much like components in a computer. However, the substructures are far more complex than even the most sophisticated computer. Considering that brains have been around much longer than modern digital computers, the many orders of magnitude in brain complexity is not surprising.

Brain substructures are composed of billions of specialized cells, called neurons. The neurons are of various types and functions. They collect, summarize, and transmit information through electrical and chemical processes. The aggregate activity of neurons is called neuroactivity.

The brain consists of three principle functional units each necessary for any type of mental activity. The units can be described as follows: a unit for regulating tone or waking; a unit for obtaining, processing, and storing information; and a unit for programming, regulating, and verifying mental activity. Mental processes in general and conscious activity in particular take place with the participation of all three units. Each unit has its role to play in mental processes and makes its contribution to their performance (Luria, 1973).

Each unit consists of at least three zones built one above the other. The zones consist of the primary area that receives impulses from or sends impulses to the periphery, the secondary area where incoming information is processed or programs are prepared, and the tertiary area, which is responsible for the most complex forms of mental activity.

A waking state is essential for normal mental processes, and being awake requires a certain level of stimulation known as cortical tone. The structures maintaining and regulating cortical tone do not lie in the cortex itself, but below it, in the subcortex and brain stem. These structures have a double relationship with the cortex, both influencing its tone and themselves experiencing its regulatory influence. The brain stem is a powerful mechanism for maintaining cortical tone and regulating the functional state of the brain and is a critical factor in determining wakefulness. In the diagram below, these structures are labeled as the brain stem, the pons, and the medulla oblongata.

The human nervous system always exhibits a certain tone of activity essential to all biological activity. However, situations exist when ordinary tone must be raised. Situations requiring a higher level of cortical tone come from at least three principal sources: internal metabolic demand, outside stimulation, and mental intention.

The first of these sources is metabolic demand. Metabolic processes maintaining internal equilibrium of the organism (homeostasis) are in their simplest forms connected with respiratory and digestive processes, with sugar and protein metabolism, with internal secretion, and so on. These are all regulated principally by the hypothalamus.

The environment is a second source of cortical tone activation. We live in a constantly changing environment. Changes, which are sometimes unexpected, require a certain level of increased awareness. This increased awareness must accompany any change in the environmental conditions, especially in the appearance of an unexpected change. Awareness must lead to mobilization for possible surprises. Consequently, environmental information is needed as much as internal metabolic information. The amygdala is one of the key brain structures that processes environmental information and activates a higher level of cortical tone. The amygdala is an almond shaped structure located in each hemisphere of the cerebral cortex. The amygdala's relevance to human conflict will be discussed later in this chapter.

The third source of activation is mental intention. Much human activity is evoked by intentions and plans. These intentions are socially motivated by external and internal speech. Every intention formulated in speech defines a certain goal, evokes a program of action, and leads to the attainment of that goal. When the goal is reached, the activities stop. If the goal is not reached, further mobilization of efforts occurs. Achieving goals requires a certain amount of energy that is possible only if a certain level of activity can be maintained.

Thus, the first functional unit of the brain regulates cortical activity and the level of alertness. This unit is a nonspecific network, which modifies brain activity gradually, step by step, without direct relationship to external information or to the formation of complex goal-directed intentions or plans.

The second functional unit of the brain receives, analyses, and stores information. This unit is located in the lateral regions of the neocortex on the convex surface of the hemispheres (on the cerebrum in the diagram below). It occupies the posterior regions, including the visual, auditory, and general sensory regions. The unit is not a continuous network, but is made up of isolated neurons. Unlike the first unit, the second unit neurons do not work on the principle of gradual change. Instead, the neurons obey an "all or nothing" rule. These neurons receive discrete impulses and relay them to other groups of neurons (Luria, 1973).

This functional unit has high modal specificity. This means that each part is adapted to receive very specific visual, auditory, vestibular, or general sensory information. For example, the individual neurons of the visual system only respond to narrowly specialized stimuli. Some cells only respond to certain colors, others to the character of lines, still others to the direction of movement. A cell responding to color will not respond to a line. This characteristic is called modal specificity.

Essentially, information is received and passed along to higher levels of brain functioning as analysis progresses. The primary zones of the second unit react to the stimuli provided by the eyes, ears, nose, and skin as well as to movement within space. The secondary zones accumulate the information passed along from the primary zones. Thus, a secondary zone might take inputs from primary visual neurons concerning color, lines, and movement to begin analyzing what is perceived. The tertiary zones are responsible for enabling groups of several analyzers to work together. The tertiary zones spatially organize the information coming from the secondary zones and convert the successive stimuli into simultaneously processed groups. Thus, the tertiary zones not only integrate information flowing from the outside world, but are important for symbolic processes.

Three laws govern the structure of the second brain unit. First, the cortical zones are organized in a hierarchical structure. The relationships between the primary, secondary, and tertiary cortical zones demonstrate how information processing becomes increasingly complex as it is synthesized.

Second, as the zones move from primary to tertiary, neuron functions become less specialized. The primary zones possess maximum modal specificity. The secondary zones are much less modally specific and convert the primary information into functional organizations. However, secondary visual neurons still only respond to visual signals from primary visual neurons. The secondary neurons consequently retain some modal specificity. The tertiary zones have the least modal specificity because their function is to integrate all of the information coming from the primary and secondary zones.

Third, as functions move upward from primary to tertiary they are progressively lateralized. At the primary level, both hemispheres of the brain operate similarly. As the information progresses up through the zones, however, functions begin to differentiate depending upon whether the information is in the left or the right hemisphere. For, example, the left hemisphere dominates speech functions at the tertiary level, but the right hemisphere does not. Thus, the left hemisphere plays an essential role in the higher forms of cognitive activity connected with speech: Perception organized into logical schemes, active verbal memory, and logical thought. The right hemisphere plays a subordinate role in these processes.

The final functional unit of the brain concerns organization of preconscious, unconscious, and conscious activities (Luria, 1973). Preconscious and unconscious activities relate to about 98 percent of mental processing occurring within the brain. Preconscious and unconscious activities involve forming intentions and plans, monitoring the performance of activities directed to accomplishing intentions and plans, and comparing or verifying the effects of actions against the original intentions. As we will see, consciousness accounts for a very small percentage of neuroactivity.

The structures of this third unit lie in the anterior portion of the brain, known as the prefrontal cortex. The most important part of this unit are the frontal lobes, found on the cerebrum in the diagram. These portions of the brain play a decisive role in the formation of intentions. They also regulate and verify the most complex forms of human behavior. The prefontal cortex also regulates activity, changing it in accordance with complex intentions formed with the aid of speech. The prefontal cortex has two-way connections with the lower structures of the brain stem and diencephalon and with all other parts of the cerebral cortex. Thus, the prefontal cortex is a tertiary cortical superstructure, performing a far more universal function of general regulation of behavior.

The three functional units do not operate independently. Human activity takes place through the synthesis of all three brain units, each of which makes its own contribution. For example, perception takes place through the combined action of all three functional units of the brain. The first unit provides the necessary cortical tone, the second carries out the analysis and synthesis of incoming information, and

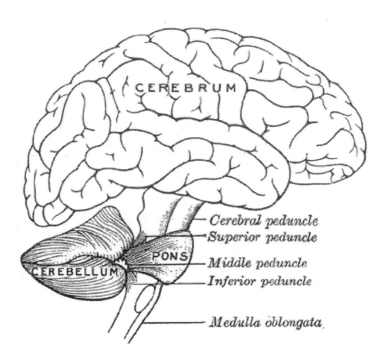

Cerebral peduncle
Superior peduncle
Middle peduncle
Inferior peduncle
Medulla oblongata

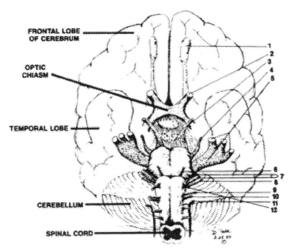

FRONTAL LOBE
OF CEREBRUM

OPTIC
CHIASM

TEMPORAL LOBE

CEREBELLUM

SPINAL CORD

1 SMELL
2 OPTIC
3 EYE MOVEMENT
4 EYE MOVEMENT
5 FACIAL SENSATION
6 EYE MOVEMENT
7 FACE MOVEMENT
8 HEARING & BALANCE

9 TASTE
10 INVOLUNTARY MUSCLES
(Heart, Stomach,
Throat, Chest,
Intestines)
11 NECK AND BACK
VOLUNTARY MUSCLES
12 TONGUE

the third directs the necessary controlled searching movements that give perceptual activities active character (Luria, 1973).

Automaticity

Automaticity refers to the principle that much of our everyday life—thinking, feeling, and doing—is automatic. People, objects, behaviors of others, settings, roles, and norms drive what we think, feel, and do without our conscious awareness. We make decisions and begin acting on them more than a half second before we are even conscious of what we are doing. Most importantly, we judge quickly, then rationalize our judgments. Bargh's research in this area has revealed important and startling insights into how humans react socially (Bargh, 1997).

For many years, cognition was based on a serial stage model. In serial stage processing, a social event occurs. We see and hear the event, then we consciously evaluate the people and their actions in the event. Based on our conscious evaluation, we consider an appropriate response and we respond. For example, Sarah arrives on time at her office to wait for John. When John appears a few minutes late, the serial model says that she consciously evaluates John based on his tardiness. She then judges whether John is rude or untrustworthy or simply uncaring. She reaches her conclusion and acts accordingly. This model places Sarah's consciousness at the center of her evaluation and response.

Bargh postulates that preconscious processes largely create the immediate psychological situation. The preconscious mind, of which we are not aware, determines how we interpret perceptions of other people's behavior, how we evaluate those behaviors based on their physical features and their actions, and how we respond to the situation. These processes operate simultaneously, in parallel, and communicate with each other. The output of one system therefore has consequences for the others. These processes operate on the same input at the same time. Consequently, they are separate processing modules.

Here is how the processes seem to work. A social event occurs, such as John arrives late. Sarah preconsciously perceives the event. In her brain, an automatic set of unconscious processes simultaneously does three things.

The first set of preconscious processes decides what all the things, people, and actions are. Sarah preconsciously recognizes

John and through her quantitative operator determines that he is late. She is not aware of this processing yet, but John's late arrival is enough to generate a preconscious interpretation of behavior. This preconscious process selects sensory information to send to the conscious mind.

The second set of processes judges whether the things, people, or actions are "good" or "bad." This is a dichotomous process with no room for ambiguity. From this process, emotions begin to be generated. Sarah's preconscious processing immediately does a down and dirty evaluation that the situation is "bad."

The research on automatic attitude activation shows that the preconscious evaluation effect is extremely general across social and nonsocial events. In research studies, automatic evaluation occurred regardless of how extreme or strong the earlier attitude toward the object. It also occurred when all aspects of intentional evaluative processing were removed. In fact, as conscious strategic processing conditions were eliminated, the automatic evaluation became more pronounced. Consequently, the researchers learned that we evaluate all social events immediately as good or bad, without intending to evaluate, having recently thought in terms of evaluation, or being aware of doing so. Therefore, we preconsciously screen everything we encounter and classify it as good or bad, within a fraction of a second after the encounter.

The third process sets a goal of interaction and initiates action. The goals are again dichotomous: To connect with the thing, person, or action or to defend against the thing, person, or action. Sarah preconsciously decides to defend and says without thinking, "Where have you been? You certainly are rude!" A half second later, as Sarah's cortex processes more information about John, she realizes that his clothes are ripped and torn. Only then can she reevaluate her first judgment and realize that John must have been delayed by an accident of some sort. The problem, socially, is that Sarah, having committed to her first down-and-dirty judgment, may now lose face if she changes judgment. Instead of a simple apology to smooth over her first comment, she stays on the track of the first, preconscious, and now obviously wrong judgment. Not realizing how her preconscious processes have misled her, she chooses an offensive assault to protect her from her obvious error.

These three preconscious processes can be summarized as perception, evaluation, and motivation. Only after these processes have begun does the conscious mind become aware of the social event.

The preconscious and unconscious have already perceived, evaluated, and chosen goals. The conscious mind through the causal operator, unaware of all of this, must rationalize, explain, and reconcile all of this. Not surprisingly, it is often wrong. Because we are only aware of what is conscious, we believe that our reactions start with conscious appraisement. In fact, conscious appraisement is nothing more than an after-the-fact attempt to figure out what happened.

As we automatically judge whether something is good or bad, we infer motives. From inferred motives, we infer intent as either intent to help or intent to hurt. Social psychologists have labeled this phenomenon fundamental attribution error. We can now see that fundamental attribution error is a biological response to external stimuli or internal memories. The judging process is outside of conscious control and occurs automatically all of the time.

Humans are prone to judge "bad" more often than "good." This predisposition may lie in the adaptive ability to deal with an uncertain, dangerous world conservatively. As a result, negative attributions are frequent even if wrong. Thousands of years ago social interaction was far less complex than it is today. Human societies were small and the task of surviving was paramount. The ability to judge quickly and automatically was useful in an environment where most everything was dangerous. In modern times, the dangers are not so apparent, since social change has occurred much faster than biological change. As a result, humans are dealing with far more complex societies while equipped with archaic biological responses. Thus, in an ambiguous situation, we are prone to judge negatively. This automatic "jumping to conclusion" results in blaming or accusation that may be unwarranted. Nevertheless, once made, the conflict cycle is initiated or escalated.

The persistence of conflict escalation can be seen in the interaction of two "judges." One person judges another negatively and reacts accordingly. The other perceives the behavior as an attack on identity and responds defensively. It takes a great deal of discipline and will not to react to identity attacks. Even then our bodies are screaming at us to defend and attack. Most people succumb to the unconscious responses, not realizing that they are playing out their biological programming. The underlying reasons for these behaviors and reactions lie in the function and structure of the human brain.

The Cognitive Operators

The human brain underlies all human experience. It is responsible for receiving information from the outside world, analyzing it, informing us what that information is, putting an emotional content to the information, creating a behavioral response to the information, and acting on the behavioral response. In fact, every human brain has a set of abilities that are absolute. Thus, despite what might appear to be extreme differences in cultures, beliefs, and attitudes, every person has a neurological physiology that is essentially identical to every other person.

The brain also is the chief organ in the central nervous system. The central nervous system is composed of nerves, the central nervous system, and the brain, and the neurochemicals modulating the system. The autonomic nervous system is the core of the central nervous system because it maintains base line physical functions. The autonomous nervous system also responds to external information and thus connects the brain to the rest of the body.

The autonomic nervous system is divided into the sympathetic and parasympathetic systems. The sympathetic system supports the approach-defend response to desirable or noxious environmental stimuli. In essence, the sympathetic system causes a sense of arousal. This system is connected to the lower brain and penetrates into the higher brain. Its principal purpose is to control short-range adaptations to events in the environment.

The parasympathetic system maintains homeostasis and conserves bodily resources and energy. Thus, it is responsible for all metabolism and growth, digestion, relaxation, and sleep.

The sympathetic and parasympathetic systems are usually described as antagonistic or inhibitory to each other. Intense activity in one system usually indicates decreased activity in the other. Neuroscientists have learned that the sympathetic-parasympathetic interaction is highly complex. The balance between the systems can also be modified through conditioning. The human baseline state at birth represents an emotional setting brought into the world. For example, a person may be initially "uptight" or "laid back." This balance can be altered, through social processes such as ritual, so that a new baseline is established.

The primary functional characteristics of the brain-mind are cognitive operators. These are specific functions performed within the brain that we experience as mind. Cognitive operators work on inputs from the environment and memory. They operate on sensory perception, thoughts, and emotions to create meaning. The cognitive operators work together to create the experience we call "mind."

Cognitive operators are the same in all people. Functions such as language, vision, movement, and thought tend to be localized in the same general areas regardless of who is examined. Similarly, cognitive operators are shared among all humans, indicating a common genetic origin.

The cognitive operators help us to understand how conflict can arise over seemingly indisputable events. A person experiencing an event with predominantly the wholistic operator will perceive and interpret the event in terms of a larger perspective. On the other hand, another person experiencing the same event with predominantly the binary operator will perceive and interpret the event in terms of dichotomy, such as good and evil or right and wrong. These people will experience the same thing objectively, but subjectively place entirely different interpretations and meanings on it. Moreover, each person believes his or her interpretation is the true reality of the situation, thus denying the other person's perspective and interpretation. Understanding the cognitive operators helps to explain many common conflict situations.

Seven primary cognitive operators comprise most of the functions of the brain. Each operation represents a specific function of the brain, but when woven together form the complexity of the human mind. These are the basic cognitive operators:

- The wholistic operator
- The reductionistic operator
- The abstractive operator
- The binary operator
- The quantitative operator
- The causal operator
- The emotional value operator

The wholistic operator allows humans to view reality as a whole. In other words, this is the process that gives people a larger perspective and places information into context. Experiments have established that this operator is located in the parietal lobe of the non-dominant hemisphere of the brain. For right-handed people, it is the upper right center part of the brain. (The dominant hemisphere is opposite the dominant hand). The perceptions generated by the wholistic operator are of a gestalt nature such that it tells us how a group of units work or fit together as a whole. Ideally, peacemaking processes try to engage the wholistic operator so people in conflict can see a larger perspective than what is immediately before them.

The reductionistic operator functions in the opposite manner to the wholistic operator. It allows humans to look at the whole picture and break it down into component parts. Not surprisingly, the reductionist operator is located opposite of the wholistic operator in the dominant hemisphere parietal lobe. It is connected to sight, hearing, and touch, as well as the language center. The reductionistic operator performs various logical-grammatical operations and gives humans their scientific, logical, and mathematical approach to understanding the world. The most accurate understanding comes from the combined operation of the wholistic and reductionistic operators. However, if the reductionistic operator dominates the wholistic operator, a person will be unable to see the big picture. This is a common problem for people in conflict.

The abstractive operator is the center of the logical induction process because it permits general concepts to be formed from individual facts. All general concepts or ideas underlying language derive from the abstractive operator. Inferences and circumstantial evidence are also processes created by the abstractive operator. It can take two facts and from them derive a third fact not proved directly. Ideas such as mathematics, government, justice, and culture are all aspects of the abstractive operator. This operator appears to be located in the inferior portion of the left hemisphere parietal lobe. This is the lower left center part of the brain. Tumors in this area prevent people from making comparisons such as "larger than," "smaller than," or "better than." Oftentimes, money will be a symbol for reparation of identity injuries. The abstractive operator will perform the processing that tells a person whether he or she is being treated fairly by the offer of a sum of money for resolution of a dispute.

The binary operator is located in the same region as the abstractive operator and orders information into opposite pairs or dyads. A dyad is a group of two elements with the opposite meanings. Dyads include right and wrong, good and evil, justice and injustice, happy and sad, and so forth. Each opposite in the dyad receives some of its meaning from its opposite. Thus, the elements of a dyad require each other for full meaning. Rigidity in conflict situations occurs because people lock into their binary operators, seeing issues in black and white terms and people as good or evil.

The quantitative operator permits us to determine quantity from the perception of multiple elements. It is the bean counter part of the brain and is located in the inferior parietal lobe near the binary and abstractive operators. This operator allows humans to number objects, to order and rank, to count, and to measure. The survival value of this operator is vital. Through it people are aware of such mundane, but critical things, as how much food is in the pantry, how much money is in the checking account, what time it is, and how long before the next appointment. Quantification is an important part of human cognition.

The causal operator permits information to be viewed in terms of causal sequences. Neuroscientists believe this operator results from the connections between the left frontal lobe and the left orientation association area. People with tumors in these areas have severe deficits in deciding why things happen. In its most basic function, the causal operator tends to create a sense of causality on all information. Thus, this operator forces humans to question why things work the way they do or why people behave the way they do. Essentially, humans are driven to know the cause of every experience and event in life. Neuroscientists call this the causal imperative: humans have a biological necessity to seek out causality in everything. This operator is at the root of much philosophical and religious thought.

Michael S. Gazzaniga, a neuroscientist at Dartmouth College, has studied the causal operator in his research with split-brain patients, people whose left and right hemispheres have been separated by surgery or disease (Gazzaniga, 1998).

The brain creates an illusion of self as it constructs its past. The reconstruction of events starts with perception and goes all the way to human reasoning. The mind is the last to know things. After the brain computes an event, the illusory "we" becomes aware of it. This is because the brain, particularly the left hemisphere, is built to interpret data the brain has already processed. The causal operator carries out one more activity upon completion of automatic brain processes by reconstructing the brain events to form a cohesive story. In doing so, the causal operator makes huge errors of perception, memory, and judgment. As Gazzaniga says, biography is fiction. Autobiography is hopelessly inventive. The important point to understand is that "rationality" is a fiction created by the conscious mind's limited perception of what the rest of the brain is processing.

A special system carries out this interpretive synthesis. Located only in the brain's left hemisphere, the causal operator seeks explanations for internal and external events. It is tied to the general capacity to see how contiguous events relate to one other. The operator, a built-in specialization in its own right, works on the activities of other adaptations built into our brain. These adaptations are cortically based and work largely outside of conscious awareness.

The causal operator creates the lies necessary to create a fiction of control. Human brains are built to remember the gist of things, not the details. The causal operator and the memory system meet in these false recollections. As the operator spins the tale, calling on the schema of past memory, it simply drags into the account likely details that could have been part of the experience. This operator is also the cause of much conflict because different people weave different stories about the same objective events. Since the causal operator is creating reality for them, they absolutely believe in the truth of their own stories to the exclusion of other stories.

The left hemisphere's capacity for continual interpretation means it is always looking for order and reason, even when they do not exist. The interpreter works beautifully to help people understand the world. It fails miserably when trying to interpret large or meaningless data sets.

The significance of this research cannot be overstated. We have assumed for too long that people's perceptions of events are accurate and rationally based. They are neither accurate nor rational. Thus, conflict arising from different perceptions and perspectives is inevitable. One key to reconciling conflict based on differing interpretations of events is recognizing the role of the causal operator in weaving stories. Each person will understand an event or experience uniquely based on the salience formed by the causal operator.

The emotional value operator, the final operator, is the most complex brain function. It must place emotional values on the responses of all the operators and, therefore is connected to all of them.

Emotions are the result of a long history of development and are part of the regulatory devices we come equipped with to survive. The biological purpose of emotion is twofold.

First, emotions produce specific reactions to situations. These reactions generally may be divided into approach or defense reactions. Approach reactions permit sexual reproduction, food gathering, and sharing of shelter. Defense reactions result in freezing, fleeing, or fighting.

Second, emotions prepare the organism for the specific reaction required by the circumstances. Preparation might include increased blood flow, changing heart or breathing rhythms, or increased arousal or sensitivity. For either dangerous or valuable environmental stimuli, a corresponding set of emotions exists. This is why, despite infinite variations, we can successfully predict emotional responses to certain stimuli (LeDoux, 1996).

Conflict, of course, is highly emotional.

Emotion

Historical Studies of Emotion

In 1878, the French neurologist Paul Broca, identified an area under the cortex that he called the limbic lobe (from the Latin word *limbus*, implying the idea of a circle, ring, or surrounding). This lobe formed a border around the brain stem, hence the name limbic. In later years the entire system would be called the limbic system. As viewed by evolutionists, the limbic system emerged in primitive mammals. The system commands certain behavior necessary for the survival of all mammals. Early theorists believed that emotions and feelings, like anger, fright, passion, love, hate, joy, were mammalian inventions originating in the limbic system.

In 1937, neuroanatomist James Papez demonstrated that emotion was not a function of any specific brain center, but of the circuit that involves four basic structures interconnected through several nervous bundles. Paul D. MacLean, accepting Papez's proposal, created the term *limbic system* and added new structures to the circuit (MacLean, 1989).

MacLean's theory was simply stated. According to his understanding of the theory of evolution, the human brain expanded to a great size while retaining the basic features of three formations that reflect ancestral relationships to reptiles, early mammals, and recent mammals. These three formations constituted a hierarchy of three brains in one or what MacLean called a triune brain.

The primitive or reptilian brain was comprised of the structures of the brain stem. MacLean called this the R-complex. The R-complex was responsible for self-preservation. In this complex, mechanisms of aggression and repetitive behavior were developed. This region was believed responsible for the instinctive reactions of the so-called reflex arcs and the commands allowing some involuntary actions and the control of certain visceral functions indispensable to the preservation of life. According to MacLean, the R-complex started the first manifestations of the phenomenon of ritualism by which an animal defines its hierarchic position inside a group and establishes its own ecological niche. MacLean's theory paralleled Konrad Lorenz's theory of ritual as a means of aggression reduction.

The intermediate, or paleomammalian, brain consisted of the structures of the limbic system. This brain corresponded to the brain of the inferior mammals.

The neo-mammalian brain consisted of the neocortex, and some subcortical neuronal groups. This brain corresponded to the brain of the superior mammals, including the primates and, consequently, humans. This rational, neo-mammalian brain was considered a highly complex system capable of symbolic language, enabling intellectual tasks such as reading, writing, and performing mathematical calculations.

These three layers appear one after the other, during the development of the embryo and the fetus, recapitulating the evolution of animal species from lizards up to Homo sapiens. According to MacLean, they are three biological computers that, although interconnected, retain their peculiar types of intelligence, subjectivity, sense of time and space, memory, mobility, and other less specific functions.

MacLean' limbic system theory of emotion has been influential in the neurosciences and clinical medicine. However, it has not been established by empirical evidence. Joseph LeDoux, a neuroscientist interested in emotion, has concluded that study of the limbic system, or more particularly, that an emotional system exists in the brain, is misguided (LeDoux, 1996). Based on empirical studies, LeDoux demonstrated the neural circuitry for the emotion of fear (LeDoux, 1995). These circuits had little to do with the limbic system, other than the amygdala. Furthermore, the centerpiece of the limbic system, the hippocampus, was implicated in nonemotional processes like memory and spatial behavior.

Assuming the theory of evolution, LeDoux believes that emotions are products of different systems, each of which evolved to take care of survival problems. Because of evolutionary requirements, LeDoux believes that different systems of the brain will be involved in different emotions. LeDoux also believes that there are basic emotions hard-wired into brain architecture. One of the advantages of a large cortex is that different hard-wired emotions can be blended together to create softer, more complex emotions, where cognition plays a greater role.

Characteristics of Emotion

From a neurological perspective, certain basic principles about emotions seem to be clear. First, emotions arise from nonconscious processes. Although we like to think that we can control our emotions, in fact all we control are some limited external behaviors. We cannot turn anger off and on volitionally, just as we cannot turn feelings of joy off and on. We may be able to recall memories that evoke anger or joy, but the actual instigation of emotion is beyond conscious control. One of the reasons we appreciate skilled acting is because actors can give the appearance of expressing and controlling emotions in artificial settings (Damasio, 1999).

Second, emotions are biologically determined processes, depending on innate brain devices. The principle adaptive purpose of emotions is to arouse us to some event, situation, or activity. Generally, the event may be judged as good if it leads to reproductive potential, food, or shelter, and bad if dangerous or unknown. Far and away, most environmental events are judged as bad so as to protect the organism from fatal surprises. Emotions play an important role in survival observable to one degree or another in all vertebra species. Emotions are more complex in higher orders of species. More complicated emotions seem to permit more subtle and varied responses to the environment, giving rise to more precise adaptations. Humans have the most complex emotional structures, allowing an almost infinite variety of responses to the environment.

Third, the brain structures responsible for emotion consist of a limited ensemble of devices beginning at the brain stem and extending into the higher brain. The cortical structures do not appear to generate but instead interpret emotion and possibly blend simple emotions into more complex emotions. In addition, the cortex creates feeling, which is the conscious interpretation of an emotional state.

Finally, all the structures are engaged automatically without conscious deliberation or control. We are not aware that emotions are being generated until at least half a second after the emotion has begun. Furthermore, the cortex cannot control emotion such as by extinguishing it or suppressing it or changing it. For example, we cannot consciously eliminate the emotion of anger. We may be able to suppress those few external signs of anger over which we have some control, but the anger will remain. Similarly, we cannot change anger into joy with conscious control. Think about it. If humans had the ability to control emotion, they would have no need for artificial stimulation such as drugs, movies, or sports. Humans engage in these activities because the activities evoke emotions not created by conscious thought. Emotionally related conflict behavior is likewise not under conscious or volitional control.

Neurological processes. Different emotions are produced by different brain systems. While MacLean believed that all emotions originated in what he called the limbic system, neuroscientists now believe that no single brain structure is responsible for all emotions. Instead, emotions probably are linked to particular brain structures. While few emotions have been directly linked to specific brain structures, the research seems to suggest a general theory of emotion. According to this theory, emotions arise in a three-step process. First, we are engaged by a stimulus, which will induce emotion. This could be an external stimulus or a memory. Second, signals generated from processing the stimulus activate all of the neural sites that are prepared to respond to the particular class of inducer. These sites are preset genetically, but may be modulated by experience. Finally, the emotional induction sites trigger signals toward other brain sites and the body to engage in appropriate action. The combined result is emotion, created quickly and unconsciously.

The fear response system. One emotion clearly linked to specific brain structures is fear, generated in a brain substructure called the amygdala, a little almond-shaped structure deep inside the temporal lobe. It is like the hub of a wheel in that it receives inputs from a wide range of levels of cognitive processing. These connections enable the amygdala to play its important role in the expression of fear. Through these connections, the amygdala is able to appraise emotional meaning and initiate reactions consistent with its appraisal.

The fear reaction system involves a parallel transmission to the amygdala from the sensory thalamus and the sensory cortex. The first information about something fearful reaches the amygdala by a direct path from the thalamus. This path, being shorter, is much faster than the parallel pathway from the thalamus to the cortex to the amygdala. The downside of the shortcut is that the amygdala does not benefit from cortical processing. Thus, the amygdala is provided with a crude representation of the stimulus and appraises it as either "good" or "bad." The advantage of this down and dirty pathway is speed—we can react to potentially dangerous events before we fully know what is going on. Eventually, the cortex processes the information and sends it on the parallel, but longer, path to the amygdala. Based on this information, the amygdala may modify its appraisal of the event.

The process can be illustrated as follows. A hiker encounters a snake coiled behind a log. Her eyes send the visual information to the thalamus for initial processing. The thalamus sends part of the information to the amygdala and part of the information to the cortex. The path to the amygdala being shorter allows a fast, unconscious response to begin. Right now the hiker doesn't know if the object is a stick or a snake, but it registers as potentially "bad," and the amygdala sends signals to the hypothalamus to arouse the organism for action. Meanwhile, the thalamus feeds information to the visual cortex, which assembles a more detailed representation of the snake. This outcome is sent back to the amygdala about half a second after the amygdala receives the first inputs from the thalamus. If the thin curved object was a stick, well, better to be safe than sorry. If it was a snake, the earlier, faster response could mean the difference between life and death. Hence, the down and dirty pathway has a powerful survival value.

The amygdala appears capable not only triggering and steering responses to danger, but also of acting on higher-level neocortical processes. First, the amygdala arouses the cortex. Cortical arousal, once established, makes concentration on anything else very difficult. Working memory becomes focused on the situation as it tries to figure out what is going on and what should be done about it. All other inputs are blocked out, resulting in impaired reasoning, decision-making and other higher cortical processes. If you have experienced a feeling of tunnel vision when emotionally engaged, your working memory is shutting out all other inputs as it tries to deal with the source of arousal.

The reason for this is strictly biological. The connections from the amygdala to the cortex are much richer than the connections from the cortex to the amygdala. This allows the amygdala literally to overwhelm the cortex, which in turn feeds the arousal back to the amygdala. This results in a vicious cycle of emotional reactivity. Thus, arousal tends to lock people into an emotional state. Once the fear system is turned on, it is difficult to turn off unless something else occurs that is significant enough and arousing enough to shift the focus of arousal. Worse, stress, as a form of arousal, helps amydalic functioning. Stress shifts us even deeper into a mode where we react to danger rather than think about it.

Thus, the amygdala is able to overwhelm the cortex and the rest of the brain so that a person not only forms emotional ideas, but also responds to them. A famous example of this is Charles Whitman, who in 1966 climbed a tower at the University of Texas and indiscriminately killed people with a rifle. Whitman had initially consulted a psychiatrist about his periodic and uncontrollable violent impulses, but was unable to obtain relief. A postmortem autopsy of his brain revealed a tumor the size of a walnut compressing his amygdala.

We can now gain some insight into conflict behavior. First, people in conflict tend to act in predictable ways. This relative uniformity of behavior suggests a common neurological basis that cuts across cultures and ethnicity. Typically, conflict can induce anger and fear. When these emotions are strong enough, they will dominate and override what we experience as consciousness. We become sensitive to our environment as we are prejudging events and situations as bad. Of course, as we react to defend, by freezing, fleeing, or fighting, we set off an emotional response in the Other. Not only are the internal neural feedback loops escalating reactivity internally, the response of the people in conflict are creating an external, environmental feedback loop. This feedback is called conflict escalation and, in extreme situations, can lead to physical violence.

Feelings. Many people confuse emotions with feelings, but emotions and feelings are quite different processes. Simply stated, feelings are our awareness of emotions. Feelings can only exist with consciousness, while emotions do not need consciousness at all. Charles Darwin demonstrated that emotions are similar across species, many of which lack consciousness. However, humans and probably other higher order primates, are conscious of their emotions. The conscious awareness of emotion is what we call feeling.

The neural patterns constituting a feeling arise from the changes within our bodies as emotions are developed. If the amygdala triggers the fear mechanism, our heart rate increases, we breathe faster, we become flushed as blood expands into skin capillaries, and as we become aware of these changes in our body state, we experience fear. Interestingly, our awareness of emotion, our feeling, occurs, neurologically speaking, much later than the onset of the emotion itself. Since emotions are triggered preconsciously by subcortical brain systems, we have no control over them. Only after we start feeling the emotion can we consciously attempt to intervene. Often, as we have all experienced, our feelings have become too strong for a conscious override and we must live through the emotion.

Why do we have feelings? First, feelings alert the organism to the problem emotion has begun to solve. While the brain has mobilized the body to take action, feelings allow our conscious self to assess the situation. If the thin curved shape on the trail is just a stick, we can start to relax and reverse the emotion of fear. On the other hand, if it is a snake, we can consciously direct our behavior to a place of safety.

The second purpose of feelings is to make us pay attention to emotions. The feeling of fear is not pleasant; it is like an alarm bell going off in our ear, except worse. We are conditioned to avoid the feeling of fear because of its unpleasantness. Hence, the feeling of fear motivates us to avoid the environment that stimulates fear.

Finally, feelings extend the reach of emotions by facilitating the planning of novel and customized forms of adaptive response. Lower order animals, lacking a conscious awareness of emotion, can only react with a limited number of preprogrammed behaviors. Generally, these are freezing, fleeing, or fighting. Once conscious awareness of emotion develops, the organism can literally choose the response most appropriate to the situation. In highly variable environments, this ability has a much greater adaptive value for survival. As a result, humans have been able to live in many environments where other animals simply could not survive.

Defining states of mind. In different states of mind, people interpret the same facts or circumstances in various ways. For example, a person may experience a conflict in one state of mind, but be completely content in another. A common experience illustrates the point. If you have left your home slightly late for an appointment at a coffee house, red lights and other drivers create a sense of frustration and conflict as you hurry to your destination. When you go to the same coffee house without a deadline, the exact same conditions, red lights and drivers, are not longer a frustration or source of conflict. The different experience is based on the difference in state of mind. Observing differences in attitude in various states of mind can clarify the nature of the conflict.

A state of mind is a combination of conscious and unconscious experiences with patterns of behavior that can last for a short or long period of time. Every person has a repertoire of recurrent states of mind, which can sometimes be identified or described. Likewise, observers can learn, with experience, to recognize the states of mind of those who are familiar to them.

States of mind index inner emotion and the degree of control one has over urgent feelings. Control ranges from excessive stifling to impulsive expression. States of mind can be considered as emotion and mood, regulation, and motivation (Horowitz, 1998).

The first category for a state of mind is its *emotional state*. Descriptions can be general, such as angry or depressed. Or descriptions can be more idiosyncratic, such as tensely vigilant or morose. People are often hard pressed to describe their feelings and emotions in verbal terms, but frequently use metaphors to express themselves.

The second type of category for a state of mind concerns *emotional regulation*. Emotional regulation comes in four states: well-modulated, under-modulated, over-modulated, and shimmering.

Well-modulated states demonstrate a relatively smooth flow of expressions. Emotions and feelings appear genuine and regardless of intensity are expressed in a poised manner. The observer may feel subjective interest and empathy, with a sense of being connected to the individual and the material presented. The observer appraises the individual as engaged in an organized process of communication without major discords between verbal and nonverbal modes of expression.

The under-modulated individual appears impulsive, uncontrolled or experiencing intrusive concepts and emotions. Intense expressions may suddenly appear as the individual experiences sudden flares, surges, or pangs of emotion. The observer may experience surges of emotion as an empathic response or perhaps feel a wish to intervene in a way that will help the patient regain control.

The over-modulated individual demonstrates excessive control of expressions. He or she is stiff, enclosed, masked, or walled-off. To an observer, the individual's emotional displays seem false. The observer appraises the individual as distant from genuine communication. Therefore, the observer may feel disconnected from the individual, even bored or inattentive.

The person in a shimmering state shifts rapidly between uncontrolled and over-controlled emotions. The observer may see inconsistencies between verbal and nonverbal behavior. The clashing signals may occur simultaneously or within a brief period of time.

The third label for states of mind is motivation. States of motivation are described as wanted (usually well-modulated), dreaded (often under-modulated), problematic compromise (frequently shimmering), and quasi-adaptive compromise (sometimes over-modulated). A configuration of motivational states can be diagrammed as four quadrants: the wanted state, the dreaded state, the problematic compromise, and the quasi-adaptive compromise.

In a conflict situation, a person may yearn for the restoration of an earlier equilibrium, which is a wanted state. Memories and fantasies about the conflict, cause the person to fear the intense and un-controlled emotional flooding confronting the conflict will entail. This is the dreaded state. The person might have anxiety during con-templation of the implications of the conflict, which is a problematic compromise state. A person may enter the quasi-adaptive compro-mise state by avoiding the conflict or the person involved with the conflict. This restores a semblance of equilibrium. Nevertheless, since the underlying issues of the conflict are not addressed, the mo-tivational state is not adaptive. Rather, it is a compromise motiva-tional state to reduce anxiety without confronting the problem.

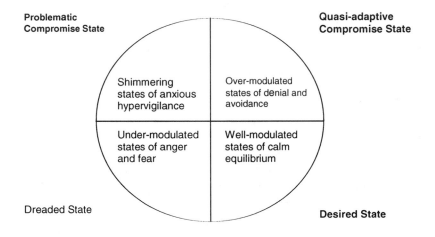

A Configuration of States During Conflict

From M. Horowitz (1998)

Conflict challenges adaptation and disturbs equilibrium. It often triggers a transition from a well-modulated state into one that is under- or over-modulated. One person might move from calmness to abrupt anger, indicating a move from a well-modulated state to an under-modulated state. Another person might move from calmness to a stony face and flat coldness, indicating a move to an over-modu-lated state.

Labeling states helps us to understand how people come to feel the way they do in conflict. Under-modulated, over-modulated, well-modulated, and shimmering states indicate a person's degree of emotional control. Well-modulated states are those in which a per-son is in self-command, appropriately spontaneous, expressive, and harmonious in verbal and nonverbal communications and is able to control impulses. Under-modulated states are those in which expressions are excessively impulsive. Over-modulated states are those in which a person is excessively veiled or pretending a role. Finally, shimmering states show contradictory emotions and controls.

Types of Emotion

Neuroscientists are still unsure of the neurological foundations for most emotions. However, emotional behaviors are well-known in psychology and a brief discussion is useful here.

Emotions can be categorized as primary or universal emotions, secondary or social emotions, and background emotions. The primary emotions include happiness, sadness, fear, anger, surprise, and disgust. These emotions are primary because they are found across species. Secondary emotions include embarrassment, jealousy, guilt, and pride. These emotions are found only in higher order primates living within social structures. Background emotions include well-being, malaise, calm, and tension.

Some emotions are short-lived, while others are persistent. Primary emotions tend to be short-lived, while background emotions tend to persist. This is not a general rule, as anger, for example, may persist over a long period of time.

Two nonemotional states are commonly confused with emotion. They are frustration and relief. Frustration arises when happiness is blocked, and relief arises when some sustained negative emotion is suspended.

Anxiety. Anxiety is a prospective emotion in that it motivates us to deal with traumatic events in advance of their occurrence. Anxiety reduction brings about relief or creates a sense of security. Because anxiety is very uncomfortable, when the stimuli that elicit it are present, we are motivated to change the circumstances. Usually this involves leaving the environment (escape) and avoiding similar environments in the future.

The capacity to become uncomfortable by the prospect of future experiences motivates us to take realistic precautions against those experiences. However, anxiety can also be disadvantageous. At its worst, it can disable our ability to deal with the uncertain future at all. Additionally, anxiety, especially in the context of conflict, can cause escalation through avoidant and contentious behaviors.

Conflict is largely caused by anxiety, and conflict behavior stems from anxiety. Anxiety is a state of uncertainty, which results in arousal. Anxiety often occurs when the source of arousal is not immediately apparent. Fear, in contrast, is usually attributable to a concrete situation or event.

Since anxiety is based on an inchoate event, it is ambiguous. Thus, anxiety-provoking events can be interpreted in more than one way. Because of the predisposition of the amygdala to negatively judge events, anxiety is often relieved by negative attribution of cause.

Anxiety is an extremely unpleasant condition for humans. Thus, humans seek relief from it as quickly as possible. Behaviors that relieve anxiety include physical action, such as escape by running, or in worst cases, physical violence. This urge to action explains why physical exercise is a good antidote for anxiety.

Physical action is usually not appropriate in social interaction. Consequently, people may relieve anxiety by becoming indignant, angry, or hostile. Again, these reactions temporarily relieve anxiety because they institute more concrete feelings. When anger or hostility is not appropriate, for example, as between an inferior and a superior, anxiety may be relieved through nervous laughter, obsequious behavior, or passive-aggressive behavior. These same behaviors are often present in peacemaking sessions.

Under Sullivan's view of self (Sullivan, 1972), a person needs power, status, and prestige as security against anxiety. For most people, this translates into a coercive, contending conflict management style. The internal dialogue may go something like this: "My power, status and prestige must come at your expense. My need to be secure from anxiety is so great that I am willing to step on you to protect me." Hence, a common reaction to the anxiety caused by conflict is contentious behavior.

Humiliation. For many people, conflict involves a threat to their self-esteem and to core elements of their self-image. The degree to which individuals feel humiliated depends on the degree of their narcissistic vulnerability—that is, on the strength and the adequacy of the integration of their self-identity.

Narcissistically vulnerable individuals have problems in their capacity to maintain self-image and a clear sense of self-identity, both of which can be easily threatened and injured. These individuals need and use others to regulate and enhance their low self-esteem, to confirm their inflated (though fragile) sense of self, and to provide a receptacle for the projected "bad" parts of themselves. They depend on other people to confirm the view of self they maintain.

THE NEUROPSYCHOLOGY OF CONFLICT / 175

For the more narcissistically vulnerable, conflict may serve as a defense against a sense of fear, rejection, and humiliation. Since the successful conclusion of a conflict can compensate for, or even repair, an injured self-image, a conflict may be waged to restore threatened self-esteem and identity. Thus, the courtroom is often perceived as an arena in which to master painful feelings of rejection, humiliation, and role loss, to reconstruct definitions of the self as good, and to recover a more positive sense of self. Unfortunately, the court process does not usually permit this identity repair to occur.

People with narcissistic vulnerabilities have a spectrum of responses to the perceived threat to self-esteem and self-integrity. They develop different strategies for dealing with these threats. These strategies involve different symbolic and defensive uses of others in the conflict, resulting in varying degrees or resistance to resolution and amenability to mediation.

Anger. Anger is an emphatic message carrying several important meanings. Anger can shout, "Pay attention to me," when a person has a need to be heard. Anger can also reprimand, as in "I do not like what you are doing" (Tavris, 1989). The message here is intended to stop some offending conduct. Anger can exhort another to "Restore my pride." Anger, therefore, is a means to gain respect from another. Anger may also signal some form of overt conflict, such as "You're in my way!" In this case, anger signals frustration when desires or goals are thwarted.

Anger has adaptive survival value because it sends a message of danger. This occurs when one feels threatened and is moving toward aggressive defense. Finally, anger can be a political or social statement, such as "Give me justice." Anger, especially in the context of collective action, is harnessed to redress power imbalances.

Despite these various messages, social attitudes toward anger are ambivalent. For example, we are told not to rock the boat, but we are also told the squeaky wheel gets the grease. So, some social confusion exists regarding the propriety and usefulness of anger. People become angry everywhere, but do so in the service of their culture's rules. That is, the rules of expressing anger are based in the norms and context of culture. Generally, people learn to live by a large set of unstated rules of behavior. These rules are frequently not even thought of as rules, but are just the ways things are done. Consequently, these unstated rules are not apparent until broken. Anger is one sign that they have been broken. Thus, anger plays an important policing function by regulating everyday social relations.

As most everyone has experienced, anger can be a serious impediment to peacemaking. In particular, people can become angry during negotiations when offers or counteroffers appear grossly unfair or disrespectful. Straub and Morrighan's wounded pride/spite model states that people with full information about a transaction who see an ultimatum offer as unfair will also become angry (Straub and Morrighan, 1995). If they become angry, they will most likely act spitefully and reject an economically valuable offer. Wounded pride refers to a personal, inwardly focused feeling occurring when self-worth is violated. When people are not given the dignity they expect, they may question their self-image and feel hurt. This is wounded pride. In contrast, anger and spite are focused outward. Anger is directed to the person deemed responsible or blameworthy for a violation or offense. Spite is a behavior generated from anger designed to hurt the offender. Spiteful actors see their reaction as just retribution, believing that revenge has its own moral imperative (Pillutla and Morrighan, 1996).

The Straub-Morrighan model suggests that the sequence for rejecting an offer is: perceiving that the offer is unfair, feeling wounded pride and anger toward the party making the offer, and rejection of the offer in spite. The wounded pride/spite model views reactions to ultimatum offers as containing cognitive, emotional, and behavioral elements.

Emotions play a central role in negotiations. People want to maximize their emotional satisfaction as well as their economic position. Consequently, people often reject small, unfair offers rather than experiencing the emotional distress associated with accepting them (Straub and Morrighan, 1995). Emotions play an even larger role when a person can attribute intentionality to the party making the offer. The more an injustice can be attributed to another person, especially a person with control, the more likely anger will arise. People value symbolic rewards such as status. Thus, analyzing conflicts simply on the basis of economic maximization models is inaccurate and unrealistic.

Anger provides a compelling short-term explanation for ending negotiations in ultimatum bargaining and other social interactions. Anger causes rejection and walkouts even though in cooler moments people may wonder at their willingness to suffer unnecessary losses (Straub and Morrighan, 1995).

Emotional Control

As we have seen, many ideas and feelings are processed preconsciously or unconsciously. Often these remain out of consciousness because more immediate or important thoughts and emotions occupy conscious representation. Unwanted memories and the emotions associated with them can be blocked from awareness. This is a defensive mechanism that can prevent the danger of emotional flooding. Nevertheless, it can become maladaptive if it prevents a full recognition of ideas and blunts the possibilities for solutions to difficult problems (Horowitz, 1998).

Three broad categories of emotional control exist: control of the contents of conscious experience, control of form of thought, and control of person schemas.

The control of contents of conscious experience can be achieved by altering topics (changing what is within conscious representation); altering concepts (changing the ideas that are chained to together to form conscious thought; altering the importance of concepts; and altering the threshold of disengagement (changing the point at which a topic is abandoned).

The control of form of thought can be achieved by altering the mode of mental representation. This means changing from verbal or lexical representation of thought to visual representation (imagery) to somatic enactions (how the body reacts). Lexical representation reduces emotion, while visual representation increases emotion. In addition, form of thought can be achieved by altering time spans. Time spans include past, present, and future. The focus can change from past to present to future to control emotion. Form of thought can also be controlled by altering logic levels. People can change the rules used to organize thought from tight logic to loose, illogical associations.

For example, people can blunt emotion by shifting from a broad logic of rational problem solving to concentrating on minor details. People may also control form of thought by altering their level of action planning. This means moving from a reflective consciousness to reflexive quickness. By altering the degree of motor activity, people can control emotion. Finally, people can control their form of thought by altering arousal levels. People can choose calming or arousing activities, drugs, or stimuli to change their form of thought.

Emotions may also be controlled through person schemas. People have a repertoire of roles. By shifting roles within the repertoire, emotional intensity can be reduced. People also have a repertoire of roles for others. By shifting those roles, emotional intensity attached to others can be reduced or increased. For example, the other's role might change from high to low status to protect self-esteem. In any relationship there may be different role-relationship models. Some may be wanted, some feared, and some use compromise to avoid dreaded states. By altering which role relationship model is active, emotion can be controlled.

All people engage in judging the actions of others. Value schemas are the tools used for judging. Different value schemas may be given different priorities in different states. When in danger of blame, as when shame threatens to destroy self-esteem, a person can control against such distress by shifting values.

Finally, emotions can be controlled by altering executive agency schema. *Executive agency* refers to the person believed to be in charge of forming plans and instigating action. Usually the executive agency is "I." In transitioning to another state, the executive agency may shift to something other than "I" such as "us" the family, "we" the work group, or "we" the community. By altering this schema, an impoverished "I" can be made larger and more important, thus controlling emotion.

Observe that in all of these control mechanisms, the actual emotion is not directly controlled. Rather, different states of mind are created to block unwanted emotions. The unwanted emotion is not eliminated, nor is the event or memory that created the emotion. Instead, the effect of the emotion on consciousness is minimized.

Neurotransmitters and Neuromodulators

Brain structures are not the only origin of emotions. In addition, animals exhibiting emotions, including humans, have a neurochemical system that by itself is powerful and when coupled with the brain, becomes extraordinary. Neurochemistry is thus a crucial component of emotional generation, continuation, suppression, and extinction. For our purposes, neurochemicals can be divided into neurotransmitters and neuromodulators. Neurotransmitters are the chemicals released at the transmitting end of a neuron, called the axon. The neurotransmitter diffuses through the minute space between neurons, called the synapse, and is picked up at receptor sites on the receiving ends of adjacent neurons, call dendrites. One axon may therefore transmit information to many nearby dendrites. The dendrite responds to the receipt of a neurotransmitter by sending an electrical charge through the neuron, which is ultimately expressed in its axon releasing a neurotransmitter. Thus, neuronal activity is both electrical and chemical (Luria, 1973).

Certain brain stem neurochemicals modify synaptic efficacy. These substances are called neuromodulators, as distinct from neurotransmitters. In other words, neuromodulators affect how fast or slow a dendrite might respond to a neurotransmitter, or whether it will respond at all. Thus, some neurochemicals engage in the raw transmission of information and other neurochemicals modulate where and when effective transmission will occur (Allman, 1998).

This system provides the essential neurochemical basis for intentionality. The neuromodulators are responsible for maintaining the global state of the forebrain, which is expressed in behaviors such as waking, the four stages of sleeping, and reactivity which is subjectively experienced in terms of awareness, motivation, mood, affect, disposition, and the state-dependence of reactions to stimuli. A large part of current psychiatric research and clinical practice is devoted to discovering the actions of these chemicals and learning ways to enhance or diminish their actions in mentally disturbed people.

The neuromodulators are grouped by their chemical structures into two main classes: the neuroamines and the neuropeptides. The lists are long and still growing. Some better-known neuromodulators and their associated behavioral contexts are listed as follows:

Acetylcholine	Memory
Dopamine	Hedonism
Endorphins	Pain relief
Histamine	Arousal
Melatonin	Alarm clock
Norepinephrine	Imprinting
Oxytocin	Orgasm
Serotonin	Relaxation
Vasopressin	Aggression

Each interacts in complex patterns with other modulators and transmitters in different contexts. Thus, the above list is rudimentary in that for every neurochemical that creates a behavior, there is at least one that probably inhibits that behavior. Thus, the neurochemistry of behavior is very complicated and still not well understood. Nevertheless, serotonin is better understood and plays an important role in behavior relevant to conflict.

The bottom structure of the brain is composed of a network of serotonergic neurons in the brain stem. The serotonergic neurons are so named because they secrete from their axon terminals the neurotransmitter serotonin.

Serotonin was discovered in 1948 by the biochemist Maurice Rapport and his colleagues at the Cleveland Clinic. Serotonin causes blood vessels to constrict. Hence the name was derived from a combination of the Latin words for blood, *serum*, and stretching, *tonus*. Later studies found that serotonin could have the opposite effect in blood vessels, indicating that serotonin has a complex modulating role. Serotonin is made from the amino acid tryptophan, which is abundant in meat and fowl, but is not created in the human body. Tryptophan is obtained by the digestion of proteins and is transported by the blood to the brain where it is converted to serotonin.

If one thinks of the structure of the brain as a house, the serotonergic neurons are located in the basement. Like the basement regulators of water and electricity, this set of neurons is fundamental to the functioning of the house, acting somewhat like the house's thermostat to maintain a comfortable equilibrium in response to outside variations. The cell bodies of the serotonergic neurons occupy virtually the same location in the basement of every vertebrate and are even in the same spot in the central nervous system of amphioxus, a primitive chordate. In humans they participate in the most complex aspects of thinking and emotion. The axons of the serotonergic neurons project to every part of the central nervous system, where they influence the activity of virtually every neuron. This widespread influence implies that the serotonergic neurons play a fundamental role in the integration of behavior. Our sense of well-being and our capacity to organize and to relate to others depend profoundly on the functional integrity of the serotonergic system (Allman, 1998).

An animal's arousal state is closely related to the activity of the serotonergic neurons. Serotonergic neurons fire less frequently as arousal decreases from active waking state, to quiet waking, to slow wave sleep. Serotonergic neurons stop firing altogether in rapid-eye-movement sleep, when most muscles in the body become inactive. When the animal increases its motor activity, the firing of the serotonergic neurons often increases just before the activity begins and continues as long as the motor activity is maintained. Thus, the increase in serotonergic neuron activity is apparently driven by the neural commands to move the muscles. Serotonin plays an important role in the maintenance of cortical tone.

Drugs that decrease the amount of serotonin increase exploratory, eating, sexual behavior, and fear-induced aggression. Similarly, when the gene that encodes one class of serotonin receptor is inactivated in mice, the mutated mice are grossly obese and prone to dying from seizures. This evidence suggests that serotonin constrains neuronal response and thus stabilizes brain activity. Obsessive-compulsive and anxiety disorders are related to deficiencies in the serotonergic system and are treated by drugs that strengthen the serotonergic modulation of neuroactivity.

Serotonin is intimately linked to social status in primates. In experiments changing the level of serotonin in monkeys, monkeys with low levels of serotonin had low social status. When the concentration of serotonin was manipulated, the monkeys' social standing was influenced. Thus serotonin levels directly affect social status. By contrast, higher status was not related to obvious physical features such as larger body size or canine teeth. During the course of the experiments, which lasted several weeks, social status changes were always preceded by changes in affiliative behavior with females. Male monkeys given drugs that increased serotonin engaged in more frequent grooming interactions with females. Increased grooming behavior was followed by female support in dominance interactions, which increased the male's social status.

Conversely, male monkeys given drugs that decreased serotonin had less frequent grooming interactions with females, and female support in dominance interactions diminished, resulting in decreased status for the male. The dominant monkeys were more relaxed and confident; the subordinate monkeys were more likely to be irritable and to lash out at other animals. The experimenters also found that the amount of serotonin was positively related to the frequency of pro-social behavior, such as grooming, and negatively related to antisocial behavior, such as fighting. Thus, serotonin seems to stabilize the relationships between the individual and other members of its social group.

Why do not all animals have high levels of serotonin and its receptors and live in the most congenial manner possible? Asked another way, what is the biological role for the higher level of risk-taking in males in some species? In *The Descent of Man*, Darwin linked male aggression to competition among males for females. This has led to the widely accepted idea that aggressive males become socially dominant. Because of their dominance, males are thought to enjoy greater sexual access to females and therefore greater reproductive success. However, there is evidence to indicate that factors other than dominance may be involved in male risk-taking.

Does aggression lead to social dominance? In the study concerning serotonin levels in monkeys, male status was invariably preceded by changes in affiliative behaviors with females in the social group such as grooming interactions. Increased affiliative behaviors led to increased female support in dominance interactions with other males, which in turn led to rising status. This investigation and others indicate that high status in primate groups is much more dependent on social skills and coalition building than on aggression.

Social competence probably counts for more than aggression in achieving either high status for reproductive success in primates. Why then are the non-caretaking males aggressive and prone to risk-taking? The answer may be that risk-takers constantly probe their world, seeking out new opportunities and detecting hazards in an always changing environment. Through their probing they generate new information that they communicate to close kin, thus enhancing their kin's survival of and the propagation of their shared genes. The risk-takers may also be crucial to colonizing new habitats during changing environmental conditions.

Low serotonin levels are related to stronger motivational drive and greater sensitivity to rewards and risk in the environment. Animals with high serotonin levels, while more stable, are less sensitive to hazards and opportunities in the environment. This may explain the diversity of serotonin levels in natural monkey populations. The low serotonin monkeys may be the first of their group to find new food sources and may serve as sentinels that detect predators. Such behaviors may endanger an individual but enhance the survival of close relatives and the propagation of genes shared with the individual.

The potential adaptive significance of genes for low serotonergic function may explain why mood disorders, which are associated with low serotonin levels, are so prevalent in human populations. Furthermore, serotonergic function helps to explain many behaviors associated with human conflict. For example, people who demonstrate a predominantly cooperative conflict may have genes adapted to higher serotonin levels. Likewise, those people exhibiting a predominantly competitive conflict style may have genes adapted to lower serotonin levels. This does not suggest that people cannot change their conflict styles or conflict behaviors, but that one possible predisposition may be based on neurochemistry.

Finally, neuropsychologists have suggested that impulsive human aggression may be modulated by the serotonergic system. Given the proper environmental circumstances, the lower the functional status of the serotonergic system, the more likely an individual is to respond to threats, frustration, or aversive events with aggression. The lower the functionality of the serotonergic system, the more severe the aggression is likely to be. Serotonin inhibits aggressive behavior. Consequently, if serotonin levels are low, individuals have a difficult time inhibiting their response to perceived verbal or physical assaults (Coccarro and Kavoussi, 1996).

Conclusion

The neurosciences provide important insights into conflict behaviors. These insights are very different from conventional wisdom and explain why we react to conflict the way we do. Summarized, some of the insights are:

Most of our everyday behavior is automatic. As Bargh and others have discovered, much of our behavior and activity is scripted by learned experiences. These scripted behaviors are created to achieve certain goals. For example, the decision to walk down the street sets in play a goal of walking down the street. The scripts that allow us to walk down the street without conscious attention are automatic. Goals are often unconsciously triggered by environmental cues. Furthermore, triggers may unconsciously put into play scripts that are inappropriate or that would not be chosen consciously.

Emotions are an unconscious process occurring outside conscious awareness or "thinking." We become aware of emotions, which awareness we call feelings, only after the emotions have begun. Generally, we are aware of emotional reaction about half a second after the reaction has begun.

Reasoning or intention cannot control emotions. Because emotions are unconscious, they are not under volitional control. The reason for this seems to be that the neural connections from the brain substructures responsible for reaction to the cortex are richer than the connections from the cortex to the substructures. Thus, more information can flow to the cortex and dominate its processes than can flow from the cortex to the lower structures. Consequently, emotions can and do overwhelm the higher cortical processes because of the rich, one-way neural connections between the amygdala and the cortex. This also suggests that once emotions are generated, they are very hard to stop because of the neural feedback loops. As a result, trying to deal with emotion by asking a person to think rationally is futile. Common experience tells us that we cannot be persuaded by reason when we are emotional. Neither can we persuade others dominated by emotion to be rational.

We judge events, people, and memories preconsciously as good or bad. We have no conscious control over this judging process and are not aware that we are even being this judgmental. Based on the initial judgment, we preconsciously decide to approach or defend. Because of the hazards of the primal environment, we are inclined to judge things, people, and events as bad and invoke a defense.

Conflict situations naturally tend to be judged as bad and defense reactions are instigated unconsciously. Only after we have reacted to our preconscious judgment, do we begin to rationalize and "make up stories" about what has happened and why. These after-the-fact justifications are often wrong when we face complex situations or we lack complete information. Because our rationalizations are made up to create order out of chaos, we defend them vigorously. Our causal operator will not give up an interpretation easily. This explains why people in conflict tend to invalidate interpretations that contradict their own. Seeing other perspectives or possibilities threatens the need for order and predictability.

Neuropsychology is still in its infancy as researchers painstakingly unravel brain function. In years to come, neuropsychology will probably aid our understanding of the causes of human conflict at a biological and psychological level that cannot be imagined today. Most importantly, neuropsychology, especially as it explains automatic behaviors such as the fear response system, provides insight into common conflict behaviors.

Reflections on Chapter Six

Marsha McClelland is the human resources director of Anodyne Industries, one of your larger clients. She has consulted with you about difficulties with the executive vice president, Peter Majora. Mr. Majora has a hot temper and is very aggressive to the point that two valuable vice presidents have resigned in the past ninety days. Ms. McClelland is fearful of wrongful termination lawsuits if Mr. Majora's conduct persists. However, he has the ear and support of the CEO, so he is not likely to leave or be terminated himself. Ms. McClelland has asked that you brief the senior management team on current developments in employment law with a particular emphasis on litigation trends. By this indirect approach, Ms. McClelland hopes that Mr. Majora will realize the risk he poses to the company.

You are now at company headquarters in the main conference room. You have been going through your Power Point presentation and the management team has been very attentive. Suddenly, Mr. Majora explodes in anger, saying, "This is all b—-s——! We have a company to run and the lawyers aren't going to run it for us." He glares at you, then strides out of the room, slamming the door behind him.

Based on the information in this chapter, what do you think is going on? Will reasoning work with Mr. Majora? Why or why not? If reasoning won't work with him, what can be done?

What types of conflicts do you think might be growing within the organization as a result of Mr. Majora's behavior?

How, as the company lawyer, can you deal with the internal conflicts to prevent escalation into litigation.

Is conflict resolution within a client organization even a part of the role of an outside lawyer? Should it be? Explain your answers.

Would your answer be different if you were house counsel? Why or why not?

What insights does this material on the neuropsychology of conflict give you in understanding what is happening at Anodyne?

CHAPTER SEVEN

IDENTITY

*T*HE PARTERSHIP DISPUTE WAS ABOUT as intractable as a business conflict can be. Partners who had been like brothers for over forty years were now spending millions of dollars in litigation costs. Because the case was taking up so much court time in pretrial matters, a discovery referee was appointed. The parties individually began to approach the referee about settlement overtures, and the referee began a painstakingly careful mediation process. Because of the intense hostility, the process was slogging, but progress was being made. The referee could see a settlement forming in two or three more weeks.

Then the plaintiff's counsel announced that his clients had run out of patience and were filing an amended complaint. The allegations of the complaint stated incendiary facts that, if true, could lead to the disbarment of one of the parties, a lawyer. The sole purpose of the amendment was to push the defendants faster toward settlement. In fact, the new pleading had the opposite effect. Instead of creating the incentive intended by the plaintiffs, the allegations so enraged the defendants, who believed their integrity was being attacked, that all settlement discussions broke off. The case went to trial and nearly bankrupted all of the parties.

Identity challenges and threats account for far more conflicts than most people suppose. This is because identity conflicts are difficult to articulate. People often viscerally react to an identity attack and do not recognize that their reaction is escalating the conflict. Sometimes people feel the emotion of the identity conflict but ascribe

186

it to some more objective cause. A conflict over money is much easier to grasp than a conflict accelerated by threats to identity. People may also avoid identity issues by asserting less inflammatory issues. In these cases, the identity conflict simmers under the surface, boiling up to thwart resolution as agreements on the less volatile issues seem close.

The psychological foundation for identity rests on order, autonomy, and relatedness (Zehr, 2000). Order describes how we form reality so that it is predictable and certain from day to day. Autonomy describes how we strive for control over our environment to fulfill basic needs. Finally, relatedness describes how we must be in social interaction with other human beings. Identity does not exist without order, autonomy, and relatedness.

How we achieve identity through order, autonomy, and relatedness determines how we respond to conflict. A relatively normal person will develop order by learning to control herself. Autonomy will be developed through the ability to create opportunities for choice and then be able to choose. Relatedness will be developed through learning to trust others. A violent person will have learned to develop order by trying to control others. Autonomy will be expressed as an assertion of power over others through physical force or intimidation. Finally, relatedness will be experienced as profound distrust of others. Thus, the difference between a normal person's response to conflict and a violent person's response to conflict is in how each develops and maintains order, autonomy, and relatedness.

Identity is also experienced along a continuum from honor to humiliation. People strive for honor and avoid humiliation. Honor implies acceptance and high regard by others. Humiliation, experienced as shame, implies rejection and lack of validation by others. In conflict, people often experience humiliation and shame. To restore honor often requires people to seek vindication, which allows them to validate themselves in a group. In this sense, crime and justice are reciprocals of each other. A criminal offense is an act of self-esteem that is boosted by committing violence against another. Justice is an act of self-esteem that shifts blame away from the victim onto the offender.

Consequently, when people speak of justice, they are seeking some reciprocity in the form of an exchange. In retributive justice, that exchange is the shifting of humiliation to the offender so that the victim may be vindicated. In restorative justice, the exchange occurs through validation of the victim by the offender and validation of the offender by the victim. Instead of a shift of humiliation, there is a transformation of humiliation. In either case, the underlying drive is protection and preservation of identity.

The problem of shame and humiliation is exacerbated in noncriminal social conflicts because each party may believe he or she is the victim. Thus, to restore personal honor, each seeks vindication from the other by the process of humiliation. Adversarial process through the courts provides an opportunity for retributive and punitive action by both parties, resulting in protracted litigation. Each party seeks vindication through the approving decision of a highly regarded authority figure—the judge, or a panel of peers—the jury. Conflicts are frequently escalated into intractability, and, when a decision is finally rendered, neither side feels vindicated or restored.

Even the most routine commercial dispute has undertones of identity conflicts. For example, the law protects expectancy interests created by contract. Profits to be realized from contracts are protected even if they have not been earned. If the expectancy of profit is lost because of a breach of contract, the injured party may easily construe the breach as an attack on identity. The problem intensifies if a lawsuit is filed because the defendant may feel wrongfully sued. The lawsuit is therefore interpreted as a threat to the defendant's identity. As a result, both sides feel victimized by identity threats. Talking out these conflicts usually will not work unless the underlying identity issues are recognized and resolved first. Thus, legal process and conventional negotiation tends to accelerate rather than extinguish identity conflicts. Compromise is difficult in identity conflicts because existential concerns such as dignity, validation, safety, and recognition are at stake. These things cannot be gained or lost through bargaining. In fact, bargaining diminishes their importance, and people would rather fight than concede. The apparently simple commercial dispute now becomes an intractable conflict.

In summary, our identities represent our core or essence. Consequently, we are very attentive to the care and maintenance of our identities. Threats to identities are serious matters because they represent a threat to survival. Identities give people a claim to group resources, both physical and emotional. If identities are threatened, claims on group resources are also threatened and the ability to survive is impaired.

The Neurological Foundations of Identity

Human identity stems from consciousness. People recognize that they have identities unique to themselves and that others have separate identities. This awareness, arising without conscious thought, is the product of a complex group of neurological processes layered one upon the other. When fully activated, these processes create a sense of "I-ness" or personal identity.

Damasio (1999) has labeled these processes the proto-self, core consciousness, and the autobiographical self. Acting together, these processes create what people experience as personal identity.

The Proto-Self

Boundaries and stability are the two precursors for consciousness because they mark where an organism stops and the environment begins. For example, cells are defined by boundaries called cell membranes. Within cell boundaries are organs and chemicals that constitute the physiology and anatomy of the cell. In the same way, the outer layers of our skin define our external boundary. Inside the skin are all of the parts that create us and allow us to live. Outside the skin is everything else.Stability means that the body will maintain itself within a narrow range of operations while existing in a widely varying external environment. The concept of homeostasis describes how stability is maintained within an organism. If our body becomes too hot, we regulate the heat by perspiring or moving to a cooler place. All organisms act to maintain internal stability.

To maintain boundaries and stability requires an internal management system. Generally, the central nervous system, including the brain, provides this service. Signals generated by neural impulses and chemicals released into the blood provide the brain with information about the state of the body. To keep track of these signals, the brain builds a representation of the body from neural patterns within the brain. These neural patterns are called the proto-self, which is the precursor to core consciousness.

The neural patterns are constructed at multiple levels from the brain stem to the cerebral cortex through a highly interconnected neural network. Thus, the proto-self is not an isolated brain function, but is the aggregate of many subsystems acting in concert. The proto-self acts automatically and preconsciously. The proto-self has no powers of perception and holds no knowledge. Through the proto-self, the brain recognizes what is "I" and what is "not I." This is the first layer of identity.

Core Consciousness

The next level of identity is core consciousness, which is the knowledge that materializes when we confront an object, construct a neural pattern for it, and discover automatically that the image is formed in our perspective, belongs to us, and can be acted on. We are not aware of core consciousness because, from our perspective, it happens instantaneously, automatically, and continuously. Neurologically, core consciousness is created through a pulse-like pattern of neurons firing as content presents itself from stimuli or memory. The neurons in core consciousness fire in milliseconds, while our conscious mind operates on the order of tens, hundreds, and thousands of milliseconds. Consequently, core consciousness operates at a much higher speed than conscious awareness. Awareness is based on the steady generation of consciousness pulses that correspond to the endless processing of objects in core consciousness.

The essence of core consciousness is the feeling of "I-ness" engaged in the process of knowing our own existence and the existence of others. Most of the time, we are not attentive to our knowing because there is little reason to allocate precious cognitive capacity to noticing that we know.

While the proto-self is a first order neural map, a second-order neural map creates core consciousness. This map creates images that account for the relationship between object and organism. While the proto-self simply reacts to objects, the core consciousness creates a nonverbal account of what is happening. Thus, the first basis for consciousness is a feeling that arises in the re-representation of the non-conscious proto-self. The proto-self is recreated in the second order neural map along with the objects it is interacting with.

So, we have a first order neural pattern that represents the physical states of the body. This pattern, if depicted in lights, would look like innumerably fast flickers over a network of neurons and brain substructures. From this pattern, a second-order or derivative pattern arises. The second order pattern receives a succession of signals related to an unfolding event that occurs at different brain sites. This succession constitutes a neural pattern that becomes the basis of an image.

This second pattern recreates the first pattern but also provides an account for the changes to the first pattern. The second pattern constitutes "knowing" and is called core consciousness. While neuroscientists are unsure of the precise locations of the second-order pattern, they believe it is implemented in multiple richly connected sites. Core consciousness is transient and ephemeral. It is engaged solely in the present. What happens when we sleep, and core consciousness naturally subsides? This leads us to the next level of consciousness, the autobiographical self.

The Autobiographical Self

In complex organisms such as humans, the fleeting moments of knowledge that pass through the core consciousness can be committed to memory, categorized, and related to other memories. The consequence of this learning is the creation of autobiographical memory.

A third neural pattern is created from autobiographical memories. This third pattern is the next level of consciousness—the autobiographical self. Thus, the autobiographical self is based on autobiographical memory constructed from memories of past experience. Autobiographical memory grows continuously from life experience, but can be remodeled to reflect new experiences.

We gradually construct our self-image of whom we are physically and mentally. Our idea of self is based on autobiographical memory and constantly subject to change. These changes are due to the remodeling of the lived past and remodeling of the anticipated future. We actually create memories of the future in the form of desires, wishes, goals, and obligations.

We are not conscious of which memories we store and which we do not. In addition, we are not conscious of how we store memories or how we classify and organize them. Finally, we are not conscious of how we relate memories of sights, noises, tastes, touches, and smells, how we relate different topics together, or how we attribute different emotional significance to memories. All of this work occurs preconsciously and outside of awareness.

Certain sets of memories are consistently and constantly reactivated moment by moment. These memories deliver to our extended consciousness the facts of our physical, mental, and demographic identities. The autobiographical self creates these identity facts. Actualization of the autobiographical self into a neural pattern is what we call personal identity.

Personal identities are biologically formed in convergence zones within the brain. These convergence zones consistently and interactively activate the fundamental data that define personal and social identities. Thus, at any moment of consciousness, a set of identity records or memories forms a backdrop for our minds. Identities thus become active and available memories for processing.

The neural substrate for identity is based on a complex interaction of various neural nets that we experience as "self" and "I." These nets maintain a relatively consistent pattern, but one that changes with experience, education, and maturity. Normally, the changes occur imperceptibly. We go to great lengths to protect these neural patterns because they truly define who we are. Information that is dissonant with, contradicts, or challenges the viability of these patterns evokes intense reactions. Think of these nets as powerful gyroscopes. When spinning, gyroscopes strongly resist forces perpendicular to their spinning planes. In an analogous way, the patterns of the neural nets comprising our identity are usually resistant to sudden unexpected change.

Cognitive Psychodynamics

Cognitive psychodynamics (Horowitz, 1998) describes in psychological terms how people develop identities and relationships and what can go wrong in the process. It builds from the theory of person schemas, a multidisciplinary collaborative research effort culminating in the book *Person Schemas and Maladaptive Interpersonal Patterns* (Horowitz, 1991).

Person schema theory is now used to answer such questions as how people form meaningful identities during development. In addition, it answers the question of how people deal with the conflict between self-striving and responsibility to others. Schema theory also explains how beliefs are aggregated into packages of information and why passionate beliefs lead to a variety of emotional or defensive states.

Cognitive psychodynamics uses schema theory to explain the irrationality that often appears in repeated relationships. The goal of cognitive psychodynamics is to explain how ideas and feeling can be modified by heightened conscious awareness, formation of new insights, and new decision-making.

Schemas

Schemas, also known as cognitive maps, are frameworks for interpreting sensory data and for forming plans. The mind has many schemas to organize reality. Smaller order schemas form into larger order schemas. For example, a schema may develop to interpret the sensory experience of seeing a nose. Another schema may develop to interpret the sensory experience of seeing eyes. Other schemas break down the many other attributes of a human face. These individual schemas are used by a larger schema, called a supraordinate schema. The supraordinate schema is a model of how several schemas fit together to make sense of the entire face. In general, schemas can be changed, but are largely preconscious processes.

Person schemas are the schemas relating to identity and relationships. They include self-schemas and other-schemas. Self-schemas combine many meanings to culminate in a sense of identity. Other-schemas construct a known figure within the mind. Role relationship models are the scripts of transactions that have occurred in the past between self and others.

A self-schema is an organized set of meanings that a person attributes to himself or herself. Self-schemas are not random attributes, but patterns of associated beliefs. Self-schemas make up a structure of unconscious knowledge that can be realistic or unrealistic in content and in links between content.

Self-schemas are active or inactive. Activated schemas influence working models, which are the current active processes of consciousness that create perceptions of reality. Working models combine with perceptions to organize representations in conscious experience. Our sense of current identity comes from self-observation of self-experiencing in reflective consciousness. Self-schema elements include—

- body image;
- roles of self;
- associated memories of self;
- emotional response style;
- scripts of action sequences;
- values and rules;
- self-regulatory style;
- future intentions and plans.

These elements will differ from one self-schema to another. Furthermore, the linkages between these elements, such as body image and role, may vary from self-schema to self-schema.

The complexity and richness of identity depends on supraordinate self-schemas, which are schemas of many schemas. People who have more supraordinate self-schemas tend to have a more integrated self-organization. However, conflict elements within the supraordinate schema can limit that integration. If the supraordinate self-schema contains beliefs on how to balance conflicted elements, the schema is integrated. If the elements are poorly connected, the schema is conflicted.

With an integrated self-schema, a person's varied roles can blend smoothly together. If the supraordinate schema is conflicted, a person may anticipate both wanted and dreaded outcomes of the same aims. The threatening and dreaded consequences can be prevented through a shift into schemas for defensive compromises. Thus, the wanted state is not achieved, but the dreaded state is avoided. This creates a wish-fear dilemma.

Relationships

People seek out relationships with others for safety, sex, warmth, stimulation, and reflections of identity. Yet many people act in ways that form and then break relationships. Many aspects of beliefs about relationships operate as unconscious person schemas. People act irrationally in relationships and wonder why they do so. The role-relationship model helps to explain how these schemas operate.

A role relationship model is a format used to define a recurring pattern in a narrative or observed transaction. The elements include self-schemas, other-schemas, transactional scripts for emotions, acts, and communications, and the values used for critical appraisals of the consequences of a transaction. A role relationship is therefore an assembly of associated meanings connecting schemas together.

Personal Identity, Face, and Impression Management

Face is the word we use to describe how we manage our identities in relation to others. Our need for face is based on two related but conceptually distinct concepts: negative face and positive face. Negative face refers to our desire to have our prerogatives respected. This is the feature of identity we call autonomy. Positive face consists of our desire to have our presented image approved by at least some important others. This is the feature of identity we call relatedness. Paradoxically, face consists of our need to be autonomous, yet to be accepted by others. We spend considerable energy maintaining face. Face-threatening acts often result in angry responses, even violence in some cultures.

Positive face is that part of identity concerned with self-esteem, self-respect, and positive views of self. Not surprisingly, the experimental research shows that we think very highly of ourselves, even when the objective facts do not support our views. Additionally, for most individuals, positive personality information is efficiently processed and easily recalled, while negative personality information is poorly processed and difficult to recall. We are much more likely to hear and recall praise than criticism.

In general, normal individuals have unrealistically positive views of themselves, an exaggerated belief in their ability to control their environment, and a view of the future that maintains that their future will be far better than the average person's.

Self-enhancement, exaggerated beliefs in control, and unrealistic optimism are associated with higher motivation, greater persistence, more effective performance, and ultimately, greater success. In other words, these illusions create self-fulfilling prophecies. They may help people try harder in situations with objectively poor probabilities of success. Although some failure is inevitable, ultimately these illusions will pay off more often than will lack of persistence. In addition, these positive illusions may be especially adaptive under adverse circumstances.

When faced with adversity, one's belief in one's competency, behaving in a world with a generally positive future, may be useful in overcoming setbacks, with potential blows to self-esteem, and potential erosions in one's view of the future. Thus, face may be an adaptation to a dangerous, uncertain, and difficult environment. Persons able to persevere through hardship are more likely to succeed than those without that attitude. Perhaps this explains why hope and faith hold such strong values in many communities.

In social situations, we look for confirmation of our preexisting self-perceptions. We implicitly signal how we want to be treated by adopting physical identity cues such as choosing what we wear, by taking on social roles that communicate our self-perceptions, and by communicating in ways that preferentially solicit self-confirming feedback. We actively seek to discourage others' mistaken impressions of us and are more likely to seek social feedback if we believe it will confirm our self-conceptions. This process is called impression management.

Impression management occurs as we attempt to project images of ourselves so as to influence the people around us. Impression management occurs because people generally wish to create a specific positive, or sometimes negative, self-identity. Impression management is achieved by strategically chosen behaviors, both verbal and nonverbal, that will cause others to view us as wanted. Impression management can be automatic and therefore preconscious, or it can be consciously controlled.

Berkeley sociologist Irving Goffman (1973) first conceptualized the phenomenon of impression management. According to Goffman, persons in social interaction function as "actors" whose "performances" depend upon the characteristics of both the situations and the audiences at hand. These "actors" on the stage of life strive to control their images or identities to obtain wanted social, psychological, or material outcomes. Goffman believed that controlling one's identity influenced the definition of situations and established expected norms, roles, and behaviors. Thus, he viewed impression management as intentional, goal-directed behavior and an inherently communicative process.

According to Goffman, impression management is an improvisational process by which we closely monitor our behavior in accordance with the cues presented by the situation and others. This stems from our desire to confirm our self-impression through social identity feedback from others. We seek feedback from others about our social identity that is congruent and consistent with our own views. Thus, we seek self-consistency or the need to ensure that others view our impression as we view it.

Because this process occurs rapidly, our cognitive load is high and we are likely to rely on social information that can be processed easily and efficiently. We process nonverbal cues much more quickly and efficiently in social encounters than verbal cues. Therefore, we rely heavily on nonverbal feedback in social interactions. Most of the nonverbal feedback we receive is processed outside of consciousness. Hence, unless we actively attend to it, we are not necessarily aware of what information we are receiving from others.

Impression management may consist of "identity enhancement," "identity protection," or "identity adjustment" activities. Each of these functions may resolve differences perceived between current and wanted social identities (Bozemand and Kacmar, 1997).

Identity enhancement describes the strategies used to strengthen the self-perception and other-perception of identity. Self-perception is the view people hold of themselves and is connected to the idea of autonomy and negative face. Other-perception is the view people believe others hold of them (my perception of how you view me) and is connected to the idea of relatedness and positive face. Identity enhancement implies that people create a clearer, more definitive sense of self. Self-enhancing impression management occurs when we have a social identity goal that, if achieved, will in some way allow us to bolster our self-esteem. Thus, we are likely to select an identity that is not only more positive than our current self-concept, but also one that we can reasonably claim and achieve. These activities are largely active and intentional.

We enhance self-perception of identity through behaviors such as self-promotion, false modesty, self-deprecation, and self-presentation. The other-perception of identity is enhanced through behaviors such as intimidation, flattery, enhancing others, conforming to others' opinions, doing favors, and being social. An identity conflict may arise if these strategies are obstructed or blocked such that identity enhancement fails. Typically this type of identity conflict arises from competition between people. When people have an interest in winning, on being on top, or on beating the other guy, some type of identity enhancement strategy is in play. At a primal level, this behavior may signify a bid for superior claim on resources. Since litigation is inherently a competitive process, parties and counsel often engage in social strategies designed to enhance personal identities and harm the opposition's identities.

When identity enhancement strategies fail, a condition of identity denial exists. In other words, our bid for improving self-esteem is rejected by others, which may cause shame, embarrassment, and humiliation.

A classic form of identity enhancement denial can be illustrated by the following case. Two real-estate developers had spent twenty-five years jointly acquiring and developing a major office and shopping center complex. They also engaged in their separate projects and businesses. Both men were very successful financially and actively involved in their community. Their conflict started when the nonmanaging partner asked for some information on the project. The managing partner believed that the information was proprietary. He feared the nonmanaging partner would use the information to compete against the project.

The conflict escalated to a bitter lawsuit. During preliminary settlement discussions, the nonmanaging partner repeatedly said in private that he had "made" the managing partner, who would be nothing today without the nonmanaging partner. Interestingly, in private pre-settlement discussions with the managing partner, the managing partner used almost exactly the same words. He said he had "made" the nonmanaging partner. The nonmanaging partner was a "lightweight" and would have been nothing without the managing partner. Both men attributed the success of the other not to the other's skill, but to the speaker's efforts.

These beliefs indicated a strong sense of denial of identity enhancement. Both men, despite their success, really needed and were looking for identity enhancing behaviors from the other. They seemed to need validation from the other of their contribution. Each man's apparent rejection of the other created a need for vindication and validation that each naively believed could be satisfied by the court.

If this analysis were put to them directly, they would strongly deny it. Neither man could or would accept his dependence on the other for identity enhancement. The strategy for dealing with this was, in a preliminary joint meeting, to ask each man to write down privately three positive attributes about the other. Then the men were invited to consider sharing those thoughts with the other privately and informally as discussions continued. The effort was resisted at first, but when executed, provided significant identity enhancement. The discussions moved from an acrimonious and competitive climate to much more collaborative conversations.

The second strategy, identity protection, is used defensively when people perceive that their identities are threatened. Those are strategies and behaviors that prevent damage or harm to our social identity in the eyes of others and are often implemented when we perceive threats to our social identity. Identity protection activities are largely, but not exclusively, reactive.

Typical protective strategies of self-esteem include disclaimers, self-handicapping accounts, excuses, and justifications. Strategies involving relatedness include apology, restitution, ingratiation or flattery, doing favors, and conforming to others' opinions. These strategies tend to protect the identities from threats. Identity threats may challenge persons' constructions of reality about themselves. Alternatively, identity threats may challenge a person's rights or claim to some group membership.

Group membership in this context is a broad concept that includes formal group membership and equivalency. Equivalency occurs when two people see themselves as equals. If one person claims equivalency with another and the other rejects that claim, an identity conflict may ensue. For example, one of the real estate partners might consider himself equivalent to his partner in wealth, community stature, success, and so forth. When identity based on group membership is threatened, the threat is usually interpreted as a challenge on claims to resources such as emotional support, recognition, or validation. It is also a challenge to a sense of entitlement to the primal needs of sex, food, and shelter.

Threats are perceived when outside information contradicts information represented in the neural patterns constituting identity. The basic strategy is defense by distancing oneself from the threat, minimizing or rationalizing the threat, transforming the threat through apology and restitution, seeking the goodwill of others, and conforming one's opinions to those held by others.

When identity threats become too great to be defused by defensive strategies, the third strategy, identity adjustment, may be invoked. As it implies, identity adjustment occurs when a person changes self-perception or other-perception to cope with the threat. Strategies involving self-perception include self-deprecation, creating opposing images, permitting a sense of strategic failure, or self-handicapping. Strategies involving other-perception include disobedience, rebellion, noncompliance, creation of opposing images, and supplication.

These strategies may be characterized as identity defeat. They lower personal views of self (lowered self-esteem) so that identity shrinks to a protective state. When the strategy is rebellion, the larger group and its resources are rejected in exchange for the ability to maintain some semblance of identity. These strategies connect to the idea of order. To maintain order, through certainty and predictability, we reduce our identity maintenance overhead to manageable levels.

We use these tactics depending on the type of feedback we receive, anticipate, or seek from others. For example, when receiving relational feed back (e.g., "You let me down"), we are more likely to respond with relational tactics such as apologies or restitution. When the feedback is content-oriented, and therefore more focused upon us than on the relationship between us and the other (e.g., "Your performance has been poor"), our responsive tactics are more likely to be content-oriented (e.g., we will offer explanations for the poor performance).

To summarize, identity conflict may arise when impression management strategies backfire. From the actor's perspective, conflict may result if the actor is engaged in appropriate impression management but is being ignored by the other. Failure to give appropriate feedback can be a form of disrespect, leading to a sense of injustice and conflict. Many people report in peacemaking sessions that conflicts escalated quickly because a letter was not responded to or was interpreted as cutting off any further communication. The actor believed he or she was acting appropriately, but was ignored.

This "insult" of apparent indifference created a need for apparent escalation, usually in the form of a lawsuit. From the target's perspective, conflict may arise if the actor engages in defective or inappropriate impression management such that it is perceived as controlling or manipulative. In these situations, the target's negative face is threatened and the target is likely not to give the positive feedback sought by the actor. Now, both parties are face-threatened and escalation is more likely

Proper impression management can also de-escalate a conflict. Apology can give both positive face and negative face to others. Although it costs the actor some face, apology can create a new impression of respect and concern that counteracts any earlier dysfunctional impression management strategies.

What is most interesting is how much effort we put into securing satisfaction of our own face needs and how little effort we seem to put into looking out for face needs of others, friends as well as strangers. Thus, in everyday life we routinely commit face-threatening acts that are intrinsically threatening to the identities of others.

In conflict, face becomes an early weapon of choice. Insults are direct attacks on face. Often, people in conflict maintain or enhance their own face by diminishing, attacking, or destroying the face of the other. The same process occurs between groups, as each group puts down the other.

Social Identity

Our concept of self has two distinct aspects. One is personal identity or face, which includes specific attributes such as confidence, talent, and sociability. The other aspect is social identity, defined as that part of our self that derives from membership in a social group. The part of the self based on group memberships is generally referred to as collective identity, while social identity refers to interpersonal and social worlds. Personal identity refers to an individual's personal values, ideas, goals, emotions, and so forth (Bozemand and Kacmar, 1997).

Social identity theory involves three central ideas: categorization, identification, and comparison. The first is categorization. We categorize objects to understand them. In a similar way we categorize people (including ourselves) to understand the social environment. We use social categories like black, white, Australian, Christian, Muslim, student, and bus driver because they are useful. If we can assign people to a category then that tells us things about those people. We couldn't function in a normal manner without using these categories. Similarly, we find out things about ourselves by knowing what categories we belong to. We define appropriate behavior by reference to the norms of groups we belong to. We can only do this if we can tell who belongs to our group.

The list of categories is endless because each person can claim a myriad of influences, factors, and components that comprise an identity. Some identities such as ethnicity are inherited; others such as gender are socially constructed. Our parents define many identities for us as children, and we try on many identities ourselves. Today we're cowboys, tomorrow astronauts. Yesterday, we were circus clowns. These apparent games and child's play are really experiments in identity creation as we work out for ourselves who we are. As we mature, we begin to assume more stable identities. Nevertheless, social identities change and must therefore not be considered as fixed immutable characteristics of an individual.

The second important idea is identification. We identify with groups we perceive ourselves to belong to. Social identity thus functions to locate "me" in "us" (Brekhus, 1999). That is, identities define our roles within groups. Identification carries two meanings. Part of who we are is made up of our group memberships. That is, sometimes we think of ourselves as "us" vs. "them," and at other times we think of ourselves as "I" vs." him or her." Sometimes we think of ourselves as group members and at other times as unique individuals. This varies, so that we can be more or less a group member, depending upon the circumstances. What is crucial for our purposes is that thinking of our self as a group member and thinking of our self as a unique individual are both parts of our self-concept. In social identity theory, the group membership is not something foreign that is tacked onto the person; it is a real, true, and vital part of the person.

The other meaning implied by the concept of social identity is the idea that we are, in some sense, the same, or identical to the other people. When we say that we are the same, we mean that for some purposes we treat members of our groups as being similar to ourselves in some relevant way. To take the most extreme example, in some violent conflict such as a war, the members of the opposite group are treated as identical and completely different to the in group. The enemy is considered deserving of death. These beliefs are not the product of a bizarre personality disorder. Under these circumstances, violent behavior is accepted and even expected.

The third idea is the notion of social comparison, which says that to feel good about ourselves, we compare ourselves with similar others. Thus, we gain self-esteem by comparing ourselves with others in our group and by seeing ourselves as belonging to a prestigious group. In this way, identities are socially protective. That is, people assume appropriate identities to obtain social acceptance, which leads to greater opportunities for social success. If a socially protective identity is challenged, people feel they are being stripped raw.

Social identities are dynamic. Identities are context-dynamic because they vary according to individuals' social settings. No one specializes in a single identity across all social settings. Thus, identities reside in the interaction between the individual and her social environment. Generally speaking, a lawyer in a courtroom will assume a much different identity than when on a vacation with her family. And being on vacation will cause an identity that is different from the identity used during the school year. All of these identities are real, but very different and all belong to the same person.

We do not choose identities haphazardly. Instead, social locales and times define how we are to feel, act, and who to "be." As a result, we seek clues from our immediate environment to decide which identities are pertinent for the moment.

Social locales and times are known as "social space." Most social space is "unmarked" and is therefore treated as "generic social space." A good example of generic social space is the supermarket. You may meet people with whom you present a completely different identity in the work environment, for example. However, your work identity is not active within the supermarket. Instead, you are just another shopper and take on that identity. Within generic social space, the full range of a person's identity expressions is restricted and policed through devices such as disapproval, discrimination, and legal controls.

People in generic social spaces closely monitor the presentation of others' identities. As a group, social extremes are therefore limited, and individuals are encouraged to blend in with the majority. They are discouraged from standing out as extreme or unique. In a sense, we are moral vigilantes for one another. One need only watch a group of teenagers to see this effect. On any given Saturday, a group of girls or boys will look the same, walk the same, and talk the same, each striving to blend in. If you ask them about this conformity, they would deny it. Furthermore, they would assert that they are expressing their unique identities among their peers. Adults are usually more sophisticated at expressing identities to blend in so that their actions are not as noticeable as the socially neophyte teenagers. Nevertheless, we generally strive to fit in, not stand out, and thereby help maintain generic social space.

Identity traits, those specific behaviors and ways of being that constitute identity, can be characterized as "marked" and "unmarked" (Brekhus, 1999). A marked trait is one that is active and highlighted at the moment, while an unmarked trait is passive, socially generic, and normal for the social context in which it is expressed. People tend to see their marked attributes as more relevant to their identities than their unmarked attributes. Thus, a law student will identify more as a "law student" if that is a marked trait than as a parent with young children residing in a suburb of a large metropolitan region.

Similarly, others are quite sensitive to marked traits and make categorical generalizations based on them. People might say, "Oh, she's a law student," rather than "Oh, she's a mother of a three-year-old and a five-year-old." This occurs because people tend to ignore unmarked traits. In conflict, people tend to focus on one or two marked traits that define their differences and completely fail to recognize that they have far more unmarked traits in common. This suggests that exploring common unmarked traits is a strategy for de-emphasizing conflict differences.

People use social space, that is, space where social interaction occurs with others, to construct, present, and negotiate their identities. Most commonly, individuals will attempt to match their spatial and temporal surroundings with appropriate identities. Thus, the surroundings will elicit repression or expression of certain traits. Denial of the use of social space for this purpose may lead to identity conflicts. In effect, one party or group is denying another party the right to a marked identity within a given social space. Within the United States, the First Amendment protects the expression of certain identities as the free expression of ideas. However, not all identities are protected in all spaces. Consequently, many social conflicts can arise without constitutional or legal protections.

Brekhus (1999) divides identity management into duration and volume. Duration refers to the time one spends presenting an identity, and volume refers to the intensity of presentation. High volume sites and settings amplify marked identities consistent with the environment, while low volume sites and settings tend to mute marked identities. For example, a young man might present an identity comprised of urbane coolness in a nightclub. The "cooler" or more "hip" the nightclub, the more the young man's identity will be amplified. Put him in a church congregation the next morning, however, and that low volume setting will mute his hipness. Information control and concealment of identity are common strategies in low volume environments. Thus, our young man, the pastor's son, is most likely interested in suppressing his Saturday night identity in front of the church elders.

Identity management suggests some of the causes for identity conflicts. If an identity presentation is appropriate to the social space, but is denied to the person, conflict may arise from rejection or outcasting. If an identity presentation is inappropriate to the social space and is denied to the actor, the denial or disapproval may act as an attack on personal autonomy, self-reliance, and the ability to control one's environment. This is a powerful stimulus to conflict.

Brekhus describes various combinations of identity management as lifestylers, commuters, and integrators. Lifestylers are high on volume and high on duration. Commuters are high on volume and low on duration (they commute to and from the identity). Integrators are low on volume and high on duration.

Brekhus studied the identity management of gay men in a suburban environment. Lifestylers were those gay men who expressed their gayness as a dominant part of their identity and at a high-volume and who kept the volume turned up all of the time. These men's identities were expressed at 100 percent volume and 100 percent duration. Commuters were those gay men who, on weekends or vacations, expressed their gayness at high volume, but kept their gayness at low volume at all other times. These men were 100 percent gay for, say 18 percent of the time. Integrators did not express their gayness at high volume at all, but incorporated their gayness into their everyday lives. Thus, they were 18 percent gay 100 percent of the time.

This taxonomy can be usefully applied to many identity types. For example, within a political group there may be lifestylers, commuters, and integrators. Lifestylers embrace and express the political ideology of the group as a major component of identity all the time. Commuters express the political ideology of the group when they are with members of the group, but not at other times. Integrators may sympathize with the political ideology, but do not express it actively. However, they hold the political ideology all the time.

Thus, disputes over identity often concern whether one should treat one's identity as a noun and live it all the time, treat it as a verb and "play it up" at marked times, or treat it as an adjective and integrate it as a portion of one's whole self.

How the Legal System Escalates Identity Conflicts

A number of legal theories protect various dignitary interests that are associated with identity. A dignitary interest is noneconomic in the sense that it is not measurable in dollars. Dignitary interests include such things as reputation, privacy, free speech, freedom of association, freedom of assembly, and freedom from unreasonable searches and seizures. These interests generally do not affect economic interests such as earning capacity or production of wealth. Instead, they are personal and go to those rights enjoyed as a consequence of being a human being in a free society.

The law protects these interests to a certain degree, by imposing duties on people not to harm them. Violating these duties may create a liability that can be prosecuted to judgment in a civil lawsuit. Typical causes of action, or legal bases for liability, include libel and slander (damaged reputation), and invasion of privacy. The usual remedy for these violations is compensation, rendered in the form of a judgment after trial.

The law does not recognize nor provide a remedy for the majority of identity conflicts. This leads to the first cause of conflict escalation: the system of justice rejects the person's claim of identity threat or damage as not based on any recognized legal right. This rejection is often construed as a further attack upon identity. The effect is to escalate the conflict, rather than provide a path to resolution. In fact, no formal institution or system exists to deal with serious identity conflicts. The tragic consequences can be found in the Columbines and Santanas of society, where high school students have suffered such extreme identity attacks that they react in violence.

A second concern is how the law translates the violation of most interests into compensation. Lawyers negotiate settlement by arguing over the "value" of the case. Evaluative mediators offer their opinions as to likely outcomes and "values." In the meantime, the clients are listening to their representatives haggle over that which is non-negotiable—-the value of their identity, their respect, and their outraged sense of injustice. The law assumes that injury to all interests can be reduced to dollars, essentially implying that identity can be repaired or restored if the price is right. When the defendant offers an amount to settle, the plaintiff sees it as absurdly low, indicating further bad faith and another rejection of identity. This is when the parties often talk about suing over the principle of the matter, rather than looking for a pragmatic agreement. When principle is at stake, identities are in play and cannot be easily negotiated away.

Two related issues emerge from the compensation method of identity protection. First, because identity conflicts are personal and highly subjective, the possibility of malingering, false claims, and fraud is very real. Since injury to identity usually cannot be measured in any objective way, people who do not mind abusing the legal system will assert claims in the hope of receiving free compensation. The reaction to this problem creates a second concern: that all identity conflicts are perceived as frivolous and that people who assert them are dishonest and unscrupulous. In cases of the actual identity conflict, this perception tends to escalate disputes because the disbelief acts as another identity attack.

The next concern arises from adversarial ideology. Lawyers are not trained to be aware of or be sensitive to identity-based conflicts. Thus, normal lawyering practices taken on behalf of a client can escalate identity conflicts. Allegations in a complaint, for example, can be insulting to a defendant's identity, even though the allegations are proper as to form. Similarly, witnesses may interpret pretrial questioning through depositions as attacks on identity. The lawyer, however, is just doing his or her job, oblivious to the escalating conflict.

One of the paradoxes of Western culture concerns our need for autonomy juxtaposed with our dependence upon others for identity and face. Because of our absorption with our own individuality, we spend much more time working to enhance our identities than to help others enhance theirs. This leads to another paradox: in highly escalated conflicts, people are highly dependent upon one another for face and self-esteem. Oftentimes, the foundation of the conflict is in the failure of the parties to extend themselves beyond personal self-absorption to acknowledge and validate the identity of others. One of the greatest challenges is recognizing this identity dependence dynamic and finding a process to transform it.

In later chapters, we will see how identity goals become important in conflict. In addition, conflict escalation is closely tied to changes in the perception of the identities of others. Thus, identities run throughout conflict, and understanding when and how identities are involved in conflict is a central task of peacemaking.

Reflections on Chapter Seven

Reread the case at the beginning of this chapter. Using the material in the chapter, construct an analysis of the conflict based on identity theory. You can add facts to flesh out the case as long as you state them clearly.

Does the law respond to identity conflicts in any meaningful way?

The remedies available in law and equity boil down to judgments for money (damages or restitution), coercive orders (injunctions and incarceration or death sentences), and declaratory judgments (declaratory relief and quiet title). Every judicial act falls within one of these broad remedial categories. Do these remedies address identity-based conflicts?

CHAPTER EIGHT

RELIGION AND CONFLICT

A True Story of Law and Religion

XIONG AND HIS FAMILY LIVED in Ban Vinai, a refugee camp in Thailand. His son, Kou, less than a year old, was born with clubfeet and a deformed hip. The American doctors in the camp suggested that an operation would help repair his feet and hips. The operation was done, but Kou was not cured.

At about the same time, Xiong's wife fell ill. Xiong sought the shaman to root out the source of these evils. The shaman was displeased. God made the boy with twisted feet. Xiong should not meddle in God's business. The doctors should leave the boy alone, or bad things would happen to the family. Further proof was forthcoming. Xiong's next two sons were born in the Thai camp with cleft lips, a signal that God was unhappy with the doctors' efforts to undo his work.

After the family resettled in California in 1988, social workers initiated a medical examination of Kou. Doctors again said surgery was the boy's best hope. Xiong allowed the boy to be examined but refused the operation. God smiled on him. A girl, Joanie, was born in September. No cleft lip. No club foot. Perfect. The couple wanted more children, and they feared that if they tried to fix Kou's problem an angry God would curse future offspring.

The County Department of Social Services sued Kou's parents to force them to allow doctors to perform a series of operations, which could take as long as two years to complete. His parents refused, saying that a Hmong medicine man, or shaman, told them that God will punish them if there is an operation. If Social Services prevailed, Kou would be taken from his parents' custody, so that the operation could be performed. If his parents won, his condition would worsen, possibly confining him to a painful life in a wheelchair.

The headlines tell the rest of the story:

ON TRIAL: BELIEFS OF FAMILY, BOY'S NEEDS HMONG CULTURE AT ODDS WITH TREATMENT (*Fresno Bee*, February 21, 1990). Testimony began Tuesday in a trial that pits the medical needs of a young Hmong boy against the cultural beliefs of his family.

JUDGE WILL RULE ON SURGERY FOR HMONG BOY (*Fresno Bee*, February 22, 1990). The Xiong family, having lost a small battle of beliefs in court Wednesday, will find out today the outcome of the war.

JUDGE ORDERS SURGERY FOR HMONG BOY (*Fresno Bee*, February 23, 1990). For all the strangeness of her native tongue and her beliefs, a Hmong mother's response Thursday to the judge's bad news was universal. She wept.

HMONG FAMILY FILES APPEAL TO COURT RULING (*Fresno Bee*, March 1, 1990). The struggle between what is best for a Hmong boy's health and what is best for his family's well-being moved Wednesday into the appellate court. An attorney for Ger Xiong filed an appeal Wednesday, six days after a lower court had ruled that Xiong's son must have surgery.

SURGERY ORDER ON BOY DELAYED (*Fresno Bee*, March 3, 1990). The District Court of Appeal issued an order Thursday indefinitely delaying surgery on a 6-year-old Hmong boy.

HMONG SUIT HEADS FOR HIGH COURT FAMILY APPEALS TO STOP SURGERY ON SON'S CLUBFEET, HIP (*Fresno Bee*, June 13, 1990). Attorneys for a Hmong boy facing surgery against his parents' wishes plan to appeal today to the U.S. Supreme Court.

HIGH COURT OKS SURGERY FOR HMONG BOY (*Fresno Bee*, June 21, 1990). The most powerful court in the United States says a young boy must have surgery on his clubfeet, but the strength of his parents' resistance may render the court powerless. In a decision made public Wednesday, U.S. Supreme Court Justice Sandra Day O'Connor refused to postpone surgery on the boy, Kou Xiong, 6.

HMONG PLEA: LEAVE BOY ALONE, CLANS ASK CHANGE OF RULING ON SURGERY (*Fresno Bee*, June 28, 1990). Representatives of all 18 Hmong clans, frustrated by government attempts to force a Hmong boy into the operating room, have asked officials to reconsider.

ANOTHER LAWYER IN HMONG BATTLE TO AVOID SURGERY (*Fresno Bee*, July 7, 1990). A Hmong boy fighting to keep from being operated on got a second attorney Friday, one who could pursue a lawsuit against doctors and social workers. At the same time, attorneys for his parents are seeking dismissal of a court decision ordering surgery. The basis for their request is that social workers have been unable to find a doctor willing to operate against the parents' wishes.

HMONG BOY APPEARS SAFE FROM SURGERY (*Fresno Bee*, September 20, 1990). It appears very likely that Hmong parents being pressured to allow surgery on their son's clubfeet will be left alone after all. The director of the County Social Services Department said the logical conclusion of the court case as it stands would be for it to be dismissed.

PSYCHIATRIST NAMED TO HELP HMONG BOY (*Fresno Bee*, September 22, 1990). A judge, trying to weigh the benefits of surgery on a Hmong boy against the harm of separating him from his parents, asked a psychiatrist for help Friday.

JUDGE APPROVES 90-DAY EVALUATION OF HMONG BOY (Fresno Bee, September 28, 1990). A judge Thursday granted a psychiatrist 90 days to evaluate a Hmong boy whose parents are resisting surgery on his clubfeet.

NO HMONG SURGERY – JUDGE (*Fresno Bee*, December 21, 1990). Ger Xiong walked out of a courtroom Thursday with one care lifted and another firmly on his back. Gone was the judge's ruling that doctors would operate on Xiong's son against his wishes. But even after the judge dismissed a legal action that had mystified and angered many Hmong, Xiong carried the weight of the entire case with him.

Introduction

For many people like Ger Xiong, though not all, religion is a strongly motivating force. Religion provides an organization and perspective that shapes personal meaning and creates reality. Religion also is a universal attribute of humanity because the human brain acts as the creator and interpreter of religious experience. Religious differences arise from the differing interpretations of a core set of experiences. These experiences can be so profound as to lead people to conclude that they experienced an Ultimate Truth. Their description and interpretation of their experience becomes the basis for religious beliefs, rituals, and practices.

Religion, when it conflicts with other perspectives, can be a fertile source of conflict. Consider this recent conflict. In rural California, a large Sikh community engages in farming and agriculture. The children of this community are brought up in traditional ways that include the religious requirement that young boys carry ceremonial knives concealed on them when they go to school. The local school district, in response to the violence at Columbine High School and elsewhere, instituted a zero-tolerance policy against any objects that could be used as weapons. The young Sikh boys attending school, who were bright, extremely well-behaved students, were found with their ceremonial knives. The boys were arrested and expelled. The outcry in the Sikh community led to media coverage. The school district eventually had to back down, but the humiliation and outrage in the Sikh community continues to this day. This story, like that of Ger Xiong, shows how ignorance, lack of sensitivity, and a failure to comprehend religious beliefs led to an entirely unnecessary conflict. Unfortunately, it is a recurrent theme in human history.

Lawyers are often unaware of religious sensitivities in disputes and conflicts. This is exacerbated by clients who intuitively feel that their religious beliefs may be irrelevant when talking to lawyers. Clients consequently will not raise religious issues, but will deal with lawyers at the lawyer's level. Lawyers as peacemakers cannot afford this luxury of ignorance.

In this chapter, we consider religion as an important, but often overlooked component of conflict and peace. The themes raised by religion include neurotheology, religion as cultural identity, religion as personal identity, cosmology or Creation stories, views of humankind, and concepts of salvation, redemption or enlightenment, and religion's perspective on peace and conflict. As important as religion is in conflict, it is a vast field. Therefore, this chapter should be viewed as the briefest introduction to some ideas of religion relevant to peacemakers.

Neurotheology

Neurotheology is a termed created by physicians Eugene d'Aquili and Andrew B. Newberg (d'Aquili and Newberg, 1999) to describe the neurological study of religious experience. Using modern brain imaging techniques, these researchers have uncovered neurological functions involved in the many altered states of consciousness commonly called religious experience. From these studies, they have proposed a neurological model that explains why humans create myths. Their model establishes the neurophysiological basis for religious experience across all cultures and faiths. The importance of this model is that humans share a basic religious identity expressed in a rich array of beliefs and faiths. At the bottom of this religious diversity are core neurophysiological processes shared by every person. Understanding this shared physiology allows people to recognize that their similarities are far greater than their differences.

At the outset, neuroscientists are quick to point that their research does not attempt to answer the question, "What is the nature of God?" Nor do they deny the existence of God. The point they make is that human religious experience in all its diversity stems from a shared neurophysiology (d'Aquili and Newberg, 1999). Furthermore, religious faith is genetically coded into the human brain through the functions of the cognitive operators. Finally, they argue that any direct experience of God must, of necessity, be mediated by the human brain. Therefore, understanding neurological processes in the context of religious experience is ultimately important to understanding the experience of God.

Religious behaviors arise from two neuroanatomical and neurophysiological mechanisms. The first mechanism results from the perception of causal sequences in the organization of reality. Humans, acutely aware of their contingent and existential nature, automatically seek control over the universe by creating causal explanations for all that they experience. Gazzaniga calls this process the interpreter (Gazzaniga, 1998); d'Aquili and Newberg call it the causal operator (d'Aquili and Newberg, 1999). Regardless of terminology, humans are driven by a causal imperative that may be described as an incessant, continuous need for meaning. This causal imperative, in conjunction with the other cognitive operators within the human brain, leads to the creation of myths to explain the unexplainable.

The second mechanism is the experience of altered states of consciousness. These altered states exist along a continuum and involve what d'Aquili and Newberg identify as the wholistic operator (d'Aquili and Newberg, 1999). Mystical experiences arising from neurological processes have been interpreted for thousands of years as glimpses into a supernatural world. Because the reality experienced in these mystical states is so different than baseline reality, they tend to confirm the power sources created by the causal operator.

Religion, from a neurological perspective, is therefore the interplay between the causal and the wholistic cognitive operators. The causal operator creates myths and ultimately the concept of deity for self-maintenance purposes. The wholistic operator aims for self-transcendence.

Myths explain ultimate reality in terms of either efficient or final causality. Efficient causality concerns creation or foundational stories, such as the Babylonian creation myth or the Genesis story. Final causality relates to salvation or apocalyptic stories, such as the Resurrection of Christ or the stories of the book of Revelation.

The interactions of the various cognitive operators create myths (d'Aquili and Newberg, 1999). To understand this process, consider that only a very few basic analytical relationships exist. These are created by the cognitive operators toform spatial, temporal, and affective relationships. The relationships include such concepts as inside-outside, above-below, right-left, front-behind, all-nothing, before-after, simultaneous-sequential, and within-without. Each of these relationships is given some affective value, either good or bad. Thus, above is viewed as good, while below is associated with bad. Inside is good; outside is bad. According to evolutionist scientists, the basis for these relationships is in their survival value. Above is good because to be high increases one's ability to spot food, evade predators, and be free of danger. On the other hand, below is bad because of the possibility of falling objects, jumping predators, and injury from falling objects. Inside is good because of protection from predators by cave walls or weather from tents. Outside is bad because of exposure to predators and weather.

Myth elements are paired in a manner similar to the basic analytical relationships. Thereford, dyads such as life-death, good-evil, or heaven-hell are essential in all myths. Myths are presented in two parts. The first part is the myth problem, which is always a problem of ultimate concern. One of the important aspects of cognitive operators is that they operate whether they have available data or not. If they lack data, they still operate, but do so by creating quasi-data to fill the voids. This quasi-data takes the form of gods, demons, or power sources necessary to provide causal explanations for the universe. Since the causal imperative drives us to order the universe in meaningful patterns, we are biologically compelled to create stories if we cannot deduce causation from available facts. Thus, the mythical problem classifies unexplainable aspects of reality in terms of opposites through the binary operator, and it classifies sequences in terms of the causal operator.

Consider Wink's Myth of Redemptive Violence from chapter 1 (Wink, 1993). In that myth, the good guy faces the irredeemable bad guy. The mythical problem is how to construct a reality that will not dissolve into chaos. The binary operator sets up the two opposites, whose tension needs resolution. Thus, the good guy is opposed to the bad guy and a conflict of epic proportions is established. Resolution of the conflict is provided by the second part of myth, the mythical solution.

The mythical solution neurologically constitutes a shift from the left hemisphere where the causal operator is located, to the right hemisphere where the wholistic operator is located. When the wholistic operator acts on the dyad created by the binary operator, it allows the opposites to be perceived as integrated or unitary.

The solution to the Myth of Redemptive Violence is violence. The good guy obliterates the bad guy, thereby restoring order to the universe. The bad guy is merged into the good guy in a highly satisfying emotional process and the myth is resolved.

To understand mystical states neurologically, we must revisit the two systems of the autonomic nervous system. These are the arousal (sympathetic) and quiescent (parasympathetic) systems. These systems are usually antagonistic, which means that increasing the level of one system leads to a decrease in the other. These systems also balance each other as controls, so that one system does not, under normal circumstances, run amok.

Under certain conditions, however, these systems begin to complement each other. These conditions require hyperstimulation of one system so that when an extreme is reached, the other system is stimulated rather than inhibited.

Mystical experience has been categorized into five neurological states based on the arousal and quiescent systems (d'Aquili and Newberg, 1999). Hyperarousal states occur in extreme physical activity such as running or swimming. Athletes often report the runner's or swimmer's "high." People in this state experience a sense of "flow" as if they were effortlessly channeling huge currents of energy. The hyperarousal state with quiescent breakthrough is experienced as orgasm, rapture, or ecstasy that can lead to a trance-like state. Intense physical rituals lead to this state.

From the other direction, hyperquiescent states occur with extreme relaxation and a sense of oceanic tranquility. This state can be achieved through deep meditation or slow chanting. Hyperquiescent state with arousal breakthrough results in a feeling of absorption and a tremendous release of energy.

Finally, in a condition of maximum activation of the arousal and quiescent systems, dissolution of the perception of boundaries occurs such that one no longer experiences a difference between self and universe or that time exists. This is the state of absolute unitary being. Absolute unitary being is neurophysiologically caused by deafferentation of the orientation area of the brain. In simple English, the part of the brain responsible for orienting us in reality and maintaining the perception of self from everything else is shut off from all outside input. It is still functioning, however, as it tries to generate orientation to time and space. When the orientation association area has nothing to work on, the resulting experience is a sense of no time and no space. Put in another way, we experience infinite space and infinite time. This is the ultimate human transcendental experience.

Another important aspect of this process concerns emotion. As a person progresses toward the experience of absolute unitary being, the emotional response to the experience intensifies. Consequently, the experience of absolute unitary being is not only profound because of the perception of oneness with the universe, but the emotional satisfaction of the experience is profoundly deep.

Human experience with altered states of consciousness falls along a continuum that corresponds to the following examples (d'Aquili and Newberg, 1999):

- baseline reality—experienced as everyday living;
- aesthetic experience—experienced when watching a beautiful sunset or listening to music;

- intense romantic love—experienced as something bigger than the couple;
- visions of divinity—experienced as a glimpse of power sources beyond normal reality;
- cosmic consciousness—experienced as oceanic bliss;
- progressive trance states—experienced as dissolution of the sense of individuality;
- absolute unitary being—experienced as oneness with the universe or with God.

Neurophysiologically, the orientation area of the brain is progressively deafferented or shut off from outside input as one moves toward absolute unitary being. Full deafferentation results in the extreme of the continuum, which is the relatively rare experience of absolute unitary being.

We now have the elements of neurotheology. The concept of deity arises from the combined effects of the binary operator creating the mythical problem and the causal operator creating the supreme power to resolve the problem. These are inherent, non-modifiable brain functions. Humans have no choice or control over these functions or their operations. The result of these operations is a subjective creation of supernatural power beings or gods.

The wholistic operator interprets the state of absolute unitary being as experiencing God. Since many people have experienced absolute unitary being over many centuries, much anecdotal evidence has collected to support the causal operator's creation of a Supreme Being. Thus, the combined effects of these mechanisms create the substrate for all of the major world religions.

Mystical states are the root of all religious experience. These mystical states are altered states of consciousness, ranging from very mild to very profound. The neurological paths to these mystical states are either top-down or bottom-up. Top-down paths are typified by meditation and very slow ritual, such as chanting. The practitioner moves from a state of baseline consciousness to an altered state of consciousness by concentrating mental activity. Bottom up paths are typified by ritual, usually through liturgy. Typically, bottom up paths are group events that move participants into mildly altered states of consciousness.

What Is Religion?

Religion is the formal and informal set of beliefs, symbols, and rituals used to articulate a religious experience. Religious experience can be viewed in several ways. From a sociocultural perspective, religious experience provides rules of life and explanations for what the meaning of life is. From a neurotheological perspective, religious experience is ultimately a neurological event arising in human brains.

Many religions express living in the context of walking a "path of life." The world's religions provide alternative orientations to how we should live. Each of these orientations is expressed in distinctive symbols. Thus, a religion may be defined as a holy or sacred symbol system. Religious experience is also an experience of life-meaning based on ultimate values. Ultimate value implies that if we dig deep enough we will come upon an underlying value that validates a person's life, giving meaning and orientation to all other interests and that answers the question: "Why am I living?" (Hutchison, 1991).

Ultimate values have priority, are spread over the totality of experience, and contain emotional components. First, ultimate values are higher than personal or cultural values. An ultimate value gives meaning, purpose, and direction to human life. Thus, in a crisis, a person willingly sacrifices every other value, including life itself, to preserve an ultimate value.

Second, ultimate values are spread over all experience. They remain constant and provide a foundation upon which belief structures can be based. Finally, ultimate values have an emotional component called holiness. The holy is a unique emotion because it is the human response to transcendence. By transcendence, we mean the ability to experience absolute unitary being. Every religion has symbolic forms for transcendence and each implicitly claims that its symbols are valid, often to the exclusion of others. The highest expression of the holy is the quality of reverence. Holiness therefore refers to experiences of transcendence. The presence or absence of the holy in human experience is an accurate indicator of religion.

Therefore, religion is a system of holy forms that are patterns of human attitudes, beliefs, or practices. They are organized, structured ways of thinking, feeling, or doing. Powerful symbolic objects and words that elicit strong emotional responses express religious experience. Religions are symbol systems that guide human existence, both socially and individually.

Religion and Cosmology

Cosmology is the knowledge about creation, and each religion has its unique rendition of the Beginning. Ultimately, the various creation stories concern the organization of good and evil within the universe. Thus, religious cosmology affects how we view others. If our cosmology is one of good versus evil, we may be more likely to view those in conflict with us as irredeemably evil. If our cosmology is based on original sin, we might be able to see the Other as evil, but redeemable. If our religion's cosmology does not see creation in terms of good and evil, we are unlikely to view the Other as evil. Three basic views seem to dominate religion: Good vs. evil (binary), evil as the corruption of good (abstractive), and a view that the universe is unitary (wholistic). Each of these cosmologies provides the foundation for a worldview and personal framework for evaluating conflict.

The Binary View: Good Versus Evil

As discussed in chapter 1, one cosmological story says that the universe was created in a battle between good and evil.

According to this story, creation is an act of violence. Tiamat is murdered and dismembered, and from her cadaver the universe is formed. Order is established out of chaos through violence. Chaos (symbolized by Tiamat) is before order (represented by Marduk, god of Babylon); hence, evil is before good. Evil is an ineradicable constituent of ultimate reality and exists before good. Evil is simply a primordial fact.

Hinduism provides another example of this type of cosmology. The oldest Hindu creation myth centers on Indra's slaying of the demon of cosmic waters, Vritra, thus releasing the cosmic waters and setting the stage for the emergence of the cosmic order.

This battle was the climax of the age-long struggle between two kinds of forces. Vritra was the champion of the demons of restraint, bondage, and nonbeing, while Indra was the leader of the forces of light, life, and being. Immediately after he was born, Indra's aid was sought for this crucial battle. He accepted on the condition that he should be king of the gods. Then he took three great drafts of soma (beer), which gave him overpowering strength and vast size. By means of these newly acquired powers, he split heaven and earth, so that he might occupy the intervening space. For the battle with Vritra, Tvashtar, blacksmith of the gods, armed him with lightning (Smart, 1984).

After a fierce struggle, Indra conquered and slew Vritra, bursting his belly and thus releasing the seven cosmic waters or rivers. These waters were pregnant with the sun, whose light and heat were essential to sustain life. Soon the earth was spread out and stabilized, and the sky attached at the four corners of the earth.

Indra reigned as supreme ruler over this order. In the course of events, human beings were fashioned as servants of the gods. Although Vritra, the chief of demons, was slain, the demons still exist in the dark underworld from which they come forth to tempt and to mislead humans. And so the age-old battle between good and evil continues.

The Abstractive View:-Evil as the Corruption of Good

By way of contrast, the Judeo-Christian biblical myth of Creation is diametrically opposed to the Babylonian myth. In the biblical Creation story, a good God creates a good creation. In Genesis 1:1-10, NRSV, we read:

> In the beginning when God created the heavens and the earth, the earth was a formless void and darkness covered the face of the deep, while a wind from God swept over the face of the waters. Then God said, "Let there be light"; and there was light. And God saw that the light was good: and God separated the light from the darkness. . . . And God said, "Let there be a dome in the midst of the waters, and let it separate the waters from the waters." So God made the dome and separated the waters which were under the dome from the waters that were above the dome:. And it was so. God called the dome Sky. . . . And God said, "Let the waters under the sky be gathered together into one place, and let the dry land appear.": And it was so. God called the dry land Earth; and the waters that were gathered together he called Seas. And God saw that it was good. . . .

Chaos does not resist order. Good exists before evil. Evil and violence enter as a result of the machinations of the serpent and the couple's disobedience. A good reality is corrupted by free decisions made by humans. Men and women were to live in harmony with God, but in asserting their independence became alienated from life with God. In this far more complex and subtle cosmology, evil emerges for the first time as a problem requiring solution (Wink, 1993).

The Wholistic View: The Unitary Universe

A third creation story sees the world as emerging from a neutral force. Representative of this belief is the Tao Te Ching. Chapter 25 speaks to something of creation when it states that

> There was something formed out of chaos,
> That was born before Heaven and Earth.
> Quiet and still! Pure and deep!
> It stands on its own and doesn't change.
> It can be regarded as the mother of Heaven and Earth.
> I do not know yet its name:
> I "style" it "the Way."
> "Great" means "to depart";
> "To depart" means "to be far away";
> And "to be far away" means "to return."
> The Way is great;
> Heaven is great;
> Earth is great;
> And the king is also great.
> In the country there are four greats,
>   and the king occupies one place among them.
> Man models himself on the Earth;
> The Earth models itself on Heaven;
> Heaven models itself on the Way;
> And the Way models itself on that which is so on its own. (Henricks, 1989)

The Way is the reality that existed before all else and out of which came the physical universe. Yet the Way is not only womb-like, it also continues to be present in each individual thing as an energy or power. This energy pushes each thing to develop and grow in accord with its true nature. Evilness, from the perspective of the Tao, is simply ignorance of the Way.

In another view of unity, the Upanishads state that a single principle underlies the entire universe. At the level of absolute unitary being, the world is experienced as an interconnected unity. In the Brihad Aranyaka Upanishad, the creation account starts with the statement "In the beginning, there was nothing but the single, unitary principle *Brahman*" (Stevenson and Haberman, 1998). However, because it was alone, it was lonely and found no pleasure. In this state of loneliness, it wanted another and so divided itself into two parts, a male and a female. The male and female here began to interact centrally, and from this was born the entire universe of diverse forms. This story exemplifies the effect of the binary operator and of the wholistic operator within the human brain. Accordingly, the Upanishads view the world we experience with our senses as a single reality, even though it is clothed with a variety of names and appearances.

Notice how these three views of cosmology are based on the interplay between the causal operator, always seeking explanation, and either the binary, abstractive, or wholistic operator. In any given cosmology, one cognitive operator seems to dominate. The relative dominance of a cognitive operator also explains why people have such a difficult time reconciling different religious faiths. Obviously, the binary operator is the opposite in function to the wholistic operator. A person explaining Creation using the binary operator will develop a completely different story than someone using the wholistic operator. Consequently, the same essential facts are interpreted in opposite ways. Layer on the neurophysiology of religious experience, the rituals and symbols used to create and support religious experience, and finally the philosophy and theology to explain it all, and conflict over religious beliefs is inevitable.

Imagine three people in conflict, each holding respectively a Babylonian, Judeo-Christian, or Taoist view of creation. The Babylonian might see the Judeo-Christian and Taoist as inherently evil. The Judeo-Christian might see the Babylonian and the Taoist as inherently good, but estranged from God and therefore evil. The Judeo-Christian would believe that the Babylonian and the Taoist could be redeemed to goodness by God's grace. The Taoist might see herself, the Babylonian, and the Judeo-Christian as having strayed away from the Way. Thus, any evil was strictly personal. Each worldview, based on a specific cosmology, directs how one person considers another. In conflict, these worldviews are often below the surface and tend to act preconsciously to filter, sort, and organize perceptions of conflict situations.

Salvation

Salvation is based on the idea that we can be saved from our current existence. Salvation as a concept assumes that our existence is unhappy, poor, and unsatisfying or that we are estranged from God and from each other. Thus, we need to be saved from our existence to be truly free and actualized as beings. Salvation occurs through a variety of processes, including redemption, faith, works, and enlightenment. No one knows if salvation actually occurs because it is a transcendent state of being. Therefore, salvation is often based on hope, faith, and trust. There are no guarantees. Each religion has its unique salvation process that is claimed to be infallible. Two people with different views of salvation can therefore find themselves in conflict because of their quite different interpretations of the same event or circumstance.

Judaism and Salvation

According to Judaism, humans have misused their God-given free will, they have chosen evil rather than good, and have therefore disrupted their relationship to God. The Old Testament is a continuing story of the tribe of Israel's sinfulness and unfaithfulness to God. Pride, selfishness, and injustice appear throughout the stories (Lind, 1980).

If God has made us for fellowship with himself, and if we have turned away, then we need his forgiveness to restore the relationship. Hence, the idea of salvation is developed. Human restoration is possible by the mercy, forgiveness, and love of God. As a result, the Old Testament evokes the promise of a savior from God who will liberate Israel from oppression and evil.

Christian Salvation

The core Christian belief is that God was uniquely present in one particular person, Jesus. God uses the life, death, and resurrection of Jesus to restore us to a right relationship with himself. Christian orthodoxy holds that Jesus was physically resurrected. The Resurrection shows the way to eternal salvation for each person (Smart, 1984).

To have salvation, each person must accept the redemption offered by God through Christ and become a member of the Church. Regeneration is started with membership in the Church, but is not completed until after death. Thus, salvation does not occur in this life, but may occur in a life after death. Christianity holds a strong belief that this life is transitory and that a better, everlasting life awaits those who have faith in Christ and God.

Islamic Concepts of Salvation

In Islam, the specter of the Last Judgment, with its eternal reward and punishment, remains a constant reminder of the ultimate consequences of each life. It underscores the Koran's emphasis on the ultimate moral responsibility of each believer. At a moment known only to God, all will be called to judgment in a great cosmic event. Islam refers to this as the day of decision or the day of reckoning. All are responsible for their own actions and will be judged according to the record found in the Book of Deeds. There is no redemption, atonement, or intercession through an intermediary. Allah, who is a merciful but all-powerful judge, consigns all to heaven or to hell as he wills. In contrast to Christianity, the Koranic payoff is not at death, but at some undefined time in the future. Thus, after death, the faithful Muslim must wait until judgment day before gaining access to heaven (Smart, 1984). The Koranic view of salvation is therefore a strict form of social control.

The vision of after life is both spiritual and physical. Since the last day will be accompanied by bodily resurrection, the pleasures of heaven and the pain of hell will be fully experienced. The garden of paradise is a heavenly mansion of perpetual peace and bliss with flowing rivers, beautiful gardens, and the enjoyment of one's spouses and beautiful, dark-eyed female companions (*houris*). In contrast to the "spiritual" images of a more somber, asexual Christian paradise, the Koran offers vivid descriptions of the delights and pleasures of paradise. The depiction of the Koranic paradise is, however, male-centric.

Hindu Concepts of Salvation

In Hinduism, religion begins with the quest for meaning and value beyond self-centeredness. It renounces the ego's claims to finality. Thus, becoming a part of a larger, more significant whole relieves life of its triviality. In supporting one's own life and the lives of others, community takes on an importance no single life can command. This transfer of allegiance from self to community marks the first great step in religion. It produces the religion of duty, after pleasure and success the third great aim of life in the Hindu outlook. Performance of duty earns respect and gratitude from one's peers. More important, however, is the self-respect that comes from doing one's part. In the end, even these rewards prove insufficient.

As long as people are content with the prospect of pleasure, success, or service, the Hindu sage will not likely disturb them beyond offering suggestions for how to proceed more effectively. Hinduism waits for the moment when these things finally lose their original charm and one finds oneself wishing that life had something more to offer.

Hinduism says that life holds other possibilities. What people really want are infinite being, infinite knowledge, and infinite bliss. These wants can be summarized into a single word: liberation, understood as release from the finitude that restricts humans from limitless being, consciousness, and lives.

Hinduism's specific directions for actualizing the human potential come under the heading of yoga. The word yoga derives from the same root as the English word yoke. Yoke carries a double connotation: to unite (yoke together), and to place under disciplined training (to bring under the yoke). Defined generally, then, yoga is a method of training designed to lead into integration or union. Yoga is designed to unite the human spirit with the God who lies concealed in its deepest recesses.

Religion, Politics, and Cultural Identity

Aside from its spiritual aspects, religion has been a major accelerant of world conflict, despite universal teachings of peace. This has been due to the identity formation associated with and propagated by religious dogma, political power supporting and supported by religious leaders, and ethnicity. The monotheistic faiths of Judaism, Christianity, and Islam developed integrated religio-sociopolitical orders based on the triadic formulae of the king, God, and the culture of an ethnic group (Hange, 1998).

In Judaism, much of the Hebrew Bible is about how life is to be lived based on the law. In addition, the prophets spoke against the excesses and idolatries of royalty, the rich, and the people. Biblical Israel followed the pattern of its contemporaries where the king, the cult, and the culture of one ethnic group ruled together as a triadic unit. The fate of each triadic unit, whether Israeli, Assyrian, Babylonian, Egyptian, or Roman, was to conquer or be conquered.

This is the story of much of the Hebrew Bible and most of ancient history. The struggle of the Jewish people was how to survive as a people and a faith. The yearning for political autonomy was the driving force behind their hopes for a Messiah. This need also drove the ideology of Zionism in the nineteenth century, culminated in the formation of the state of Israel in 1948, and continues to affect Middle Eastern dynamics to this day.

The early Christian movement avoided the triadic pattern. The followers of Jesus confronted the Roman Empire with a distinctive worldview that has been called *sectaria* (Troeltsch, 1931). They saw themselves as a distinct minority group with voluntary membership, set against the larger social order. Highly disciplined, concerned for faithful obedience, they claimed no power base from which to change the world. Their gospel of peace was demonstrated in nonresistance to the point of martyrdom.

But the triadic pattern asserted itself at the beginning of the fourth century, when Constantine declared himself a Christian, and the Roman world was Christianized. This was the beginning of church-type Christianity, which sought to be inclusive in geography and membership, to dominate the social order, and to extend its saving ministry through sacramental participation. Church-type Christianity intended to establish peace in the world, or at least some kind of order, by legal and military power (Burkholder, 1988). Thus, King, God, and Culture dominated church-type Christianity.

Regarding Christians and war, Canadian Baptist theologian Douglas John Hall (1988) has written,

> Under the conditions of Constantinian Christianity (which is to say during the greater share of its history) the Christian church allowed its message to undergird, cultically, the political bravado of successive empires. The church sought to achieve its mission by aligning itself with power. It would have power through proximity to power.
>
> What this has meant in practice is that the church has had to sanction war. For empire only sustains itself finally through military might. . . . Thus the concept of "the just war" has not been incidental to the theology of Christendom, as is sometimes thought; it is an integral aspect of the whole posture of Christendom vis-à-vis worldly power. The just war follows from Christian triumphalism as naturally as heat results from fire! When the triumph of the Christ is tied to the triumph of this or that imperium, then the triumph of the Christ is also tied to the logic of war.

Many teachings of Christ were too difficult for the state churches to maintain or emphasize so they were relegated to monastic life. Thus, by the time of the expansion of Christianity into the Holy Roman Empire in Western Europe and in the development of alliance of church and state, integrated religio-sociopolitical orders had been established. Vestiges of these orders survive in the state churches of Western Europe, the Christian nationalism in North America, and the attempts to restore "symphonia" in post-Soviet Eastern Europe.

Today, church-type Christianity seeks to dominate the political order by getting its people into places of power. Government is a tool for establishing the earthly equivalent of God's kingdom. The church claims the right to impose religious values, even by coercion or force if necessary.

In contrast, classic sectarian peace groups, exemplified by the Anabaptists and the Society of Friends, take a much different attitude toward the state. The Anabaptist movement started when a group of young Protestants questioned authority. Did Scripture or the Zurich city council have the last word in matters of faith and practice (Kraybill and Hostetter, 2001)? The group decided that Scripture was what dictated faith, not government. From this then extremely subversive and radical viewpoint, the various Anabaptist sects emerged. Mennonite confessions of faith appeal to the teachings and life of the Jesus of the Gospels. The words of Jesus have precedence over all other authorities. Thus, the Christian's responsibility is to pray for government, "for kings and all who are in high positions, so that we may lead a quiet and peaceable life" (1 Timothy 2:2, NRSV).

However, Anabaptists are prepared to disobey rulers if necessary to remain faithful. Furthermore, Anabaptists have no intention to use force or military power to shape the whole society according to Christian principles. Following Jesus' instructions to love enemies and not to resist evildoers, the Anabaptists practiced a nonresistant love that rejected force and violence to order human relations. They were willing to suffer in the face of injustice.

These pacifist convictions have been tested in North America in the Revolutionary War, the Civil War, and in World War I. In 1935, representatives of Brethren, Mennonite, and Quaker groups gathered in Kansas to declare their opposition to war and form an alliance of Historic Peace Churches (Kraybill and Hostetter, 2001).

In recent decades, this posture has changed, particularly for mainstream Mennonites. Although all of the Anabaptist groups affirm the importance of peacemaking, its centrality in theology and practice varies. For some groups, peacemaking is a core understanding of Christian faith while for others it is peripheral. For some, peacemaking means quiet nonresistance to evil; for others it means assertive peacemaking in the face of injustice. Consequently, social activism in the form of peace building, community building, and supporting the oppressed is now a dynamic component of the Mennonite mission.

In contrast to Christian history, Islam has supported religio-sociopolitical unity from the beginning. In the words of Manzoor Ahmed Hanifi: "The word *Islam* suggests more than a system of theology. It stands for a distinctive civilization and a socio-politicoeconomic order, based on a form of practical theology. It has been evolving since the days of the Holy Prophet and spreading in all corners of the world" (Hanifi, 1988, p. x). Fuad Khuri puts it this way: "Islamic jurists, especially the Sunni, consider *din* (religion) a formulation of public policy where religion, state, and faith merge in a single form of action. The emphasis on a religion as public policy has given rise to two related processes: the supremacy of the *shari'a* (law) in Islam (Sunni), and the sovereignty of the Islamic community, the sovereignty of religion. . . . A society, any society, becomes Islamic if it fulfills two conditions: officially recognizing Islam as the religion of the state and being governed by a Muslim" (Khuri, 1990, p. 29, 34).

The Islamic nation, which had initially conquered an area greater than the Roman Empire, was conquered by nations of Christian Europe and Christian Eurasia. Since the mid-twentieth century, Islam has been reclaiming political, cultural, and religious territory.

As religion becomes more prominent, it will factor more significantly into national and international conflicts. This process could be seen as a re-sacralization of national structures that were themselves created by religious forces. As Khuri notes,

> Few nationalistic formulations have emerged in the world without religion playing a major role in clarifying its contents. Consider the rise of English nationalism and its association with the Anglican Church; or German nationalism and Lutheranism; or the French, Italian, and Spanish nationalisms and the consolidation of the Catholic Church; or Greek nationalism and the Orthodox Church of Byzantium; or, for that matter, American nationalism and the Protestant Churches. Religious symbols are part and parcel of the total symbolic heritage in which the national pattern is embodied. (Khuri, p. 218)

All three monotheistic faiths have patterns of development that create political entities prone to conflict, regardless of the faith's theology regarding violence. For each faith, a visionary leader formed religio-political faith communities. Each of these communities has a deep and unchangeable sense of holy history that transcends national boundaries and defines the vision and ethos of the people. Each of these communities initially formed in opposition to other religio-political communities: Moses led an exodus from Egypt that set

Yahweh and himself against the gods of Egypt and the pharaoh. Roman imperial forces in collusion with religious leaders in Jerusalem killed Jesus. Furthermore, Jesus' title Lord was in opposition to Caesar's position. Mohammed and his Islamic followers exerted religious and political efforts against idolatry and political structures not in submission to Allah's way. Therefore, the core identity of these communities was formed in a context of contention with other religio-political communities.

The formation of these faith identities has led to patterns of thought that make religious conflict difficult:

- Current conflicts are seen as similar to, or an extension of, a given "holy history's" past struggles.
- Quotes or contexts from Scriptures describe current conflicts.
- Resentment of the other group's political or religious gains generates fear connected to the primal persecution phase of the "weaker" faith.
- Because of the singular focus of monotheistic faiths there is a difficulty in coexisting without one faith community asserting or assuming superiority.
- Aggression and atrocities against the religious "other" are easier to carry out because the initial phase of each faith included contention with other faiths.
- For each group, survival and witness centers on sacrifice and suffering (exile/holocaust, persecution/cross bearing, lesser jihad/greater jihad). This faith struggle easily translates into conflict when the struggle is corporate. Members of these groups experience and interpret their survival as repetitions of past history. The crudest example of this translation is that the Crusaders were literally "cross bearers" in both name and practice, as a symbol of redemptive suffering (the cross) was turned into a symbol of redemptive violence.
- Finally, each religion's faith is based on an alternative allegiance to whatever political structure it may be living under. This alternative allegiance periodically comes to the fore in attempts to form a religious state: a Jewish Israel, the Islamic Republic of Iran, or a Christian America.

Lawyers, Peacemaking, and Religion

American law students are trained in Constitutional Law class about the separation of church and state. A classic separation case is

Wisconsin v. Yoder, 406 U.S. 208 (1972). In *Yoder*, three Amish families sued the state of Wisconsin over its requirement that children be enrolled in school until the age of sixteen. The parents refused to comply by removing their children from school after they completed the eighth grade and were convicted of violating the law. The families claimed that their rights to exercise their religion freely were not being respected. The Wisconsin Supreme Court found in favor of the Amish parents. The Supreme Court agreed with the lower court that Wisconsin's law violated the families' rights to free exercise of religion. The court's decision prevented states from asserting an absolute right to institute compulsive high school education. By preventing parents from removing their children from school, the state was intruding into the family and preventing them from instilling their faith in their children.

Law students study this case and are questioned by "what-ifs?' from their law professors. For example, what is a religion? What if a religion tolerated incest? Would it be protected? Did the court side with the Amish because the Amish value structures were unassailable? What if a religion maintained values antithetical to mainstream beliefs? For example, how does *Yoder* comport with Ger Xiong's case? Law students learn to abstract principles from cases like *Yoder*, but in so doing lose the crucial elements of the conflict.

Because the separation of church and state is an important element of the Bill of Rights and demonstrates constitutional issues arising between powers reserved to the people versus powers given to the government, a fair amount of class time is spent on the subject. Beyond the constitutional issues, which are thorny and therefore perfect for teaching, law students are not exposed to the interplay of religion and conflict. At best, the separation of church and state becomes an exercise in dialectic argument.

In the real world, however, religion plays an important, if usually hidden role in people's lives. People belong to faith communities. Family and faith traditions dictate observances repeated year after year, And the existence of church, mosque, temple, or synagogue provides a focal point for social activity. In conflicts, people often resort to religious metaphor or to relevant scriptural teachings to justify, explain, rationalize, or guide their decisions.

Religion also seems often intertwined with conflict. Many regional and national conflicts are described in religious terms because religion provides an easy, simplistic label for journalists and political analysts. Oftentimes, religion is treated as nearly synonymous with culture in that different religious groups have different cultural practices that may conflict. In these cases, the actual theologies are not as much in conflict as the cultural practices. Nevertheless, religion is the label given to the conflict.

Furthermore, religion creates worldviews and perspectives that influence conflict behavior. Religion in this context is more subtle and important than a label or descriptive cause of conflict. If a follower of Islam sees the world one way, that person's reaction to conflict will be colored by that viewpoint. Thus, when people of different faith traditions engage in conflict, an unseen layer of complexity may be added to the problem.

Religion does not provide any easy answers to conflict. Despite the fact that each religion professes beliefs against violence and conflict, each, as a manifestation of human action, has engaged in contradictory conduct. Furthermore, the essential teachings of peace are easily ignored by adherents of the faith on the basis of rationalizations such as those of just war theory or of jihad. The concept of peacemaking must, therefore, recognize the importance of spiritual teachings without permitting religiopolitical dynamics to dominate disputes.

While it is clearly a conflict accelerant, religion may also be a resource for peace. Each of the major faith traditions embraces the Golden Rule. Each professes peace as a great aspiration. Each tradition places relationship with others and relationship with God or an Ultimate Reality at the head of religious achievements. Consequently, whether a party in conflict believes in Native Spirits or the Resurrection, he or she is striving to understand and exemplify a higher way of living. Buried in these beliefs lie resources available to peacemakers who are sensitive to the realities of the people they serve.

Perhaps the most basic belief of a religion is its expression of the Golden Rule. Consider the following statements and ponder the universal nature of the Ultimate Reality:

- CHRISTIAN (Matthew 7:12, \): In everything do to others as you would have them do to you; for this is the law and the prophets.
- ISLAMIC (Sunnah): No one of you is a believer until he desires for his brother that which he desires for himself.
- TAOIST (T'ai Shang Kan Ying P'ien): Regard your neighbor's gain as your own gain and your neighbor's loss as your own loss.

- BRAHMAN (Mahabharata 5:1517): This is the sum of duty: Do naught unto others which would cause you pain if done to you.
- JEWISH (Talmud, Shabbat 31a): What is hateful to you, do not to your fellow man. That is the entire Law; all the rest is commentary.
- ZOROASTRIAN (Dadistan-i-dinik 94:5): That nature alone is good which refrains from doing unto another whatsoever is not good for itself.
- BUDDHIST (Udana-Varga 5:18): Hurt not others in ways that you yourself would find hurtful.
- CONFUCIAN (Analects 15:23): Surely it is the maxim of loving kindness: Do not unto others what you would not have done unto you.

Finally, consider again the case of Ger Xiong. Who was following the Golden Rule? Is it not possible that the social workers and court were considering its application by thinking, "If I were in the position of the boy, I would want someone to intervene and help me." On the other hand, Ger Xiong might be thinking, "My beliefs forbid surgery for my child. Why are they subjecting me to this torture? I would not do this to them so why are they doing it to me?" So the application of the Golden Rule may not be so simple, especially when cultural heritages and beliefs are very different. We examine this aspect of conflict next.

Reflections on Chapter Eight

Consider this situation and its ingredients:

- A group of Islamic businessmen have filed applications with the city to build a mosque in one of the wealthier neighborhoods in the city.
- The pastor of a nondenominational fundamentalist Christian church located in the same neighborhood has vocally opposed the application.
- The issue is beginning to polarize the city. The city council has requested that you intervene in the dispute.

Based on the materials in this chapter, how might you prepare for the peacemaking assignment?

Is this a religious-based conflict? Why or why not?

What questions might you ask both sides to comment on in preliminary meetings?

Who should be included within the peacemaking process?

How would the law address this conflict? Would a court challenge by the pastor to the application process provide peace or escalate the conflict?

CHAPTER NINE

CONFLICT AND CULTURE

C ULTURE DRIVES CONFLICT AS SURELY as any interpersonal differences. First, culture provides a repertoire of behaviors and standards of reference to evaluate the actions of others. Culture also shapes what people consider valuable and worth fighting over. Culture invests particular goods, social roles, official positions, or actions with meaning and is the vehicle for which many conflicts are played out. Cultural interpretations of particular acts or settings become highly emotional, as symbols involved in the dispute quickly become associated with control, autonomy, power, and, most important, identity, hopes, and fears. Finally, conflict behavior is often highly structured because culture encourages certain actions taken to pursue individual or group interests and discourages other actions.

The sad reality is that conflict resolution systems, especially the legal system, ignore the chronic dissatisfactions, frustrations, and angers caused by culture. Oftentimes, correctly assessing the origins of conflict requires an astute analysis of the cultural underpinnings of the problem.

Defining Culture

Culture has been described and defined in many ways. For the purposes of understanding conflict, culture may be defined as a set of beliefs, norms, rituals, and perspectives that people share within a

233

group. This definition emphasizes cognition over structural description because we are interested in understanding how common perspectives affect conflict.

Culture establishes some basic ground rules within a group. It allows everyone to see the world in about the same way and, therefore, provides efficient group operation. People do not have to waste time or resources when they share common understandings of how things are supposed to be. Thus, rules for behavior, dress, carriage, language, decision-making, impression management, etc., are all predefined within a given culture. Because these cultural beliefs are accepted without question, they tend to disappear from consciousness. In fact, much of what we call culture is the script created from automatic behaviors discussed in chapter 6.

Culture comes from individual experience and is passed socially from peers or predecessors. We are not born with culture in us. As children, one of our most important tasks is to be socialized into the group so that our behaviors and beliefs will conform to group norms. This conformity is critical to survival because it reduces the anxiety of uncertainty. A fully functioning member of a culture can be expected to behave in predictable ways given a known social event or situation.

This definition of culture also supports the idea that individuals embody multiple cultures. The culture of a family, a work group, a faith community, a political entity, or a social group all make up various cultures experienced by any individual. In this sense, culture is an outward expression of the multiple identities people develop within society.

Misconceptions about Culture

In decades past, culture was viewed in a much less expansive way. In one usage, culture related to artistic endeavors, such as music, opera, painting, sculpture, and literature. One was "cultured" if one understood and appreciated these art forms. This narrow view of culture was elitist and exclusionary, as only those who could afford the leisure and expense of education could become members. Those who were cultured looked down upon those who were not. Similarly, whether a society was "civilized," depended upon whether it expressed artistic endeavors at a level equal or superior to the existing order. Under this view, Roman and Grecian societies were civilized and cultured, while Native American societies were uncivilized and uncultured. This hubris has led to extraordinary violence and conflict between human societies.

Other misguided definitions of culture were based on political ideologies. The medieval Japanese saw themselves as highly advanced compared to other Asian and Western societies. Similarly, dying European monarchies of the nineteenth century were considered cultured when compared to the rough and tumble growth of democracy in the United States.

These views are inadequate because they fail to reflect the complexity of culture. Furthermore, they are connected to an ideology of superiority. Six misconceptions about culture seem to persist:

First, people often believe that culture is homogenous and free of internal paradoxes and contradictions. This idea of culture views a society as being consistent within itself. The truth is that cultures are composed of humans, each of whom carries his or her multiple perspectives and frames. Culture is rarely consistent and can better be described as a set of rules of thumb, under which a group of people tends to operate.

Second, people often believe that culture is a thing that can be acquired or possessed or ascertained. In fact, culture is merely a term for describing a complex set of more or less shared perspectives, behaviors, expectations, and unstated rules.

A *third* view of culture assumes that it is uniformly distributed among members of a group. Thus, if one knows a culture, one can predict what any member of that culture will do in a given situation. This is a fallacy of inductive generalization from an insufficient sample or inappropriate analogy. As we saw earlier, people within a culture may carry or assume different types of identities, such as the Lifestyler, the Commuter, and the Integrator. All of these individuals may be members of the same culture, but express the culture in quite different intensities and duration. In short, culture is never perfectly shared by individuals in the population.

A *fourth* mistake is to assume an individual has only one culture; that membership in a culture is synonymous with group identity. The fact is that individuals belong to many cultures and are consequently far more complex than this one-dimensional view permits.

Fifth, people often believe that culture is simply based on custom and is synonymous with traditional ways of behaving and surface level etiquette. While tradition and ritual play an important role in culture, culture is far more complex and subtle.

Finally, people believe culture is timeless and unchanging. Actually, culture is dynamic and highly responsive to new circumstances. Culture from the inside appears stable because the members are all changing at about the same rate. Thus, the degree and speed of change is not apparent. One can, therefore, say that because my culture appears constant, all cultures must be constant. To an outsider, however, cultures may change quickly and dramatically. For example, the structure of South African apartheid collapsed in a matter of a few years, completely changing the country.

These six views of culture are reductionistic because they distill a complex and subtle process into a simplistic, easy to understand formula. When conflict and culture come into play together, this simplification can cause severe escalation and destroy peacemaking efforts.

Culture is often an ideological resource for contestants, justifying positions and behaviors. When culture is a conflict accelerant, one strategy for resolution is deconstructing all of the inadequate ideas of culture. In this process, we make sense of culture through analysis of its interplay with conflict.

Analyzing Culture and Conflict

Analyzing the interplay between culture and conflict varies according to what is being observed. If the conflict is between persons of the same basic culture and the peacemaker is from outside that culture, the peacemaker's goal is to understand that culture's implicit and explicit rules regarding conflict behaviors and attitudes. On the other hand, if the conflict appears to be between persons of different or dissimilar cultures, a higher order of complexity exists. Not only must the individual cultures be assessed, but also their interaction and differences must be considered. When two people meet who have different models for recognizing and dealing with power and conflict, and when their respective models are backed up in their eyes by some special authority, authenticity, or feeling of rightness, then we may begin to speak of cultural difference.

Cultural analysis begins with some simple axioms. These axioms can be stated as follows:
- Culture defines what people value.
- Culture defines what people are likely to gather into disputes about.
- Culture defines appropriate ways to behave in particular kinds of disputes.
- Culture defines institutions in which disputes are processed.

Values are typically stated ambiguously within a culture, but may be based on views of human nature, religion, economic theory, and political ideology. For example, the term "family values" in vogue with some American politicians embodies a general statement that nearly everyone agrees to. However, the precise meaning of family values—just exactly what they are—may vary dramatically. People in a same sex, stable, monogamous relationship may fervently believe in family values, yet are condemned by those who see family values exemplified by the mid-twentieth century "nuclear family," consisting of heterosexual married partners and children.

Values are often expressed through the use of symbols such as flags and monuments. When these symbols are used effectively, they tend to enforce group solidarity. Threats to these symbols, such as flag burning, are viewed as threats to the culture and are, therefore, repressed. If religion is part of the cultural issue at play, ultimate values may be invoked. Ultimate values, especially as found within religion, are those values that will be given up last. In some cases, people will surrender their lives rather than give up ultimate values.

Finally, values are inculcated and strengthened by ritual, ceremony, and sacralization. Culture provides the ritual process by which people jointly share, express, and experience values. If a value becomes sufficiently transcendental, it becomes sacred and is enshrined in powerful ritual.

Culture also defines what people are likely to dispute about. Conflict over resources, power, and relationships may vary from setting to setting. Since culture helps people separate the relevant from the irrelevant, culture helps define what issues are important. An incident with stray cows may cause riots in one culture but little fuss in another. An insult to character in one culture may be a compliment in another. Affronts to autonomy and individualism may be offensive in one culture and irrelevant in another. In essence, what is culturally important is what people will dispute about.

The third axiom states that conflict behavior is defined by culture. Different types of conflicts may call for different types of behaviors. In rural Albania, honor to a family is restored through an intricate set of rules of revenge embodied in the *kunan*. In some indigenous South American cultures, conflict is never to be overt, whereas in urban Afro-American families, conflict might be placed out in the group for everyone to see and evaluate.

Finally, culture defines the institutions that process conflicts. In Palestine, the tradition of *sulha* offers an informal mediation process.

In the United States, the small claims court is a semi-formal way to resolve small legal disputes, while neighborhood justice centers provide a range of services from mediation to arbitration. Some conflicts are resolved through formal legal process, others through private means. Each culture defines for itself what conflicts are to be determined by what types of process and institution. The culture of conflict refers to specific norms, practices, and institutions associated with conflict in society.

Conflicts can be seen as a process of social communication whose messages are interpretable because disputants share a common frame of reference. Conflicts escalate when a common frame of reference is small because each side relies on its own understanding of what is going on, reading unintended meanings into a situation. Thus, objective situations alone do not cause overt conflict. Rather, the subjective interpretation of a situation is more likely to be a force in the escalation of conflict.

Culture affects conflict behavior, and conflict can also be understood as cultural behavior. Culture frames people's understanding of their social worlds, how they classify people, how they evaluate possible actions, and culture sanctions certain responses. Conflict reflects cultural priorities, but it can also be used to alter them. Culture is political because control over the definition of actors and action favors certain people and groups over others. The culture of conflict both summarizes the society's core values and reflects prior conflicts that favored some individuals and groups over others.

Conflict theorists have identified two types of theories for understanding conflict within a cultural context. The first, called structural theory, considers conflict-limiting approaches such as offering incentives, payoffs, or societal reorganization as a means of conflict resolution. A structural analysis of conflict hypothesizes that the stronger the ties of kinship, economy, and politics in a society, the lower the chances of conflict among individuals and groups (Avruch, 1998).

The second, called psychocultural theory, alters the images and metaphors of the conflict or alters the relationships between key parties. A psychocultural analysis considers that much social action is ambiguous. Therefore, it stresses the importance of the interpretation of words and deeds to explain why some disputes unleash intense conflict sequences, while others do not (Avruch, 1998).

Psychocultural dispositions are deep-seated, internal representations widely shared by members of a society. Relationships early in life often create a model for later relationships. The early relationships provide a set of standards by which groups and individuals evaluate their social worlds. Dispositions learned early in life are not only relevant on the perceptual level; they are also implicated in the automatic behaviors that serve one throughout life, such as how to respond to perceived insults, when to use physical aggression, or whom to trust. Culturally shared interpretations of the self and social world also serve as a filter for interpreting others' actions as well as guiding one's own behavior.

Structural and psychocultural theories of conflict are more complementary than contradictory. While psychocultural dispositions account for a society's overall level of conflict and violence, social structural conditions determine the selection of conflict targets. Each conflict source suggests contrasting strategies for managing conflict successfully. Both social structural interests and psychocultural interpretations shape a society's culture of conflict, but in quite different ways. Specific individual and group interests connect social structure and conflict. Shared interpretations of the world link psychocultural dispositions and conflict. Psychocultural theory is more relevant to the intensity of conflicts, whereas structural theory explains the specific ways conflict and cooperation are organized.

Culture and Emotion

We know that emotions are similar across cultures and even species. Regardless of language, custom, or beliefs, humans experience the same fundamental emotions. This is why art and literature can cross cultures with ease—they tend to evoke the same emotions in every person. While culture does not affect the basic repertoire of emotions, it profoundly affects how emotions are expressed.

Every culture establishes display rules that govern how emotions are expressed. In some cultures, the display rules require that emotions not be overtly displayed. In fact, we only have control over some of our facial muscles and some of our musculoskeletal system. Thus, even in cultures requiring no overt displays of emotion, emotion is still displayed. However, the discipline exerted to minimize the display is highly valued. In other cultures, the display rules are much more relaxed so that people can exhibit what they are experiencing.

Display rules are culturally created, not biological necessities. The stoicism of the stereotypical Marlboro cowboy is a cultural creation. Violation of display rules leads to the typical discouragement and even punishment of the nonconformist. Display rules, like other norms, provide an indication of group membership so that violation of the rules threatens group solidarity.

Cultural Schemas

Two people may experience the same social event, but perceive it differently. For one person, the incident is brushed off with a laugh. For another, the event creates intense and instant conflict. The problem is that the images on our retinas may be similar, but how we use our visual cues to turn these images into what we "see" depends on our natural and human-made environments. Part of the problem arises because the social world is more ambiguous than the physical. Social perception is therefore subject to just as much or more preconscious processing than is "physical" perception. In addition, how we act on the world is likely to follow cultural scripts.

Dov Cohen demonstrated the power of cultural schemas in perception (Cohen, 1997). Cohen argued that Southerners belong to a culture of honor in which insults and affronts must be answered—often violently—or else "face" is lost. In a series of laboratory experiments, Cohen invited Southern and Northern students at the University of Michigan into the lab and provoked them. As subjects walked down a narrow hallway, they were bumped by a confederate of the experimenter and called an "asshole."

From the qualitatively different set of reactions, emotions, cognitions, and physiological responses, the meaning of the insult and implicit rules for what to do about it were profoundly different for Northerners and Southerners. Southerners responded to the insult by getting angry, while Northerners were more likely to be amused by it. Southerners were more likely to show more hostility and dominance in their thoughts and actions, while Northerners were not. And Southerners seemed to think the insult would damage their reputation in the eyes of onlookers, while Northerners did not.

Perhaps most strikingly, Southerners and Northerners showed different physiological responses to the insult. Using a cover story about monitoring blood sugar levels as they performed mechanical aptitude tests, Cohen took saliva samples from Northerners and Southerners before and after being bumped. He measured the samples for testosterone and cortisol. Southerners showed significant increases in both hormones; Northerners showed increases in neither.

The differences between Northerners and Southerners on many measures were not just a matter of degree. The two groups were showing entirely different patterns of responding, yet they were exposed to the same social event.

Cohen failed to find conscious attentiveness by any of the subjects. Debriefings with some subjects uncovered justifications of righteous anger based on a sense of moral superiority. In many other cases, they produced a lot of confused blustering as subjects groped for why they did what they did or why it was important or not important to act tough. For some subjects, after a number of probing questions, it was obvious that the bedrock answer was "just because." Their goals, actions, and definitions of masculinity were activated by virtue of the situation they were in. It was not a matter of conscious deliberation; they were just following their cultural script.

This study suggests that conflict can be triggered by chronic automaticity. That is, goals, perceptions, and beliefs can become embedded by virtue of culture. When appropriately triggered, the goal sets into action its predetermined plans and strategies. If those strategies are aggressive, conflict is likely.

The issue is actually even subtler than cultural influence. As we have seen, a nonconscious connection between a current and past situation can trigger an automatic emotional reaction. If the reaction is triggered on the basis of peripheral or irrelevant features of the two situations, explaining the emotion can be difficult. Furthermore, such a reaction may be impervious to rule-based reappraisal. In other words, the reaction may not be modifiable through rational analysis of the situation. To observers for whom the situation does not seem to justify emotion, the reaction may seem irrational. Finally, because the connection between the preloaded situation and the current situation may be unconscious, may not be linked in time or place, and may not be open to scrutiny, attempts by others at rational analysis will not be helpful.

In contrast, reactions elicited from perceived events can often be undone by reappraising the situation. Suppose that one's feelings were hurt by a critical comment. Then one learned that the comment was directed to someone else. Usually, the interpretation of the comment would change and the hurt feelings would go away. In fact, anger and aggression appear to act in this way. If a person is self-aroused such that he or she is focusing on the angry meaning of the situation, angry behavior reduces the emotion only if it decreases the activation of the event that triggered the anger. The catharsis view, which depends on a pool of energy to be drained off, has never been established empirically. Venting, in other words, is not what happens when people express their anger.

Conflict can arise when two people react to the same social stimulus in different ways. If they have been culturally attuned to respond differently, what they observe the other person doing in response to the stimuli is not only wrong, it may be quite offensive.

Suppose that Erin is raised in a culture that breaks its eggs on the small end. Over time, Erin's skill at egg-breaking becomes automatic and she assumes it the correct and only way to break eggs. Erin begins to date Roger, who was raised in a culture that breaks its eggs on the large end. Of course, Roger's egg-breaking skill is automatic, correct and natural to him. Erin and Roger have a discussion about the importance of correct egg-breaking. Erin insists on the small end of the egg being broken. Roger, recognizing the immediate cultural difference says nothing, but reminds himself that this is important to Erin.

One day Roger, wishing to show his affection for Erin, breaks eggs for her. Erin, watches in shock as Roger, intending not to offend and having every intention of breaking the egg from the small end, breaks the large end of the egg. She is in turn embarrassed, humiliated, and angered at Roger's insensitivity, coarseness, and general incivility. Roger is completely nonplussed why he broke the egg at the large end when he knew to break the egg for Erin at the small end. He too is embarrassed at his lapse.[6]

What happened was more than force of habit or inattentiveness. Roger had developed an automatic goal of breaking eggs from the large end in the presence of people who supported, loved, and affiliated with him. He literally acted thoughtlessly, meaning nonconsciously, despite his conscious intention to the contrary. Erin's presence triggered a goal of seeking affirmation and support in Roger. In turn, the goal automatically produced behavior that, in the past, had led to satisfaction of the goal. Unfortunately for both Erin and Roger, Roger's automaticity was inappropriate for Erin.

Erin, too, was a victim of cultural automaticity. She perceived Roger breaking the egg at the large end and categorized him as uncouth and insensitive. Simultaneously, she instantly and nonconsciously evaluated the event as bad, which triggered emotions. Again, simultaneously, she became motivated to respond with avoidant behavior. Several milliseconds later, she became aware of her judgment and emotions, consciously labeled them, then ascribed her reaction to her consciousness. In fact, her conscious awareness was about one-half second behind her perception, behavior, and emotion.

If Roger and Erin were questioned after this incident, we would probably learn that (1) Roger did not intend to offend Erin, (2) he did not realize he had broken the egg at the large end until it was too late, and (3) he could not explain why he did it. From Erin we would learn that (1) she believed what Roger did was a gross insult to her, (2) that he would not have done it if he truly cared for her, and (3) she could not explain why she was so offended by his act. Erin thus assumed intentionality when, in fact, automaticity was operating.

From an objective perspective, Roger meant no harm. In fact, he intended precisely the opposite—he was seeking to approach Erin. From Erin's subjective position, however, Roger's intentions were readable only from his conduct. Since the conduct was reprehensible, the logic of the situation dictated that Roger was purposively insulting and disrespectful to Erin. Roger was therefore a bad person. Erin had no control over her reaction to Roger and although her rational mind might be able to understand what really happened, her emotional unconscious was more powerful. Thus, even the memory of Roger breaking the egg on the large side would be enough to trigger a negative judgment. Consequently, forgiveness would be difficult for Erin.

Culture also puts an initial frame on issues; this initial frame is very difficult to change once set; and this frame starts reactions that can activate automatically (knee-jerk reactions may be an appropriate metaphor). Loaded issues—those involving abortion, affirmative action, gun control, and so on—are likely to trigger such responses. Thus, politicians try to control the vocabulary and imagery of the debate so that they can impose the frame they want. They seek to control the "if" part of the "if-then" conditional—defining the world in a certain way—because the wanted behavioral reaction can then flow much more easily.

As an example, framing affirmative action as either involving racial justice or reverse discrimination will produce profoundly different effects. Even subtle differences—such as framing just the opposition to affirmative action as based either on opposition to (a) reverse discrimination or (b) unfair advantage—has significant effects on people's attitudes. Slight changes in the wording of survey questions can produce large changes in opinions about topics where one would guess that people's attitudes have long ago crystallized. If af-

fective and cognitive reactions can be triggered by such subtle framing changes in survey questions, it is not hard to imagine the effects
that are triggered by the framings and over-learned associations that
are a part of culture. Culture primes us to think of issues in certain
ways and prepares us to accept the frames that are put on issues by
rulers.

Gender and Conflict

Gender pervades all aspects and levels of conflict because it carries expectations for conflict behavior and for rights and responsibilities in conflict negotiations. Because gender is so pervasive, its influence is often unseen. It becomes a subtext that supports other assumptions and conclusions. Most scholars recognize that gender is a
social construction; thus, gender is distinguishable from biological
sexual differences. Sex refers to the biologically based distinctions
between woman and man that are chromosomal and hormonal. Gender refers to the cultural, social, and power implications of sexual differences. Sex differences in social behavior may be viewed as inherent in the nature of men and women, whereas gender originates in
the social system (Taylor and Bernstein Miller, 1994).

Conventional wisdom states that men and women in Western
cultures deal with interpersonal conflict in different ways. Typically,
men are expected to emphasize a competitive all or nothing approach, while women are expected to engage in a problem solving-
collaborative approach.

In fact, conventional wisdom is wrong. In the *Social Psychology of
Bargaining and Negotiation*, Rubin and Brown (Rubin and Brown,
1975) reviewed 100 studies that focused on the relationship between
sex and bargaining behavior. They found that the results divided
into three categories. One set of studies did not establish any difference in bargaining performance between men and women. A second
group of studies showed that men behave more cooperatively than
women, and a third group of studies indicated that women behave
more cooperatively than men. Women and men do not differ in their
abilities and skills of bargaining, but are sensitive to different cues in
the bargaining situation. Women are more attuned to interpersonal
aspects of the relationship while men are more interested in the task
of maximizing gains.

Keashly (1994) reviewed studies after Rubin and Brown. She
found that in close relationships, there are more similarities than dif-

ferences between women's and men's conflict behavior. Both men and women engage in accommodative, avoidant, compromising, collaborative, and competitive behavior in conflict situations. Conflict styles are largely interchangeable between men and women. Conflict management behaviors depend on the degree of the emotional connection, relative access to power, and the gender of one's partner. Studies of conflict management in work relationships also reveal no gender-based behaviors (Euwema and van de Vliert, 1994). Research on work relationships reached conclusions similar to those based on the research about personal relationships. Men and women engage in an equally extensive range of conflict behaviors, but the conflict and characteristics of the relationship, such as hierarchy, status, and role influence their behaviors.

Social psychological research therefore provides little evidence of gender differences in conflict management abilities or skills. Sex-role expectations appear to influence behavior and perceptions of behavior in particular circumstances. Thus, gender-linked conflict seems to occur most often when a relationship or a situation is vaguely defined. Within the workplace, structural basis of power, experience, and job status are stronger influences on behavior than gender.

In general, the studies imply that women are not worse negotiators than men. Given a reasonable degree of situational power, women are likely to be as oriented toward winning against their opponents as are men and as successful at doing so. Women are not nicer negotiators that men in terms of being more fair-minded or compassionate. Thus, gender differences in conflict and negotiation behavior are an artifact of power and status differences between men and women rather than a result of sex-role socialization.

Three Themes of American Culture

We now move from the general to the specific to understand how American culture contributes to chronic interpersonal conflict. Three themes describe the core of American culture. Together they create an unseen, chronic condition that easily accelerates conflict when conditions are proper. These themes— competition, individualism, and republicanism— form the bedrock of American society and contribute to the litigation mindset of the American people.

Competition and Conflict

Those of us living in the United States experience a competitive society. The advocates of competition argue that it is efficient and fair. Competition theoretically allows each person to advance in society based on his or her merit, hard work, and ambition. Hence, it justifies a fundamental concept of justice: equal opportunity for all. As we will see, however, competition carries some heavy costs, especially in regards to its tendency to encourage negative and destructive conflict.

Competition as a model of culture emerged with the new trading class within European feudal society. Trading itself tended to be an isolated way of living. It involved taking things that had been made, mined, or grown in one place and selling them at another place for a cost higher than the cost to make and transport them. The trader was not a part of a larger society. He was often the outsider, set apart from the natural rhythms of the seasons that still governed the lives of most people. People engaged in trading developed ideas that the larger community's values and needs should not be the highest guide to life. Instead, individuals should be able to determine for themselves what was best (Bellah, Madsen, Sullivan, Swidler, and Tipton, 1996).

As people came together, forming towns alongside the medieval castles of Western Europe, they developed a sense that they should be free of the restrictions and prohibitions that the larger society placed upon them. They insisted "private" or "personal" needs should be equally legitimate with communal needs. The goals of the community should include the fulfillment of the needs of the individual.

This development was extremely valuable. Too often the communities of the past had been dominated by small groups of people who forced their special interests upon everyone else. Asserting that the needs of all individuals should also be taken into account was an important corrective.

However, the rising class of traders met with tough opposition from the landed aristocracy and the church. They were forced to define themselves and their "rights" even more clearly. In the struggles from the fourteenth through the eighteenth centuries, this class began to assert the needs of the individual as the highest goal. It demanded that all external constraints on individuals be removed. Eventually, this included the demand that religion, ethics, and philosophy be purged of all elements that could challenge the rights of the individual to do whatever he or she chose to do, regardless of its effects on the larger body politic. Emphasis was shifted from the community to the individual. The larger society was seen as valid or deserving of allegiance only to the extent that it served the needs of the individual.

These ideas were antagonistic to the established religious and ecoomic elite. For hundreds of years, ideas about individual rights were seen as revolutionary. Eventually, through the triumphs of the American and French revolutions and the less bloody conquest of power in England, the middle class became the new ruling class. Its ways of regarding reality became enshrined in the universities, churches, and mass communication. The pursuit of individual wants was not only protected from state intervention, but became the criterion by which all other activities should be evaluated.

To provide a foundation for this approach, theories of the world were developed from Hobbes to Freud to contemporary economists. Foremost among these was John Locke. The essence of Locke's position was that the individual was before society, which comes into existence only through the voluntary contract of individuals trying to maximize their self-interest. Locke and other theorists assumed that rational self-interest was the "natural" inclination people would follow if left to their own devices. Egoism was not simply an historical aberration, but a biological and psychological necessity (Bellah, et al., 1996).

From the concept of individualism, a further proposition developed. While people pursued their own self-interests, some people were better at it than others. They were smarter, more energetic, more motivated, or more something than others. These people ended up receiving the greatest rewards in society. As a result, an incentive structure was established to push people to compete against one another for fame, wealth, and prestige. This incentive structure provoked enormous scientific, artistic, and political advances, but at a hidden cost (Kohn, 1992).

Under the ideology of competition, only a few could actually succeed. Consequently, the culture of competition meant that there were masses of less successful people who suffered from a psychology of self-blaming. If you are not good at pursuing your own self-interest, you have no one but yourself to blame. Your anger should be directed at yourself. The retributive aspect of this position, that "it's your own fault—so now live with what you made" seemed morally fitting to those who succeeded. Morality was based on the assumption that, "You are just out for yourself anyway, trying to get what is best for you without regard to anyone else. You have no right to complain to the rest of us if you do not do well in the scramble for self-interest." This, in turn, flowed from the view that a competitive way of being was the core of human nature (Lerner, 1986).

While we can see how this ideology developed from a revolutionary idea to a moral truth, it is simply wrong. Competition is not a part of human nature.

Some argue that competition is an evolutionary process. Herbert Spencer, Darwin's apologist, was the first to apply adaptive evolutionary theory to culture. According to Spencer and many that followed him, survival of the fittest justifies competition in modern society. Spencer was wrong. In fact, there is no necessary relationship between natural selection and competitive struggle. The equation of competition with success in natural selection is a cultural prejudice. Evolutionary success is defined as having more offspring. This reproductive success means that the genome is carried forward into future generations. However, reproductive success can be attained by a large variety of cooperative strategies. Thus, there is no *a priori* preference in the general statement of natural selection for either competitive or cooperative behavior. Nothing about evolution requires competition. In fact, natural selection discourages competition because survival demands that individuals work with, rather than against, each other. Spencer's arguments, based on the theory of evolution, were nothing more than justifications for the ruling class to maintain their positions through continued control of economic power, status, and political power. By saying that they were the successful competitors was an after the fact justification, not an explanation.

Competition is a learned phenomenon. People are not born with a motivation to win or to be competitive. In the United States, however, we are carefully taught the morality of competition. The result is that, except for the visible cooperation required for any society, we are uniquely uncooperative as a people. The message that competition is appropriate, desirable, required, and even unavoidable is drummed into us from nursery school to graduate school. It is the subtext of every lesson (Kohn, 1992). This theme should not be confused with games played competitively for recreation or enjoyment. The fundamental difference between our cultural obsession with competition and game playing is that the former is forced upon us while the latter is freely chosen. This fact is missed when people use game metaphors to describe a sale, a trial, or a company's success.

What are the costs of competition? We can identify three reasons why competition leaves us insecure and anxious. The first and most obvious is apprehension about losing. The second concerns feelings of apprehension about winning. The third concerns our apprehension about the reactions of others to our winning. Thus, competition is a pervasive cause of anxiety in our culture.

If we are in competition, there can only be one winner; the rest are losers. Competition immediately sets up every person except the winner as less worthy, less human, and less desirable. While many competitions are trivial, over time the balance of wins and losses becomes wearing. Eventually, people give up and accept themselves as less worthy of success (Kohn, 1992). Deep inside, however, these people know that they are good and are frustrated at a culture that puts them down. Every trial lawyer feels the pressure of competition and knows that he or she is only as good as the last big win. Thus, the pressure to win becomes enormous. More significantly, it outweighs other possibilities, such as restoration of peaceful relationships between the parties.

What if we do win? We are placed in a position of momentary glory and bask in admiration. The problem is that the glory is short-lived. If we live for the glory, we soon begin to define ourselves in terms of winning and losing. We become apprehensive about the contest, which creates anxiety, frustration, and necessarily conflict.

How do people react to us if we do win? Jealousy, envy, the need to put "him" or "her" back in place, is a common reaction to the winner. People resent winners because winners are living proof of the losers' unworthiness. The winners clearly receive the brunt of negative reaction. They may feel bad and thus not compete as hard next time. More likely, they will defend themselves by declaring their personal superiority (Kohn, 1992). The losers become inferiors, not deserving of respect or love. Again, conflict ensues. Many lawyers can relate how, after winning a big case, they have created strong jealousies within their law firms. Rather than being applauded and encouraged for their success, they are marginalized because they have threatened the self-esteem of other members of the firm.

One of the problems with competition is dichotomous thinking. In a contest, there are only two possible results: win or lose. When there are only two choices, typically one is seen as good and the other as bad. Everything is neatly sorted as rational or irrational, righteous or satanic, progressive or reactionary, reasonable or radical. The brain's binary operator dominates the other cognitive operators. A world that can be reduced to such simple terms is a much more manageable, comfortable world, one that does not ask us to grapple with tough moral questions. It is also a world of intense, inherent, and chronic conflict.

When dichotomous thinking is competitively generated, there is a tendency to be concerned about what is the best. People are either number one or they are unworthy. Thus, the brain's quantitative operator joins the binary operator to create a compelling worldview. When people perform this kind of value-laden division, they place themselves on the good side. They want the good to triumph over the bad. A gulf opens between them and us, which invites aggression. From seeing right and wrong as the only two possibilities, they claim righteousness for themselves and see the opponent as an evil non-self. Such polarity not only implies superior-inferior; as it denies complementarity, it also invites battle. Thus, superior tends to become pitted against inferior.

Competition as a cultural theme is therefore a foundation for significant conflict.

Individualism and Conflict

Individualism lies at the very core of culture in the United States. Americans believe in the dignity, indeed the sacredness, of the individual. Anything that would violate our right to think for ourselves, judge for ourselves, make our own decisions, live our lives as we see fit, is not only morally wrong, but is sacrilegious. Our highest and noblest aspirations, not only for ourselves, but those we care about, are closely linked to our individualism. Yet some of our deepest problems both as individuals and as a society are also closely linked to our individualism.

The capitalist revolution of the late eighteenth century seemed to promise a very different world. No longer would there be an authoritative allocation of rewards. Each person was, in principle, free to make whatever they could of themselves. Where one ended up would be a reflection of one's own efforts and capacities.

Self-employment decreased from 50 percent in the 1860s to less than ten percent in 1980. During this period, the media played up the mythology of endless opportunities for advancement on the part of those who were investors and smart. Since some people really did have this experience of "making it," and since almost everyone saw some part of their life growing better, the general celebration of "endless possibilities" was enshrined in the American unconscious.

The ideology of society focused on social mobility. People could make whatever they wanted of their lives. From this, the dominant justification for capitalism could be accepted. Where one ends up is a function of how much effort one expends and how much talent one has. This is called the theory of meritocracy: Advancement in the social hierarchy is a function of individual merit (Lerner, 1986).

The post-World War II years saw a dramatic increase in acceptance of the ideology of meritocracy. With this belief came an important, but hidden corollary: If you are in a stressful job, you have no one but yourself to blame.

For almost every adult American, the majority of one's waking hours are involved with getting ready for, transiting to and from, and performing at work. Work fills a massive amount of waking energy. The emotional dynamics that emerge at work have a huge impact on the rest of people's lives. The way people understand and interpret their stressful conditions generates a deep and abiding self-blaming process that often spills over into "personal life." Because people blame themselves for their stress, they often feel terrible about themselves. That feeling shapes their family and personal life.

Many people systematically shut out work environments that frustrate their human capacities (Lerner, 1986). This enables them to survive in jobs to earn money for food and rent. Given their perception that nothing can be changed, they have no reason to keep themselves "open" and "sensitive to their experiences." They know that people who remain sensitive and open simply cannot function in "the real world." To survive, one learns to deny and repress awareness of parts of oneself that have, in any event, never been validated or given much opportunity to develop.

How does work do this to people when all are supposed to live within the ideology of meritocracy? First, work makes people feel powerless over their lives. They have no control over how they spend the majority of their day.

Organizational theory recognizes that organizations neither require nor desire the full range of human behaviors and relational capacities. Only behaviors and relations that are functional to the organization have a proper place in the organization. What is functional is determined in terms of the articulation of the division of labor and the coordination of roles. The division of labor creates a rationalized hierarchy of specialized tasks. The coordination of roles operates as a system of interdependencies enforced by expectations, rewards, and sanctions. The division of labor and its coordination define the proper place of any individual in the organization. This proper place is not merely a structural location described by behaviors and relations, but is also an organizational culture and a mode of occupying organization space. Employees are typically restricted to the use of institutionalized formats based on a strong and bureaucratic rationality (e.g., standardization of format and content, etiquette of address, and personal voice, neatness, etc.). Although these restrictions are expressed as a concern for clarity, efficiency, and professionalism, they actually impose a discipline that discourages variation.

Control has become so central to the psychology of management it is thought to be an independent psychological dynamic. Managerial control is power over other people, imposing managerial goals and actions in place of those that workers might choose. In our society, people have power when they have this kind of control. To the extent that people's jobs require that they control other people, they rationally develop controlling types of personality structures. These personalities help them get better jobs and higher salaries. Thus, society rewards those who most effectively control others. Society consequently reinforces and re-creates the need for control. People who develop a controlling personality structure find themselves succeeding in the economic marketplace. However, these same people may also find themselves having deep problems establishing loving relationships and enduring friendships in their personal lives.

There are three major forms of control over the work force (Lerner, 1986). First is direct control exercised by a supervisor or foreman. Foremen and supervisors often develop an interest in the power of their positions and the right to it. Consequently, they tend to put workers down. In seeing workers as somehow inferior, potentially incompetent, and untrustworthy, these managers justify to themselves the right to have more power and exercise control.

Direct control generates unnecessary opposition from the workers. Foremen and supervisors often use their power arbitrarily, in ways that generate resentment and resistance. A foreman's insecurity can lead to the development of obnoxious or insensitive personality traits to which workers strongly react. Senior managers have tried to deal with this problem by providing special courses on communication and conflict management for their lower level managers. However, the model of direct control relies too heavily on the personalities of those in these lower level positions. These people remember all too well when they were workers and do not want to go back into the ranks. They are, therefore, willing to do anything to look good to their superiors, usually at the expense of their workers.

A second form of control is based on the technical organization of the workplace itself. People are controlled by the needs of the work itself rather than by management. The assembly line is a perfect example of this principle. The advantage to management is that control is more mysterious to the employees. Lower level managers do not appear to be exercising arbitrary authority; they are only doing what the machines require.

The third form of control, bureaucratic control, is the most sophisticated form of management. In a bureaucracy, rules and regulations replace supervisors' commands. Work is governed by a set of rules that seem to stand independent of the wills of individual supervisors. Each job is prescribed by rules that tell people how their performance will be judged, the rewards for doing the job correctly, and the penalties for inadequate work. Rules seem to provide "fairness" to the whole process.

Bureaucratic control, experienced as inflexible and uncaring, reinforces self-blaming. Workers come to feel that their problems are caused by their own failures to adjust to reality. They blame themselves for aspects of their situations that are built into the structure of their economic world.

The three methods of control often coexist in the same work situation. They mutually reinforce feelings of failure and incompetence, and provide a daily experience why people are incompetent to run things, do not deserve to have power, and should just leave the big questions to those who know better.

The second debilitation of work is the effect of "de-skilling" (Lerner, 1986). In light of management's overriding need to control, the workplace is organized so that people have fewer opportunities to use their intelligence and creativity. Job tasks become increasingly narrowed. As production becomes increasingly complex, working people actually become less and less skilled. This process is called "de-skilling."

In contrast, senior managers receive more information and increased decision-making powers. Their job becomes more interesting and challenging. This experience helps make them oblivious to any humanly destructive aspects of the de-skilling process. After all, if the employees wanted interesting jobs, they would have gotten their lives together more effectively to take the interesting jobs the senior managers now find available.

De-skilling destroys worker self-esteem and sense of power. Work that requires only certain specialized skills does not provide workers with the chance to develop a sense of their ability. Many workers come away from work believing that they are not capable or intelligent. Their work gives them no opportunity to use and develop their abilities to think and be creative. Gradually, they become so unused to using their intelligence that they become afraid to try.

Most people want to work, but want work that is meaningful and for which they are respected. As they become socialized to the world of work, they learn that their actual jobs will give them neither opportunity to be creative nor opportunity for respect. Eventually, they develop various ways to resist and to reclaim their dignity. Typically, this is done by not giving all that is wanted by management. If they cannot have their real needs met, they will assert their autonomy and a measure of power for themselves by refusing to go along with programs set by others.

The psychological result is that many workers feel anger and rage at themselves. When the rage is kept inside, it is often managed through drugs or alcohol. When it explodes irrationally at work, the angry worker becomes isolated from fellow workers and puts his or her job in jeopardy. A worker's anger makes that worker even more distrusting of himself, confirming his self-blame (Lerner, 1986).

These problems are not unique to the working class. The same ideology of meritocracy, based on competitive individualism, creates an atmosphere conducive to conflict in the professional classes and in management. Professional and management people sell themselves and their products. To make themselves into attractive commodities, they must carefully study the latest trends in their fields and then look and act in the "appropriate" way. The person on her way up in the corporate world is continually in competition with others. This dynamic increasingly dominates lawyers, doctors, mental health professionals, real estate and insurance agents, managerial personnel, clergy, teachers, college professors, and people in publishing and government.

As people tailor their attitudes and lifestyles to fit their needs for success, they become increasingly alienated from themselves and their own feelings. Their daily reality forces them into a competitive and distrustful mode with everyone around them.

These people are afraid of getting close to others and afraid that others will swallow them up should they do so. This fear is due to their acute sensitivity to their economic world. Fear of intimacy is not just paranoia. It is the correct perception that other people will take advantage of them (Lerner, 1986). Other people will use any weakness as a weapon in the ongoing struggle for success. In every sector of society, people feel desperately alone, unhappy, and frustrated. They also feel terrible about themselves for feeling this way. They are convinced that their own failure in the work world is much greater than that of others. Then they go home to find further frustrations and disappointments.

People suffer much pain in personal life. The fantasy of a magical relationship with someone who will make all of the pain go away is rarely fulfilled. Most people end up with relationships that do not meet these expectations. Instead of understanding how the original fantasy could not be fulfilled, people see themselves as having failed again. The self-blaming at work is now massively reinforced by self-blaming about their failures to create a good personal life. In their frustration, they become angry with their spouses, lovers, children, and parents. Ultimately, these are most typically manifestations of the deeper anger at themselves. They come to see themselves as the source of their own continuing failures and unhappiness.

Work has a deep and profound effect on how people feel about themselves even when they are not at work. People typically return home feeling tense, upset, sometimes depressed, and almost always with a deep sense of frustration at their failure to create a fulfilling life. They blame themselves for these frustrations, but are often filled with rage that has been suppressed all day. They are afraid of losing control over this rage. Typically, these feelings are layered over by a surface level of calm and relief at getting home. Most people present themselves as not "letting it get to them" (Lerner, 1986). They pretend that they are unaffected by stupid bosses, arrogant supervisors, new techniques for processes that they are not quite sure they can master, sales that did not go through, people who they are not sure they have impressed enough, co-workers with whom they must compete for praise or promotions, or people with whom they work who are not doing their part of the work competently and thereby making it harder for everyone else. In fact, they are worn out, stressed, and profoundly unhappy.

To drown their frustrations, tensions, exhaustion, and rage, people watch television. Sometimes they allow themselves to experience some limited set of feelings evoked by the programs. Mostly, television helps them numb themselves to all feelings. The rapid succession of programs does not allow for time to reflect or to get too deeply attached to the meanings and feelings of any one program. The beauty, the vivid colors, the quick movements, the rapid succession of images all help to create a world of fantasy within which nonwork hours can be lived. The narcotizing effect is powerful as people escape the paralyzing feelings brought home from work by living through this fantasy world (Lerner, 1986)

People use alcohol or drugs—the "royal road" to forgetting the frustrations at work. People engage in frenetic activity in sports, religion, and politics. Too often these activities serve a destructive function for working people. They are used to escape from the feelings of pain of the work world. This is particularly true of people who throw themselves into these activities, allowing their entire emotional lives to be consumed and leaving no space for reflection, introspection, or time to calm themselves down.

Television, alcohol, drugs, sports, and frenetic activity provide ways for people to stay out of touch with their pain, anger, and self-blaming. Because these activities succeed at repressing painful feelings, they also ensure that personal lives will be unfulfilling. Fulfilling relationships can only be built through deep connection and communication. The emotional energy put in to repressing the alienation, self-blaming, and anger experienced at work leaves too little energy to develop emotional connection. Equally important, people who are regularly out of touch with their feelings simply do not have the skills to suddenly jump into open and honest relationships. Nor do they have the capacity to deal with conflicts constructively when conflicts become acute.

The sad part about the mystique of individualism is that it is carried like a bad gene from generation to generation. Children, more than adults, suffer from the ideology of individualism.

A child's relationship with his or her parents is from the start a process of misrecognition. The child's human essence is not acknowledged. Instead, the parent conveys to the child that the child has a set of roles. Anything more will be too much for the parent to handle. The parent offers an implicit deal: "You will get love and recognition from me of the sort I have available only if you become a thing, the assortment of roles, in which I am seeing you. If you will be that thing, then I can give you as much love as I have to give" (Lerner, 1986, p. 123). Human essence is repressed in the process, but is not obliterated.

Children learn quickly that something is not right in the world— it is they. Most children try to mold themselves to their parents' expectations. But no matter how they try, their way of being does not give them the love and recognition that they need. When children discover this, they typically begin to feel deep pain about themselves. Most children become painfully aware that their parents are not really there for them and do not love them for who they are. They feel deep shame about their inability to elicit love from the people who know them best.

Experiences at school typically confirm a child's worst fears about themselves. The starting assumption in school is that everyone is just fine at home. In school, the myth of meritocracy is first generated. The teacher will supposedly treat everyone equally. How a child does in these circumstances will be a reflection of his or her worth, talents, and merit. By being "fair" in this way, the actual experience of the child in family life is "expunged from the record."

This seeming equality is not real and educators know it. But they have limited resources, both physically and emotionally. Consequently, for self-protection, the myth must be carried out. The differing levels of pain that children bring to the school have a dramatic consequence on their behavior and their ability to learn. In addition, the pains and problems of family life shape the roles children assume in social interactions with each other and school authorities.

Children receive a very strong message from school: "If you are having a problem, if you are upset, this is some personal issue, and certainly not shared by the rest of us, who are all doing very well. You had better keep control of what is bothering you, because your problems are more troubling than those of others. You would be making yourself look foolish to try to have your needs and hurts be discussed with the other kids" (Lerner, 1986, p. 137). Children learn to develop an external personality that can connect with other kids, but not get too close. Learning in school is learning how to deny one's real feelings and upsets. Children learn to participate in a shared world distant from one's real feelings.

Any hope that the natural tendency for love and solidarity could break through the false school reality is quickly smashed by the dynamic of competition. Schools emphasize individual achievement, often at the expense of other kids. Sports and other games reinforce the competition built into the classroom. By the time the child has been in school a few years, he has learned that this is "just how the world really is."

Adolescence is no picnic either. The adult personality is formed during adolescence. The drive to create a personality acceptable to parents' is now transferred on to a peer group. Each teenager will adopt group values and concerns with passion, fueled by desperation for recognition and love. Consequently, teenagers develop a facade corresponding to his or her sense of what would be "acceptable." Teenagers present this personality to the group, hoping the group will love them. On the other hand, teenagers know this validation is superficial because their real, underlying, childhood personality still feels ignored and unloved.

The cost of individualism is not acknowledged, but it is extensive. Many people are isolated and alienated from one another. They are angry, frustrated, and unhappy. They are distrustful and suspicious. Because they have never connected deeply with anyone, they lack the skills to deal well with interpersonal relations. They especially lack conflict management skills.

Most of the time, people are unaware of their repressed angers. But when they get into fights, or arguments, or other conflict, much of the emotional fervor is an expression of their chronic distress. When they have the opportunity to strike back, they do. Hence, lawsuits in the workplace have become commonplace and divorces are nastier and nastier.

Peacemakers must come to know and understand this chronic, unstated, low level conflict. It manifests itself in nearly every conflict in Western society and accelerates manageable conflicts into intractable ones. It is subtle and therefore difficult to transform.

Politics and Conflict

One of the great pillars of American culture is the concept of republicanism. Jefferson, perhaps the greatest republican, believed that political equality could only be effective in the republic when the citizens actually participated. To him, the ideal republic was a self-governing society of relative equals in which all participate.

Politics is conceived of in three ways. First, politics is a matter of enacting the moral consensus of community through democratic process. This view of politics is exemplified by the politics of community. A second view of politics sees it as the pursuit of different interests according to agree-upon neutral rules. This is the politics of the special interest, often euphemistically called pluralism. The politics of special interests is frequently seen as a necessary evil in a large, diverse society and as a reluctant second best to consensual democracy. Special interest politics is not seen as morally virtuous because inequalities of power, influence, and moral probity often determine political outcomes. Inside connections are rewarded and the strong appear to be favored at the expense of the weak.

The third view is the politics of nation that sees statesmanship and the high affairs of national life as transcending particular interests. The politics of nation embodies the idea of impartial governance according to law with leadership given the task of uniting a highly diverse society to a national purpose.

Many Americans have a limited capacity to understand the economic and social organization of the United States because their chief moral language is limited by a narrow view of individualism. Under the traditional view of individualism, anything that is not under the control of individual choice cannot be encompassed in the moral calculation. Thus, in a society that assigns people their places and relative power, conditions of inequality, lack of power, privilege or esteem cannot make coherent moral sense. This raises a problem of invisible complexity.

Because people cannot make moral sense of the significant cultural, social, and economic differences between groups, they lack means for evaluating the different claims each group makes. Thus, the conflict of interests become troubling and people are tempted to translate group claims and interests into the language of individual rights. Groups or categories of individuals begin to insist they are entitled to certain benefits, help, or entitlements as a matter of right. When their claims are not accepted as matters of justice, the outcome of the conflict is widely interpreted in terms of power. Thus entitlements are satisfied in terms of the power of those seeking the rights.

Power and influence are not viewed as legitimate because they fall outside the dominant ideology of individualism. Under this ideology, every person is presumed free to pursue in open competition his or her own interests. To the extent that institutions, corporations, and labor unions transcend or step out of the free market, they become highly suspect. Thus, lawyers who are able to defend wrongdoers successfully on the basis of legal technicalities are not viewed as legitimate because they are sidestepping the basic ideology of American culture. Similarly, plaintiffs' lawyers who "hold up" large corporations in class action lawsuits or seek large verdicts in employment disputes are seen as interfering with the autonomy of individualism and the right to make a profit. They are demonized as the antithesis of American competitiveness.

Conclusion

As we have seen from the chapter on the neuropsychology of conflict, almost our entire behavior comes from goals that are triggered without conscious thought. Thus, one way of looking at culture is as the accumulation of consistent, automatic goals shared among people. Processes, evaluations, and interpretations that seem to be automatic, uncontrollable results of the social environment drive behaviors. When everyone in the group shares a common understanding, strikingly similar behaviors result. These complex behaviors constitute what is commonly referred to as culture. These behaviors are acquired from individual experience and from peers and ancestors. Once acquired, these "cultural" goals do not require conscious focus to become activated. Instead, they are triggered by events or people, bypassing awareness altogether. Culture is not a reductionistic way of grouping people, but is a shorthand term for a complex set of shared understandings, experiences, histories, and rules of behavior.

Gender is culturally created, not inherent in biological sex. Women and men are not different in conflict management or negotiation behaviors, contrary to common beliefs. Differences in conflict behavior are due to differences in power, status, and role as opposed to gender-based distinctions.

Three themes of American culture create a chronic conflict that accelerates acute conflicts. These themes, competition, individualism, and republicanism, appear as core values, but carry deep, hidden costs. The legal system is designed to support these themes so there should be no great wonder that litigation is not a peacemaking process.

Finally, the legal system generally either ignores the subtleties of culture or assumes that culture is homogenous. Thus, lawyers generally do not consider the interplay of culture and conflict in the disputes that clients bring to them. If they do consider culture and conflict as relevant to a dispute, they rarely have the tools to understand how to deal with it. A lawyer as a peacemaker, on the other hand, will be sensitive to the possibility that culture and conflict are intertwined in a dispute.

Reflections on Chapter Nine

You are the chair of a large nonprofit private social services agency. Your board of directors is extremely diverse, reflecting the broader community. The board consists of three Afro-Americans (one man and two women), three Hispanics (two men and one woman), a Cambodian man, a Hmong woman, two white males, and three white females. A conflict has developed within the board over decision-making processes. Some board members tend to dominate the discussions, leaving others feeling like they are being pressured to remain silent. Others are uncomfortable with the apparent lack of cohesion and consensus building. Some members seem to thrive on vigorous and loud arguments, while others are repelled by that type of behavior. The agency provides important services to the community; therefore, a strong, committed board is essential.

Using the materials in this chapter, prepare an analysis of how the cultures of the board members might be contributing to the conflict.

If you suspect that the cultural diversity might be one cause of the divisiveness, what techniques, processes, or ideas can you develop to transform the conflict?

How does the law deal with conflicts arising from cultural diversity? When are legal solutions effective? When are they ineffective?

CHAPTER TEN

JUSTICE

*T*HE DISPUTE WAS BETWEEN an owner and a contractor. The contractor had agreed to build a turnkey gas station-market for the owner with a completion date of June 1. The completion date was important because it would allow the owner to capture a large seasonal business. By June 1, the project was not complete, but the parties agreed that the owner could take possession so as to not lose the summer business.

Nevertheless, the ongoing construction made operations difficult and inconvenient for customers. Furthermore, the computer system operating the entire business was discovered to be giving away free gasoline. The owner requested a conference with the contractor. At the meeting, the contractor denied liability. The owner refused to pay any further on the contract, and the contractor pulled off the job. Litigation ensued.At mediation, the owner stated that he would not pay a dime to the contractor. "It just isn't fair that he receive a dime more!" the owner exclaimed. The contractor said, " I know you are unhappy with the job, but most of the problems were caused by you. I want simple justice. Just pay me what I'm owed and we'll call it quits."

The case settled, but not quickly and not easily, because principles were more important than money.

Introduction

Strangely enough, unless law students take a class in Jurisprudence or Theory of Law, they are not exposed to theories of justice.

Instead, they seem to absorb an understanding of justice from the many cases they study. In a recent class of senior law students, I asked the question, "Someone please give me a definition of justice." No student could come up with an answer and many felt embarrassed. Their embarrassment was understandable, but their ignorance was not their fault. Other than learning the substantive development of due process and equal protection, law students learn little about justice.

At best, their understanding of justice is incomplete. As lawyers, they learn soon enough that the court system is not interested in administering substantive justice, having a hard enough time assuring everyone that procedural justice is reasonably fair.

If peacemaking holds to higher values, then surely one of its values must be to work toward justice. But the problem is, what justice? Defined by whom? And how is justice, if achieved in a peacemaking process, to be measured.

This chapter does not answer those questions, but it does provide some foundational knowledge about justice from which answers might be developed. We will look, for example, at the three classical theories of justice: Positive Law, Social Good, and Natural Rights. These theories of justice are mutually exclusive from one another, yet their threads are woven into the fabric of common understandings of justice.

Theory is well and good, but how do people perceive justice. The sociological research divides into the instrumentalist and subjective schools of study. Instrumentalists claim that delay, cost, and poor outcomes are objective reasons why people are unhappy with lawyers and the civil justice system. The subjectivists, on the other hand, contend that subjective evaluations of justice in a given dispute are more strongly influenced by whether the disputants feel they have been heard. Outcome and delay do not seem, at the end of a conflict, to matter as much as being listened to. We look at some of this research.

Alternative Dispute Resolution in general and mediation in particular has critics. A group of scholars, legal and otherwise, assert that mediation does not help the poor and disenfranchised. Furthermore, by diverting cases out the court system, some critics contend that informal procedures deprive society of the ability to develop the law. These critiques have suggested that justice is not always served by non-adversarial process, particularly in cases of extreme power imbalances.

Why Justice?

The basic problem that has to be solved by social cooperation is that everyone cannot have everything they want at the same time. Similarly, people cannot act as they please or live in families, groups, or communities that always follow the policies they prefer. Finally, people cannot always have their preferred status or social position. Thus, people must be willing to accept outcomes, policies, and status that are not personally most desirable for themselves or their group.

Justice has evolved as a concept to regulate cooperative efforts between people within a group and between groups of people. Justice specifies reasonable solutions to conflicts that arise among people trying to coordinate their values and behaviors. Principles of justice, therefore, govern the coordination of social interaction (Tyler and Blader, 2000). The fundamental question is whether the rules of social coordination specified by justice effectively manage conflict resolution. Finally, for justice to be effective, it must shape people's behaviors, separating judgments about what is right from what is personally beneficial. Justice must motivate acceptance of decisions and efforts to help the group even when those decisions and efforts are contrary to individual or group self-interest. Thus, in terms of social coordination, justice has little value if it does not influence how people feel and what they do.

Common Threads of Justice

To begin our consideration of justice, think about how the word is used. In one respect, justice is a social norm (Bird, 1967). Justice sets forth a standard of conduct or behavior, such that a person, act, or decision may be called just. As will be seen, justice as a social norm varies according to the theory of justice. In Positive Law theory, for example, justice as a norm means conformity to law, while in Social Good theory it means good for the most.

In another respect, justice is approbative. That is, we measure someone or some act as good or bad based on our ideas of justice. We say that a person is just or the decision is just, implying that the person or decision is good. In this sense, justice is descriptive of a character or attribute valued by society.

In a final respect, justice is obligatory because of a duty to do justice. Similar to justice as a social norm, the obligatory aspect of justice varies according to theory. In Positive Law theory, justice as an obligation simply means obedience to law. Under Natural Right theory, justice as an obligation means respect for the rights of others.

Justice also involves the idea of rights. A right is a command or claim for something due and which other agents are obligated in conscience not to frustrate. This definition contains three elements. First, there is an object, something that is due by possession of a right. As the owner of my house, I have the right to privacy, to be secure against trespass, to sell it, or give it away. The objects in these cases consist of forbearances by others or actions that I can perform such as selling or conveying.

Second, there is the subject of the right, the agent who possesses it. Thus, I, as the owner of my house, possess the right to it. The right is something, therefore, that someone possesses.

Third, there is an obligation imposed upon others to respect my right and to observe it either by way of forbearance or positive action. Thus, corresponding to the possession of my home ownership, there is a duty imposed upon others not to interfere with my quiet use and enjoyment of my house.

A problem in discussing justice and peacemaking is understanding the aspect of usage. Are we considering justice as social norm, approbation, obligation, or a combination? Are we discussing justice in terms of rights? If so, what aspect of rights is in contention? To make matters more complicated, people and scholars tend to confuse the aspects of justice as defined by the particular theories of justice. Thus, justice may mean to one person that the law is obeyed, while to another it means equitable distribution of wealth. If these two try to evaluate whether peacemaking attains justice, they will be doomed to endless argument. Thus, the first step is to establish some clear vocabulary and a common conceptual framework of justice.

Classical Theories of Justice

The Positive Law Theory of Justice

Positive Law makes three claims. First, justice depends on law. Justice is therefore supremely objective and measurable. Second, because the law takes precedence over justice, justice cannot measure law. That is, no law can be unjust. Finally, the law provides the whole measure of justice so that justice is nothing more than conformity to law. A person who obeys the law is said to be just and a decision that conforms to law is said to be a just decision, regardless of outcome.

Positive Law theorists have a distinctly negative view of the nature of humanity. Cooperation is not considered a natural state. Instead, humans are considered essentially aggressive, and, lacking controls, would oppose each other for their own advantage. Thus, Thomas Hobbes, a Positive Law advocate, claimed that the life of all in a state of nature is "solitary, poor, nasty, brutish, and short" (Hobbes, 1651, p. 65). The "state of nature," exists when there is no society or civilization. It is a state of brutal, personal competition and therefore a state of war. In Hobbes' view, the only possible way out of this condition is through law. Consequently, peace equates to law. In this sense, Positive Law theory aspires only to a negative peace, not a positive peace.

Law, to be meaningful, must be supported by coercive power. Hobbes wrote that "there must be some coercive power to compel men equally to the performance of their covenants." As long as "there is a fear of not performance on either part," there can be no justice. Thus, justice depends on a superior, coercive power.

Power derives from government, formed by men and women to order their relations with one another. Consequently, Hobbes called government the Leviathan to emphasize its superior power over individuals. A "social contract," or common agreement among people to abandon their "state of nature," creates the Leviathan. According to Hobbes, each person implicitly says to every other person, "I give my right to govern myself to this assembly on the condition that you too surrender your right to govern yourself to the assembly. From this covenant, a governing legislature is created—the Leviathan. The Leviathan has so much power that it can overwhelm any person breaking the covenant. It therefore maintains peace through coercion. Punishment becomes necessary to enforce the social contract because without punishment, the power of the Leviathan is nonexistent.

From this proposition, Positive Law theorists develop the entire scheme of property rights, individual rights, and government rights. Without a superior coercive power, these rights cannot exist. In a state of nature, rights only exist for those individuals with superior power.

Since justice depends on law, for different civil societies there are different justices. Because each society defines its own laws, justice is relative not absolute. Thus, a democratic society has "democratic justice," an oligarchic society has "oligarchic justice," and a totalitarian society has "totalitarian justice." Positive law is not concerned with "goodness" or "rightness" except insofar as it relates to law as a means to order (Bird, 1967). An oppressive law is just because it is law. As will be seen, this view is sharply criticized by many social justice advocates.

Positive Law theory uniquely claims that positive law, independent of any other measure, establishes the only norm of justice. However, law is independent of justice, and justice is not an ideal that positive law realizes in practice. Hobbes claims that "no law can be unjust." Stated more precisely, no positive law can be legally unjust. Therefore, the purpose of the law is not to pursue justice in the sense of equality, equity, or need, but to pursue order.

This axiom is counter to many people's views of justice. Most Americans, for example, are taught as school children that the legal system is the source of justice in civil society. Justice in this sense is taught as an equivalent to moral correctness. The Pledge of Allegiance ends with the phrase, "with liberty and justice for all." No one bothers to explain or correct the error later in life, and people are left with a false impression of the law and the legal system. In fact, justice is not a goal or objective of legal positivism. A judicial decision is just when it has been made in a regular fashion and in conformity to the system of rules in force. Outcome is not important, and Positive Law theory does not measure justice by it. In other words, Positive Law theory does not concern itself with the substantive moral correctness of a judicial decision.

In contrast to a judge, a legislator's actions can never be measured as just or unjust. Since justice is determined by conformance to a rule, the legislator's act of creating a rule is above justice. Thus, Positive Law theory restricts many traditional principles of justice to the work of a judge. That work is constrained to deciding cases in conformity to law without regard to moral correctness in the individual circumstance.

In identifying justice with conformity to the law, the Positive Law theory expressly denies the ancient definition of justice as rendering each to his own—*suum cuique,* meaning that one is entitled to a fair share. In essence, Positive Law theory denies the Natural Right theory of justice because natural rights are based on moral obligation. Since moral obligation is subjective, it is always a matter of dispute. According to its advocates, Positive Law is clear, objective, and determinate. It is, according to its advocates, a scientific and empirical standard of justice.

Positive Law theory does recognize an approbative factor in justice. When a person says a law is just or unjust the person is approving or disapproving the law. A Positive Law theorist would not say,

"This law is unjust." Rather, she would say, "This law is unjust because I oppose it" (Bird, 1967). To Positive Law theorists, however, invoking injustice is an emotional expression that turns a demand into an absolute postulate. Therefore, justice has an objective, normative meaning only when it is identical with legality. If justice is attributed to anything but law, it cannot be more than an expression of emotion and subjective belief. Value judgments framed in terms of justice are therefore subjective statements of emotion.

Justice in Positive Law theory consequently has two characteristics. First, justice implies an objective norm of social action. Second, when used approbatively, justice is subjective and relative to the individual.

Positive Law theory also deals with "ought." In other words, it provides an answer to the question, "Why obey the law?" First, positive law embraces a punitive "ought" based on physical punishment. "I ought to do X because if I do not, I will be punished." Second, Positive Law theory embraces an approbative "ought": "I ought to do X because I approve of it."

The punitive aspect of Positive Law requires coercion. Positivists believe that, without coercive power, people will not obey the law. Positive Law theorists, using the language of utilitarianism, contend that if punishment is greater than the benefit obtained from the breach, individuals will be deterred from misbehavior. They soften the coercive necessity required of Positive Law theory by stating that, although justice rests on might, it is also based on the agreement of those who live under it.

Legal positivism, a strand of Positive Law relating directly to law and legal systems, stresses the separation of law and morals (Hart, 1958). Legal positivism states three propositions about the nature of law. First and most important, the law does not have inherent moral value: its existence is independent of the standards that may be used for its evaluation. Second, a legal system is primarily a system of rules. Logically all rules are alike: either their operative facts occur and they apply, or their operative facts do not occur and they do not apply. Finally, the existence of law is a social fact. The question of its existence is empirically ascertainable in the practices of the community (Hart, 1958).

In summary, the Positive Law theory of justice is concerned with order, not with fairness. Justice is measured by obedience to the law, which is presumed to be objectively determined by judges. The Positive Law theory of justice is therefore the narrowest view of justice.

The Social Good Theory of Justice

The Social Good theory of justice is associated with the classical utilitarian philosophers. The Social Good position falls between the Positive Law and the Natural Right theories of justice and shares something with both.

The Social Good theory differs from the Positive Law theory in the relation between justice and law. Social Good theory refuses to identify justice with conformity to law. First, not all violations of law are unjust. Second, law does not completely create justice. Instead, justice furnishes a standard by which laws are declared just or unjust. Finally, some conduct lies outside the law, but is nevertheless measured by justice. For example, a parent may be just or unjust to children in matters where the law leaves the parent free to act without interference.

While Positive Law theory denies a "natural justice" separate from law, Social Good theorists find nothing wrong in such an idea. Hume argues for "natural justice" as a condition of society without civil government and positive law (Hume, 1751). For Hume, unlike Hobbes, both society and justice precede government, and "the state of society without government" is not only conceivable, but it is also "one of the most natural states of man." In this state, contrary to Hobbes, justice is necessary for society.

Under Social Good theory, justice provides a criterion for measuring positive law. When laws become unjust so as to cross all interests of society, Hume declares that they lose all authority. Thus, laws themselves may be just or unjust, opposing the Social Good theory to the Positive Law theory of justice.

Social Good theory claims that justice must be decided in terms of social utility. The origin and basis of justice lies in the good of society; that is, in a good greater than any individual for private good, achievable only through people acting in common, and one in which individuals can find their own good. All laws are just or unjust according to how they promote the social good.

Justice, like the morals of society, evolves out of the demands of living together. This theory emphasizes people and their needs. Unlike the Natural Rights theory, individuals are not naturally just. Instead, like Positive Law, all the rights and rules of justice are entirely made and conferred by society. Consequently, there is no natural right underlying justice.

The judgment that "X is just" says that X conforms to the social good. Thus, it is not a subjective emotion as asserted by the Positive

Law theory. Justice, apart from legality, has an objective basis. Justice is a rule of conduct and a sentiment that sanctions the rule. Sanctions can be both internal and external. Internal sanctions are identified with feelings of duty or conscience; external sanctions are identified with punishment.

The norm of justice is also a moral rule declaring what ought to be done and creates a serious moral obligation. What is just must be done and not merely because failure to do so will result in punishment. The obligation of justice is a duty owed to society resting on the responsibility for the social good.

The Natural Right Theory of Justice

The difference between the Natural Right and the Social Good theories of justice is their basis of justice. While the Social Good theory bases justice on the social good, for Natural Right theory, justice rests on natural rights. Under the Natural Right theory, natural right provides the ultimate criterion of law, furnishes an objective norm for human action, and makes the observance of justice obligatory.

The Natural Right theory is the most complex of the classical theories of justice. More variation is found among its proponents than among those of the other theories. There are three aspects identifying the Natural Right position. The theory denies, first, that justice is identical with legality. It also denies that justice is defined by what is good for society. Instead, Natural Right theory asserts that justice is based on human nature. Thus, justice answers not only to the needs of law and society, but also to the needs of people (Bird, 1967). Human needs underlie the relation of justice to law and to society.

Natural Right proponents deny that justice is exclusively a matter of law and of the social good and assert that justice must serve the interests of humanity. Most, but not all, proponents also assert the existence of natural law.

Natural rights are frequently declared as a number of specific rights. For example, the American Declaration of Independence asserts "that all men . . . are endowed by their Creator with certain inalienable Rights, that among these are Life, Liberty, and the Pursuit of happiness." The French Declaration of the Rights of Man and of the Citizen claims "natural, inprescriptible, and inalienable rights." Natural rights are sometimes understood as rights that people possess as individuals before they form a political society. They belong to people in a state of nature before civilized life. This view of human nature is opposite that of the Positive Law theorists.

Natural rights are also social, since they can only be claimed, exercised, and acknowledged within society. Such rights involve interpersonal relationships, but they are not made by or for society. Natural rights exist because humans are conscious of their existence and able to communicate this consciousness to one another. Although a natural right may exist only in human society, a person possesses it because of innate humanness and not because of citizenship in a given society.

Among some Natural Right theory proponents, equality is paramount. Aristotle is the leading representative of this strand, followed by Aquinas and other writers in the Aristotelian tradition. Equality is most often considered a principle of justice with respect to the exchange and distribution of material goods. For Aristotle, the exchange of goods provides the standard case of justice or injustice. The unjust person, he writes, is the person who "takes more than his share, not of any and all goods, but of those on which good and bad fortune depend" (Rackham, 1934). Aristotle calls such a person unjust. Justice is established, in such a case, when the shares are redistributed so as to bring about equality.

Equality requires a standard of measurement. This standard, Aristotle says, is "in reality demand, which holds everything together, since if men cease to have wants, or if their wants alter, exchanges will be no longer, or will be on different lines." Money has come to represent demand and "provides the measure which makes things commensurable and reduces them to equality."

Equality also represents equal treatment among all human beings. Any departure from it calls for justification. In this sense, the right of equals to equal treatment is what some authors call a prima facie right that cannot be denied or taken away without some justification.

All Natural Right theorists agree that justice provides a criterion of goodness for both society and law. Constitutions, as well as laws, according to Aristotle, "must be good or bad, just or unjust." Constitutions can be classified according to their justice, the best state being the one that has "men who are just absolutely and not according to some particular standard." As possessors of natural rights, people have a basis from which to judge society and its laws. Thus, justice, according to Natural Right theory, is not entirely dependent on law. Some natural right authors, like Locke and Jefferson, claim that natural rights are self-evident. Thus, the task of law is merely to secure their observance.

All Natural Right proponents agree that justice is broader than law. Questions of justice can arise independent of any question of law. Consider the case of an employer who agrees to pay workers a certain wage and then lives up to the agreement, or the case of the chief of a tribe who is hard and severe, but who treats each member impartially according to his or her deeds. In each case there is no question of law at all, but the employer and the tribal chief are just. These are examples of what Aristotle and Aquinas call commutative and distributive justice—justice between private individuals and justice between the head of the community and its members.

Justice, under Natural Rights theory, is an objective norm of human action. Not all justice may be reducible to natural right, but nothing can be just that goes against a natural right. The objectivity of justice derives from human knowledge of fundamental moral principles. Knowledge of such principles is to some a form of rational knowledge. To others, knowledge of moral principles is innate. Under either view, humans have dignity such that what is ultimately due is logically before a social agreement, public law, or institution.

Obligation is an essential element of right because a right requires others to respect it. Obligation in Natural Right theory arises not from the fear of punishment, but from a rational apprehension of what is correct behavior. According to Natural Right theory, one need only appeal to human conscience instead of to the social good or the sanction of law. The Natural Right position does not deny that law and society may enforce justice. Justice concerns an external, objective act that may be done entirely from compulsion and fear of consequences. However, the just act, when coerced, is not the act of the just person because it does not arise from the virtue of justice. It is legal only, and not moral.

What Is Justice?

Each of the three theories has its measures of justice. Accordingly, justice is defined as conformity to the law or doing what is useful for the social good or rendering to each what is one's own or due by right. The following table summarizes these measures.

THEORY	MEASURE	OBLIGATION
Positive Law	Conformity to law	Obedience
Social Good	Most good for the most people	Promote good of society
Natural Rights	Preservation of individual rights	Recognize human rights

The first definition, developed by the Positive Law theory, is the simplest of the three. It claims that justice is nothing more than conformity to law. Both the Social Good and the Natural Right theories disagree with this analysis. One theory asserts that justice is based on social good or social utility, while the other theory asserts natural right.

All theories agree that justice obligates people to do something that is good and that concerns another. Stated in terms of obligation, each theory says justice obliges people to obey the law; justice obliges people to promote the social good; justice obliges people to render to each what is a natural right.

The Natural Right theory asserts all three propositions, but sees the third as controlling. The Social Good theory asserts the first and second proposition, but denies the third, claiming that there is no such thing as a natural right. The Positive Law theory asserts only the first proposition and denies the second and third propositions (Bird, 1967).

The fundamental difference between the theories concerns the relation between justice and society. For all theories, justice is a social virtue and a norm governing one's conduct toward others. One group of theories holds that justice is based exclusively on society and ordered to the good of society or its laws. In contrast, the other group maintains that justice is ultimately based on people, and not on their society.

Classical Justice and Peacemaking

Peacemaking is value-based, meaning that it assumes that relationships are as important as individual rights. The ancient Hebrew concept of shalom expresses the goal of peacemaking: establishing right relationships between people. Peacemaking looks for full or partial reconciliation, apology and forgiveness, recognition and empowerment. Peacemaking helps disputants rise above the tunnel vision created by conflict.

In contrast, Positive Law theory resolves conflict without regard to relationships and solely through application of the law to the facts. Interpersonal relationships are not important; recognition and empowerment are not important; and reconciliation is not important. Applying the justice conceived by Positive Law theory precludes any form of justice based on the relationship of the parties. Instead obedience to law is paramount, with the corollary that coercion to compel obedience is, therefore, justifiable. Positive Law theorists claim that this is fair because it is objective. Moreover, Positive Law focuses disputants on their individual rights and obligations to the exclusion of the other. Thus, Positive Law favors competition over cooperation as a means of resolving conflict.

Social Good theory resolves conflict through an analysis of what is good for society, not for individuals. Thus, specific relationships may be sacrificed for the greater good. Two of the problems with the Social Good theory of justice are defining what is good and who shall be the arbiter of goodness. Peacemaking assumes that the parties themselves are best able to determine how a conflict should be resolved. In peacemaking, reference to a greater good is therefore unnecessary. To the extent that the Social Good theory of justice promotes any activity that tends to benefit society, it will tend to support peacemaking. However, justice in peacemaking is broader than the justice conceived by Social Good theory.

The Natural Rights theory resolves conflict by upholding the inherent rights of individuals. Because of this, however, the theory does not respond well to conflicts arising between natural rights. In addition, the extreme form of Natural Rights is individualism to the exclusion of communitarianism. Therefore, the Natural Rights theory is not necessarily supportive of peacemaking. It may agree with peacemaking as a form of justice as long as natural rights are upheld. If peacemaking requires any compromise of individual rights to achieve reconciliation, the Natural Rights theorists would probably reject it.

Justice, Identity, and Cooperation

One of the basic problems of social living and a root cause of conflict is the constant tension between self-interest and cooperation within groups. Cooperation generally means that a person will put aside his or her self-interest for the betterment of the group. Why do people cooperate, and what conditions cause people not to cooperate? In researching this question, social psychologists have found a strong link between justice, social identity, and cooperation. Thus, justice has importance beyond the theoretical and abstract notions presented in classical theory. Justice fundamentally drives cooperative behaviors.

Those unfamiliar with the academic literature on justice judgments are usually skeptical when hearing that fairness concerns may outweigh the desirability of favorable outcomes when shaping feelings and behaviors within groups. Intuitively, people are expected to be most concerned with how much of a resource they receive, rather than with the processes by which they received it. This outcome-based intuition has led to the myth of self-interest (Miller and Ratner, 1996), which reflects the widely held view that people cooperate to obtain better outcomes. This belief, however, does not correspond to the reality of human motivation.

While people will say that what they seek from groups is goods and resources and will rarely mention fairness, in dispute resolution studies, a favorable outcome plays a small role in post-experience evaluations. Despite the fact that outcome considerations dominated their pre-experience choice among dispute resolution procedures, fairness and quality of treatment weighed far more heavily than the outcome when people evaluated the totality of their experience. Three strands of justice research support this finding: relative deprivation theory, research on distributive justice, and research on procedural justice.

Relative deprivation theory argues that satisfaction in social situations is not a direct function of the objective quality of the rewards or resources received from others. Instead, satisfaction is determined through comparisons between one's own outcomes and some type of standard. Thus, the same objective outcome can be satisfying or dissatisfying depending upon which standard it is compared to. Subjective experience is therefore shaped by the choice of comparison standards.

The research on relative deprivation theory suggests that notions of entitlement or deservedness establish comparison standards. These standards derive from conceptions of a just or fair outcome. In other words, people judge outcomes based on what they think is fair. If people think the outcomes are being fairly distributed, they are more satisfied with the outcome.

Another strand of research concerns distributive justice, or how people view what is a fair distribution of resources. The primary principles of distributive justice are equity, equality, and need. Each principle describes a way to balance contributions against distributions of resources. Morton Deutsch related equity, equality, and need to three crucial but divergent social goals. Economically-oriented groups used the principle of equity to allocate resources. Solidarity-oriented groups used the principle of equality for allocation decisions. Caring-oriented groups based justice on the concept of need.

(Deutsch, 1975). Distributive justice theories focus whether parity exists between the distribution of outcomes and some standard for distributing the outcomes, be it contribution, need, or equal division between the parties.

Distributive justice norms can resolve coordination problems if the norms are accepted and people defer to them when they receive less than what they think they deserve. To the degree that people defer to distributive justice decisions because the decisions are perceived as fair, judgments about distributive justice create social harmony. However, because of the inherent human tendency to exaggerate one's value, achieving subjective fairness through distributive justice is difficult.

Because of the difficulties of distributive justice theory, researchers began to examine procedural justice. Procedural justice theory argues that people will accept outcomes based on the justice of the decision-making procedures. Many studies have confirmed that when third-party decisions are fairly made, people are more willing to accept them voluntarily (Tyler and Blader, 2000). Procedural justice judgments have been found to have an especially important role in keeping agreements. Pruitt and his colleagues studied the factors that led to performance of mediation agreements. They found that the procedural fairness of the initial mediation session was the central cause for people adhering to the agreement six months later (Pruitt, Peirce, McGillicuddy, Welton and Castriano, 1993).

Two explanations have been proposed to describe the importance of procedural justice. One develops from Thibaut and Walker's control model of procedural justice (Thibaut and Walker, 1975). Thibaut and Walker argued that that people want to maximize their control over the decisions determining outcomes. By having influence over the decision, people can control them in way that they perceive is fair to them. However, people usually do not have direct outcome control and must therefore resort to indirect control via procedures that allow presentation of evidence to the decision-makers. Decision control refers to control over the decision, while process control refers to control over the presentation of evidence. According to Thibaut and Walker, how people view justice relates to the control between them and the third-party decision-maker.

In their original analysis, Thibaut and Walker emphasized decision control, viewing process control as an indirect means of exerting decision control. Later research has suggested that process control is often more important to people than decision control (Lind, Lisak, and Conlon 1983). The results of the Lind, Lisak, and Conlon study showed that decision control did not affect fairness judgments. Whether decision control was available or not, process control increased people's perceptions of fairness.

When do people claim injustice? A field study of court-annexed arbitration procedures found that disputants expressing unfairness felt they had too little opportunity to tell their story (Adler, Hensler, and Nelson, 1983). Tyler (1987) showed that process control enhanced procedural justice even when the decision-maker was seen as biased, when he or she was seen as acting in bad faith, and when the outcomes were important. The only sense of injustice arose when the decision-maker did not appear to give consideration to the respondents' views.

In other words, the decision-maker must be seen as giving due consideration to the views expressed, even if he or she is not influenced by those views. The opportunity to tell one's side of the story is a potent factor in enhancing the experience of procedural justice (Conlon, Lind, and Lisak, 1989).

In contrast to Thibaut and Walker, Tyler and Lind have developed a second model to explain feelings of subjective justice. Their relational model (Tyler and Lind, 1992) suggests that evaluations are linked to social bonds. The relational model assumes that people are predisposed to belong to social groups. Consequently, they are very attentive to signs and symbols about their status within groups. People want to understand and maintain the social bonds that exist within their groups and will establish connections if given even the most tenuous basis for group identification. This occurs because positive connections enhance self-esteem.

People are also remarkably sensitive to the politeness and dignity they experience with authorities. Respect signifies status within a group. Consequently, people wish decision-makers to accord them equal status in disputes and conflicts. When they are not treated politely or with dignity, people will complain of injustice.

Finally, evaluation of the authorities' trustworthiness influences judgments about procedural fairness. Group members wish to understand the underlying motivations of authorities, so that future behavior can be predicted. For this reason, trust is a key component of legitimacy. Trust involves questions of security, that is, people's efforts to predict how the authorities will act in the future. Ethical trust is far more important than trust in the authority's competence.

Tyler and Lind's group-value model states that people place importance on three aspects of procedure: the neutrality of the procedures, inferences about the trustworthiness of the motives of the authorities, and the degree to which people are treated with dignity, respect, and politeness during the process. These aspects of process convey identity-relevant information to the parties, such as status, self-esteem, and validation. They are therefore powerful forces in the perception of justice and exceed the importance of both control- and outcome-oriented judgments (Tyler and Blader, 2000).

Can Peacemaking Provide Justice?—Critiques

In any discussion of justice and peacemaking, one must sooner or later confront the Alternative Dispute Resolution (ADR) critics. From 1984 through 1992, in law journals from Yale, Wisconsin, Harvard, Iowa, George Washington, Florida State, and *Law and Social Inquiry*, among others, some scholars seriously questioned both ADR's purported benefits and prevailing methods for evaluating ADR's risks. More particularly, certain critics expressed concern about the effect of informal dispute resolution on racial minorities, women, and the poor. Those critics worried about situations where the participants were of unequal power, the issues were volatile or involved "public rights," and the decision-makers were unconstrained by public scrutiny or a formal record. The critics concluded that ADR was not appropriate for all cases and participants, emphasized the need for access to adjudication, and questioned the political dimensions of ADR.

In this section, we will review the critiques of three scholars: Richard Abel, Owen Fiss, and Richard Delgado. These three provide a useful counterpoint in considering how peacemaking relates to justice issues.

Richard Abel. Richard Abel, a member of the Critical Legal Studies Conference, calls nonjudicial dispute resolution "informalism." He criticizes informalism because, in his view, it reinforces power and authority in society. In Abel's analysis, ADR disempowers rather than empowers people. In an early article, Abel asserted that informalism inhibits social change by persuading disputants to sacrifice their grievances in the interests of peace and cooperation. Informalism "presupposes a high degree of normative consensus on the substantive norms that control behavior outside the legal system" (Abel, 1980, p. 40). He views dispute resolution as depending upon shared values. Abel challenges the assumption of shared values, contending that there is disagreement about social and political values. By concealing this disagreement, Abel contends that ADR stifles have-nots from improving their position. (Delgado, Dunn, Brown, Lee, and Albert,1985)

Abel's later views are more Marxist. In *Conservative Conflict and the Reproduction of Capitalism: the Role of Informal Justice*, Abel argues that informalism shifts power to the more powerful elements in society. Abel contrasts formalism, a product of classical liberal theory, with informalism, which

> expresses positivist theories . . . which justify domination, authority, [and] the exercise of control from above . . . . Classic liberalism is the ideology of the revolutionary phase of capitalism, whereas positivism is the ideology of capitalism triumphant. The movement from formalism to informalism thus reflects and carries forward a shift in power from the less privileged to the more. (Abel, 1981, p. 256)

In another article, Abel argues that "informal institutions neutralize conflict by responding to grievances in ways that inhibit their transformation into serious challenges to the domination of state and capital" (Abel, 1982, p. 280). First, informalism allows the state to control new areas of conflict by attracting disputes that otherwise would have been settled outside the system. As informalism frees up formal state resources, the state can garner more power by assuming control over a greater breadth of cases. Further, informalism fosters dependence , thereby strengthening the state's control over conflict in society.

Informalism neutralizes potentially destabilizing conflict in a third way. By directing conflict into safe channels, the state renders conflict "conservative." Conservative conflict becomes predictable and manageable. By creating an environment that emphasizes cooperation, informalism denies the existence of many conflicts and transforms others into simple misunderstandings. When informalism is unable to suppress conflict, it minimizes the political and structural aspects by controlling who and what can be claimed, where it can be claimed, and against whom claims can be made. Informalism directs attention to interpersonal, neighborhood, and intraclass disagreements, ignoring the conflicts that are important to the oppressed (and likely to threaten the powerful)—conflicts between labor and capital, consumer and producer, polluter and inhabitants of polluted environments. As a result, opportunities for liberating conflict are intentionally suppressed.

For Abel and others, the tension between informalism and justice is irresolvable. Without legal power, the imbalance between individuals and corporations or government agencies cannot be redressed. One cannot have equity and informality at the same time.

Owen Fiss. One major critique asserts that informalism serves private interests at the expense of public interests. This harms minorities, the poor, women, and other disadvantaged groups to the extent that they benefit from formal legal processes.

Owen Fiss is the principal spokesperson for this view (Fiss, 1984). For Fiss, the settlement process may distort justice in a number of ways. First, wealthier parties having access to better counsel and more information are better able to predict litigation outcomes, giving them a superior bargaining position. Second, the poorer party may be in financial need and thus forced to settle for a smaller sum rather than wait for litigation. Finally, the poorer party may be forced to settle simply because she cannot sustain the cost of litigation.

Fiss also warns of the increased danger of conflicts of interest between disputants in settlement proceedings and their representatives. In settlement negotiations, the negotiator shapes the settlement. Fiss implies that lawyers as negotiators will put their personal interests ahead of their clients. In contrast, juries and judges make independent judgments by considering the information provided by representatives. The judicial process, according to Fiss, is less likely to subordinate the interest of the disputant to that of the representative.

Fiss' final concern is that settlement does not support the substantive public goals of adjudication. For Fiss, peace between the parties is not as important as development of the law through litigation. He asserts that judicial officials are

> not to maximize the ends of private parties, nor simply to secure the peace, but to explicate and give force to the values embodied in authoritative texts such as the Constitution and statutes: to interpret those values and to bring reality into accord with them. This duty is not discharged when the parties settle. (1984, p. 1085)

Litigation embodies public values. Fiss points to *Brown v. Board of Education* as an example of the public nature of adjudication, describing that case as an example "in which the judicial power [was] used to eradicate the caste structure." For Fiss, "[c]ivil litigation is an institutional arrangement for using state power to bring a recalcitrant reality close to our chosen ideals" (1984, p. 1089). Because the "chosen ideals" of a liberal democracy include equality and because ADR does not advance those ideals as well as litigation, ADR may harm the disadvantaged.

Richard Delgado. In 1985 and 1988, Richard Delgado and his colleagues examined ADR's informal structure and highlighted the risks of biased treatment for racial minorities, women, and the poor (Delgado, Dunn, Brown, Lee, and Hubbert, 1985). Drawing upon social-psychological theories and studies, they concluded that people are more apt to act on their prejudices in an informal ADR-type setting. In contrast, they argued that the formal structure of the courtroom suppressed biases.

Delgado asserted that informalization may increase class-based prejudice. He observed that the risk of prejudice is greatest where there is direct confrontation between disputants of different power, there are few rules governing the interaction, the setting is closed, and the issue is highly personal.

According to Delgado, informal process is most apt to incorporate prejudice when a person of low status and power confronts a person or institution of high status and power. Delgado says that the dangers increase when the mediator is a member of the superior group or class. In these situations, Delgado believes that minorities and members of other out-groups should choose formal adjudication. In addition, the justice system ought to avoid pressuring them to accept an alternate procedure. Thus, Delgado would restrict ADR to cases involving parties of comparable power and status.

Informal processes also risk prejudice when the issue touches a sensitive or intimate area of life such as culture-based conduct. Thus, Delgado says that many landlord-tenant, interneighbor, and intrafamilial disputes are poor candidates for ADR. When the parties are of unequal status and the question concerns a sensitive, intimate subject, the risks of an outcome colored by prejudice are especially great.

Unlike other critics, Delgado offers suggestions on preventing prejudice from distorting ADR processes. He would require rules that clearly specify the scope of the proceedings. He would forbid irrelevant or intrusive inquiries. Proceedings would be open and subject to some form of higher review. The third-party facilitator or decision-maker should be a professional acceptable to both parties. Any party desiring one should be provided with an advocate, ideally an attorney, experienced with representation before the forum in question. To avoid atomization and lost opportunities to aggregate claims and inject public values into dispute resolution, ADR mechanisms should not be used in cases that have a broad societal dimension. Instead, Delgado states that they should be forwarded to court for appropriate treatment.

Critiques of informal justice disappeared from the academic landscape by the mid-1990s. The fears first raised had not materialized as mediation and arbitration became accepted within the legal community. First, conflicts and disputes were not being diverted out of the courts on a wholesale basis. Parties had to agree to mediation before it could take place. Second, the nature of the mediation process gave the parties more control than they had in court. Finally, user satisfaction seemed to grow with little or no complaints about unfairness or disenfranchisement of the disempowered.

Restorative Justice

Another strand of justice, predominantly relating to criminal justice, has emerged in the form of restorative justice.

A brief history of criminal justice will provide a context for understanding the importance of restorative justice. Early legal systems emphasized restitution between offenders and victims. What we call crimes today were primarily offenses to victims and their families. Thus, while the community had an interest in seeing that the wrong was acknowledged and the offender punished, the offense was not seen as a crime against the state (Van Ness, 1986).

This began to change when William the Conqueror took over all of the land of England after the Norman Conquest. King William parceled the land out to his political supporters and the church and began to assert control over offenses. While ancient justice systems prevented families and communities from destroying each other with violence, William and his descendants were concerned with controlling legal process as a means of political control.

Thus, William's son, Henry I, issued the *Leges Henrici* in 1116, which created thirty judicial districts in England. Jurisdiction in these districts was granted over offenses to the King's Peace—arson, robbery, murder, counterfeiting, and crimes of violence. Criminal violations for the first time were not seen as requiring restitution between victims and offenders, but as offenses against the government. The most serious crimes became known as felonies because they were considered breaches of the fealty owed by all people to the king as guardian of the realm (Berman, 1983). As the king usurped power over criminal offenses, victims lost their ability to have a voice in, or obtain restitution from, offenders. The state's interest was in fixing responsibility for criminal conduct and punishing those found responsible.

Out of the struggle between the kings of England and the nobility came a series of protections for those accused of crimes. The struggle between the monarchy and the nobility for political control lasted for centuries. At times, the nobility was able to extract concessions from the monarchy. The Magna Carta is one notable example in which the concept of a trial by a jury of peers was established. Sometimes, the pendulum swung the other way, such as when Henry VII created the Star Chamber to control rebellious nobility through confessions obtained secretly and by torture. The corrective to the Star Chamber was the Habeas Corpus Act of 1679 and establishment of the English Bill of Rights in 1688 (Berman, 1983). Eventually, these protections were included within the United States Constitution Bill of Rights.

After the state gained complete control over crime and punishment, the field of criminology emerged. Criminology is the study of crime, criminals, methods of punishment, and methods to reduce criminal offense. The classical school of criminology arose in the eighteenth century and emphasized free will, rationalism, and utilitarianism. Punishment was seen as a deterrent on the assumption that people were rational decision-makers and would avoid pain. Thus, people would not commit crimes if the punishment for the crime were sufficiently severe (Van Ness, 1986).

Classical criminology was challenged in the late nineteenth century by the positivist school of criminology. Founded by Italian sociologists, this school believed that there were biological and environmental explanations for crime.

The ultimate objective of both schools of criminology was to reduce crime through punishment. Punishment is the intentional infliction of pain by the state on a human being and is justified by those who believe it helps to define values that we live by. In addition, punishment is said to protect freedom by punishing those who break the law. At various times in modern history, punishment has been used to deter criminal conduct, to rehabilitate offenders, and to incapacitate offenders.

The problem with the criminal justice system is that it simply does not work. If deterrence were effective, we would have less people in prison rather than the record numbers of prisoners present today. If rehabilitation were effective, crime rates and recidivism would be falling, not rising. Finally, if incapacitation is the purpose, why does the state imprison so many people who are either guilty of. social crimes such as drug use or who are people unlikely to recommit an offense. Furthermore, the burden on the taxpayers is staggering. Finally, the victim's voice has been lost.

The restorative justice movement arose as a response to these concerns. Restorative justice describes both a movement and a philosophy, but is not well defined from a theoretical or legal viewpoint. The literature describes restorative justice in terms of participants (Zehr, 1990), purposes (Van Ness and Strong, 1997), and processes (Umbreit, 1994), emphasizing the roles of the victim, offender, and the community. Restorative justice purposes include such concepts as reconciliation, shalom, and tsedeka (Bianchi, 1991). Restorative justice processes are embodied in victim-offender reconciliation, victim-offender mediation, negotiated restitution, community justice conferencing, family justice conferencing, and reintegrative shaming (Braithwaite, 1989).

In essence, restorative justice is a way of responding to conflict, misbehavior, and crime that makes things as right as possible for all affected. Restorative justice includes recognizing the conflict or harm, repairing the damage (physical and relational) as much as possible, and creating future accountability plans and agreements that will prevent the same thing from happening again.

Restorative justice is based on a number of philosophical principles (Claassen, Kader, Tilkes, and Noll, 2000). First, restorative justice is about making things as right as possible for all people. Restorative justice recognizes that conflict causes injury for every person entangled in it. Therefore, the primary goal should be to restore relationships. In contrast to retributive justice, restorative justice is not interested in punishment for punishment's sake. People are healed not by watching "justice" meted out by verdicts or imprisonment, but by working to understand each other and honestly trying to make things right.

Restorative justice responds in ways that build safe and healthy communities. Restorative justice believes that the government has the duty to maintain order, while the community has the duty to maintain peace. Thus, restorative justice processes encourage community participation and involvement in all conflicts affecting the community and its members. Restorative justice empowers disputants, offenders, and their communities to assume central roles in recognizing harm, repairing damages, and creating a safe and civil future. Restorative justice also recognizes and encourages the role of community organizations— including the academic, education, and religious/ faith communities—in teaching and establishing the moral and ethical standards that build up the community.

Restorative justice prefers to deal cooperatively and constructively with conflicts, disputes, and offenses at the earliest possible time and before they escalate. Nevertheless, restorative justice is not permissive. In this regard, restorative justice holds disputants and offenders accountable to recognize the harm they have caused and to repair damages as much as possible.

Restorative justice prefers maximum use of voluntary and cooperative response options and minimum use of force and coercion. Under restorative justice, governmental authorities provide oversight, assistance, and coercive backup when individuals are not cooperative.

Restorative justice is measured by its outcomes, not its intentions. Do participants emerge from the restorative justice response feeling respected and safe? Are they motivated and empowered to live constructive and civil lives? Are they living in community in a way that demonstrates an acceptable balance of freedom and responsibility? Are responses by authorities, community, and individuals respectful, reasonable, and restorative for everyone?

Restorative justice is contrary to many of the propositions asserted by the classical theories of justice. Restorative justice rejects positivism outright, claiming that justice is measured by outcome, not intentions. Restorative justice is strongly relational and communal. It therefore does not concentrate on the social good, but on the relationships between the disputants. Restorative justice assumes that if personal relationships are right, the community will be a better place. Restorative justice also deviates from positivism and social good theory because it rejects coercion as the principal tool of social control.

Restorative justice does not focus on natural rights either. Natural rights theory leads to a strong preference for individual freedom and autonomy. Restorative justice prefers community to individualism, reconciliation over technical assertion of rights, and attention to the other rather than attention on self.

Conclusion

Audi alteram partem: "Hear the other side."

Justice raises a number of questions. Some of them are:

What values should peacemaking serve? Does peacemaking fulfill the classical theories of justice? How should we measure the "quality" of justice? Does peacemaking provide a subjectively favorable experience of justice? Does peacemaking respond to Abel, Delgado, and Fiss? If so, how? When is peacemaking appropriate? When is adversary process appropriate?

Peacemaking, by its very philosophy, cannot meet all definitions of justice. If peacemaking strives to serve positive law theory, then the peacemaking process is relegated to seeking obedience to laws, without regard to outcome fairness. If peacemaking strives for social good, the definition of what is good must be answered. Furthermore, can peacemaking tolerate a poor outcome for one party that in the larger context is good for society? If peacemaking strives to elaborate justice based natural rights, how are conflicting rights reconciled? If one side's natural rights must be subordinated to the other side's rights, has justice been met?

These questions cannot be answered in the abstract. Each conflict presents its own challenges and measures of justice. Thus, no objective measure of justice is possible or desirable. What seems most important is to realize the ephemeral and subjective nature of justice. Justice is what a person feels is fair to him or her. In peacemaking, we should therefore strive to see that each party to a conflict is dealt with as objectively and fairly as possible and has the opportunity to feel that justice was achieved. We should be deeply concerned whenever a party in a peacemaking process feels injustice at the hands of the peacemaker.

When dealing with injustices arising from the conflict, peacemakers should keep in mind the slippery nature of justice. By understanding the theories of justice, peacemakers can help parties articulate their feelings of injustice. One possibility is to encourage parties to talk about their notions of justice. People can be engaged to discuss justice in terms of fairness and equal treatment. Oftentimes, a strong sense of injustice will be intertwined with identity issues, such as loss of face and disrespect. Once stated explicitly, the injustices can more easily be separated, respected, and processed appropriately.

Justice implies a different perspective for peacemakers than is held by lawyers in general. In peacemaking, the perception of substantive justice, being treated fairly and equally, is as important as procedural justice. Lawyer peacemakers cannot easily shrug off a compromise settlement that ends a lawsuit, but does not address deeper injustices. This is especially true when the parties will have a future relationship. Thus, the responsibility to assure that the parties are experiencing justice in the peacemaking process is much greater than found in traditional lawyering.

Reflections on Chapter Ten

In what circumstances will the parties be able to formulate an agreement to a dispute that each sees as fair and just?

Does the law guarantee justice? Analyze this question carefully.

What do clients expect when they are asking for justice?

What questions might you develop in helping clients to articulate their justice goals?

How does American culture create justice conflicts?

How can you, as a lawyer-peacemaker, explain justice to eighth graders without allowing them to become cynical?

CHAPTER ELEVEN

CONFLICT BEHAVIOR

Theoretical Considerations

IN CONFLICT, PEOPLE ENGAGE EACH other with, among other things, their words, tone of voice, and actions. These are called conflict behaviors and can escalate, suppress, ignore, or resolve disputes. Conflict behaviors are generally not consciously chosen, but emerge as a repertoire of actions that have been learned since childhood from everyday encounters, arguments, and disputes. Most people use their full range of conflict behaviors to one degree or another but, depending upon the nature of the conflict, prefer particular behaviors over others. Most conflict behaviors are automatic. They occur without conscious choice, but are explained and rationalized after the fact by the causal operator. In thinking about conflict behaviors, keep in mind that the parallel model of cognitive processing involves the simultaneous events of perception, evaluation, and motivation.

Many factors influence conflict behaviors, including the other party's behavior, the context of the conflict, the goals being sought, the concerns for one's own goals versus one's concern for the other party's goals, and so forth. Because conflict is emotional, conflict behavior occurs preconsciously and without conscious control or choice. As we become aware of how we are acting, we can choose to change. Nevertheless, because of the intensity of the moment, consciously changing behaviors may simply be too difficult. Furthermore, we may intend to deal with the conflict in one manner only to find ourselves reacting to the style of our antagonist in a different manner. This is because much of our conflict behavior is preconsciously triggered and is scripted by our experiences during childhood emotional development and adult life experiences.

Conflict Schemas

Schemas are an examples of automaticity at work. As we have seen, schemas are storage systems that preserve specific emotional learning such as resentment at feeling treated unfairly. Within these storage systems are the corresponding range of behaviors that we have been learned to be sensitive to, as well as how to act when the experience is triggered. These storage systems preserve what has been learned, but are continually updated by life experience. They lie dormant in the preconscious mind waiting for a trigger, then release the old feelings and old responses automatically, without conscious thought or choice.

A conflict schema is a powerful set of negative thoughts and feelings that develop because of unpleasant, threatening, or debilitating relationship experiences. Many schemas develop during childhood and persist through adulthood. To keep these schemas in check, people develop schema strategies or defenses. The strategies provide at least partial solutions to an early life problem—such as working hard to please a critical parent or being gregarious to avoid rejection by other kids (Bennett-Goleman, 2001). Every conflict schema is an attempt gone awry to fulfill basic needs of life: safety, connection to others, autonomy, competence, and so forth. When these needs are met, a child will thrive. When they are denied, conflict schemas take root.

Each conflict schema has its own emotional, gut wrenching feeling that takes over when the schema grips a person. These feelings may repeat the emotions experienced during earlier traumatizing events. During conflict schema episodes, people once again plunge into abject fear, rage, or depression. The paradox of conflict schemas is that they revolve around compelling needs, but lead people to act and think in ways that keep those needs from being fulfilled.

Bennett-Galeman (2001) identifies a number of maladaptive schemas. They are maladaptive because they usually trigger feelings and behaviors that are inappropriate for the context in which they arise. Because they occur preconsciously and automatically, however, people have difficulty controlling them.

Abandonment results from reactions to loss. The constant fear is that one will be abandoned. This schema can arise from childhood experiences, either actual—such as a parent dying or divorcing— or symbolic such as an emotionally distant parent. For people with this schema, the prospect of being alone brings up deep feelings of sadness and isolation, with resulting fear and panic.

Deprivation creates a deep sadness and hopelessness stemming from the belief that one will never be understood or cared for. People with deprivation schemas often feel angry about their needs being ignored. Their anger covers an underlying loneliness. This schema is characterized by unrelenting demands that cannot be satisfied.

Subjugation concerns the feeling that one's needs in an intimate relationship never take priority. People with this schema will give up easily but build a reservoir of resentment that will develop into anger and then outrage. This schema will be triggered by preconsciously perceived threats to autonomy by outside authorities. Strategies include not making commitments or decisions because they symbolically invoke the old feelings of entrapment. In conflict, these people would rather prolong the dispute than make a decision to resolve it.

Mistrust derives from a core belief that people cannot be trusted. Along with mistrust comes its emotional component, quickness to not just anger, but rage. People with this schema are constantly vigilant, fearing that they will be exploited or betrayed. The mistrust schema can be primed in several subtle ways. It can take the form of an ongoing belief that people have ulterior motives. Thus, any outreach will be rejected as manipulative.

Unlovability manifests itself in bouts of shame and humiliation. Two strategies dominate this schema. Some people give in to their deep sense of unworthiness and lack any self-esteem or self-confidence. Others hide their feelings with arrogance, bravado, and public recognition.

Exclusion concerns how people feel about their status in groups, whether at work, in the family, in circles of friends, or even at meetings or parties. The core message interpreted through this schema is, "You are not like us, and we do not like you." Typical emotions include anxiety and deep sadness at being alone. Anxiety over being scrutinized makes this person socially awkward. The schema strategies are again paired. One strategy is simply to withdraw. Another strategy is to concoct an in-your-face outcast role, such as those some adolescents adopt. The message is, "I'm different, I don't belong, and I don't care." This type of statement is, of course, an internal lie.

Vulnerability is caused by a sense of loss of control. People in the grip of this schema feel that some catastrophe is about to strike as ordinary fears escalate out of control. As an important adaptive behavior, worrying prepares people to weigh risks. However, it becomes maladaptive as a schema when it paralyzes action.

Failure invokes feelings of deep self-doubt and sadness. While the unlovability schema stems from feeling flawed as a person, the failure schema centers on achievement and career. One feels that success is undeserved. In conflicts, the failure schema is often accompanied by avoidant behavior. The sense is, "I am not competent to handle this conflict. Therefore, to avoid being the fool, I will avoid it."

Perfectionism is the other side of failure. While the failure schema invokes a sense of inability, the perfectionism schema creates a sense needing to meet unrealistically high standards. To blunt the possibility of criticism, these people drive themselves to work much harder than they have to. Of course, no matter how hard one tries, it is never good enough. This schema drives workaholics, whose slightest imperfections or failures result in self-criticism and self-reproach. Some of these people try to hold others to the same high standards they apply to themselves. As a result, they are critical of what they perceive as the failings of others, even when those people have done a perfectly adequate job.

Entitlement schemas are particularly difficult. People with these schemas feel so special that the rules do not apply to them. Entitlement schemas place people above the rest such that social conventions and laws simply do not apply to them. This schema should be distinguished from the healthy confidence that genuine ability creates. Well-grounded pride allows people to stretch themselves toward more difficult challenges. In contrast, the entitlement schema leads people to exaggerate their abilities by a false pride. The emotional behavior accompanying this schema is anger when people deny requests or set limits.

These schemas tend to operate in clusters, making maladaptive behaviors more complicated. However, schemas tend to be repetitive in that reactions to triggering events become predictable. Furthermore, schema attacks occur without conscious thought. The telltale signs of a schema attack are an overreaction that is very quick, very strong, very inappropriate, and on closer examination, reveals a symbolic meaning that triggers the schema. The neurological basis for schema attacks lies in the amygdala, which we learned about in chapter 6. The amygdala seems to act as a schema warehouse and contains past emotional traumas and the reactions to them. When a match occurs between a past distressing event and the amygdala's perception of the current situation, the schema is activated or triggered. As we have seen, the problem is that the amygdala's processing is down-and-dirty so that it is often inaccurate in its perception and reaction. This is fine for avoiding rattlesnakes, but not so adaptive in ambiguous social situations. Brain studies show that a hot amygdala, one that is highly activated, impairs our ability to turn off negative thoughts and emotions. Consequently, against conscious choice, we engage in maladaptive behaviors. This process is the primary cause of conflict behaviors.

Blake and Mouton's Conflict Management Grid

In 1964, Blake and Mouton (1964) proposed five ways managers handled organizational conflict. Those ways were described as avoiding, accommodating, compromising, competing, and problem solving. In 1970, they expanded their idea by stating that these five behavior types covered all possible conflict strategies. They defined each strategy on a two-dimensional grid showing how the relative concern for one's own goals versus one's concern for the other's goals determined conflict behavior. The grid looked as follows:

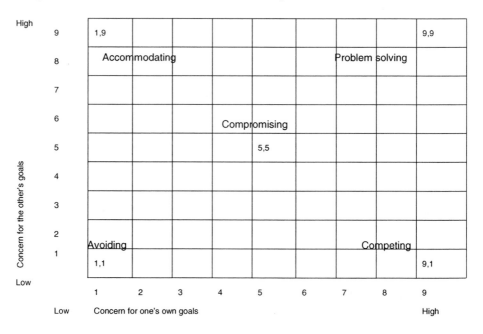

Blake and Mouton developed their theory based on five locations of conflict behavior: 1,1 (Avoiding), 1,9 (Accommodating), 5,5

(Compromising), 9,9 (Problem solving), and 9,1 (Competing). These five behaviors resulted from low, intermediate, and high levels of concerns for personal and the other person's goals.

For example, in the 1,1 corner, a person has a very low concern for both personal goals and the goals of others. Typically, this person will stay away from controversy, will turn away from disagreement, or will remain neutral. Likewise, high concern for the goals of another and low concern for one's own goals, shown as 1,9, demonstrates accommodating behavior such as cajoling, appeals to reason, and appeasement.

A critically important point must be reemphasized: these conflict behaviors are not rationally or consciously chosen. They are only descriptions of observed behaviors, not explanations for what triggered them. In other words, most people do not consciously weigh their concern for personal goals against their concern for another person's goals, then decide what conflict behavior is most appropriate. Schemas invoke schema strategies, which are then described as conflict behaviors. Thus, preconscious brain processing is the source of conflict behavior, not rational, conscious choice. Nevertheless, examining these conflict behaviors is important so that they can be recognized and dealt with.

Van de Vliert (2000) observed that the grid really portrayed four aspects of conflict behavior. The first aspect of the grid is a five part typology of conflict behaviors, illustrated as follows:

Accommodating		Problem solving
	Compromising	
Avoiding		Competing

This aspect emphasizes descriptions of what people do in conflict.

Competing. Competing is satisfying one's own concerns while disregarding the other's concerns. This is usually a preconscious reaction based on how a schema cluster filters a situation. Parties often make their own demands apparent, then hide their true motives and any other information that might weaken their position. Competing people are quite active in conflict and aggressively pursue personal goals. A competing style is typically not very flexible as people avoid sacrificing any goals (Rubin, Pruitt, and Kim, 1994). Competing is typically seen in two strategies. The first, *forcing*, occurs when one party simply coerces others to go along. There is neither concern for understanding other's position nor any attempt to build a future re-lationship.

The second form of competing is *contending*. Contending is softer than forcing because it has an element of flexibility. Typically, a con-tender will be flexible as long as flexibility does not block her goals. A contender may also express understanding and sympathy for other's feelings. Unlike forcing, contending shows concern for future relationships.

Superiors typically use a competing style over inferiors when the outcome of the conflict is important to the superior. Conscious com-peting, especially forcing, is particularly useful in emergencies or when a decision must be made quickly. Competing is disadvanta-geous, however, when future working relationships are important or where the cooperation of the other is required. No person enjoys re-strictions on personal autonomy, and every person wants both posi-tive and negative face to be respected. The coercive nature of com-peting therefore carries a heavy cost of surveillance and the need to enforce threats when resistance is met. Competing is also not partic-ularly effective in conflicts between equals because resentment will result in a breakdown of the relationship (Rubin, et al., 1994).

Accommodating. Accommodators give in to others to preserve a bad relationship or improve a good relationship (Rubin, et al., 1994). Accommodators are highly flexible, as they will accede to the other's demands. They tend to empower others while suspending personal control. Again, this is usually the result of preconscious schema clus-ters being triggered by some aspect of the current situation.

Yielding is the first variation of accommodation (Rubin, et al., 1994). Yielders will demonstrate apathy toward the conflict, showing no concern with their own needs. They tend to accommodate the other's needs entirely, allowing the other to control the outcome of the conflict.

The second variation of accommodation is conceding. Conced-ers maintain contact with the issues and accommodate now to build a better future relationship.

Accommodation is a useful strategy when relationships are more important than the issues underlying the current conflict. Skill-fully employed, accommodation can convey an understanding of the other's needs to improve the relationship. On the downside, ac-commodation may be seen by the other as weakness and encourage a more competitive approach. Accommodation is also a poor style when it results from the fear of facing difficult conflict issues.

Avoiding. Parties who avoid conflict do not demonstrate concern for their own or other's interests. Avoiding prevents these interests from being aired and addressed. Of course, if one expects to lose a conflict, avoidance is not a bad choice. Even in this circumstance, however, issues will remain unresolved and latent conflict will boil beneath the surface. Avoiding disputes disempowers others by denying the possibility of dealing with the conflict. Thus, avoidant behavior can escalate a conflict because it can be so frustrating for others to deal with.

The first variation on an avoiding style is protecting (Rubin, et al., 1994). Protecting emerges when parties wish to avoid conflict at all costs. They build a shell around themselves and respond with a strong counterattack designed to warn others off. Protecting involves very low disclosure and flexibility, as people in this style do not want to work with the conflict at all.

A second variation on the avoiding style is withdrawing (Rubin, et al., 1994). In withdrawing, parties keep issues off the table, but show somewhat more flexibility than protectors. Withdrawing is more subtle than protecting as withdrawers find ways to change or leave the conversation.

Smoothing is a third duration of avoiding (Rubin, et al., 1994). Smoothers play down differences and emphasize issues on which there are common interests. They avoid issues that might cause hurt feelings or arouse anger. Sometimes, this behavior is appropriate to keep the situation relatively calm. It becomes a problem when used to evade difficult issues.

Sometimes parties avoid conflicts because they have the power to simply ignore issues. In cases such as these, the other party is forced to escalate, oftentimes to litigation, to provoke a response. In such cases, avoiders become indignant and quite often turn into competitors.

Compromising. Compromising requires both parties to give up some of their needs to fulfill others. The compromiser looks for an intermediate position in which some important goals can be reached in exchange for trading off others. Compromisers show moderate flexibility as they do relent on some of their demands. They empower themselves and others because shared control is necessary to the give and take necessary for compromise.

Firm compromising offers tradeoffs, but shows limited flexibility and low-to-moderate disclosure (Rubin, et al., 1994). In this style, compromisers push, showing a tough approach designed to motivate others to cooperate. Firm compromisers are actively involved in the conflict and often take the lead in hammering out agreements.

Flexible compromisers tend to share thoughts and decisions, seeing give and take as an evolutionary process (Rubin, et al., 1994). They tend to have less well-defined positions and may allow others to take the initiative in negotiation.

Compromising is often confused with problem solving because tradeoffs and exchanges seem like integrative behavior. Compromising is advantageous when two equally strong parties are locked in impasse. However, compromise often results in a low commitment to agreements because parties must give up something they value. In many types of litigation, cases are settled through compromise. While the lawyers may be satisfied with the result, clients are often displeased with the agreements and processes used to reach them.

Problem Solving. Problem solving has received attention because its goal is to meet all the important needs of both parties. Successful problem solving does not have any significant disadvantages. Problem solving is difficult to maintain during a conflict because the emotions of the situation trigger other schema strategies. Nevertheless, parties are generally pleased after successful problem- solving sessions, and this satisfaction promotes a high commitment to keep agreements.

Problem solvers are highly concerned with both their own and the others needs. They are involved in the conflict, seeking understanding of every issue and exploring all possible integrative solutions. They are flexible because they do not rigidly adhere to positions. However, they are also committed to achieving their goals and will not sacrifice them. Problem solving works best when parties have high aspirations for the outcome of the conflict, insist that their goals and needs be satisfied, and are flexible about how this is done (Rubin, et al., 1994).

Problem solving requires a high degree of information about issues, needs, and interests. Thus, problem solving requires an open, safe, and secure communication climate. Problem solving also requires mutual empowerment without sacrificing individual power bases. This is most easily accomplished when both parties have common power resources.

Problem solving requires a great deal of time and energy. Creativity is not easy. Consequently, it does not work well when time is limited or there is pressure to act immediately. In some circumstances, problem solving favors the stronger party and, therefore, raises fairness and justice concerns. In addition, problem solving can increase aspirations so that if a timely solution is not achieved, the process may be abandoned. Finally, apparent problem solving may be used to cover up or justify the use of force by a stronger party.

Style Effectiveness. Studies in organizational development show that forcing is generally more successful when there is one best solution. Forcing also works when a value conflict exists between a superior and an inferior. Inferiors often accept forcing if the superior is fair and can give objective reasons for forcing a solution.

Problem solving has been most successful when the parties are highly interdependent and must work together in the future. Problem solving is also effective when there is mutual awareness of the potential for destructive conflict. Problem solving works when people are open-minded and willing to ignore power issues. Problem solving has also worked when the conflict is detected early, and one or more parties initiate problem solving before conflict escalates. Finally, problem solving is effective when focused on a common problem rather than defeating or adopting one party's preferred solution.

One last word about conflict styles: Different styles are likely to work differently in different cultures. Generally, high-context cultures, such as those in Asia, favor avoidance and accommodation over forcing and compromise. Low context cultures such as the industrialized West tend to favor competition and compromise.

Integrative and Distributive Outcomes

The second aspect of Blake and Mouton's grid, which Van de Vliert calls the X-cross model, shows outcomes of conflict behaviors. This aspect is derived from drawing two lines diagonally across the grid. The X-cross model demonstrates how concerns for goals and conflict behaviors relate to the distributive versus integrative dimensions of conflict. This aspect of the grid looks as follows:

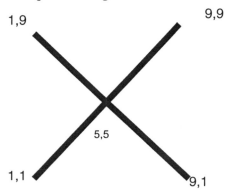

If this X-cross model is carefully examined, two relationships become apparent. The first relationship is the line moving upward left to right. In the conflict management grid, the line would be defined by 1,1-2,2-3,3-4,4-5,5-6,6-7,7-8,8-9,9. This line represents the extent to which a conflicting party minimizes or maximizes the outcomes for both parties in the conflict.

As Van de Vliert describes it, the size of the joint pie is at stake. The variable sum of the pie ranges from 2 (1+1) to 18 (9+9). Both parties are treated equally and the issue is how far up the line they can find agreement. This type of outcome is called an integrative outcome because agreements are reached on the basis of reconciling and integrating the interests of the parties in conflict. The key factor to integrative outcomes is a mutual concern that all parties' goals be achieved.

The second relationship is the line moving downward from left to right and defined by 1,9-2,8-3,7-4,6-5,5-6,4-7,3-8,2-9,1. This line represents the extent to which the conflicting party minimizes or maximizes his or her relative gain or loss versus the other party. The end state is usually a winner-loser or an equal split. The line coordinates represent a constant sum of 10. This type of outcome is called a distributive outcome and represents such concepts as competition, and zero-sum results.

The meaning of compromise at 5,5 becomes very interesting in the X-cross model. Along the integrative line, compromise is a mixture of avoiding and problem solving, while along the distributive line, compromise is a point of balance between accommodating and competing. The position of 5,5 is clear along the integrative path, but ambiguous along the distributive path. Compromise could, in a distributive situation, be neither accommodating nor competing, a mixture of accommodating and competing, or alternating accommodating and competing.

This aspect of the conflict management grid highlights the dilemmas that people face in conflict behaviors. By its very nature, conflict presents each party with two evaluative choices. The first choice is whether to interpret the situation as either a fixed pie or a joint pie definition. The second choice is between equal or different treatment between oneself and the other party. Fundamentally, these choices represent the "good" or "bad" evaluation of the amygdala and the nearly simultaneous choice to approach or defend. Likewise, these evaluative choices are made outside of conscious processing— they are almost always preconsciously made.

Each option has advantages and disadvantages. For example, integrating will tend to preserve and enhance relationships, but may cost a party economically. Integrating behaviors may also build trust at the expense of competitive advantage. Further, integrating behaviors involve the risk of losing image, position, information, or the opportunity for distributive behavior. In contrast, distributive behaviors may result in competitive advantage, but may also undermine potential agreements reached in negotiation and harm future relationships. Again, these evaluations are not generally carried out consciously. Instead, they occur preconsciously and quickly.

A second dilemma concerns the effects of the other party on distributive and integrative behaviors. To move along the integrative line requires appropriate reactions from both parties to the conflict. Generally speaking, movement along the integrative dimension requires behavioral symmetry. That is, one cannot successfully avoid, compromise, or problem solve if the other person does not also avoid, compromise, or problem solve. Both parties must engage in the same conflict strategy; hence, their behaviors must be symmetrical. This presents challenges because the conflict behaviors are so often preconscious, rather than explicitly chosen strategies. In contrast, movement along the distributive dimension requires behavioral complementarity. For example, one cannot successfully accommodate if the other party does not want to win. In distributive situations, the conflict strategies will be effective only if they complement each other.

If the parties adopt strategies that are neither symmetrical nor complementary, the conflict will escalate or reach an impasse. Thus, in a lawsuit, both parties may be highly competitive. No movement toward resolution can occur unless the behaviors align along the grid. These dilemmas are resolved by blending and alternating integrative and distributive moves. People may move distributively, then integrate, or engage in integrative behavior until the other person acts distributively, in which case a distributive countermove may be invoked. In either situation, the X-cross model shows how these various behaviors are related in terms of integrative and distributive actions.

Goal Concerns and Conflict Goals

The third aspect of the conflict management grid is what Van de Vliert describes as the L-model. The L-model provides an explanation for why conflict behaviors occur. The L-model looks as follows:

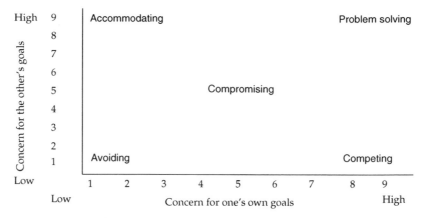

Any person in social conflict is concerned with achieving goals. This concern has two directions: achieving personal goals and attaining the goals of the other person in conflict. A party's conflict behavior is always determined by both concerns, even when the goals are preconsciously chosen. As the L-model shows, little concern for one's goals and for the other's goals leads to avoiding both integrative and distributive behavior (1,1). Accommodating behavior results if one cares little for personal goals and has a strong concern for another's goals, (1,9). Moderate and strong concerns for both self and other result in compromise (5,5) and problem solving (9,9). Finally, when one strongly cares about personal goals, but shows little concern for others' goals, fighting ensues.

Concerns for goals are not goals themselves. Instead, concerns for goals are the motivations to accomplish personal goals and the other's goals. Because the two concerns for goals operate at the same time, they create a motivational dilemma. On the one hand, people do not like to give up their goals. On the other hand, human decency generally requires people to avoid obstructing or irritating others. In other words, how does Sarah look out for her own interests without selfishly interfering with Tom's interests. The dilemma is resolved through decisions about the attractiveness and feasibility of outcomes. If an outcome requiring one to show little concern for the goals of others is very attractive and very feasible, then we would expect to see a high concern for personal goals and a low concern for the other's goals. The calculation of costs and benefits, often unconscious, results in competing behaviors.

Conflict Goals

All conflicts incorporate at least one of four types of goals, described as content, relationship, identity, and process goals (Wilmot and Hocker, 2001). The magnitude and intensity of the conflict issue at stake determines what conflict goals will be pursued.

Content goals are most familiar to lawyers because they involve substantive rights and obligations. A dispute over money is a typical content goal; one party claims damages and wants payment while the other denies and resists payment. Each party is focused on the goal of compensation. Without diminishing their importance, content goals rarely are the sole cause of human conflicts. Often, content goals are granted substantially more importance by parties and counsel than they deserve. For example, a demand for money might be higher than is realistic or fair, not because the plaintiff is seeking a superior negotiating position, but because the demand for money is symbolic of other conflicts occurring between the parties.

Relationship goals ask the question, "Who are we in this conflict?" Many times, parties feel a deep sense of injustice and offense. In civil cases, both sides often feel victimized. Parties to conflict are said to have relationship goals when they seek relief from the injustices they feel. The injustices are not subject to legal analysis. Consequently, the goals are left unstated or stated vaguely. Many times clients complain, "It's not fair," or "I've been taken advantage of." Relationship goals, being emotionally based, are sometimes difficult for clients to articulate. Therefore, clients tend to project their relationship goals into content goals. This is how content goals become symbols for other conflict goals.

Identity goals concern self-esteem and face and ask the question, "Who am I in this conflict?" Conflicts that have escalated into litigation commonly involve clients whose self-esteem or face has been threatened or injured. This goal is extremely powerful because it involves a threat to a person's psychological existence. The deeper the challenge to self-esteem, the more likely a defense reaction will occur. Like relationship goals, identity goals are often not well articulated. Hence, identity goals too can be projected onto content goals. If both relationship and identity goals are projected onto a content goal, one can see why a party may seem unreasonable in a demand for compensation or refusal to pay.

Process goals concern how parties prefer to deal with conflict. Lawyers see resolution of conflict from an adversary ideology. Sometimes, this orientation can exacerbate a conflict. If party A wishes to fight and party B wishes to avoid, B's reluctance to fight may turn to intransigence. Clients often say that they do not want to sue, but if they do, it will be all-out war. Other clients may relish the idea of a good fight and have little interest in other processes. Thus, a conflict can arise simply through different process goals.

Goals may also be positively or negatively interdependent. The word *interdependency* describes a relationship between my goals and your goals. If our goals are positively interdependent, we will stand or fall together.(Deutsh, 1973) The critical factor is whether we can perceive our ultimate goals as positively linked. When positive interdependency is recognized, integrative conflict behaviors are supported because self-interest requires negotiation and joint problem solving. Positive interdependency tends to equalize concern for oneself and for the other because the attractiveness and feasibility of outcomes are similar, if not identical for both parties. Thus, positive interdependence creates common ground and a shared perception that mutually beneficial agreements can be reached.

If our goals are negatively interdependent, we will perceive them as incompatible with each other. Deutsch called this condition contrient interdependence (Deutsch, 1973). Typically, parties perceive that they want the same thing, but must settle for different things. In this competitive situation, one party will swim as the other sinks. Negative interdependence occurs when one's gain is perceived as the other's loss, such as in scarce resource conditions. Resources not only include money, but also access to space, position in a hierarchy, information, attention, social power, and status. In many conflicts, due to personal and environmental effects, people perceive that goals are negatively interdependent when they are not. This is caused by a perceptual distortion known as the fixed-pie error—the parties expect their counterpart's interests to be opposed to their own. This cognitive error increases as the conflict intensifies (Rubin, et al., 1994).

Conflict issues characterized by negative interdependence favor distributive rather than integrative behaviors because self-interest requires a win-lose attitude over withdrawal or reconciliation.

Conflict Escalation

Conflicts are dynamic until a stalemate or resolution occurs. If emotions intensify, a conflict is said to escalate. Conflict escalation can be viewed as a social process and as a psychological process. As a social process, conflict escalation is described by an aggressor-defender model and a conflict escalation model. As a psychological process, conflict escalation passes through five stages corresponding to a regression in personality integration. Both views offer important insights into conflict behavior.

Social Processes

Aggressor-defender model. In the aggressor-defender model, the aggressor seeks change that places him or her in conflict with the defender. The goal may be to take something from the defender, to alter reality at the defender's expense, or to stop the defender's annoying behavior. The aggressor ordinarily starts with mild contentious tactics because this is the least risky approach. If these fail, the aggressor will move on to stronger tactics and continue to escalate until the goal is achieved or the cost of escalation is greater than the value of the goal. The defender reacts, escalating its efforts in response to the aggressor's level of escalation. This process persists until the aggressor either wins or gives up (Rubin et al., 1994).

The aggressor-defender model fits some cases of escalation, but is given too much weight in everyday thinking. Typically, this is the only model that people use in understanding escalation. The aggressor-defender model is popular because it satisfies the need to look for origins and people to blame. However, many examples of escalation do not fit the aggressor-defender model because it postulates a unidirectional causal sequence. In the aggressor-defender model, the defender is reacting to the aggressor's behavior. In many conflicts, however, the escalation follows a more circular process with each party reacting to the other's behavior. Thus, the conflict spiral model has been developed to explain circular escalation.

Conflict spiral model. The conflict spiral model of escalation sees disputing as a vicious cycle of action and reaction. Contentious tactics encourage contentious reaction, provoking further contentious behavior, completing the cycle and starting it over. The conflict spiral model accounts for the fact that escalating conflicts often move from small to large. Issues proliferate and the parties become more absorbed in these issues. Retaliation provides a new issue for the target of the action. Consequently, the list of transgressions grows longer and longer as the spiral continues. Each new grievance intensifies the sense of crisis (Rubin et al., 1994). The nature of conversational dynamics contributes to the spiral. In addition, certain psychological processes lead parties into destructive cycles.

Psychological Processes

Stages of escalation. Conflict escalation at the psychological level is a gradual regression from a mature level of emotional development to an immature emotional level (Spillman and Spillman, 1991). The psychological process of escalation does not take a chaotic course, but develops step by step in a strikingly reciprocal way to emotional and cognitive development. The decline and disintegration of emotional and cognitive patterns proceeds in each conflict escalation stage according to specific characteristic principles. In other words, as conflicts escalate through various stages of intensity, the parties show behaviors indicating regression of their emotional development.

Escalation to a new level takes place when one of the parties' acts is unacceptable within the current escalation stage. *Five stages of escalation have been identified* to correspond with precise cognitive regressions (Spillman and Spillman, 1991).

Escalation to *Stage One* forms part of normal everyday life. Even in good relationships there are moments of conflict. These can only be resolved with great care and mutual empathy from true perspective taking. In this phase, people are aware of tensions but make efforts to find objective solutions in a cooperative manner. If a solution is not found, especially because one of the parties sticks obstinately to his point of view, the conflict escalates to the next stage.

In *Stage Two,* the parties fluctuate between cooperative and competitive positions. They are aware that they have common interests though one's own wishes predominate and increase in importance. Dealing with information becomes limited in favor of one's own arguments. The matters in dispute are extended. Logic and understanding are used to convince or win over the opposing side. At this stage, each party does everything possible to prevent the weakening of his or her position. The temptation to leave the field of mere argument increases until the conflict escalates because of some action taken by one of the parties.

By entering *Stage Three* , the field of concrete actions, the parties each individually fear that the grounds for a common solution of the problem could be lost. Interaction becomes more hostile and irritable. All logic has focused on action replacing fruitless and nerve-wracking discussions. This change is satisfying because it temporarily reduces inner tensions and anxieties. Paradoxically, the expectations of the parties are such that they believe through pressure and resolution they will change the other party. At the same time neither is prepared to yield voluntarily. Thus, the contradiction in this stage of escalation evolves so that one party sees measures to bring about a change taken by the other as a signal toward escalation.

In stage three escalations, pressure to conform increases. This pressure is one of the first visible warning signals of intensifying escalation. Differing opinions become less acceptable, forcing group members with differing views to remain silent and become bystanders. The increasing uniformity of opinion causes the group to narrow its own perception and to reduce the potential of action and thought. Thus, a mature, complex view of reality is sacrificed for a reductionist, simplified version that is more easily sustained emotionally. At this level, the actual issues of the conflict become blurred, while the general characteristics of the opponent become the center of attention. Stereotyping is applied as negative identification of the opponent. Power becomes important

To decrease internal tension and anxiety, people are tempted to turn to action to obtain a better leverage against the opponent. Thus, both parties refuse any kind of empathy and thereby become primed for escalation to stage four.

At *Stage Four,* something has happened to invalidate a party's core sense of identity. As a result, the party perceiving invalidation experiences threat. Invalidation of core identity constructs is threatening because it destroys meaning and one's ability to predict events. Conflict intensity will be particularly high when identities of two or more parties invalidate each other. At this level, cognitive functioning regresses substantially as the amygdala overwhelms the neo-cortex with threat warnings. One is aware of other perspectives, but is no longer capable of considering the thoughts, feelings, and situation of the other. Emotionally, black and white judgments predominate so that everything that is not-I is threatening and evil. Oppressive emotions are attributed against the opponent along the lines: "Because I am afraid, you must have threatened me."

Distortion is another psychological response to threat evident at stage four escalations. Typically, a person aggressively forces meanings onto the construct system to deal with the threat of invalidation. Distortion may take several forms. For example, the threatened individual may simply deny the incoming, invalidating information or may redefine the nature of the information. In either case, information is manipulated to protect identities from further threats.

As events are distorted, threatened individuals develop increasingly rigid interpretations of the world. As this process continues, characteristics about the other party that were originally seen as "like-self" become threatening. The other party is increasingly perceived as and treated like someone entirely different from "self." New information that could lead to seeing the other as "like-self" is aggressively distorted or is simply not processed.

Rigidity separates the "invalidated" party from the "invalidating" party, putting distance between the self and the threat. Not only are the behaviors or demands of the other party threatening, but also the other's beliefs and characteristics are unrelated to the original threat.

Rigidity can have psychological, social, or physical manifestations. Distance may be increased by such mechanisms as shutting down communications between the self and the invalidating other, by construing the other as bad in various ways, or by physical separation. In effect, rigidity secures the boundaries of the self to protect identity against further attack. Psychological defenses are built up, alarm systems are installed in the home, and military forces are mobilized along national borders. Self and other become mutually exclusive categories.

At this level of escalation, both sides are forced into certain roles from which they see no escape. Each side provokes and combats a certain behavior of the opposing party. If the conflict cannot be halted at this stage, the escalation reaches a dramatic increase in intensity. Escalation results when one side commits or threatens to commit some action that is felt by the opposite side as a loss of face that has to be dealt with forcefully.

At *Stage Five*, progressive regression appears in the form of a comprehensive ideology of antagonistic perspectives. Sacred values, convictions, and superior moral obligations are at stake. The conflict assumes mythical dimensions. Sometimes the parties fantasize omnipotence. In object relations terms, the escalation has reached a hallucinatory-narcissistic sphere. The entire self-conception is drawn into the conflict such that individual perceptions and evaluations disappear. Power and violence assume impersonal forms, and the perception of the opponent freezes into the rigid image of the enemy. As separation increases, the process of dehumanization may begin to occur at both the individual and group levels. When some other group is dehumanized, its members are evaluated as being "bad" or "evil."

Dehumanization is one of the basic processes hypothesized to maintain the domination-submission relationship, which can occur between low and high status groups such as men and women or persons of different racial backgrounds. Low-status groups are defined as objects by high-status groups, as less than self, less than human. As we saw in chapter 5, Buber spoke of this through the "I-Thou" and "I-It" distinction.

Dehumanization makes violence more tolerable because of the ease of harming something or someone construed as not human. The dehumanization process reduces one's ability to process objective information about the "enemy." Both validating and invalidating information is rejected as reliance grows on a psychological construction of the other.

By threatening and creating fear, both parties strive toward total control of the situation and thereby escalate the conflict further. To remain credible and to restrain the enemy from an act of force, the threatening group feels compelled to commit acts of force itself. This, in turn, proves to the threatened group the aggressive nature of the threatener and provokes counterforce and further escalation.

As the separation between parties becomes more extreme, the conflict takes on greater importance. Both parties behave in ways that are consistent with maintaining the conflict. In this sense, they collude in prolonging the conflict. This behavior may or may not be explicitly stated or intentional.

Collusion presents an interesting paradox, because the conflict becomes a part of each party's identity. Collusion may, over time, be manifested in formal social, political, and economic structures within and between parties. The conflict becomes institutionalized in both obvious and subtle ways. Many will recall that when the Cold War was declared "over" politicians and journalists fretted over the absence of an enemy to rail against. Part of the Cold War phenomenon rested in its identity definition for political and military leaders in the United States as well as in the Soviet Union.

As rigidity increases, the collusion process takes hold. Both parties are hostile, rejecting and criticizing the other. They become sole behaviors of the relationship and validate the distortions that created the behaviors in the first place. In other words, the effect of distorting the other group is to make the other group behave consistent with the distortions. Thus, conflict becomes a defining characteristic of the identity of the parties.

Collusion may be manifested in various ways, most of which serve to formalize and crystallize the conflict. Formal rituals may emerge within each party that sanctify the struggle and celebrate the victorious and noble efforts of the self or self-group. In many ways, the conflict is institutionalized, both within and between parties. At this stage, the prospect of ending the conflict threatens to invalidate the self. This contributes to the intractability of the conflict to any effort of resolution or reconciliation.

Rational Thinking and Intractable Conflicts

People think that if they can just reason through the problem, the conflict can be resolved. In fact, practical reasoning often leads to intractable conflict. This discussion is especially pertinent to law students and lawyers, who rely heavily on reasoning to find solutions to conflicts. In mediations of litigated disputes or in judicial settlement conferences, lawyers use logical arguments to persuade each other of the merits of their respective positions. As we have seen, using logic, argument, and persuasion indicates Stage Two escalation. What is not as well known is how logical argument, the primary tool of the lawyer, can exacerbate and escalate conflict, rather than reduce it.

To explore the rule of reasoning in conflict, first consider some fundamental principles of argument.

An argument is a set of assertions, such that one or more of the assertions provide support for another assertion in the set. In classical theory, arguments do not have truth-value. That is, there is no such thing as a true or false argument. When an argument is deductive, it will be either valid or invalid. When an argument is inductive, it will either be strong, moderate, or weak.

Arguments always have two parts. One part provides the evidence. This part is called the premise or premises. The other part provides a claim. This is called the conclusion. An argument only exists if it contains both a premise and a conclusion. Premises and conclusions do not have to be explicit. They may be implied.

Deductive arguments are those in which the conclusion is true, assuming the premises are true. In deductive reasoning, the premises provide conclusive grounds for the conclusion. Because of the nature of deductive reasoning, we can guarantee that the conclusion is derivable from the evidence, if the argument is correct in deductive form and the premises are true. While we say the conclusion or claim is true, we do not say that the argument that leads to the conclusion is true. The argument, if deductive, is either valid or invalid. If the deductive argument is valid, then the claim or conclusion will be true. *Deductive reasoning* has the following characteristics:

1. The scope of the conclusion does not exceed the scope of the evidence.
2. The evidence provides conclusive grounds for the conclusion.
3. The conclusion must be true if the evidence is true.

Inductive reasoning, in contrast, has the following characteristics:

1. The scope of the conclusion transcends the scope of the evidence.
2. The evidence does not provide conclusive grounds for the conclusion.
3. The conclusion might be false even if the evidence is true.

Inductive arguments are evaluated on content, rather than form. An inductive argument is never valid or invalid, nor is it true or false. The only evaluation of inductive argument is whether it is strong, moderate, or weak, indicating the degrees of probability that the conclusion is true. There can also be inductive fallacies, but these simply indicate a weak argument.

Unlike inductive reasoning, a clear demarcation exists between good and bad deductive reasoning. While we evaluate inductive reasoning in light of content, we evaluate deductive reasoning by its form or structure. The content of deductive reasoning is immaterial to evaluation of the argument. Thus, deductive arguments are either valid or invalid, based on their form.

The seduction of the deductive argument is its ability to provide clear and definite responses to the question, "Is this a good argument?" However, deductive reasoning cannot tell us anything new about the world. It cannot identify a true conclusion unless the truth of the premises is established. This means, ultimately, that any valid deductive argument is dependent upon some inductive argument.

First semester law students learn a formula for analyzing legal problems. The formula is a mnemonic called IRAC and stands for Issue Rule Analysis Conclusion. Examination of the formula shows that it is a combination of inductive and deductive reasoning.

The issue states the problem: Was John guilty of battery?

The rule states the applicable rule of law: Battery is a nonconsensual touching of another.

The analysis considers the facts of the case: John kissed Sally while she was asleep.

The conclusion answers the issue: John is guilty of battery.

Generally, IRAC is deductive in overall structure. However, both the Rule and the Analysis sections rely heavily on inductive reasoning. First, there may be several legal rules to choose from. Inductive reasoning will be the process used to choose the best rule. Second, the facts may contain ambiguities or inconsistencies, or be incomplete. Lawyers have to deal with all of the problems the facts present. Again, this is an inductive process. Once the rule is chosen and the facts selected the lawyer moves back into the deductive mode of IRAC.

For the lawyer, then, deduction is the end of the game. The premises are where the battles are fought and won. Establishing the premises is solely within the realm of inductive reasoning. Once the premises are established, the final argument can be constructed. The power of the deductive argument is that if the premises are accepted and the argument is in proper form, the conclusion must be true. This has enormous persuasive power in human affairs.

The choice of inductive arguments used to create the major and minor premises of a deductive argument are solely within the discretion of the person constructing the argument. One result of this discretion is the evolution of intractable disputes grounded on the inability of practical reasoning to resolve disputes. Two parties to a conflict can be perfectly rational and advance logical arguments for their positions, yet be completely polarized. The fact that each argument is valid in form and possibly strong in content persuades the advocate of the righteousness of her position. Thus, considering other equally valid and strong arguments becomes difficult. When two arguments compete, neither argument will dominate, and the conflict is ripe for escalation to stage three.

In the abortion dispute, for example, pro-life and pro-choice advocates agree on the principle that proscribes taking human life. But they disagree on the minor premise. The pro-life person describes the fetus as having human status; the pro-choice person does not.

At bottom, the abortion dispute is arbitrary, which makes it possible for the adversaries to be rational and diametrically opposed to each other. Both the multiplicity of starting concepts and their elasticity explain the occurrence of rational conflict and the difficulty of resolving disputes on rational grounds.

Intractable conflicts can thus be explained in terms of the capacities of reasoning to admit contrary conclusions and by the empirical fact that individuals do arrive at different conclusions on contrary, though logically rational, rules and criteria.

Conclusion

Lawyers tend to look at human behavior in terms of how it interferes with rights and obligations established by law. For example, they will ask, "Did John perform his contract obligations?" To answer this question, lawyers will examine the contract and try to ascertain what exactly John did. John's actions will be categorized as either complying with the contract or breaching the contract. This is a narrow perspective on human behavior.

Peacemakers take a broader perspective. They might ask, "What were John's conflict behaviors when he performed (or failed to perform) his contract obligations?" By understanding John's conflict behavior, peacemakers can gauge John's commitment to cooperation and his motivation to engage with other people in the conflict. Peacemakers might also consider what environmental or attitudinal changes might be necessary to resolve the dispute. How, for example, can John be moved from a contentious behavior to a cooperative behavior, if that is what is necessary for true resolution of the conflict.

In addition, peacemakers may look at conflict behaviors as indications of what conflict goals are being pursued by the parties. For example, contentious conflict behavior may reveal that one party has identity goals that need exploring and resolution. By linking conflict behaviors to conflict goals, peacemakers can penetrate the apparent irrationality of the conflict and help to create some order from the chaos.

Finally, conflict behaviors are benchmarks for escalation levels. As we saw in chapter 4, the appropriate mediation orientation is very closely related to the conflict escalation level. At lower levels of escalation, evaluative mediation may be more efficient. At higher levels of escalation, transformative or narrative mediation might be necessary. Conflict behavior provides clues as to where the parties are in escalation, which then suggests the appropriate orientation to process.

In summary, if we are interested in a determination of right and wrong, we view behavior against some objective standard such as a rule of law. If we are interested in resolving a conflict through peacemaking, we are interested in conflict behavior as information about what led to the conflict and how it might be transformed into peace.

Reflections on Chapter Eleven

Michael was a successful entrepreneur in his late 60s. He owned a national business service organization that had afforded him the cash flow to invest in many other businesses. He was intelligent and shrewd about business deals and had been able to buy distressed companies, turn them around, and profit handsomely.

In 1990, he bought a real estate firm that was losing money. He saw an enormous potential if the firm could be infused with new life. For the next five years, he invested $5 million into the firm, and it slowly started to grow.

In 1995, the firm had grown to the point that it needed a full-time manager. After a search, he hired JoAnn, who had been working as a turnaround manager at a competing firm in the region. JoAnn was very energetic and charismatic, so Michael was convinced she would be perfect for the business. Michael and JoAnn negotiated an employment contract that provided for very generous bonuses if certain performance criteria were met.

For the next five years, JoAnn and Michael worked on growing the business. Michael hated conflict and avoided confrontation at all costs. He was not a good speaker and needed time to reflect on things before making decisions. In contrast, JoAnn was an aggressive workaholic. She was very rough on staff to the point of almost being abusive. Employee turnover was high, but those who stayed were top performers. Michael often saw things that he did not like, but was afraid to confront JoAnn. JoAnn was not happy about Michael's unwillingness to take on issues with her. However, their mutual goal of developing the firm allowed them the luxury of suppressing their dissatisfactions.

In 2000, their hard work paid off. The business generated net after tax revenues of over $175 million. JoAnn's bonus was well over $3 million. The problems started when Michael casually handed her the bonus check on December 31st without as much as a thank you. JoAnn interpreted that as a sign of the disrespect she had been feeling for months. Over the next several weeks, Michael and JoAnn had increasing hostile flare-ups leading to where they communicated by passing notes under their office doors. Finally, JoAnn retained legal counsel, and the matter escalated again.

You have been retained as a peacemaker to attempt one last try at reconciliation.

When did this conflict begin?

Using the materials in this chapter, analyze the conflict behaviors exhibited by the principles.

Describe the probable conflict escalation process in this conflict? At what level is the conflict now?

What techniques might you consider using to overcome the effects of these conflict behaviors? How might you de-escalate the conflict?

Part Four

Conflict
Analysis

CHAPTER TWELVE

CONFLICT THEORY

*L*AWYERS LOOK AT HUMAN CONFLICT in terms of rights, obligations, and remedies. Although facts are important, client problems are analyzed from the perspective of the law. Thus, rules of liability, causation, and damages govern the lawyer's view of human conflict. Similarly, lawyers look at various legal procedures for the means to enforce or defend against claims. Sometimes, this analytical approach works well, but other times it does not. The typical analytical approach is usually unsatisfactory when the conflict is deeper than just pure rights and remedies. Most lawyers recognize when issues other than rights are driving a conflict, but may have difficulty penetrating to the forces below these issues.

The difficulty for lawyers lies in legal training. Law school specifically intends to abstract human conflict into resolution through application of legal principles to objective facts. This process is necessary to master legal reasoning, but is inadequate as a method of training lawyers to be competent in dispute resolution.

Conflict theory, as recognized by sociology and social psychology, provides a much richer analysis of social conflict. This is because conflict is not abstracted into intellectual principles. Instead, social scientists try to observe carefully, describe what they see, and develop theories to explain what they describe. The conflict interaction is never abandoned or translated as it is in the law. Instead, it is studied in place as it occurs or has occurred.

For lawyers, understanding conflict theory can provide insight into the dynamics of the issues client face. These insights can lead to innovative and creative solutions that pure legal analysis may ignore or miss. Consequently, this chapter explores some of the leading traditions in sociology and conflict theory to acquaint students with some broader perspectives.

Sociology and Conflict Theory

Conflict theory attempts to understand the deeper causes of disputes between people and between groups. Like other scientists, sociologists who study conflict want to know "why?" Specifically, sociologists want to know why societies form. What are the underlying mechanisms of society? What happens when social structure breaks down? Why are some societies apparently successful while others are not? What are the attributes and causes of dysfunctional societies? Why does conflict arise between humans? Thus, sociologists explain human interaction that, when it becomes dysfunctional, may lead to conflict. In addition, sociologists explain when conflict is functional and healthy within a society.

Of the many theories that have been advanced, several traditions help sociologists understand how society operates. The oldest tradition, developed first by Marx then by Weber, viewed society as arising from and containing internal conflict between socioeconomic classes. In another theory, known as exchange theory, conflict was the manifestation of social power and was therefore seen as a struggle. This theory saw society as functioning from a rational person, utilitarian perspective. Under this view, those with more social power tended to avoid or suppress conflict so as to preserve their power. Finally, the interactionist tradition considered society from the perspective of the symbols and interactions of everyday life.

A word about the relationship between sociology and social psychology. Social psychology developed after World War II as a melding of sociology and psychology. Social psychology studies how people relate to each other through empirical investigation. Thus, social psychologists spend much of their time devising inventive experiments to eke out an understanding of how humans behave toward one another in social situations. Sociologists do not seem to be as experimentally inclined. They tend to observe social interaction and devise explanations and theories from their observations. At the risk of oversimplification, sociologists tend to take a macro view of social interaction, while social psychologists tend to take a more micro view of interaction. Both disciplines are valuable to understanding human conflict, but little academic effort seems to have been expended to integrate their separate ideas into a coherent body of knowledge.

Marx and Weber—The Conflict Tradition in Sociology

The conflict tradition in sociology says not only that society consists of conflict, but that when conflict is not openly taking place, processes of social domination exist. In this vision of social order, groups and individuals try to advance their own interests over others. There may or may not be overt outbreaks of conflict or violence, but the underlying theme is one of struggle to gain superior position over others. This conflict tradition provides a macro view of how societies operate and perspectives on the conflicts within societies.

This vision of society is not popular. Prevailing views of society have usually stressed a more benign picture based on religious or secular beliefs in the goodness of one's rulers. To conflict sociologists, these softer views are ideologies cloaking the real self-interests of the groups hiding behind them.

Despite its unpopularity, the conflict viewpoint has emerged whenever there have been politically astute observers or whenever intellectuals have seriously tried to write history. Machiavelli, for example, was a conflict theorist to the extent that he viewed maintenance of social order as a game of power domination.

Two very different theorists define the conflict tradition of sociology: Karl Marx and Max Weber.

Karl Marx, more than any other thinker, was the center of the tradition that dramatized societal conflict. Our concern is not with the politics engendered by Marxist thinking, but with Marx's understanding of the world as a place of domination and conflict. Marx drew heavily on the philosophy of Hegel pertaining to historical development. In addition to Hegel's influence, Marx discovered classical economics, which in his day, rested on the labor theory of value. This theory stated that human labor created value through the transformation of the natural world. In addition, property was a key element of classical economic theory. Owners of land and capital confronted workers who owned nothing but their labor. These "factors of production" became the major class actors in Marxist theory (Collins, 1994).

Marx argued that labor was the source not only of economic value, but also of profit. In a pure market system, operating under supply and demand forces, everything exchanged for its own value.

Profit came from labor because labor was the only factor of production that could be bought for less than the cost of reproducing it. This is the "exploitation of labor" for which Marxist theory was noted. If a factory owner was able to work his laborers 12 hours, but pay them for 8, he was able to squeeze more profits from them.

Marx believed that capitalist competition impelled manufacturers to introduce labor saving machines, which in turn would hurt them. Because profit came from exploiting labor, the profit basis would shrink as machines replace labor. Small or inefficient businesses would be driven out of business and industries would consolidate into monopolies. As this consolidation process continued, Marx believed profits would collapse, creating a series of business crises. The productive technology would be completely at odds with the legal property forms of capitalism and the ideological and political superstructure would collapse. A class confrontation and political revolution would follow the ensuing economic crisis (Collins, 1994).

Marx also constructed a theory of social classes. Together with Frederic Engels, Marx wrote a series of works stating that social classes are economic and therefore founded on a material base. Marx and Engels saw a crucial social relationship binding the material, ideological, and political aspects of society. This relationship, called property, is the legal right, enforced by the state, to own and control material goods.

Every society has its distinctive forms of property and, hence, social classes. Classes fight economic and political struggles, make alliances, and produce historical change. Each class has its own culture and its own outlook. Thus, the ideas and beliefs of each era are determined by its lineup of social classes.

Engels and Marx showed that conflicts and alliances among social classes pursuing different economic interests defined political struggle. They also proposed a general scheme of social classes to show the conditions under which classes arise.

Max Weber, another German, was born in 1864 and developed intellectually in the 1880s and 1890s, the period when Engels and his followers influenced German intellectual life. Weber's father was a member of a middle-class political party representing large manufacturers. Prominent politicians, lawyers, and academics met at the Weber home, and he learned backstage power politics early. Weber was also influenced by his mother's devout Protestant beliefs. He studied economics, practiced law, knew much about the history of the world, and was aware of the role of religion as a force in history.

While Marx was concerned with the economic laws of capitalism, its crises, and future breakdown, Weber was concerned with the background of capitalism and how it came into existence in the first place. Weber believed that capitalism was produced by the influence of religious ideas, asserting that capitalism came from the drive of Puritans to work out their anxiety over salvation or damnation.

For Weber, conflict was an expression of the differences between groups, interests, and perspectives that made up the world. Weber consequently saw history as a process of conflict on many fronts. He did not believe in reductionistic notions of evolutionary stages that theorists imposed on the complexities of historical reality. Instead, he created ideal models of bureaucracy and class that captured the complex historical reality. Weber also developed a three-dimensional model of stratification based on class, status, and party. These are interest groups that fight among themselves and against each other, but are also connected to each other.

While Marx and Engels deal with the conflict between the capitalist and the worker, Weber incorporates the conflict of lenders against borrowers and sellers against consumers. While Marx defines class in terms of ownership of the means of production, Weber builds his class theory on the struggle to control markets. For Weber the issue is not property ownership. Instead, social classes are based on control over markets: money and credit, land, manufacturing industries, and labor. The dominant classes are those who manage a tight monopoly on some lucrative market; less dominant classes hold only partial monopolies or monopolies in less desirable kinds of markets.

Marx states that classes simply cloak themselves in ideology. Weber agrees with this, but adds that ideology and culture are essential for a group to become more than a set of persons with the same economic position. In other words, ideology is necessary for a real social community to exist, and status-group organization becomes an economic weapon. Their very lifestyle and outlook depend on their economic resources and social position. For example, the upper class puts on debutante balls and contributes to symphony concerts and art museums as a process of turning economic capital into "cultural" capital. This creates status positions from which political power can be wielded to protect market position. Thus, class and status complement each other.

Even religious propensities are affected by class position. According to Weber, the highest social classes always prefer a dignified religion, full of stately ceremony, but not calling for too much personal commitment. The middle classes prefer an ascetic, moralistic religion to bolster their respectability and to motivate them to work hard. The lower classes treat religion as a form of magic or supernatural intervention to bring good fortune and strike down enemies.

These different cultural worldviews make higher and lower status groups seem alien to each other. They also cloak the economic differences between the groups. The dominant group, organized as a status group, always idealizes itself, claiming that it is different not because of wealth or power but because of greater nobility, politeness, artistic taste, technical skills, or whatever status ideology prevails at the time.

Possessing this kind of status ideology makes monopolizing economic positions easier for the group members. Outsiders can be excluded and competition limited automatically because only persons who seem like "the right kind" are allowed into the preferred positions. The growth of the modern "professions" shows how much the workforce has become permeated by these kinds of monopolies. Computer engineers are really just engaged in a form of specialized labor, but have cut themselves off from the rest of the working class by building an elaborate occupational culture based on highly technical and arcane knowledge. The same can be said for any licensed professional such as doctors, certified public accountants, and licensed civil engineers. Lawyers especially have this type of professional monopoly.

In short, Weber sees economic struggle as more complex than Marx. Classes become subdivided into status groups and gain control of particular markets. A secondary market for status attributes blurs economic distinctions. The economic struggles are less visible but are at the core of the system.

Weber provides a richer explanation of society than Marx. For Weber, society self-organizes according to economic class This leads to status groups to preserve the hierarchy. Human conflict can be analyzed in terms of power struggles between people of the same or different economic classes. The legal system protects economic interests by providing rights to property owners. Thus, landlords tend to have more power than tenants because the law protects the landlord's right to collect rent or evict, over the tenant's right to an affordable, habitable place to live.

The term *conflict theory* also applies to a different tradition of analysis begun by one of Weber's contemporaries, Georg Simmel.

Simmel's analysis was revived and formally expounded by Lewis Coser in the 1950s and 1960s. Simmel considered hierarchy as a fundamental topic of social order and argued that sociology should analyze the structural forms underlying society. For Simmel, conflict did not produce social change. Instead, it was another structural relationship embedded within social systems.

Simmel did not become a part of a larger conflict theory tradition until Louis Coser reformulated his ideas. Coser purified Simmel by extracting principles having wide-ranging application to all kinds of conflicts. Conflict sharpens the sense of group boundaries. Conflict is most intense between individuals or groups already closely related, because it is most threatening to the group. On the other hand, external conflict makes a group cohesive. Consequently, leaders of groups frequently seek external enemies to maintain internal order. Antagonists become bound to one another much as, when in an arms race, the military on both sides depend on each other for their influence. And conflicts tend to spread as each side tries to bring neutral parties into a coalition. Coser's formulation began a modern school of research on the process of conflict itself, which today is called conflict theory.

The conflict tradition in sociology has useful analytical application when dealing with intergroup conflicts. By using Weber's class, status, party structure of society, the reasons for apparent diverging social interests are more easily identified. Conflict theory does not, however, address elements of interpersonal conflict.

Exchange Theory

A second sociological tradition has developed around interpersonal relationships. This tradition, exchange theory, assumes that much of what is needed and valued in everyday life can only be obtained from others. People engage in cooperative behavior because they think they will be rewarded for it. Thus, the process of exchange is the basis of social interaction on which social life is constructed.

Exchange theory says that people provide rewards to others to induce rewards to themselves. Social interaction thus becomes a complex exchange of activities in which receiving benefit is contingent on a returned favor. Needs, anticipations, and predictions of others' behaviors become important ingredients in personal decision-making (Molm, 1997).

Exchange theory also assumes people have needs that when fulfilled constitute rewards. Behavior becomes positively reinforced when it is associated with the experience of reward and negatively reinforced when associated with punishment. Unlike microeconomic theory, which assumes one-time transactions, exchange theory assumes enduring dependent relationships. People maximize rewards and minimize punishment even though they may not be aware of this reinforcement process in any given situation. Exchange theory also assumes that actions associated with anticipated future rewards are more likely to occur.

Exchange relations are also power relations. One person's dependence is another person's power. If Aaron is in a position to provide Kim with a benefit Kim needs and cannot obtain elsewhere, Aaron can make Kim provide benefits as an inducement, i.e., Aaron can modify and influence Kim's actions. A balanced exchange relationship is one in which Aaron needs Kim's services as much as Kim needs Aaron's. An unbalanced relationship exists when the benefits exchanged are of unequal value. This gives power to the one who can provide the superior or more needed benefits. Social interaction consists of a continuous balancing and rebalancing of power. This takes the form of reducing needs, acquiring by force, providing inducements, or seeking out alternative sources for rewards.

From a social exchange perspective, conflict can arise from a number of sources. First, Aaron may develop an expectation that Kim is willing to negotiate. If Kim shatters Aaron's expectation by refusing to talk, a potential conflict develops. The conflict may be further exacerbated because Aaron is dependent on Kim and therefore feels powerless against Kim's refusal to exchange. Social psychologists label this the equity principle. People expect to be treated fairly by equals. In the language of exchange theory, reciprocity is expected. Aaron feels a sense of injustice when Kim denies the reciprocal exchange. The injustice can lead to conflict if Aaron acts to correct the perceived wrong.

In a relationship based on reciprocal exchange, a conflict may develop when reciprocity ceases or is considered inadequate. The feeling of powerlessness arising from unbalanced exchange relationships can defeat self-esteem, face, and lead to deeper identity-based conflicts.

Lawyers are familiar with a formal exchange—the contract. Unlike other social exchanges, a contract is a promise enforceable at law. The promise must meet certain minimum requirements as an enforceable promise, notably mutual assent and consideration. Typically, contracts are negotiated, either expressly or implicitly. The breach of obligation creates a conflict in the relationship, and may also cause economic injury. Lawyers stop analysis at the financial injury and fail to consider other aspects of the conflict. For example, if Kim breaches a contract with Aaron, the breach may lead to identity-based conflict. The judicial system provides processes for evaluating economic injury, but does not address relational or identity-based conflicts arising from contract disruptions. This is one of the reasons many people are dissatisfied with outcomes after trial.

Exchange theory also views conflict as a consequence of imbalances in the reward and power structure. These imbalances arise when vested interests, powers, institutionalization, or the internalization of cultural values maintain "undeserved" rewards for those in privileged positions. Traditionally institutions, endowed by values with symbolic significance, tend to defy innovation and reform even when changes in social conditions have made them obsolete. Consequently, powerful groups defend their vested interests regardless of the value of their "service" to society. Conflict arises when society struggles to eliminate the imbalances. The same is true at the interpersonal level. Under social exchange theory, conflict arises when an imbalance in power or resources results in a struggle to rebalance the exchange relationship.

If Aaron's exchange relationship with Kim is imbalanced, but Kim denies the imbalance, exchange theory suggests that the conflict will be resolved on the basis of dependency and power. If Aaron's sense of imbalanced exchange arises from a dependence on Kim, Aaron must change the dependency. Otherwise, Kim will dictate the resolution of the conflict. In this sense, Kim has power over Aaron. To the extent Aaron changes the dependency, the power relationship with Kim is rebalanced. In this process, the exchange relationship becomes less valuable to Aaron and, presumably, more valuable to Kim, until a new exchange balance is reached.

Exchange theory in the context of interpersonal conflict has some limitations. First, the theory is descriptive, not predictive. While it can describe interpersonal relationships as they have developed, it cannot tell us how those relationships will interact into the future. Second, exchange theory cannot tell us what people value. It explicitly excludes any assumptions about the value inherent in exchanges. Therefore, exchange theory does not help people discover, weigh, and balance interests and injustices. Third, there is no easy way to analyze exchange relationships. In particular, reciprocal and indirect exchanges may be highly subjective. Consequently, if a conflict arises from a sense of unequal treatment, exchange theory does not offer any way of probing for the violated expectation.

While exchange theory describes relationships in terms of power, it does nothing to correct gross power imbalances. As a descriptive theory, it may isolate examples of power imbalances that cause conflict, but it does not provide any prescription for remedying the situation. For example, in a depressed economy, if Aaron is employed by Kim and Aaron's earnings are essential to the survival of Aaron's family, Aaron may not be able to change the dependency. In this case, a severe power imbalance exists. In some egregious situations, such as sexual harassment, gender discrimination, or racial discrimination, the law protects the less powerful. However, many extreme power imbalances exist for which no legal protection is afforded. In these situations, exchange theory does not provide any prescriptions about rebalancing the exchange relationship.

Finally, exchange theory is based on behaviorist principles and a rational person model, both of which are outdated and incomplete views of human motivation. Humans are largely emotional creatures, with rationality being limited to those unusual situations justifying high cognitive overhead.

Despite these limitations, exchange theory is a dominant framework for understanding social interaction. It remains a central feature of empirical research into organizational behavior, decision theory, game theory, and social psychology.

Social Constructionism and Symbolic Interactionism

Another broad sociological tradition has been variously called social constructionism and symbolic interactionism. This tradition starts with the idea that humans, just by existing, interact with each other and their environment. In this process, each inevitably influences the other. Thus, a person's action influences the social environment, which then changes to influence the person (Duncan, 1960).

The environment has its own reality, but humans selectively perceive and react to it. This selectivity means that people create meaning by choosing those things that are subjectively important. Therefore, personal reality is also subjective. The struggle to find and define shared meaning is experienced as conflict. Conflict is therefore a creation between people arising out of a search for shared meaning.

Interaction is symbolic in that people respond not to some inherent quality in others' actions but the significance imputed to them. In other words, we do not respond to John's lateness because of the lateness. Instead, we respond to his lateness because we attach a social significance to being late. Meanings shared in this symbolic way form the basis for human social organization.

Society consists of overlapping networks of symbolic interaction, and only exists as individuals construct interactions through symbolic meanings. At the same time, society exists before the individual member. Consequently, each of us is born into an existing society, and our society sets the institutional parameters for our self-development, so self and society develop together in a dialectical mutual transformation. In this tradition, knowledge is derived from perspectives that are relative to particular cultural or social versions of reality. Thus, knowledge can never be final, and the frame from which something is viewed is as important as what is being viewed. Understanding reality then requires understanding the perspective from which it appears as well as understanding the thing itself.

Social constructionists do not say that people have thoughts or feelings that precede their expression, but that language makes up subjective experience. Language is therefore a precondition for thought as it provides the concepts and categories used when thinking. Furthermore, language has meaning in its use rather than its correspondence with events in the world. Language "speaks" us into existence and constitutes identity as much as it is used to communicate with others. Since language is inherited from one's culture, individuals are not viewed as prime movers in their own worlds.

If persons are constructed from language, then everyday interactions should be the focus for understanding behavior. In these interactions, the world is constructed as people express what lies within them and what they perceive outside. Such constructionism contradicts the traditional psychological view that language is a vehicle by which thoughts and feelings are expressed and actions are described.

In this tradition, conflict arises from the enormous variation in people's lives. Because there is no single, definable reality in the ways that people create their lives, differences in the multiple constructions of reality create conflict between people. Conflict is therefore understood as the by-product of diversity, rather than the result of personal needs or interests.

Conflict is also an inherent quality of society. Conflict does not just happen to people, but is created in situations that people experience as conflict. This means conflict is socially created. Likewise, conflict resolution is socially created by reconstructing situations and social structures. This reconstruction is inherently temporary because it changes the social worlds for self and others, thus resulting in a need for a new reconstruction. Balanced social states depend on imbalances in other social states. Forces that restore equilibrium in one state do so by creating disequilibrium in others. In this continuous process, conflicts arise, are resolved, and give rise to new conflicts.

From a lawyer's perspective, social constructionism seems hopelessly subjective. The whole idea of the law is to be objective and predictable. If, however, the lawyer's goal is to help people work through difficult conflicts without necessarily resorting to legal principles, social constructionism can be a useful concept.

In a breach of contract case, for example, a pure legal analysis would inquire as to the creation of the contract, the nature and extent of consideration to support the promises, the obligation created, whether the obligations were performed, whether excuses or defenses to the obligations are present, and finally, what the appropriate legal or equitable remedy should be.

A broader social constructionist examination of the breach of contract might inquire about the shared perspectives of the parties created when the contract was formed. It might seek out the meanings they imparted to each other's words and actions before and during their interaction and how they experienced their relationship without conflict. Finally, it could explore how they created conflict from a set of meanings, what their interaction might look like without the conflict, and what new meanings would have to be created to reconstruct the situation to one of resolution.

Such inquiry yields information about the parties and conflict, but no process assures a decision. Likewise, no objective standard can be used to evaluate the parties' actions. In traditional lawyering, this is unsettling. How do we advise clients if we have no sense of outcome? Here is a difference between lawyering and peacemaking. Lawyering permits advice about process and outcome based on legal standards; peacemaking permits self-exploration, insight, and choice based on dialogue between parties. The lawyer's view of conflict tends to disengage the parties, while the social constructionist view of conflict tends to engage them.

A Social Power View of Conflict

The Nature of Social Power

The idea of power in human interaction is really a metaphor from the physical sciences. Power, from a physics perspective, is the capability of affecting an object. In human affairs, when we think of power, we think of the ability to have our own way with others.

Every individual has power in the sense that she can force her world to recognize her and to cause others to adjust and compensate to her. Simply by existing, people have the power of identity. This power unconsciously pressures the outside world to notice and to compensate and is known as identive power. People also intentionally affect the world by their actions. This power is known as assertive power. One type of assertive power is physical, such as punching, tickling, or caressing another. Physical power used without consent is called force and is one of the most visible manifestations of conflict. These four powers, identive, assertive, physical, and force, are nonsocial powers (Rummel, 1991).

In contrast, social powers are those forms of power directed toward another. A person is said to have power if she can induce some change, either voluntary or involuntary, in another person. The exact nature of the social interaction varies depending upon one's views of social power. Social power explains the changes in a person's (the target) cognitions, emotions, or behaviors caused by another person (the agent). Theories of social power agree that the change in the target would not have occurred without some interaction between the target and the agent.

Each person has his or her nonsocial and social powers. Each of the social powers has a direction, a base, and determination (Rummel, 1991). Direction describes the purpose and interest in exercising power. If Sarah wants her teenage daughter to be home by 10 p.m. for safety reasons, Sarah's use of her parental power has a specific direction. Without direction, social power cannot exist. People have a purpose for exercising power, otherwise they would not use it.

Base describes capability or actual capacity to use power. This capacity is what most people mean when the say, "He is a powerful person." Without base or capability, social power cannot exist. Interestingly, perception of capacity is as important as the actual capacity itself. If you believe I have power, your belief is just as good whether I exercise the power or not. The trick is for me to perpetuate your belief without having my bluff called. Base may exist with or without intention by the party possessing it. For example, persons who are taken as role models may have a large base without being aware of it.

Determination describes the motivation to exercise power. Some people may have much base or capacity, but little determination. In this case, they have little actual power because unwilling to use what they have. Others may have little base, but intense determination. Even these relatively powerless people can gain power through sheer force of will. Gandhi, a London-trained lawyer, had no base, but an unflinching determination to see his people treated as equals in South Africa. His enormous discipline and will power magnified his limited base of power. From his experiences in South Africa, he was prepared to take on the larger challenge of overthrowing the British rule in India forcefully, but without violence.

Thus each person exercises power according to his or her unique interests, capabilities, and will. As a result of the dynamics of everyday life, people's interests shift, their capabilities alter, and their determination varies with their relationships with each other. These changes create a gap between mutual expectations and underlying interests, capabilities, and wills. As a result of this gap, friction builds up in the relationship. People began to feel tension and sense that something seems not quite right. Suddenly, some small event triggers a disruption in expectations, and conflict erupts as one or both parties decide to change the order of things.

As each person exercises power, clashes of power occur. The process of balancing power in these clashes is called conflict (Rummel, 1991). Thus, conflict occurs by engaging another person's powers, which is, in effect, engaging each other's interests, capabilities, and will. Balancing interests, capabilities, and wills results in the balancing of powers. Balancing powers does not have to be a balancing of equal weights or like forces on both sides. Nor does it have to be a balance between similar powers. Will may balance interest, desire may balance capability, knowledge may balance authority, or promises may balance threats.

Conflict ends when neither side has the further determination, purpose, or capacity to improve the outcome. The outcome may be acceptable or not, but, for the time being, the power relationships have been stabilized into a new constellation.

Sources of Power Capacity

French and Raven proposed a limited model of social power consisting originally of five bases social power, and now consisting of six bases of social power (Raven, 1992). These elements are information power, reward power, coercive power, expert power, referent power, and legitimacy power. These are differentiated by the target's relationship to the agent as socially independent (informational power), socially dependent requiring surveillance (reward and coercive power), or socially dependent without requiring surveillance (expert, referent, and legitimacy power).

Informational power is related strictly to the content of the communication and is thus independent of source characteristics or future consequences. Cognitive change is the main factor in informational power. If the agent provides or withholds information, the target will act accordingly. The target is not acting because of anything the agent does, but because of the information the agent discloses or conceals. The agent and target are said to be socially independent.

Reward and coercive power stem from the agent's ability to control consequences to the target. These two bases of power typify the opposite of informational power because they require social dependence and surveillance of the target by the powerful agent. Social dependence means the target is related to the agent such that the agent can provide or withhold something the target wants. Exchange theory is based on this idea of power. For reward and coercive power to be effective, the agent must have a way of ensuring the target's compliance. Without surveillance, the agent cannot compel obedience or punish effectively for disobedience. While many people think reward and coercive power are attractive, these power bases exact a heavy price on agents. Much energy must be spent on maintaining social dependence and developing effective surveillance.

Expertness, referent, and legitimacy are also socially dependent forms of power, although they do not rely on surveillance. Expert power stems from the target's attribution of superior knowledge or ability to the agent. Referent power stems from the target's identification with the influencing person, or at least his or her desire for such identification. This is colloquially known as "star" power. Finally, legitimate power stems from a target's acceptance of a role structure relationship with the influencing agent. Typically, legitimacy is conferred on superiors in hierarchical relationships such that inferior targets acquiesce to or obey the agent's decisions.

French and Raven's model of social power is the most widely cited in the social psychological literature. However, this model may be more useful as a conceptual tool than as a model of reality. At the very least, it fails to consider how different power sources interact, how one chooses what power source to use, and the effects of the agent or target emotionality and the attribution processes.

At the heart of the social power model is the idea that when a human need or interest is frustrated, conflict results. According to this view, conflict occurs when interests of one party are perceived to be incompatible with interests of another party. Opposition created by competing interests hardens into positions around which polarization occurs. The parties then concentrate on defending these positions while attacking or undermining the other party's position.

Several assumptions underlie the social power model of conflict (Winslade and Monk, 2000). First, conflict is based on a psychology that focuses primarily on the individual rather than a social view of human beings. Individuals are prime movers and communities are made up of distinct human beings acting independently and who are accountable for their choices.

Second, the social power conflict model assumes that individuals are driven primarily by internally generated needs. These needs have their origin in human nature. Each party in the conflict is pursuing a path of self-interest such that a successful resolution of conflict requires that both parties meet their respective needs. Individual need theory relies on a set of assumptions that have been accepted in many psychological theories. For example, Freud's account of the individual's psychodynamic struggles and Maslow's hierarchy of needs assume an inherent self-interested, pleasure-seeking principle as a basic level of human motivation.

These assumptions frame how people construct their needs and desires. They influence expectations and behavior, affect the way people respond to one another, and inform what is acceptable about social arrangements. Expectations construct understandings of what moves or responses are possible and what outcomes are desirable.

Other Theories of Conflict

Human Needs Theory

Another theory of human conflict arises from a belief that depriving people of basic needs motivates them to fight. John Burton has been a major proponent of the human needs theory of conflict (Burton and Sandole, 1986). Burton's thesis is based on Abraham Maslow's hierarchy of needs. Maslow has argued that people strive to fulfill needs in a particular order, starting at physiological needs and moving up the scale to end at self-actualization (Maslow, 1987). Maslow implies that each level must be reasonably satisfied before the next need can be.

Burton asserts that people seek to fulfill a set of deep-seated, universal needs, restrained only by desire to protect valued relationships. Burton took this one step farther by asserting that if needs are obstructed or thwarted, conflict will result. Depending on how fulfilled a person is—in terms of stability of position or direction and pace of movement—she or he can be characterized by competitive or cooperative processes of solving approaches to conflict and by distributive bargaining or problem-solving approaches to conflict resolution.

Conflict is assumed to happen because individual needs are not being met. Disputes arise when individuals, while attempting to fulfill their needs, encounter others who believe that their own needs are threatened. When needs are frustrated, a sense of deprivation arises to motivate needs satisfaction. Thus, deprivation is considered to be the underlying motivational drive for conflict. If the deprivation is satisfied the conflict is considered to be resolved.

Burton rejects the idea that conflict relates to allocation of scarce resources or that most conflicts must be resolved in a distributive way. While he acknowledges that resources may be scarce, scarcity relates to means, tactics, and metaphors, not to goals. For example, Burton says that identity is not a scarce product nor is security.

Burton's theory has deficiencies. First, he does not provide an adequate description of human needs nor an adequate definition of need. Second, his theory does not account for emotionality and non-rational preconscious behaviors. Third, he discounts the importance of culture and context within a conflict. For Burton, the key is to define the needs, agree on how to fulfill them, then act. If these conditions are met, Burton believes conflicts can be resolved.

Integrating Theories

Marc Howard Ross (Ross, 1993) recognized that human conflict is rooted in structural and psychocultural origins. Structural origins relate to the interests of the parties in conflict, while psychocultural origins relate to the interpretations given to conflict by the parties. Conflicts can be seen as a process of social communication whose messages are interpretable because disputants share a common frame of reference. Conflicts escalate when a common frame of reference is small because each side relies on its own understanding of what is going on, reading unintended meetings into a situation. Conflict is most successfully resolved when both structural and psychocultural origins are recognized.

Structural analysis of conflict hypothesizes that the stronger the ties of kinship, economy, and politics in a society, the lower the chances of conflict among individuals and groups. Thus, structural theory looks at the relationships within a society to predict whether conflict will emerge in the first place. In addition, structural analysis considers the underlying interests of the parties. Some interests are defined through the inequalities of power and resources inherent in particular levels of social complexity. Other interests are formed through interaction and exchange. Structural analysis includes such concepts as exchange theory and social power within its framework.

In contrast, a psychocultural analysis of conflict considers that much social action is ambiguous. Therefore, it stresses the importance of the interpretation of words and deeds in explaining why some disputes unleash intense conflict sequences, while others do not. Psychocultural analysis is based on social constructionism and psychology. Psychocultural theory is more relevant to the intensity of conflicts while structural theory explains the specific ways conflict and cooperation are organized.

Psychocultural dispositions are the widely shared, deep-seated, socially constructed internal representations of one's social world. These dispositions are developed through early relationships and ripen into standards by which groups and individuals evaluate their social worlds. In addition, these predispositions provide the basis for the interpretation of others' actions as well as a guide to one's own behavior. Dispositions learned early in life are also implicated in specific behavioral patterns that serve one throughout life, such as how to respond to perceived insults, when to use physical aggression, or whom to trust. Thus, conflict behavior scripts are learned from infancy and embedded in the repertoire of automatic behaviors.

In summary, social structural theory emphasizes the competing interests of groups as prime motivators of conflict. Psychocultural conflict theory explains conflict in terms of psychological and cultural forces that frame beliefs about self, others, and behavior. From a psychocultural perspective, objective situations alone do not cause overt conflict. Instead, the interpretation of situations is central to understanding the intensity and duration of conflict. The two analyses complement each other and are necessary for truly understanding the dynamics of human conflict.

Conclusion

Legal theory provides an explanation, justification, and direction for understanding the purpose and application of rules of law to particular disputes. Thus, legal theory is abstract and removed from the dispute itself. In contrast, conflict theory attempts to model conflict by examining the social interaction within human societies. While legal theory provides guidance as to how a decision should be reached, conflict theory explains why the conflict arose in the first place and suggests what might be done about it now. The various strands of conflict theory provide insights into the nature of disputes that help peacemakers in understanding and responding to them.

Reflections on Chapter Twelve

1. The two couples sat across the table from one another. They were involved in a conflict over the sale of a business. The sellers, the Sauls, had agreed not to compete with the buyers. The buyers, the Burtons, paid $5,000 down and gave the Sauls a promissory note for $45,000 payable monthly over 5 years. The Burtons had paid like clockwork for two years when they learned that the Sauls had signed up with an Internet company to conduct a business that looked suspiciously like the Burtons' business. The Burtons consulted their lawyer, who, at their request, sent a strongly worded, inflammatory letter to the Sauls. The letter accused the Sauls of fraud, breach of contract, and other assorted wrongful conduct and demanded that the Sauls take specific steps to stop their affiliation with the Internet company. Although the Sauls believed they were well within their rights to affiliate with the Internet company, they wished to avoid any conflict. They promptly complied with the Burtons' demands.

Unfortunately, the Sauls' actions did not satisfy the Burtons, and the Burtons stopped paying on the note. The Sauls, seeing no alternative, filed a lawsuit to enforce the note, and the Burtons, naturally enough, filed a cross-complaint, claiming the Sauls to be deceitful and dishonest.

a. Perform a brief legal analysis of the issues presented.

b. Now, analyze this conflict using the conflict theory principles of this chapter.

c. How do the two analyses differ?

d. What insights does a conflict theory analysis add to a legal analysis?

2. Imagine you were mediating between a master and a slave. What should be the issues? How would conflict theory help define the issues?

CHAPTER THIRTEEN

GAME THEORY

*I*N PUCCINI'S OPERA *TOSCA,* corrupt police chief Scarpia has condemned Tosca's lover Cavaradossi to death. Scarpia lusts after Tosca and offers her a deal. If Tosca will make love with him, he will instruct the firing squad to use blank bullets and spare Cavaradossi. Tosca consents. As much as she despises Scarpia, saving her lover is more important than withholding her favors.

Should Tosca go along with the deal? The two parts of the bargain are effectively simultaneous. Tosca does not have sex with Scarpia until he has given irrevocable orders to use blanks (or real bullets). The story, of course, ends in mutual betrayal. Tosca betrays Scarpia by stabbing him as they embrace. Scarpia, ever corrupt, does not tell the firing squad to use blanks and Cavaradossi is executed. Tosca leaps off a parapet to her death as the police arrive to arrest her for murder (Poundstone, 1992).

This story, like so many stories in literature, illustrates a classic Prisoner's Dilemma—a form of conflict studied by mathematicians and social scientists under the rubric of game theory (see pp. 340).

Game theory is the study of mathematical models of conflict and cooperation between intelligent, rational decision-makers. Game theory helps us understand how people react when they must make decisions with incomplete information, but does not necessarily predict or guide people toward the best decisions. Furthermore, game theory illustrates how decision-making can be inefficient because of poor information exchange.

John Von Neumann, in collaboration with economist Oskar Morgenstern, founded game theory. Von Neumann (1903-1957) was born in Budapest in 1903. During the 1920s and 1930s, his work included quantum theory, mathematical logic, continuous geometry, and abstract algebra. He was professor in the school of mathematics and the Institute for Advanced Study at Princeton University from 1933 until 1954. Von Neumann first became known internationally for his work in developing the digital computer. Working with the team at the Moore School of Electrical Engineering in Philadelphia, in 1946 he constructed ENIAC, the first digital computer. Von Neumann set out the design principles for digital computers that in essentials remain unchanged today. After ENIAC, von Neumann designed a smaller and much more powerful computer fifty times faster than ENIAC. New storage methods were designed and new programming techniques suggested, leading to the present-day digital computers. The first four generations of digital computers are now called Von Neumann machines since they all followed Von Neumann's earliest design. As a result, nearly all modern computer languages are Von Neumann languages (Roth, 1993).

Von Neumann's most famous work was *The Theory Of Games and Economic Behavior* (published in 1944. The book developed a general theory of the rational behavior of two or more people in what are basically conflicting or competing situations. First, von Neumann developed the theory of two-person, zero-sum games, in which one player's gain is the other player's loss. He then suggested the concept of equilibrium, known as the minimax solution. In this solution, one player minimizes the maximum loss the other player can impose upon him. The solution of a game depends on the players using mixed strategies where the actual moves are chosen at random.

Over the years, games for many players have been devised. The special case of the Prisoner's Dilemma was defined, and thousands of studies have explored the various aspects of game theory in a wide variety of contexts.

Economic Theory vs. Game Theory

Economic theory assumes that human beings are absolutely rational in their choices. Specifically, economists assume that each person maximizes his or her rewards in the circumstances that she or he faces. This hypothesis serves a double purpose in the study of the allocation of resources. First, it narrows the range of possibilities of choice because rational behavior is more predictable than irrational behavior. Second, it provides a criterion for evaluating the efficiency of an economic system. If a system leads to a reduction in the rewards coming to some people without producing more than compensating rewards to others, then something is wrong.

In economic theory, the rational individual faces a system of institutions, including property rights, money, and competitive markets. These are among "circumstances" a person takes into account when maximizing rewards. Normally, an individual does not consider her interactions with others. She need consider only her own situation and "conditions of the market." The assumptions of economic theory are also its limitations. The theory does not apply when competition is restricted (but there is no monopoly) or when property rights are not fully defined. Also, classical economic theory does not account for decisions made outside the money economy.

In contrast, game theory provides a theory of strategic behavior when people interact directly rather than "through the market." Games have always been metaphors for interaction in human society. In game theory, the individual's choice is essentially a choice of strategy. Unlike economics, in which outcome is determined by aggregate forces working in the market, the outcome of a game depends on the strategies chosen by each of the players in the game.

Like economics, game theory assumes intelligent, rational decision-makers. A decision-maker is rational if decisions are in pursuit of his own objectives. Game theorists assume that each player's objective is to maximize the expected value of his own payoff measured on some utility scale. Maximum expected utility payoff is not the same as maximizing expected monetary payoff because utility values are not necessarily valued in money. For example, a person will receive more incremental value (or utility) from an extra dollar when poor than she would receive from the same dollar if wealthy.

Game theory also assumes that players are intelligent. A player is intelligent if he knows everything that the theorist knows about the game and can make any inferences about the situation that the theorist can make. This assumption is obviously not satisfied in real life. However, if a theory predicts that some individuals will be systematically fooled or led into costly mistakes, the theory will tend to lose its validity as those individuals learn from experience.

Cooperative vs. NoncooperativeGames

In game theory, gaming types are cooperative or noncooperative. Players can make binding commitments in a cooperative game but not in a noncooperative one. Cooperative game theory is axiomatic and appeals to fairness and equity. Noncooperative game theory is more economic, with solutions based on players maximizing their own positions. Cooperative game theory models bargaining and negotiation; noncooperative game theory models strategic choices in the absence of ability to make binding commitments.

The difference between cooperative and noncooperative games does not lie in the presence or absence of conflict. The following situations illustrate this point (Rasmussen, 1994):

A cooperative game without conflict: Members of a work group decide which of several difficult tasks to work on so as to best coordinate their efforts. In this case, the workers make binding commitments to work together (cooperation) and develop mutual goals (no conflict).

A cooperative game with conflict: Bargaining over price between two monopolists. The monopolists are bargaining, which is cooperative, but have competing interests in setting price (conflict).

A noncooperative game with conflict: The Prisoner's Dilemma (see next page).

A noncooperative game without conflict: Two companies set a product standard without communication. Acne and Beta, corporations independently choose a software platform for their computers. No bargaining occured so the process was noncooperative. Their interests are not so adverse so there is no conflict.

Elements of a Game

Game theory requires four components:
- The Players—individuals who make decisions;
- The Order of Play and the Actions available to each play at each point in the game;
- The Information available to players at the time they make decisions; and
- The Outcomes and Payoffs resulting from different combinations of actions.

Once the rules of the game are defined, the game must be "solved." Solving a game means finding the best strategies for each player and the equilibrium that will result if each player selects her best strategy. To solve the game, the theorist must decide what constitutes the equilibrium of best strategies, using what is called an equilibrium or solution concept. The most common equilibrium is the Nash Equilibrium, which is described later in this chapter.

Two representations of games have developed over time. The older form, prevalent in the 1950s and 1960s, is called the normal form. The normal form of representation uses a matrix to relate strategies and payoffs. The extensive form of representation uses a decision tree consisting of a series of nodes. Each node represents a decision point where the player must take action.

The matrix representation suppresses the dynamic nature of the game and the information that is revealed as the game is played. In contrast, the extensive form of representation demonstrates when players have imperfect information. Thus, the extensive form representation is appropriate for games with asymmetric or incomplete information. In these games, some player has useful private information—information that is not directly observable by the other players. In a game of incomplete information, at least one player is unsure about any or all of the different parts of the game: players, strategies, or payoffs.

1,1	2,1
2,1	2,2

Matrix Form of Game

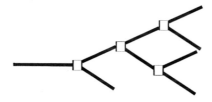

Extensive Form of Game

The Prisoner's Dilemma

While the publication of *The Theory of Games and Economic Behavior* was a critical beginning step in game theory, the invention of the Prisoner's Dilemma was even more important.

In January, 1950, Melvin Dresher and Merrill Flood, while at the Rand Corporation, conducted an experimental game that has become known as the Prisoner's Dilemma. Later that year, at Stanford, visiting professor A.W. Tucker discussed the experiment with an audience of psychologists to illustrate the difficulty of analyzing certain kinds of games. He called the game the Prisoner's Dilemma, and it has since spawned a vast body of literature in subjects as diverse as philosophy, ethics, biology, sociology, political science, economics, and game theory. More than 2,000 published studies have involved the Prisoner's Dilemma and its variations (Roth, 1993).

Tucker began with a little story. Two burglars, Bob and Al, are captured near the scene of a burglary. They are interrogated separately by the police. Each has to choose whether or not to confess and implicate the other. If neither person confesses, then both will serve one year on a charge of carrying a concealed weapon. If each confesses and implicates the other, both will go to prison for ten years. If one burglar confesses and implicates the other, and the other burglar does not confess, the one who confesses will go free while the other person will go to prison for 20 years on the maximum charge.

The burglars have two strategies: confess or do not confess. The payoffs, which are penalties in this case, are the sentences served. In game theory, the strategies and the payoffs of a game for its participants are summarized in a payoff table. The payoff table is constructed as follows:

Strategy Number 1

Al Confesses	Al gets 10 years
Bob Confesses	Bob gets 10 years

In strategy number one, if both Bob and Al confess, they both will get the intermediate sentence. Their difficulty is in knowing what the other will do. Since the police have separated them, they cannot communicate with each other to coordinate a strategy that will maximize their payoffs. Each must ask himself, "Do I trust the other guy or not?"

Strategy Number 2

Al Doesn't Confess	Al gets 20 years
Bob Confesses	Bob goes free

In strategy number two, if Bob confesses and Al states silent, Bob goes free while Al gets the maximum sentence. This is Bob's best payoff and Al's worst payoff. Bob's first choice would then be to confess, as long as he is assured that Al will remain silent.

Strategy Number 3

Al Confesses	Al goes free
Bob Doesn't Confess	Bob gets 20 years

In strategy number three, the situation is reversed from that of strategy number two. If Al confesses he goes free as long as Bob does not confess.

Strategy Number 4

Al Doesn't Confess	Al gets 1 year
Bob Doesn't Confess	Bob gets 1 year

Finally, in strategy number four, if neither Bob nor Al confess they each get a relatively light sentence of one year.

The full payoff table looks as follows:

		Al	
		Confess	Do Not Confess
Bob	Confess	10, 10	0, 20
	Do Not Confess	20, 0	1,1

What strategies are "rational" if both men want to minimize the time they spend in jail? Al might reason as follows: "Two things can happen. First, Bob can confess or Bob can keep quiet. Suppose Bob confesses. If I do not confess, I get 20 years. If I do confess, I get ten years. Therefore, if Bob confesses, my best choice is to confess. On the other hand, suppose that Bob does not confess. If I do not confess, I get a year. If I do confess, I can go free. Whatever Bob does, my best choice is to confess. Therefore, I'll confess." Al is acting rationally when he decides to confess because from his perspective, confession minimizes the worst outcome, a 20-year prison sentence.

Bob will presumably reason in the same way. Consequently, they will both rationally conclude to confess, and they will both go to prison for ten years. Had they acted "irrationally" by keeping quiet, they each could get off with a one-year sentence. Economists characterize the "rational" result of this decision-making as inefficient because the optimal result for both Bob and Al was not achieved.

Note that Bob is minimizing his worst outcome instead of seeking the best outcome for him and Al. This is the idea of minimax. Much of how people deal with conflict involves making the best of a bad situation. This natural defensive attitude prevents disputants from seeing possibilities for mutual gain based on cooperation. In the Prisoner's Dilemma, like most other conflicts, the cost of misplacing trust in the other to cooperate is so high one can only seek the best possible result for oneself. Thus, the Prisoner's Dilemma models why people may be uncooperative when cooperation will yield a higher payoff. It explains the difficulty of achieving peace.

The payoff table also illustrates a conceptual description common in game theory that has been transported into general language usage:

		Al	
		Confess	Do Not Confess
Bob	Confess	Lose, Lose	Lose, Win
	Do Not Confess	Win, Lose	Win, Win

The term *win-win* comes from this type of game theory payoff table in which one of the payoffs maximizes benefits to both of the participants.

Equilibrium

Definition

Players are assumed to seek for themselves the highest payoffs. However, their payoffs are always affected by the choices of the other player. Players therefore work through the various combinations of their choices and the possible choices of the other players to decide what strategy will be best. In the Prisoner's Dilemma, for example, we saw how Bob's thinking took him through the choices. After considering all of the combinations, Bob decided on a strategy: Confess. Confessing would provide him a minimum sentence, no matter what Al did. Thus, confessing is Bob's equilibrium strategy. Similarly, Al goes through his analysis and concludes that Confessing is his best strategy. Al's equilibrium strategy is therefore to Confess.

Equilibrium is defined as a strategy profile consisting of the best strategy for each player in the game. Equilibrium is therefore the collection of the individuals' separate rules for choosing what they perceive to be their best action. There are several equilibrium definitions important in game theory, two of which are the Dominant Strategy and the Nash Equilibrium.

Game modelers use mathematical expressions to solve for the equilibrium of a game. The modeler's primary objective is to find the equilibrium in a game, which can then be used to predict the likely outcome of the game.

Dominant Strategy

The Prisoner's Dilemma poses the question, "Why did Bob and Al individually chose a strategy that made them both worse off than if they had cooperated?" If neither confesses, both receive light sentences. What has happened here is that the two prisoners have fallen into "dominant strategy equilibrium."

The dominant strategy of any game occurs when the player, facing multiple strategies, individually decides that the same strategy will maximize his payoffs no matter what the other participant does. This is demonstrated by Al's reasoning. Al first considered his strategic choices if Bob confessed. Under that condition, Al decided that confession would be his best option. Al then considered his choices if Bob did not confess. If Bob did not confess, Al's best option was still to confess. Thus under every combination of choices, Al saw his strategy as being the same: To confess. Confession was therefore Al's dominant strategy.

If both players have a dominant strategy, and if each player selects the dominant strategy, than the combination of strategies and payoffs constitutes the *dominant strategy equilibrium* for that game. In the Prisoner's Dilemma, to confess is a dominant strategy. When both Bob and Al confessed, then the game reached *dominant strategy equilibrium*.

One might argue that Al and Bob, recognizing their dilemma, should make a leap of faith and trust each other to decide unilaterally to cooperate. But just as Al (or Bob) says to himself, "Well, maybe I should cooperate and gamble that Bob will cooperate as well," he realizes two things. First, if Bob is rational he will confess, and second, even if Bob wants to cooperate he will have to count on the fact that Al is rational and will confess. Al therefore confesses and acts out the logic of the Prisoner's Dilemma.

Whenever the parties to conflict face choices that hurt all of them, the first thought should be of the Prisoner's Dilemma. The challenge is to explain the situation to the parties so that they are motivated to build a foundation of mutual cooperation rather than relying on self-interest. Cooperation is sometimes difficult to build because of the fear of exploitation. Just like the Prisoner's Dilemma, if one party cooperates and the other does not, the non-cooperator will achieve a tremendous gain at the expense of the cooperator. If neither cooperates, both are assured of something less than the maximum loss, but do not achieve the potential maximum gain.

One of the reasons peacemaking is conceptually difficult for lawyers is their fear that clients will be exploited. Consequently, minimizing the risk is often more important than maximizing the gain.

The Nash Equilibrium

From the relatively simple Prisoner's Dilemma game, more complex games can be developed to illustrate problems of strategic choices. Consider the following problem of procurement.

Acme Corporation is considering a new Web-based ordering system. It has a choice between two technologies, one of which is established and proven, the other of which is advanced and not yet accepted in the marketplace. Beta Company designs and develops Web-based ordering systems. It is assessing the marketplace and is trying to decide whether to go with the advanced technology or remain with the proven technology. In this example, Acme and Beta are not talking to each other, but have to decide which direction to pursue. If they both decide to pursue the advanced technology, which Beta will produce and Acme will purchase, both companies will profit. If they both decide to remain with the proven technology, they will profit, but not as much. If one decides to pursue the advanced technology and the other decides to remain with the proven technology, both will lose.

The payoff table for choices and strategies might look like this:

		Acme	
		Advanced	Proven
Beta	Advanced	20, 20	0, 0
	Proven	0, 0	5, 5

Both companies will be better off if an advanced system is installed. The worst case is if one party commits to an advanced system, while the other commits to a proven system. In that case, no deal can be reached and there are no payoffs for anyone. To reach the optimal decision, Acme and Beta must agree on a compatible standard. Since the choice of standard is a strategic choice, their strategies must mesh.

This game has no dominant strategies because the best strategy for each participant depends on the strategy chosen by the other participant. In other words, neither company can choose a strategy that will maximize its payoff across all possible choices.

When no dominant strategies exist in a game, the concept of the *Nash Equilibrium* comes into play. A Nash equilibrium exists if each participant chooses the best strategy, given the strategy chosen by the other participant. More precisely, a strategy profile is a Nash equilibrium if no player will deviate from his strategy given that the other players do not deviate (Rasmussen, 1994).

In this game, if Acme chooses the advanced system, then Beta should do so also. Consequently, Advanced-Advanced is a Nash equilibrium.

Similarly, if Acme chooses the proven system, Beta should also choose the proven system. Based on Acme's choice to remain with the established system, Beta's best decision is to follow suit. Thus, Proven-Proven is also a Nash equilibrium.

The way to find a Nash equilibrium is to propose a strategy profile, then test each player's strategy against the other players' strategies. If the tested player's strategy is a best response, it is a Nash equilibrium strategy.

This game demonstrates the possibility of more than one Nash equilibrium in the set of choices available to the participants. The question is how to decide which Nash equilibrium to select. If Acme believes that Beta will choose the proven system because Acme thinks Beta is conservative, then both players will be best off to choose the proven system. Both companies will therefore assume the other company is conservative. This is the danger of a class of games called coordination games. Of course, Acme and Beta do not have to remain silent, as they may sit down and talk it out. From their discussions, they can agree on a standard and enter into a contract.

When more than one Nash equilibrium exists, game theorists classify them as either strong or weak. A strong Nash equilibrium requires that a player be indifferent to other strategies. A weak Nash equilibrium suggests that, given a choice, a player would prefer one equilibrium to another. In the Acme-Beta game, the Proven-Proven outcome is a weak Nash equilibrium, while the Advanced-Advanced is a strong Nash equilibrium. This is because the players would prefer the higher payoff available with Advanced-Advanced.

The Nash equilibrium assumes correct and consistent beliefs across players. It also assumes some form of communication about intentions.

Focal Points

When there are multiple Nash equilibriums, focal points offer clues as to which strategy will be chosen. A focal point is a Nash equilibrium that, for psychological reasons, is compelling. In coordination games, the players have to coordinate their responses to maximize their outcomes. In deciding what action to choose, players will often seek out the response they think the other person would choose. For example, assume you and your friend are asked to split a pie, but you each will get nothing if the proportions add to more than 100 percent. That is to say, you must choose a percentage and your friend must choose a percentage, the total of which cannot exceed 100 percent. If you cannot talk to your friend, the focal point will probably be a Nash equilibrium of 50/50.

In repeated games, focal points are suggested by history. If you split the pie last year on the basis of 60/40, that becomes a focal point for the split this year.

Boundaries are focal points. A nation may move up to one inch of its boundary and not evoke a hostile response from the neighbor. Should the nation cross the boundary, the neighbor declares war. Boundaries also convey information: a boundary incursion conveys intent to invade and take over. On the other hand, staying within boundaries conveys an intention to respect sovereignty.

Focal points often arise during settlement negotiations in litigation. When lawyers decide to attempt settlement, they are interested in two things. First, they want to settle the case because an efficient settlement satisfies clients. Second, they want to settle the case so as to gain maximum utility for their client. For the plaintiff in a personal injury action, this often means settling for the highest amount possible. Conversely, the insurance company seeks settlement at the least cost. Offers and counteroffers convey subtle information about where each side sees potential settlement. After several rounds in the auction, astute lawyers look for a point of future convergence. This point then becomes a focal point upon which a possible settlement might rest. Focal points can also be points of resistance. For example, the plaintiff's lawyer in a sexual harassment case might place a settlement value of $150,000 on the case, but the defendant's lawyer will not pay over $99,000. Thus, $100,000 becomes a focal point, giving the plaintiff the decision whether to settle or go to trial. If the plaintiff insists on $150,000, the focal point indicates a place of impasse and settlement negotiations will break off.

Equilibrium and Mediation

The Prisoner's Dilemma demonstrates how conflict can be inefficient. By inefficient, game theorists mean that the players cannot find strategies that will offer each player maximum utility. If Bob and Al each decided not to confess, they would have been better off. Since the Prisoner's Dilemma forced the burglars to confess, they were not able to choose the best mutual strategy. As we have seen, an equilibrium strategy is the means by which a game theorist predicts the game's outcome. When an equilibrium strategy exists, it represents the individual players' best perceptions of how to maximize their own utility given the nature of the game and choices faced by other players.

If the players cannot communicate, a mediator can suggest equilibrium to them. Typically, the mediator will suggest a settlement amount somewhere between high and low that the mediator believes will be acceptable to all parties. Without the mediator's intervention, the parties would have had difficulty finding this equilibrium point for themselves. Consequently, in the absence of a focal point upon which to establish an equilibrium, mediation and communication become important.

Game Theory and Social Dilemmas

The Prisoner's Dilemma illustrates one common type of social dilemma. As it turns out, game theory also describes another social dilemma common in conflict situations and called Chicken (Poundstone, 1992). Chicken is an important model for a wide range of human conflicts. The name comes from the teenage automobile challenge made famous in a series of 1950s and 1960s low budget juvenile delinquent Hollywood films the most notorious of which was "Rebel Without a Cause." In that movie, L.A. teenagers drove stolen cars to a cliff. The drivers jumped out at the last minute, but the one who jumped out first was "chicken" and lost. The game changed from racing over a cliff to two cars accelerating toward each other down a highway centerline. The first car to swerve was the loser.

The outcomes of the game are clear. The worst outcome is for neither car to swerve, which case there is highway carnage. The best outcome from the perspective of either driver is for the other car to swerve first, thereby proving the non-swerving driver's superior courage. The next to least attractive outcome is to swerve. The swerving driver may be taunted as being a coward, but at least he or she is alive to take it. The fourth alternative is a cooperative outcome: both drivers can swerve at the same moment. Both come out alive and no one can claim the other chickened out first.

Chicken differs from the Prisoner's Dilemma in that mutual defection (both drivers stay on course and crash) is the worst outcome (Poundstone, 1992). In the Prisoner's Dilemma, the worst outcome occurs when one player cooperates when the other player defects. The players in a Prisoner's Dilemma are better off defecting no matter what the other player does. In Chicken, on the other hand, cooperation leads to the best result, either by unilaterally missing or by both swerving at the last moment. Another curious feature of Chicken is that both players want to do opposite of whatever the other is going to do. If one knows the other will swerve, the incentive to drive straight is high. In Chicken, swerving (cooperation) minimizes the maximum harm the other player can inflict. In the Prisoner's Dilemma, defection is the minimax solution.

In games of Chicken, played out in real life conflicts, face-saving measures are called for. When one side can find an excuse, even if flimsy and transparent, to back down, the dilemma ceases.

The Prisoner's Dilemma and Chicken models are disturbing because the common good is subverted by individual rationality. Each player desires the other's cooperation, yet is tempted to defect. In general terms, this means that each player would prefer to cooperate if the other cooperates (CC) over cooperating only to have the other player defect (CD). In both the Prisoner's Dilemma and Chicken, this preference is clear. Likewise, each player would rather defect if the other side cooperates (DC) than have both players defect (DD). If the four payoffs are ordered and analyzed such that there is either an incentive to defect when the other player cooperates (DC>CC) or there is an incentive to defect when the other party defects (DD>CD), four games are defined (Poundstone, 1992). Each is has its own name.

DC>DD>CC>CD	Deadlock
DC>CC>DD>CD	Prisoner's Dilemma
DC>CC>CD>DD	Chicken
CC>DC>DD>CD	Stag Hunt

Each game is common in human conflict and each is therefore a social dilemma. All are closely related in that they are derived from the Prisoner's Dilemma by switching two of the payoffs in the order of preference. Chicken is a Prisoner's Dilemma in which confession and silence reversed. The Stag Hunt is the Prisoner's Dilemma with the preferences of reward and temptation payoffs reversed. Deadlock is a Prisoner's Dilemma with the reward and punishment payoffs switched.

Deadlock looks like this:

	Cooperate	Defect
Cooperate	1,1	0,3
Defect	3,0	2,2

Deadlock occurs when two parties fail to cooperate because neither really wants to. They just want the other player to cooperate. The difference between Deadlock and the Prisoner's Dilemma is that the parties prefer mutual defection to mutual cooperation. The only way to solve Deadlock is to increase the utility of mutual cooperation so that it is more attractive than mutual defection. The problem is that if cooperation leads to a payoff that is lower than either CD or DC, the players shift into a Prisoner's Dilemma.

Stag Hunt is described by Poundstone (1992) in the following story. It's late May, next to the last day of school. You and a friend decide it would be a great joke to show up on the last day of school with some ridiculous haircut. Egged on by your clique, you both swear you will get the haircut.

A night of indecision follows. As you anticipate your parents' and your teachers' reactions to the haircut, you start wondering if your friend is really going to go through with the plan. The best possible outcome is that you both get the haircut. The trouble is that it would be awful to be the only one showing up with the haircut. On the other hand, it might be kind of fun to see your friend's embarrassment at being the only one with the weird haircut. If you didn't get the haircut, but your friend did, and looked like a real jerk, that would almost be as good as if both of you got the haircut. After mulling things over, you decide that it really wouldn't be so bad if no one got the hair cut. Maybe everyone will just forget about it. (This is what mother says will happen.)

The outcomes in preferred order are to cooperate (both get haircuts), unilateral defection (friend gets haircut, but you don't), mutual defection (both decide not to get haircut), and unilateral cooperation (you get the haircut, but your friend does not). The payoffs look like this:

	Cooperate	Defect
Cooperate	3,3	0,2
Defect	2,0	1,1

You should certainly cooperate because that guarantees that both of you will get the highest payoff. But it also assumes that you are both rational. The problem is that your friend may not be so rational and may chicken out. If that happens, you want to chicken out too.

The reason the game is called Stag Hunt is because it illustrated the same problem in the ancient hunt. If the hunters wanted to kill a stag, everyone had to remain at assigned posts, but if a rabbit went by, any hunter might take off after it. Having caught the rabbit, the lone hunter would little care if the others failed to catch the stag.

Stag Hunt illustrates the situation when mutual cooperation is a Nash equilibrium. No one can do better no matter what. The temptation to defect only arises when a player believes the other player has reason or motivation to defect. For this reason, the dilemma is most acute when the rationality of the other player is in doubt or in large enough groups of people such that some defection is likely.

Consider the issue of wearing seat belts. Everyone is better off by cooperating and wearing seatbelts. However, the inconvenience and sheer nuisance of the device meant that many people simply refused to wear them. Only when laws requiring seatbelts were passed, did people cooperate.

The final complication with social dilemmas occurs when the players have different preferences. In each of the four games, the players held symmetric preferences in that each would prefer the same outcome over another outcome. However, preferences do not have to match up. In this case, the game is said to be asymmetric. For example, one player's preferences could be that of a Prisoner's Dilemma, while the other player's may be those of a Stag Hunt or Chicken.

The game of Bully is a cross between Chicken and Deadlock (Poundstone, 1992). One player has the preference of Chicken because unilateral defection is preferred and mutual defection is dreaded. The other player has the Deadlock preference of mutual defection no matter what. These preferences set up a game that looks like this:

		Deadlock Player	
		Cooperate	Defect
Chicken Player	Cooperate	2,1	1,3
	Defect	3,0	0,2

Bully is a model for a legal conflict in which one party prefers to go to trial while the other party sees trial as a catastrophe to be avoided at all costs. To the extent that this model is accurate, it provides a gloomy prediction because the belligerent party will likely get its way. The conciliatory party will be exploited to maintain the peace. This model also explains the results of power imbalances created by greater resources, patience, or stubbornness.

Information

Information inefficiencies are common barriers to resolving conflict. Information inefficiency occurs when information is unknown to one or both sides of the conflict. Without complete information, people must speculate. Under the assumption of rationality, each disputant will select a choice that, based on all information known and unknown, will maximize utility.

Game theorists treat information on the basis of who holds it. The information itself is irrelevant to the information conditions of the game. Information conditions include common knowledge, perfect vs. imperfect information, symmetric vs. asymmetric information, and certain vs. uncertain information. Symmetric vs. asymmetric information is the most important information condition in conflict and will therefore be taken up separately.

Common Knowledge

Information is common knowledge if all the players know it, if each player knows that all the players know it, and if each player knows that all the players know that all the players know it. This condition exists in litigation when full discovery has been completed by or under the supervision of a seasoned trial lawyer.

Perfect vs. Imperfect Information

A condition of perfect information means that a player knows every choice made by the other player. Imperfect information would exist if a player knew that the opponent had made Choice A or Choice B, but did not know which specific choice had been made. The larger the information set, the more imperfect the information condition. This condition might exist if defense counsel knew that plaintiff's counsel had retained two experts, but did not know which expert might testify at trial.

Certain vs. Uncertain Information

A game of certainty has no moves by nature (luck) after any player has moved. Moves by nature are pieces of information that remain outside the control of the parties. Essentially, nature is the probability of the occurrence of an outside event. If nature has made its last move, the information condition is defined as certain. Otherwise the game is one of uncertainty. In the context of a lawsuit, the information condition is uncertain until the verdict is read. The jury's decision is, in game theory, a move by nature, because the disputants cannot control or predict it with certainty. After the verdict, the information condition becomes certain. Of course, the judgment is appealable, so the information condition might still be uncertain because another move by nature (the appellate court) is possible.

Symmetric vs. Asymmetric Information

In a game of symmetric information, at each decision point, a player's information is identical to that of every other player. Otherwise, the game is asymmetric. The essence of asymmetric information is that it is useful private information available to one, but not all players.

Asymmetric information is a primary reason for impasse. Nearly every conflict is an asymmetric information condition because each disputant knows privately how he or she desires resolution. Unless the disputants somehow communicate their private information to each other, conflict resolution is difficult.

If resolution is reached in an asymmetric information condition, parties will wonder if they made the correct decisions. This can lead to buyer's remorse, to recriminations, and to renewed hostility. Consequently, transforming a conflict from an asymmetric information condition to a symmetric information condition is important to the potential for resolution.

Complete vs. Incomplete Information

In a game of incomplete information, nature moves first and is not observed by at least one of the players. Otherwise, the game is one of complete information. Notice the difference between complete/incomplete and certain /uncertain information conditions. In uncertain conditions, nature makes the last move and no one knows what it will be. In incomplete conditions, nature makes the first move, but that information is not known to at least one of the disputants.

These concepts may be illustrated by the game of Poker (Rasmussen, 1994). In Poker, players make bets on who will have the best card hand at game's end. The best hand is determined by a preestablished ranking.

Here is how Poker can help us understand the concept of information:

All cards are dealt face up.	Perfect, certain
All cards are dealt face down and a player cannot look at her cards before betting.	Incomplete, symmetric, certain
All cards are dealt face down, and a player can look at her own cards.	Incomplete, asymmetric, certain
All cards are dealt face up, but each player then scoops up her hand and secretly discards one card.	Complete, asymmetric, certain
All cards are dealt face up, the players bet, then each player receives one more card face up.	Perfect, uncertain
All cards are dealt face down. Each player scoops up her cards without looking at them and places them on her forehead so everyone can see them but her (Indian Poker).	Incomplete, asymmetric, certain

In case number one, everyone sees everyone else's cards, so the information is perfect. Because no more cards will be dealt (i.e., nature or luck will not act), the information is also certain.

In case number two, the information is incomplete because no one knows what she holds. The information is symmetric because all are equally ignorant. The information is certain because all cards have been dealt—nature or luck will not act again. Notice that information content is not important here. Rather, it is the state of knowledge of the players. Even though all of the players are ignorant of the hands, the information is symmetric because they are all ignorant.

In case number three, the standard Poker game, the information is incomplete because the players do not know what the other players hold. The information is asymmetric because each player has private information about her own hand. Finally, the information is certain because no more cards will be dealt.

In case number four, the information is complete because everyone has seen everyone else's hand. The information becomes asymmetric when each player secretly discards a card, and the information is certain because no further cards will be drawn.

In case number five, the information is perfect because everyone sees all the hands, but the information is uncertain because nature will act once more to deal out another card.

Finally, in case number six, Indian Poker, the information is incomplete because the players do not know their own hands. The information is asymmetric because they have private information (each player's information is unique and personal), and the information is certain because no further cards will be dealt.

Dynamic Games with Asymmetric Information

Asymmetric information, and in particular, incomplete information, is important in game theory. In dynamic games, when players have moved several times in sequence, the earlier moves may convey private information relevant to the other players' decisions. This occurs frequently in negotiating settlements of litigated disputes. The lawyers know that the first demand and counteroffer set the boundaries of future bargaining. They are very sensitive to the messages being sent at each stage of the exchange. Revealing and concealing information are basic strategies in negotiation and explain actions that would otherwise be irrational in a nonstrategic world. Two asymmetric information conditions are relevant to conflicts—moral hazard and adverse selection.

Moral hazard is caused by hidden conduct. Because of moral hazard, insured people are more likely to take risks than uninsured people. In game theory, moral hazard occurs when Smith and Jones begin with symmetric information and agree to a contract. Then Smith takes an action unobserved by Jones. Information is complete, which means that nature has not made a move unobserved by either player. However, the information is also asymmetric because Smith has information not available to Jones.

Adverse selection is caused by hidden information that distorts the terms of a contract. Because of adverse selection, for example, ill people are more likely to purchase life insurance than healthy people. The insured's health is hidden information (assuming no fraud on the insurance application). Adverse selection is common in conflicts and negotiations. Potential buyers and sellers, for example, know how they personally value a good or service. This value is known as their reservation price. Fisher and Ury (Fisher et al., 1981) describe the reservation price as the "Best Alternative to a Negotiated Agreement" or BATNA. Because each party takes care not to disclose reservation prices, the information is "hidden" before an agreement is reached. This hidden pre-contractual information can create the problem of adverse selection.

Adverse selection involves pre-contractual information while moral hazard involves post-contractual information. In both cases, an asymmetric information condition exists because the disputants are able to hide information about each other. Both conditions impede efficient settlements. Adverse selection is inefficient because parties hide their valuations and settlement objectives before they reach agreement for fear of being exploited by the other side. As a result, opportunities for agreement are lost.

Moral hazard presents a different type of inefficiency known as the problem of coordination. In a coordination situation, disputants' must coordinate their activities to maximize their respective utilities. In a moral hazard condition, the parties cannot observe each other's behavior, making coordination difficult

Information and Efficiency

Game theorists and economists believe that if parties had symmetrical information, bargaining would be less costly. If both parties to a negotiation knew the other side's reservation price, both would immediately know if a gain could be made from a transaction. Second, if both sides knew their respective bargaining power, they could avoid bargaining inefficiencies by quickly agreeing how to divide the gains from trade. When reservation information is withheld, the parties do not know if any gain from trade is possible. They waste time and resources trying to discover if there are gains to be made and, if so, waste even more time and resources trying to divide the gains.

Typically, parties inflate initial demands or minimize initial offers to give themselves "bargaining room." While this is a time-tested negotiation strategy, from an economic perspective it is inefficient. The parties must laboriously go through rounds of offers and counters, called an auction, before they can finally decide if gains from agreement can be made. Furthermore, the parties may break off discussions prematurely if they decide that gains will not be possible. This leads to lost opportunities for mutual gains, which is also inefficient. In asymmetric information conditions, game theorists have demonstrated that caucusing is an effective technique for eliciting and channeling private information.

Mediators can increase information efficiency in three ways. First, they can commit the parties to break off negotiations when private representations indicate no gains from trade are possible. Second, they can commit the parties to divide equally the gains from trade. Finally, mediators can commit to send "noisy" information disclosed during private caucuses.

Each of these commitments allows a mediator to increase the amount and accuracy of private disclosures of information. This reduces the effect of private information and lowers adverse selection. Most significantly, game theory demonstrates that a mediator can actually improve information efficiency with imprecise communication. This is called "noisy" information in gaming terms. When a mediator commits to imprecise translation of private information given by one side for transmission to the other, the party with the private information is induced to disclose more information. The mediator's imprecision reduces the ability of the other disputant to use the private information against the party disclosing it

Game theory has created some provocative issues for mediation. First, the models suggest that a mediator have the power to call off negotiations if the mediator can see no mutual gains from trade. The purpose of this is not that the power would be exercised, but that it motivates parties to disclose their true reservation values earlier in the negotiation. If parties who want to settle know that the mediator might shut down the discussions if he or she can see no overlaps, they are more likely to be accurate in disclosing their private valuations. The technique is therefore thought to be useful for eliminating the early extreme positions taken by parties. This power is contrary to conventional beliefs because mediators generally do not have the power to shut down unilaterally settlement discussions. Furthermore, those who fall on the facilitative side of mediation would find the directedness of this commitment inconsistent with their values of mediation.

The idea that mediators not only disclose private information, but also be imprecise about it, is also contrary to normal practices. Mediators are normally bound to a standard of strict confidentiality. Furthermore, mediators place a high value on trust and integrity. The idea that a mediator would disclose private information even if imprecisely is therefore unsettling to conventional mediation practices. Nevertheless, models developed to test mediation functions in conflict have established that some form of controlled disclosure is central to any economic rationale for mediation.

Cooperative Games

Games in which the participants can make commitments to coordinate their strategies are "cooperative games." The solution to a "cooperative game" is a "cooperative solution." In a cooperative game, the rational person's problem is to answer the question, "What strategy choice will lead to the best outcome for all of us in this game?" This is the reason for integrative conflict behavior.

There are always two "rational solutions," to a cooperative game. The first is a "noncooperative" solution in which each person maximizes his or her own rewards regardless of the results for others. The second is a "cooperative solution" in which the strategies of the participants are coordinated so as to attain the best result for the entire group.

If people can arrive at a cooperative solution, any nonconstant sum game can in principal be converted to a win-win game. How, then, can a noncooperative outcome of a nonconstant sum game be rational? The obvious answer is that it cannot be rational; the cooperative solution is the only true rational outcome in a nonconstant sum game. Yet noncooperative interaction describes real outcomes that occur every day.

Noncooperative solutions occur when participants in the game cannot make credible commitments to cooperative strategies. This is a very common difficulty in many human interactions. Games in which the participants cannot make commitments to coordinate strategies are "noncooperative games." The solution to a "noncooperative game" is a "noncooperative solution." In a noncooperative game, the rational person's problem is to answer the question, "What is the rational choice of a strategy when other players will try to choose their best responses to my strategy?" This is the reason for distributive conflict behavior.

The basic Prisoner's Dilemma game assumes a one-time interaction. What would happen if the participants played multiple rounds of the Prisoner's Dilemma? In many settings, the same two individuals may meet more than once. If an individual can recognize a previous player and remember some aspects of the prior outcomes, then the strategic situation becomes an iterated Prisoner's Dilemma. A strategy would take the form of the decision rule that will specify the probability of cooperation or defection as a function of the history of the interaction.

Robert Axelrod, a leading game theorist and political scientist at the University of Michigan, conducted a computer tournament for the Prisoner's Dilemma to test what types of strategies could survive and thrive (Axelrod, 1997). He invited game theory professionals from all over the world, including people who had published articles on the Prisoner's Dilemma, to submit computer programs for playing a round robin, iterated version of the Prisoner's Dilemma. Each program would play every other program, a clone of itself, and a random (i.e., coin flipping) program, two hundred times. Fourteen game theorists in economics, sociology, political science, and mathematics submitted strategies, with programs ranging from the very simple to the moderately complex.

When the tournament was over, the simplest program, called "Tit for Tat," had won. Tit for Tat cooperated on the first play of the game, and mimicked its opponent on each successive play. If the other player defected, Tit for Tat punished it on the next play by also defecting. If the other player cooperated, Tit for Tat rewarded that move on the next play by also cooperating. Thus, Tit for Tat was a strategy of cooperation based on reciprocity. At the end of two hundred rounds, the highest average score was attained by the simplest of all strategies, Tit for Tat.

A second round was solicited. In this tournament, there were sixty-two entries from six countries, people of all ages and levels of expertise, and from eight different academic disciplines. All of the entrants were familiar with the results of the first round, and yet Tit for Tat won again. Tit for Tat was still able to evoke cooperation when other more sophisticated programs were not, even after these other programs saw Tit for Tat operate.

Axelrod traced Tit for Tat's robustness to four qualities. Tit for Tat (and successful strategies generally) succeeded because it was nice, provocable, forgiving, and transparent. It was nice in that it was never the first to defect. It was provocable in that it did not let a defection go unpunished. It was forgiving in that it punished each defection only once. Finally, it was transparent in that its playing patterns were easy to figure out. Opponents did not see it as defecting randomly or behaving obscurely, and thus they were not suspicious of it. The combination of initial trust in the opponent (never be the first to defect), a capacity for certain, but restrained, retaliation for transgressions (defect once and then forgive), and clarity of purpose (be transparent), accounted for Tit for Tat's success.

Axelrod then ran a series of hypothetical replays of the tournament in which the environment of each replay was determined by the results of the previous one. A program's score indicated its fitness, and fitness determined the number of progeny the program had in the next round. As the tournament progressed through generation after generation, the environment gradually changed. At the beginning, poor programs and good programs were equally represented, but as time passed, the poorer ones dropped out and the good ones flourished. The rank order of the good programs changed, however, because goodness was no longer measured against the same universe. Programs whose success came from interaction with other good programs continued to succeed. But programs that won because they were able to exploit dumb programs found their base of support eroding as dumb programs were gradually squeezed out, and eventually they suffered the same fate.

Tit for Tat fared spectacularly well in this "ecological tournament." After a thousand generations, its rate of growth was greater than that of any other program, even though it did not outscore a single one of its rivals in any of its encounters. Tit for Tat succeeded because it was able to elicit cooperation from the greatest number of other players. Axelrod concluded that Tit for Tat was able to do this because

> [O]ther rules anticipate [its] presence and are designed to do well with it. Doing well with [Tit for Tat] requires cooperating with it, and this in turn helps [Tit for Tat]. Even rules . . . that were designed to see what they could get away with, quickly apologize to [Tit for Tat]. Any rule which tries to take advantage of [Tit for Tat] will simply hurt itself. [It] benefits from its own nonexploitability. . . . (Axelrod, 1984, p. 53)

On the basis of the ecological tournament, Axelrod offered preliminary answers to three questions about the evolution of cooperative bargaining norms that had long troubled bargaining theorists.

The first asks how cooperation gets started in an environment of unconditional defection. The answer is through the invasion of small clusters of conditionally cooperating bargainers. In Axelrod's words, "[Mutual] cooperation can emerge in a world of egoists without central control by starting with a cluster of individuals who rely on reciprocity." Small clusters of cooperators can propagate even in a hostile environment, provided that they defend themselves in Tit for Tat-like fashion. Programs that are just nice (i.e., they are passive pacifists), on the other hand, will not survive.

The second question concerns robustness: What strategy does well in a shifting and unpredictable environment? The answer is that any strategy with the traits of niceness, provocability, forgiveness, and transparency will do so. Such strategies, once established, tend to flourish in an ecologically evolving world.

And the final question is about stability: Can cooperation protect itself from invasion? The ecological tournament proves that once cooperation is established it becomes permanent. As Axelrod puts it, "[T]he gear wheels of social evolution have a ratchet" (1984, p. 21).

The payoffs in the Prisoner's Dilemma characterize real life dispute bargaining. Successful defection, where one party exploits the other's unilateral disclosure, forbearance, or concession, time after time, without fear of retaliation or loss of cooperation, produces the largest returns in life as well as in games. Similarly, mutual cooperation results in bigger payoffs for both sides than mutual defection because bargaining stakes are divided between the parties rather than wasted in ego battles, or left on the table out of exhaustion or polarization (Condlin, 1992).

Unilateral cooperation produces the poorest returns because it is usually exploited. Real-life negotiators take what they are given, even when it is overly generous, and rarely think to ask if they should refuse part of it, or give some back.

The idea of bargaining to elicit cooperation from the other side may even be counterintuitive. Lawyers typically believe that good bargainers get disproportionately large settlements most of the time. The idea that one could win by losing or tying is not so widely grasped. In Axelrod's words:

> [Tit for Tat] won the tournament, not by beating the other player, but by eliciting behavior from the other player which allowed both to do well. . . . [I]n a non-zero-sum world you do not have to do better than the other player to do well for yourself. This is especially true when you are interacting with many different players. Letting each of them do the same or a little better than you is fine, as long as you tend to do well yourself. There is no point in being envious of the success of the other player, since in an iterated prisoner's dilemma of long duration the other's success is virtually a prerequisite of your doing well for yourself. (Axelrod, 1984, p. 112)

The problem faced by lawyers as negotiators is that they are compelled to maximize gains for specific clients. If the clients are one-shot players, lawyers have a hard time considering the long-term, strategic consequences of their bargaining behavior. On the other hand, if the lawyer represents clients over many negotiations, strategic negotiating behavior becomes more important. Thus, a plaintiff's lawyer representing an injured party in a one-shot case is less likely to be care about strategic behavior than the insurance defense lawyer who represents the insurance company in many cases.

Conclusion

While game theory provides some insight into the nature of cooperative and competitive behaviors, it is a limited model of human conflict. The limitations imposed by game theory are designed to reduce the variables to be studied. Consequently, theorists are very well aware that their simplified games do not model reality. Too often, theorists outside of game theory have failed to recognize these limitations and have relied on the game situation as representative of human conflict.

The game only provides two choices for each player. In real conflict, people rarely have two choices and usually face many choices. Game theory also assumes certain payoffs, without considering other possibilities. The payoffs are imposed by the theorist, while in real life many other payoffs are available and possible.

Game theory assumes rational self-interest. It does not account for emotion, hurt feelings, or any sense of injustice. It does not deal with relationship or identity issues. It does not deal with cultural issues. In fact, game theory does not model most of the underlying dynamics of conflict.

Game theory does not allow for communication between the parties nor intervention by a third party. Real conflict involves communication between parties, whether hostile or productive. In addition, many conflicts are resolved through the intervention of third parties.

Game theory assumes perfect knowledge of all strategic circumstances and all available strategic choices. Of course, in real conflict, the strategic circumstances are vaguely understood and choices are not always well defined or well known.

Finally, game theory does not model interpersonal conflict in its entirety, but only the conflict of interest between competition and cooperation. It does not provide insight into conflict behavior or the causes of conflict.

Nevertheless, game theory as explored through Axelrod's studies reveals the power of cooperation. The Tit for Tat strategy in Axelrod's games demonstrated how, over the long term, a conservative cooperative strategy tends to do better than purely competitive strategies. Thus, game theory lends support to other experimental studies showing the superiority of cooperation over competition.

Game theory is also useful in understanding the problem solving techniques people use in conflict situations. Many people in conflict fall back on game theory to simplify what they perceive as a complicated problem. This reductionistic approach is dangerous because it ignores the many subtleties of conflict and opportunities for peace. For example, many people view conflict as a zero-sum game in which one side must win at the other's expense. This narrow view precludes consideration of other options.

Finally, game theory demonstrates how people can make apparently rational choices, but miss opportunities for even greater gains. It develops the minimax solution to conflict as an alternative explanation to the economic assumption of rational self-interest. In real life, people perceive their strategic situation as minimizing the maximum amount of harm others can do to them. Hence, their conflict strategies do not follow a strategy of maximizing personal utility.

Reflections on Chapter Thirteen

You have been assigned to mediate a breach of contract matter. Both sides and their lawyers appear highly competitive. Using the lessons of game theory, construct some arguments to convince them that cooperation is better than competition.

Describe a conflict situation for each of the social dilemmas described by Prisoner's Dilemma, Chicken, Deadlock, Stag Hunt, and Bully.

If cooperation produces superior results to competition, why do people persist in unprofitable competitive behaviors? Provide some written explanations for this phenomenon.

Is seeking cooperation a sign of weakness? Write out what feelings are evoked by this question?

How might you seek cooperation from an adversary, but protect yourself from exploitation?

CHAPTER FOURTEEN

CONFLICT ANALYSIS

Introduction

MOST PEOPLE THINK THAT CONFLICT is a messy, chaotic social environment. However, conflict is as susceptible to analysis as any other complicated problem. The essence of conflict analysis is observation and application of principles to those observations. Sometimes, conflict analysis can be done upon reflection, but most often it is done on the fly during an intervention.

Conflict analysis is a logical, structured approach to understanding what is going on between the parties. Conflict analysis can be accomplished by assessing the overall system, determining recurring patterns in the system associated with conflict, and identifying individual content contributions to the system. Data developed from conflict analysis can provide background for constructing useful conflict interventions.

Systems Approach to Conflict Analysis

General systems theory provides a framework for understanding the workings of organizations, small groups, and families. Systems theory provides a way to understand conflicts by giving information about patterns, interlocking sequences, and functions of the parties, and methods of processing information. Rather than focusing on one person as the cause of the conflict, systems analysis looks for repeating sequences of conflict within the system.

In a systems approach to conflict analysis, the system itself must first be defined. Generally, a system will be a group of people in relationship to each other. Families, work groups, congregations, and boards of directors typify various groups that might be considered as systems for analytical purposes. The next step is to identify the conflict participants and place them within the larger system.

Once the conflict participants and the relevant system are defined, the parts of the system must be defined. With groups functioning as systems, the parts are defined as roles. When a person enters a system, he or she is programmed into a specific role. Generally, roles operate at several levels. At one level, roles define responsibilities and explicit relationships. In this sense, roles are usually task-oriented so as to avoid duplication of effort and promote system efficiency. Typically, this role programming is explicit because it is either defined by the system member or predefined by the system for the member. At another level, roles define the quality and kind of personal relationships between system members. At this level, roles are not explicit, but usually develop through unstated "understandings." Because roles are multi-layered and complex, the system tends to label them. Labeling identifies roles in a simple, comprehensible way. However, labels keep people from changing and may perpetuate conflict behavior.

Roles can be analyzed by first asking system members to describe them and then comparing the descriptions to what is observed. Diagramming and flow charting the roles in an organizational chart style may be helpful at this stage of the analysis.

One of the by-products of role programming is the creation of triangles. Triangles tend to form in systems when relationships are close and intense. When one person feels lower power, her tendency is to bring in another person to bolster her position. This maneuver forms an alliance if the resulting relationship is an open one or a coalition if the relationship is hidden. Since the person brought in maintains multiple relationships in the system, interlocking triangles begin functioning over and over in predictable ways. If these triangles lead to destructive behavior, they are termed toxic triangles. Thus, the next step in systems analysis is to identify the major triangles. Triangling will vary and change depending on the issues and attitudes of the parties. However, identifying the presence of triangling provides useful information about the system. In essence, we are looking for the alliances and coalitions present in any group and identifying those that seem destructive.

When the essential nature of the system is understood, the analysis can turn to the conflict situation. The first step is to understand the rules of engagement. Rules in this context mean the underlying communication structure between the parties. Usually, no one person dictates the rules. Instead, the rules guide behavior in more subtle ways. They are the way things are done in a family, a business, a department, or a group of friends. A rule indicates what behavior is obligated, preferred, or prohibited in certain contexts. Usually these rules of communication remain implicit.

Repetitive, unsatisfactory conflicts often operate on a set of unstated, but very powerful rules. These rules, no matter how dysfunctional, are followed as long as the basic structure of the system does not change. In systems analysis, the task is to make the rules explicit so that they can be understood and changed. One of the important characteristics of a rule is that some implicit message against knowing or stating the rule directly is present. Consequently, explicitly listing system conflict rules may not be easy.

To make the rules explicit, they should be stated as prescriptions for behavior such as "When in context X, Y must/must not occur." Rules must not be stated in evaluative language.

Rules may be elicited in some of the following ways:

List explicit and implicit rules that have prescribed your own and others' behavior in conflicts.

Think of times when the rule was broken. How did you know the rule was broken? How was the violation communicated? Write about the prescription that became obvious upon breaking the rule.

Generate rules both for behavior that must and must not be performed.

Write rules even for obvious communication patterns.

Code each rule as to the following: Whose rule is it? What keeps the rule going? Who enforces the rule? Who breaks the rule? What function does the rule serve?

When this work is completed, a discussion about how the rule helps or harms peace within the system can educate the system members about their collective behaviors. In a natural way, they will present themselves with a choice of whether to change by considering new rules for adoption.

Another related form of systems analysis involves micro events. Micro events are similar to rules but describe behavior instead of dictating behavior. The "here we go again" theme identifies micro events. Typically, systems members will experience patterns of conflict over and over. These micro events can be decoded by asking some simple questions about the patterns. Micro events can be analyzed by focusing on:

Who initiates conflict events and in what way?

Who responds to conflict events and in what way?

Who else is present but not identified as a party to the conflict?

Does anyone "speak for" someone else? If so, does this keep the participants embroiled in the conflict?

If there were no conflict, what would be missing? Who would not be connecting with whom? How would the parties structure their time?

Once the underlying structure of the micro event is decoded, the system members are again faced with a natural choice about changing their behaviors. The important point is to make very explicit those sequences of behaviors that have remained hidden to the system members.

The systems approach to conflict analysis is wholistic. Its strength is in flushing out unstated, assumed, and implicit ways of behaving and thinking. The challenge to the systems approach is the resistance to change. This resistance may be manifested by refusal to participate in exercises, by disdainful comments and statements, or by outright hostility. Many people will view systems techniques as inappropriately therapeutic and will therefore discount or discredit them.

Often people criticize such techniques as "too touchy-feely." The fact of the matter is that this intervention is touching on feelings and relationships that many people do not care to examine. Thus, when resistance is encountered, the importance of conflict to the system members must be carefully considered. Conflict may be a substitute for other forms of intimacy and connection, for problem solving, or for expression of dissatisfaction. Never assume that members of a system want the conflict to be resolved. They may fear a vacuum in their interaction if the conflict is no longer serving its particular function. Although almost everyone will claim that they want to end the conflict, the fact that people keep conflicts going, sometimes for years at a time, indicates that some system function is served by it.

Consequently, systems work must be introduced carefully and thoughtfully. The parties should be prepared for this work by some discussion of systems theory. The tone of the intervention must be consistent with the environment and the expectations of the parties. For example, a conflict between a board of directors and the chief executive officer may require a tone of deference, solemnity, and dignity that may preclude some systems exercises. Used appropriately, however, systems analysis of conflicts can be a powerful tool to help parties unravel the mysteries of their dispute.

Structural Approaches to Conflict Analysis

A structural conflict analysis describes the conflict parties, analyzes the conflict goals of the parties, examines the power relationships between the parties, explores the history and context of the conflict, assesses the conflict climate, and describes the escalation history.

Conflict Parties

Sometimes, conflict parties are obvious. Most of the time, however, all the parties affected by the conflict are not so obvious. Therefore, identifying the parties is essential. We divide parties into *primary, secondary,* and *tertiary groups.*

Primary parties. The primary conflict parties are those people appearing to be directly opposed to one another. In the litigation context, the primary parties would typically be the plaintiff and the defendant. Sometimes, the primary parties are apparent rather than real. These situations exist when the primary parties are simply representatives of other parties. The legal concept, real party in interest, demonstrates this idea. The real party in interest is the person or entity the most affected by the conflict outcome, but is not the named party in the conflict.

When the primary parties are organizations, such as corporations or governmental agencies, their representatives in the conflict must also be considered primary. In addition, there are circumstances when attorneys representing organizations must also be considered primary parties.

After the primary parties have been identified, using any information is available, their conflict management style should be ascertained. Recognizing that each person manifests different styles in different types of conflicts, a determination should be made whether each party is predominantly competitive, accommodating,compromising, avoidant, or collaborative. Furthermore, the reasons behind the choice of particular conflict management styles can be useful information. In appropriate cases, simply asking the parties why they are acting the way they are will elicit important information.

Secondary parties. Secondary parties are those people not directly involved in the conflict, but affected by its course and outcome. Secondary parties might involve spouses or family members, coworkers, business colleagues, and so forth. Secondary parties are important for several reasons. First, they may provide an audience to the primary parties. Audiences influence conflict behavior by providing or withholding support. Thus, primary parties will often play to their audiences during conflict to gain support, be validated, or solidify their positions. Many times, primary parties do not want to show weakness to secondary parties. This is a manifestation of self-esteem and self-image. Primary parties may be defining a core identity on their relationship with secondary parties. Consequently, primary parties will not agree to actions that might compromise their identity as defined by the relationship to secondary parties. In these cases, secondary parties must be brought into the intervention to "give permission or consent" to the primary party to act.

Secondary parties are also important because they often instigate the primary conflict. For example, if a primary party is faced with an ambiguous situation and is deciding between pressing a claim or not, secondary parties, to gain influence, show support, or increase self-esteem, may advise the primary party to escalate the claim to a conflict. By showing solidarity with the primary party, the secondary party encourages and supports the primary party in the conflict. Oftentimes, this means that the secondary party must be dealt with in the peacemaking process. In particular, the self-esteem of the secondary party must be maintained so that the secondary party does not lose face with the primary party. A common situation occurs when a spouse is a secondary party. In this case, the ongoing relationship after the conflict requires that the secondary party be given a face-saving exit along with the primary party.

Secondary parties may also be a moderating influence on primary parties. A more collaborative secondary party may influence a strongly competitive primary party to engage in collaboration.

The conflict management style of secondary parties is as important as what primary parties. Oftentimes, primary conflicts generate secondary conflicts between primary and secondary parties. Understanding the secondary parties' conflict management styles can provide insight into the behaviors of the primary parties in the conflict. For example, a secondary party showing a strongly competitive conflict management style may force an otherwise collaborative primary party to be competitive also.

Tertiary parties. Tertiary parties are parties not directly involved in the conflict nor directly affected by the conflict, but who may otherwise be influenced by the conflict or have some influence on primary or secondary parties. Tertiary parties can be advisers, friends, or confidants. Tertiary parties may also be larger groups of people who are relying on the primary and secondary parties to resolve the conflict for them.

Tertiary parties can play several roles in a conflict. Like secondary parties, tertiary parties may provide an audience for the primary parties. Since tertiary parties are usually not directly connected to either primary or secondary parties, face-saving and self-esteem is not as important. However, tertiary parties often manifest a sense of justice or injustice, fairness or unfairness, relating to the course and outcome of the conflict. If these broad themes are present, the process must help the primary parties construct solutions that do not offend the sensibilities of tertiary parties.

Since tertiary parties are often outside of the communication process, they are often uninformed about the progress of discussions and negotiations. Therefore, they will tend to adapt more slowly to change. If the pace of change occurs too dramatically or too quickly, tertiary parties will resist, creating impediments to resolution. Thus, the need for confidentiality and privacy in direct interventions must be balanced with the need to educate, inform, and obtain feedback from tertiary parties. Many good resolutions have been sidetracked or postponed because tertiary parties were not sufficiently prepared for the changes implied by the resolution. Fisher and Ury's concept of ACBD, "Always consult before deciding" is relevant in this situation (Fisher et al. 1981). This advice is sound when there are secondary and tertiary parties standing behind the primary parties.

Conflict Goals. The second step in structural conflict analysis considers the conflict goals of the parties. In chapter 11, conflict goals were identified as involving content, relationship, identity, and process (Wilmot and Hocker, 2001).

Content goals. Content goals concern the substantive issues in the conflict. Typically, conflict goals involved disputes over money, possession of property, or other tangible rights. Content goals also will frame the issues for the parties. Issues can be defined as power-based, rights-based, or interest-based(Urly, Brett, and Goldber,1988). Power-based issues typically relate to positions within a hierarchy, decision-making authority, and governance. Decision-making processes such as elections, votes, or physical violence decide power-based issues, if the issues cannot be resolved mutually and consensually. Power-based issues almost always implicate relationship goals in the conflict. Abuse of power often leads to conflict. When people feel treated unfairly or unjustly, they resist decisions based on power. Resistance may be overt, but usually is covert, passive, and difficult to detect.

Rights-based issues concern choices between conflicting activities. Typically, the activity given the higher social value will prevail in a rights-based dispute. Rights are developed by groups to assure that group members are treated fairly by the group as a whole. If the group ignores a right, conflict will ensue. Thus, a claim by an ethnic minority that it has been disenfranchised from an election process because of antiquated voting machines raises rights-based issues. Rights-based issues implicate relationship and identity goals as well as content goals.

Interest-based issues involve satisfaction of parties' needs. In contrast to rights-based issues, interest-based issues rarely present an either-or choice. Instead, interest-based issues invite collaborative problem solving to satisfy all interests of all parties. Reframing power-based and rights-based issues into interest-based issues is an important step in moving the parties to collaborative solutions.

Content goals can also be expressed as evaluative or intellective. An evaluative conflict might be a dispute over which manufacturing process to use whether supervisors should receive salary increases. Intellective conflicts are more abstract. A typical intellective conflict is deciding which rule of law is applicable to a given situation.

Relationship goals. Relationship goals ask, Who are we in this relationship? Relationship goals typically concern issues of hierarchy, social roles, equity and equal treatment, and fairness. Hierarchy issues arise when positions within a hierarchy are challenged. Thus, if an inferior challenges the position of the superior, conflict is bound to occur. Furthermore, if a group does not have norms or standards for succession within the hierarchy, when a higher member departs, conflict can arise as inferiors struggle against each other for the higher position. Conflict arising out of the politics within organizations frequently involves hierarchy disputes and issues.

Conflict over social roles typically arises when the demands of roles conflict with each other. The apprenticeship of young lawyers often requires long hours and weekend work that may conflict with family life or social life. Role conflicts may consequently develop between professional career and family obligations. Role conflicts also develop when a person is expected to act within one role that is inconsistent with the person's other, equally important roles. The relationship conflict often arises between the group demanding a choice between conflicting roles and the person faced with the choice. Economic survival often means that employees will choose work roles over other roles. However, the choice is not freely made and the conflict will still boil under the surface. This is a large source of employment-related litigation.

Conflict over equity and equal treatment occurs when people feel that they are not being treated fairly. Typically, people expect to be treated differently depending upon whether they are superior, equal, or inferior to others in a hierarchy. Expectations of fairness are greatest between equals and least between inferiors and superiors. Conflict analysis requires consideration of both the objective facts and subjective perceptions of the parties involved in relationship goals. Objectively, the parties may be in a superior-inferior position. Subjectively, the inferior may feel equal to the superior, giving rise to a sense of inequity if there is disparate treatment.

Identity goals. Identity goals ask the question "Who am I in this relationship?" Identity goals concern face, self-esteem, and impression management. Typically, identity goals are raised when a party feels disrespected, ignored, unimportant, or worse. While identity goals arise because of the violation of relationships, they typically are unilateral goals. That is, parties with identity goals seek to improve their self-esteem or status with others. Identity goals drive the most serious conflicts. Maintaining identity is a key psychological process in human survival. As discussed earlier, identity defines "me" within "us." When one has identity, she has a primal claim on the right to food, shelter, and reproduction. When identity is threatened, survival is threatened because others deny the primal claim. For this reason, people can react violently to disrespect, reputational damage, or other identity injuries.

Process goals. Process goals ask the question, "How are we to resolve this conflict?" Process goals involve choices concerning how conflicts should be handled. Consider the Four-Way Model of conflict resolution in chapter 3. Conflicts or process goals can arise when people with different conflict styles unilaterally choose processes without consulting others. Thus, a person with a competitive style may choose an adversary process such as Model One or Two, while a person with an accommodating or compromising style prefers discussions, such as Model Three or Four. The accommodator could be offended by the competitor's choice of process, creating a process goal conflict that also implicates relationship and identity goals.

Power Analysis

The third step is power analysis. Power analysis is a three-step process that consists of assessing power, evaluating power imbalances, and ascertaining power tactics.

Assessing power. Assessing power first requires an examination of the relative power positions of each party. A number of barriers prevent accurate diagnosis of power. First, people are usually unwilling to talk about power or provide an honest assessment of their own or others' power. Open use of power is not socially sanctioned because of a cultural emphasis on equality and fairness. Furthermore, because power depends on endorsement, powerful parties often attempt to keep their power unobtrusive so as to not alienate those they influence. If the weaker parties cannot see the power or do not understand it, they can do nothing to upset the power balance. Finally, power depends on relationships between parties rather than properties of individuals. Consequently, determining the source of power is difficult. If power stems from relationships, identifying a particular person who holds power is misleading. The more important question may be who assents to the use of power or who withholds endorsement. These barriers make assessments of power a complex process.

One way to assess power is to determine the possible power resources in the situation and identify who holds them. Is one party more powerful, or are the parties relatively equal? This question is answered by looking at the primary power resources of each party. In each situation, the three components of power—direction, base, and will—should be analyzed and described.

Coercive power exists when parties are using threats and promises against each other. Does the party exercising threats and promises have the ability and the resolve to exercise the threat or promise? Are the threats and promises real or idle? Furthermore, if the threats and promises are exercised, is the consequence as good or bad as the party with the power wishes it to be? Oftentimes threats seem more powerful before they are executed and promises appear more enticing than when they are fulfilled.

Information control concerns possession of information, the ability to gain better information, and the ability to withhold or disclose information. Parties tend to have more information control power when they have better access to information and can control information disclosure. Information becomes important when it leads to better decision-making and more certain about future outcomes. Recall that the asymmetric information condition in game theory means that one party has hidden information.

Special skills and abilities become power resources when they are needed by the other party or when they provide one party with an advantage in controlling resolution of the conflict. If one party is more skilled or has greater abilities relevant to the conflict than another, that person may hold more power.

Similar to skills and abilities is expertise about the task. An experienced disputant looking at the conflict as a familiar situation will have more power than an inexperienced disputant. The experienced party will be less anxious, probably less reactive, and more disciplined because she will have a better sense of the certainty of outcomes.

Personal attractiveness and likability are important, but often overlooked power resources. Numerous studies have demonstrated that attractive people tend to be evaluated more positively. Furthermore, the human tendency to relate and to seek approval tends to bind people to those who are attractive and likable. Thus, attractiveness and likability lower defenses and resistance to that person's preferred outcomes.

Moral standing is an important power resource when there are secondary and tertiary parties involved in the conflict. Moral standing refers to a superior or preferred position based on notions of fairness, justice, equity, and other approbative norms. People seek moral standing because of identity needs. For example, a person may be seen as having a more righteous position in a conflict because of moral standing. Moral standing is not as important in the absence of secondary and tertiary parties because the other party will discount moral standing significantly. As between two parties, each will assume a superior moral position against the other. Thus, the power of moral standing is diminished by offsetting attitudes. When a audience is involved, however, audience approval and support for the party with the greater moral standing can be a significant power resource.

Legal standing provides the most power when the law is clear and the facts are unambiguous. In this case, the predictability of the judicial outcome is high. The validity of a promissory note involves clear facts and clear law. When the law is unclear or the facts are ambiguous, legal standing provides less power. Generally, the power is limited to forcing a reluctant party to respond to a claim. Oftentimes, people mistake this limited power for a greater power to coerce settlement or a decision. In other words, people believe that since they have filed a lawsuit, they are entitled to a favorable decision. Thus, people perceive a false sense of power arising from legal standing.

Legitimacy and recognition constitute another form of social power. Legitimacy and recognition imply that secondary and tertiary parties identify with and approve of the recognized party. Thus, the party with less legitimacy or recognition must fight a public relations battle.

Parties may gain power from external support mechanisms. Again, secondary and tertiary parties play a role in this type of power. They may provide support emotionally as well as financially, thereby giving an advantage to one side over the other.

Hierarchical position, by definition, constitutes power or lack of it. The higher a person resides in a hierarchy, the more power she wields. People lower in the hierarchy will tend to defer to superiors and will seek leadership services from them. Thus, inferiors challenging superiors face a power imbalance based on the existing social structure. The inertia of that structure and the security it provides are advantages for the superiors.

Loyal allies and coalitions provide another source of power. Coalitions form as a way of balancing power between two strong opponents. Typically, a coalition is formed between a strong power and a weak power such that their combined power is greater than the opponent. Loyal allies provide support—emotional, political, and financial—to primary parties. People have much more courage in conflict when they know they have people standing by their side.

Persuasive skills provide power to those who can convince others of the righteousness of their position. Persuasion is an effective source of power because it does not involve coercion and indicates a high level of communicative competency.

Control over resources is a final source of power. Resource power can be illustrated by the following situation. The city council had been arguing over whether it should invest in a stadium financed by the city. The mayor was opposed to the project and instructed his city manager to so inform the city council. When the city council, on a close vote, approved the project, the mayor directed the city manager to make certain that staff was not available in the planning department to process zoning changes and building permits.

Furthermore, building inspectors would now find themselves sent off to far parts of the city when inspections were called for at the stadium project. By controlling these resources, the mayor and the city manager managed to thwart the project despite not having final decision-making approval. Typically, people who believe they have power oftentimes underestimate the fact that inferiors in the hierarchy control the resources necessary to effectuate decisions. Thus, resource control can be a power source in a conflict.

In addition to assessing the power resources of the parties, conflict analysis requires a study of the effects of power. Is power being used judiciously? If not, why not? Is power exercise having the wanted influence on other parties in the conflict? What types of resentments are being generated because of the exercise of power? Within the conflict, which side is using power most conservatively? How is that conservatism being demonstrated? And why is a party restraining the use of power?

Power tactics. One of the most important power tactics in conflict is issue control. A number of questions illuminate this tactic. Are any issues being hidden? Who is hiding them, and why? Are any issues being withdrawn from consideration? Who is withdrawing them and why? Are any issues not being raised? Are the issues not being raised because the parties do not see them? Or are the issues not being raised because the parties do not want to face the difficult work the issues require? Are any issues being mischaracterized or trivialized? Is any party misdirecting attention away from issues? Is one person controlling the criteria for decisions?

Another indication of power control is power denial. For example, is any party denying that anything was communicated? Is one party denying that something was communicated? Is anybody denying that something was communicated specifically to another party? Is one party denying the situation in which a communication occurred? In all these cases, denial indicates a desire to exercise power surreptitiously. People oftentimes deny power to avoid the possibility of retaliation, to maintain face by appearing reasonable and fair, or simply to covertly manipulate another.

History and Context

The history of the conflict is the next step of analysis. When were the parties not in conflict, and what lead them into conflict. People will deny they were the cause of the conflict so careful listening and questioning should illuminate how their perspectives clashed with others. When possible, primary, secondary, and tertiary parties should be interviewed separately and privately. Good note taking is an essential skill, because memories fade quickly. Notes of interviews should be transcribed into a coherent narrative from the impressions and provisional hypotheses about what the conflict is about.

The context of the conflict describes the background environment. For example, is this an employment conflict arising in the context of a workplace dispute? Or is it a family business conflict involving both personal and business relationships? As we have seen, context is important for defining identity and relationships. Therefore, describing the context in some detail is essential to a thorough conflict analysis.

Climate

Climate refers to the general emotional tone surrounding the parties. It is a relatively enduring quality of a group situation experienced in common by group members. Climate arises from interaction and behaviors between individual members of a group. Climate is not psychological in the sense that it is an intangible belief or feeling in members' minds. Instead, it is a quality of the group itself because it arises from individual interactions (Folger, Poole, and Stutman, 2000).

Perceptions of climate are strongly influenced by positions within the group. Thus, factors such as positions in the authority hierarchy, length of membership in the group, and degree of interpersonal communication between group members all contribute to climate. No one person is responsible for creating a climate. Nevertheless, one or two people can set a sufficiently dominant tone to affect the interactions of the rest of the group.

Climates are relatively enduring in that they persist over time and do not change with every interaction. In some groups, the same climate may prevail for years. For example, employees often observe a consistent tone or attitude in their work environment that has evolved over time and seems likely to persist into the future. The "life-span" of a climate is determined by the relative stability of its themes, which are reinforced in day-to-day group interactions.

Climate can best be described as a set of general themes running through interaction as Folger et al. suggest (Folger et al., 2000). One category of themes revolves around authority relationships. These themes are concerned with a set of questions concerning how the group ordinarily deals with the distribution of power and respect. Is power concentrated in the hands of a few, or is it accessible to all members? To what extent is power used to mandate decisions or to resolve disagreements, as opposed to discussion and argument? How rigid is the power structure? Can members readily shift roles or are some members always in control?

A second category of themes concerns the degree of supportiveness in the group. For example, are members friendly toward each other? Can members trust one another? Can members safely express their emotions? Is there tolerance for disagreements and different points of view?

A third category of themes concerns the sense of group identity. It covers questions such as: Does the group hold an identity of its own or is it just a collection of individuals? Do members feel ownership of the group accomplishments? How great is individual commitment to the group? Do members know about and trust in each other's commitment? Themes related to these questions provide members with information allowing them to protect the consequences of conflict for the group. For example, if a group lacks a definite identity and commitment is low, the group may fracture into subgroups if conflict comes into the open. Members with an interest in preserving the group might try to hide conflict to prevent this.

A final category of themes concerns the type of interdependence among group members. These themes address the motivational set of the situation. Can all members gain if they cooperate or will one member's gain be another's loss? Do members normally take a competitive attitude toward each other?

Finally, what are the causes of this climate? Are the causes within the control of the parties or not? For example, the workplace environment may have a hostile, competitive climate fostered by a superior who believes that it produces higher productivity. In such a case, parties in conflict will not be able to modify the climate easily, making a conflict more difficult to transform.

Group members face uncertainty about how to act and about what the consequences of their actions will be. Uncertainty is natural in conflict because many people are not as accustomed to conflict as they are to other situations. People simply do not think or learn very much about conflicts. People have two ways to respond to this uncertainty. Some people may reduce their uncertainty by becoming rigid. In this situation, a person will respond to all conflicts in the same way regardless of circumstances. Rigid behavior can take many forms but there are two common examples. First, people may get defensive, flushing out anyone in their way. Others try to avoid or ignore all conflict regardless of how important the conflict is. These behaviors tend to perpetuate themselves and can be frustrating for those who have to deal with them.

The second strategy for dealing with uncertainty is to diagnose the situation and react in a manner appropriate to it. Because exact prediction is impossible, members must project their actions and estimate how others will respond to them. This projection may either occur consciously or unconsciously, but always involves guesswork about the future. Climate is indispensable in this process because members use their sense of climate to gauge the appropriateness, effectiveness, or likely consequences of their behavior. The prevailing climate of the group is projected into its future, setting a standard for conflict behavior.

In addition, climate provides an important role in understanding the conflict behavior of others. The process by which people draw conclusions about others from their actions is called attribution. Climate plays a critical role in promoting attribution bias. For example, when people in business describe conflicts, they tend to exaggerate their cooperativeness while exaggerating their opponent's competitiveness. Thus responsibility for the conflict is blamed on the other. Climate can exacerbate this type of bias by preconsciously priming goals. As we saw it in chapter 6, priming dramatically affects behaviors after the priming event has occurred. Thus, in a climate of cooperation, people will be primed to perceive each other as friendly, while a competitive climate will prime people toward hostility. Thus, the prevailing climate of a conflict situation affects interpretations of one another, encouraging certain types of behavior and reinforcing the climate itself.

The interaction-climate relationship is complex and works on several levels. Climates are maintained and changed through specific actions relevant to particular issues and concerns. A dominant and critical group member may implicitly tell other members that their suggestions may be criticized or rejected out of hand. At a second level, changes in one theme can generalize to other related themes. At a third level, interaction can create a climate that is temporarily overshadowed by more enduring qualities of the group. These shifts can be beneficial or destructive.

Because climate persists and becomes a part of the prevailing group mentality, it tends to become second nature. Members forget that climate depends on how they interact and assume that the way they treat each other is "just that way." When this happens, climate becomes what Folder et al. call a trained incapacity (Folger et al., 2000). Members forget that they can control climate by their own interaction and instead become controlled by the climate.

Climate themes can only be identified by observing the entire group for an extended period. To diagnose climate, interactions must be closely watched and group members must be interviewed about their perceptions of social interactions. In some cases, group members will be biased because they are unaware of their own behavior and do not see themselves as part of the problem. While individual accounts provide initial insights, observing how members interact with each other must verify the accounts. If interaction is inconsistent with the individual reports, the inconsistency itself is an important source of information about the group. Metaphors used by group members are particularly fertile source of climate themes. Because the precise details of meaning are only implicit in a metaphor, people will use them when they cannot provide an explicit description of the climate.

Escalation History

Escalation history backtracks through the conflict to understand the processes resulting in the current situation. In performing this analysis, two symptoms should be investigated: avoidance and escalation.

Avoidance symptoms typically involve some of the following behaviors and situations. At some point in time, the parties demonstrate a significant decrease in their commitment to solving the problem. Phrases such as "Why should we care?" or "It's not worth it" indicate a lack of commitment and avoidance of conflict. Avoidance is also indicated by quick acceptance of suggested solution. People will also stop themselves from raising controversial issues or will tune out of interaction. Avoidance will also be found when unresolved issues keep emerging in the same or different forms. Indications that group members are not sharing information with each other or that outspoken people are noticeably quiet are other indications of avoidance. Finally, when no plans are made to implement the chosen solution, allowing the problem to continue, avoidance is present.

In examining escalation history, understanding why a party is avoiding the conflict becomes critical. Oftentimes, avoidance arises due to a fear of uncertainty or the natural desire to reduce anxiety.

Taking a detailed history of how the conflict was avoided may provide insights as to how to redirect parties from work of avoidant activities.

Escalation symptoms generally follow the five stages of conflict escalation discussed in chapter 4. In Stage 1, the parties will report that an issue is taking much longer to deal with than anticipated. Somewhere between Stage1 and Stage 2, parties will repeatedly offer the same argument in support of a position. At Stage 3, parties tend to overinflate the consequences of not reaching agreement and use threats to win arguments. The parties will report a palpable sense of increasing tension and anxiety. At midlevels of Stage 3, the parties seem to be working fiercely but are not getting anywhere. Stage 4 emerges with name-calling, ad hominem attacks, and personal arguments. The parties become immediately polarized on issues and some form of coalition formation is observed. Typically at Stage 4, there is hostile eye gaze or less direct eye contact between the parties. Disrespect is shown through sarcastic laughter, inappropriate humor, defensive body language, accusations, and veiled insults. The parties have heated disagreements on pointless or trivial issues. At Stage 5, the parties see each other as nonhuman and irredeemably evil.

Preparing a Conflict Map

Conflict mapping is a technique of conflict analysis that commits the analysis to an organized examination of the dispute. At its simplest, a conflict map is simply an outline of the major components of conflict written in some narrative fashion. A conflict map disciplines the conflict analysis process by requiring some thinking about what is being observed. Furthermore, like any checklist system, a thorough conflict map prevents importance issues and facts from being overlooked.

The extent of a conflict map depends, of course, on the nature of the conflict, the nature of the intervention, time, and the motivation of the person creating the analysis. Preparing the map is, however, a valuable exercise in any conflict. First, it takes away the mystery of the conflict and puts the conflict into understandable terms. Second, and most importantly, it shows where intervention strategies might be most effective.

Conflict analysis, whether performed from a systems or structural approach, is crucial part of conflict intervention. The temptation to jump over this step because of the time investment is great, but the rewards from successful intervention based on a complete analysis of the conflict make the investment worthwhile.

Reflections on Chapter Fourteen

1.Think about a recent conflict. It can be personal or it can be a conflict of some type described in a newspaper or newsmagazine. Prepare a conflict analysis.

2.Pick a case from one of your other classes and prepare a conflict analysis. Now prepare a case brief. Does your case brief look different than previous case briefs? How does the conflict analysis differ from the case brief?

Part Five

Peacemaking

CHAPTER FIFTEEN

ETHICS

Introduction

*E*THICS CONCERNS THE IDEA of what is right and wrong. Within a professional context, ethics concerns values and attitudes embodied either in principles or in more prescriptive rules of conduct. As we will see, the various mediation codes of conduct provide little assistance on difficult ethical issues. Instead, peacemakers are generally guided by their own values and the rules of professional conduct regulating whatever underlying profession they belong to.

As mediation becomes more professional, there will be problems with conduct, choices, and attitudes. This chapter draws upon legal ethics and considers some of the issues that might arise during the peacemaking process or in the context of the relationship between the peacemaker and the parties in the dispute.

Ethical Codes Generally

Ethics are understood in terms of intrinsic value or instrumental value (Coyle, 1998). Intrinsic value is the independent value ascribed to acting ethically, while instrumental value is summarized by the cliché "it pays to be ethical." Professionals want to satisfy the demands of their consciences, but also recognize that ethics directly affect client demand for services. People will simply not retain "unethical" professionals for important personal services.

Codes of conduct separate professions from other endeavors. As the dictionary definition indicates, ethics and professionalism are inextricably connected: professional—"characterized by or conforming to the technical or ethical standards" of a calling requiring specialized knowledge. Ethical codes consequently reflect the importance of consumer protection and professionalism.

Mediation codes of ethics represent efforts to describe and dictate appropriate behaviors for mediators. These codes generally establish moral guidelines defining minimally acceptable standards of mediation conduct. The promoters hope that they will clarify issues, reduce uncertainty, and constrain individual mediator behavior.

Codes of ethics also provide a common vocabulary and express shared beliefs for both the practitioners and the general public. Codes of ethics promote public awareness of the field or profession. They reassure the general public, some of whom will be current or potential clients, that practitioners are responsible and accountable.

Existing codes of mediation ethics universally condemn mediating cases when the mediator is self-interested in a particular outcome. The underlying theme in the various codes is impartiality and neutrality. The mediator's commitment must be to the parties and the process. Pressure from outside of the mediation process should never influence the mediator to coerce parties to settle.

There are complaints about the various codes of ethics. They provide little practical guidance; they typically present lists of proscriptions and prohibitions that do not fit real life situations. They are too abstract or broad and thus difficult to apply, or else too selective, focusing on only one dimension of an ethical problem. They may not fully explain the prescriptions they do contain. Codes of ethics are often vague, which make them hard to enforce or even to follow. Furthermore, codes of ethics, despite claims to the contrary, may merely reflect the considered thinking of the groups who composed them. Thus, they may provide only the illusion of a unified consensus.

With this overview in mind, let us examine some of the sources of ethical codes applicable to mediators and peacemakers.

Sources of Ethical Standards

SPIDR-AAA-ABA Model Standards

The Model Standards were developed between 1992 and 1994 by a Joint Standards Committee formed between the Society of Professionals in Dispute Resolution (SPIDR), the American Bar Association (ABA), and the American Arbitration Association (AAA). The Model Standards cover the following nine ethical issues.

- *Self-Determination:* A mediator shall recognize that mediation is based on the principle of self-determination by the parties.
- *Impartiality:* A mediator shall conduct the mediation in an impartial manner.
- *Conflicts of Interest:* A mediator shall disclose all actual and potential conflicts of interest reasonably known to the mediator. After disclosure, the mediator shall decline to mediate unless all parties choose to retain the mediator. The need to protect against conflicts of interest also governs conduct that occurs during and after the mediation.
- *Competence:* A mediator shall mediate only when the mediator has the necessary qualifications to satisfy the reasonable expectations of the parties.
- *Confidentiality:* A mediator shall maintain the reasonable expectations of the parties with regard to confidentiality.
- *Quality of the Process:* A mediator shall conduct the mediation fairly, diligently, and in a manner consistent with the principles of self-determination expected by the parties.
- *Advertising and Soliciting:* A mediator shall be truthful in advertising and soliciting for mediation.
- *Fees:* A mediator shall fully disclose and explain the basis of compensation, fees, and charges to the parties.
- *Obligation to the Mediation Process:* Mediators have a duty to improve the practice of mediation.

The mediator's role under the Model Standards is to help a voluntary resolution to the dispute, the fundamental principle being self-determination for the disputing parties. The Model Standards place less emphasis on a mediator's substantive expertise in the underlying area of the dispute and more credence to a mediator's ability to satisfy the parties' reasonable expectations of a fair process.

Standard 1: Self-determination. The Model Standards define self-determination as a "fundamental principle of mediation" based on "the ability of the parties to reach a voluntary, uncoerced agreement." Under this standard, the charge of mediators is limited to "providing information about the process, raising issues, and helping the parties explore options. The primary role of the mediator is to help a voluntary resolution of a dispute." In comments on this standard, the mediator is advised to "make the parties aware of the importance of consulting other professionals . . . to help them make informed decisions."

Standard 1 fails to address several issues. It does not state what ethical obligations a mediator owes the parties concerning the choice of mediation models. At the least, the mediator should explain the differences between mediation, litigation, and arbitration, and that the mediator will not decide any issues for the parties. The mediator should also inform a participant of their right to withdraw from mediation at any time and for any reason, except as is required by law.

Furthermore, a mediator should discuss the different mediation models with the parties and obtain their informed consent before proceeding (See chapter 4) The disclosure obligations of the selected model necessarily include disclosure of the model that the mediator will use. This does not appear to be a common practice among mediators. To the extent that such informed consent is practiced, it is done in a cursory fashion, directing the parties toward the mediator's preferred model, be it facilitative or evaluative.

Standard 2: Impartiality. Impartiality is the foundation of mediation. Mediators must maintain neutrality and conduct an impartial process for mediation to work. All parties expect the mediator to be neutral. If they suspect otherwise, the parties are unlikely to value the mediator's involvement and ability to make a meaningful contribution to the resolution of the dispute.

Suppose a power imbalance occurs because one party dominates the discussion with superior language skills. Many mediators would take some action to ensure that the power imbalance does not threaten the weaker party's full participation in the mediation. Yet, power-balancing strategies, such asking the dominant party to listen for a few minutes or directing more questions toward the weaker party, may jeopardize the appearance of impartiality. Unfortunately, Standard Two does not advise mediators on how to deal with such difficult power imbalances. Furthermore, the comments provide little additional guidance because they simply state similarly broad, basic ideas (e.g., "A mediator shall avoid conduct that gives the appearance of partiality toward one of the parties.").

The impartiality concept raises some additional issues. Can a mediator ethically agree in advance to accept full payment from only one side of the mediation? The answer, at least as to existing common practice, is yes, with the appropriate premediation disclosures and informed consent of all parties.

What are the ramifications of a repeat player—for example, an insurance company—using the same mediators routinely? A "reasonable person" obviously would see this as a question of impartiality. Thus, mediators are obligated to inform both parties of the frequency with which the mediator mediates for a given party, institution, or advocate. This at least discloses the possibility of any perceived bias in favor of the repeat player. The parties can then give informed consent to a mediator's current or past affiliations.

What is the role of the mediator, if any, in protecting the public interest if the only parties at the table are private interests? The answer to this question may depend on the mediator's ethical code and the parties' fully informed decisions.

Finally, the impartiality standard raises some fundamental, but unanswerable questions. Can a mediator ever be truly impartial? If one is truly neutral, does this conflict with the concept of achieving a fair settlement when a fair settlement requires rebalancing power? In addition, how does a mediator hold the concept of fairness? Is not fairness a subjective criterion? Can the process really be self-determinative if the mediator directs the process? The process would not work without a degree of direction, general advice, and education of the parties, but neither would it work without impartiality, neutrality, and self-determination. At some level, these concepts conflict, and a mediator must grapple with the balance that must be achieved between them. Mediators need to know their own biases, and disclose them to the parties, and continuously assess whether they can continue to mediate if the bias obstructs neutrality.

Evaluative mediation can also pose ethical problems. Most third parties would agree that informing parties of their legal rights and responsibilities can almost never be neutral—the law, after all, almost always requires interpretation and application to specific facts. Nevertheless, there may be an important role for the neutral third-party to be sure that knowledge of the law (even if it gives an advantage to one party) is part of the decision-making process. The law, after all, is likely to provide the parties with some sense of their alternatives to a mediated agreement and is relevant in deciding whether to settle or to litigate.

The philosophical differences between evaluative and facilitative mediation track the competing views regarding whether communicating a legal statement constitutes offering "legal advice" or "legal information." The former is the predicted application of the law to the facts at issue. The latter is a generic statement of the law without reference to how that law will be applied to the facts of the case being mediated (Coyle, 1998). For example, a mediator in a land-use appeal may say, "The appeal period in a land-use action is 21 days." This statement is legal information. If the mediator says, "The appeal period in this case is 21 days, which has run, giving you a complete defense," the mediator is giving legal advice.

The matter becomes more complicated, however. In the land-use mediation, the mediator has separated the parties in separate rooms. The mediator knows that the appeal period is twenty-one days and has learned that the period has passed without an appeal being filed. Should the mediator remain silent about the obvious legal defense? If the party whose appeal time has expired asks the mediator, "What are the chances of winning the case?" does the mediator say "Your appeal time has expired, which means you have no chance of winning?" This will certainly create an incentive for the party to reappraise and lower his expectations and demands. Especially in the face of a stubborn party, an evaluative mediator will be tempted to do this. But what are the mediator's obligations to the other party? If the mediator tells the same thing to the other side, that person will recognize the power imbalance and hold out for a better deal. Impasse will loom. Many mediators probably would not reveal the defense, yet is that being truly impartial and neutral? Furthermore, if a truthful evaluation will polarize the parties, can the mediator only evaluate for one side (and that negatively), without breaching any ethical duty to the other side?

This raises the core ethical problem of evaluative mediation. In a nutshell, the most difficult ethical issues posed by evaluative mediation are caused by the tendency of evaluative mediators to give the parties stunted legal advice (Stark, 1997). Stunted legal advice may express concerns about the weaknesses of their cases but not the strengths. It may be advice about the "four corners" of the parties' complaint and answer, but not about how each party could strengthen his or her legal position. Stunted advice is intended to bring the parties closer together, not push them further apart. This sort of incomplete and potentially misleading advice is understandable given mediators' desire to reduce tension and conflict, avoid the appearance of bias, and promote settlement. But it undermines the parties' self-determination through informed consent.

Stunted advice poses three conflicting ethical imperatives. First, the mediator owes a duty of impartiality to each party, and concerns about the appearance of partisanship may constrain the type of advice a mediator is likely to give. Second, the mediator may feel a professional obligation to bring the parties closer together, reduce tension, and, if possible, resolve their dispute—imperatives that also substantially limit advice giving. On the other hand, the mediator owes a duty of fairness and good faith toward each of the parties in her evaluation. She evaluates in the first instance because she believes in the importance of party empowerment and informed consent. Providing anything less than maximum information is therefore uncomfortable for her, and her ethical conundrum becomes especially acute when less than complete information has the capacity to mislead.

The ethical problem is not that competent evaluative mediators lack the expertise to provide material information to the disputants or that they cannot ensure well-informed choices. The ethical problem is that they may not choose to do so, given their desire to settle the case (Stark, 1997). This desire causes some of the most misleading advice given by evaluative mediators. And it is this sort of misleading advice, not advising per se, that makes evaluative mediation controversial and sometimes gives it a bad name.

Standard 3: Conflicts of interest. Under the Model Standards, a conflict of interest is defined as "a dealing or relationship that might create an impression of possible bias. The basic approach to questions of conflict of interest is consistent with the concept of self-determination."

The ideal of the completely disinterested mediator is often achievable, but mediators often know a party or a witness or have some knowledge of the underlying facts or issues. If the relationship to persons or facts is substantial, the proposed mediator should step aside. If the mediator believes the interest is slight, the parties should be advised of all relevant information and decide for themselves whether to disqualify or to waive.

Under the Model Standards, the mediator has a duty to disclose all actual and potential conflicts that are reasonably known or that could reasonably be seen as raising a question about impartiality. The mediator also is to guard against prejudice based on "personal characteristics, background, or performance at the mediation."

There are essentially two types of disclosures: prior case experience and relationships. Prior case experience is information relating to previous peacemaking assignments with either the lawyers or the parties in the current case. Generally speaking, mediators should disclose the number of previous cases handled for counsel or the parties. This disclosure is designed to eliminate any unfair advantage that repeat players may have with the peacemaker by virtue of a continuing business relationship. Relationship disclosures are broader and relate to familial, social, professional, or representational relationships that might indicate bias in favor of one party or counsel. California Code of Civil Procedure section 1281.9, applying to arbitrators, illustrates the degree of disclosure that might be required for mediators. Section 1281.9 requires disclosure of all cases in which the arbitrator has served in which either party was involved, or in which the arbitrator was a party representative, the date of the assignment, the outcome of the assignment, and the names of all parties and counsel for parties. Any attorney-client relationship the proposed arbitrator has or had with a party or a lawyer for parties to the proceeding must be disclosed. Finally, there must be disclosure of any professional or significant personal relationship the proposed arbitrator's spouse or minor child living in the household has or has had with a party or lawyer for a party to the proceeding.

The mediator's ethical obligation to disclose biases or interests may cause parties to question the mediator's impartiality. This is because parties and their advocates, if any, may not trust any intervention that may limit their control. If they perceive the mediator favoring one party over another, they are less likely to explore the issues fully, are more likely to be guarded in their exchange of information, and will not be as open to exploring possible settlement points.

Again, the only plausible solution in determining whether a conflict of interest exists is to inform the parties that the possibility may exist and let them determine bias for themselves. This applies regardless of the mediator's style. Full disclosure prevents a violation of this Standard.

Standard 4: Competence. As with any profession, competence is a prerequisite for a meaningful outcome. The Model Standards state: "A person who offers herself or himself as available to serve as a mediator gives parties and the public the expectation that she or he has the competency to mediate effectively." Whether the mediator is facilitative or evaluative, some subject matter understanding usually is required simply to help the parties communicate effectively and reach resolution. Efficient communication would be thwarted if the parties had to explain terms of art, customs, or standards of the community or industry of which the mediator was ignorant. For example in litigated disputes, attorney mediators are generally retained because they have process familiarity and subject matter expertise.

Competence goes beyond substantive and process knowledge. How much conflict training has a mediator received? To what degree should mediators be encouraged to take on additional theoretical and academic training in the various disciplines that touch on conflict. Should nonlawyer mediators take some law classes? Should lawyers take classes in sociology, psychology, and conflict studies? Most mediators take a minimum of 40 hours of introductory courses, then learn by trial and error what works for them. A license to cut someone's hair in most states takes more hours of study and practice than it takes someone to become a mediator. Is this lack of specific standards and educational requirements desirable?

The Model Standards skirt around proper mediator training and qualifications. Standard 4 does not define "necessary" or "reasonable." The comments state that parties may choose a mediator if they are satisfied with that individual's background and qualifications, but acknowledge that training and experience often make a mediator more effective. In addition, the description of the standard also provides that "in court-connected or other forms of mandated mediation, it is essential that mediators assigned to the parties have the requisite training and experience." The key word "requisite," however, is also undefined. The broad, vague adjectives, such as "necessary," "reasonable," and "requisite," may reflect disagreement over the proper extent or nature of mediator training. Although there appears to be consensus that mediators should have "requisite" training, there is no agreement as to what type or amount of training is sufficient. The Model Standards take no stand on that question and, therefore, are not helpful with the difficult issues surrounding mediator training and qualifications.

Standard 5: Confidentiality. Maintaining confidentiality is critical to the integrity of the mediation process. Confidentiality encourages candor, allows a full exploration of the issues, and increases the likelihood of settlement. It also minimizes the inappropriate use of mediation as a discovery technique.

Under the Model Standards, a mediator is not allowed to disclose information a party expects to be confidential "unless given permission by all parties or unless required by law or other public policy." When appropriate, researchers may gain access to statistical data and, with the parties' permission, may review files, observe mediation, and interview participants.

The general rules are modified to allow "the parties [to] make their own rules with respect to confidentiality, or the accepted practice of an individual mediator or institution may dictate a particular set of expectations."

Confidentiality is, however, a complex problem. Issues concerning confidentiality are discussed later in this chapter.

Standard 6: Quality of the process. The Model Standards state, "A quality process requires a commitment by the mediator to diligence and procedural fairness." Additionally, "The parties decide when and under what conditions they will reach an agreement or terminate a mediation." Thus, the parties should decide the appropriate role or mediation model for the mediator. Offering any advice, whether legal, financial, psychological, or religious, while mediating disputes is strongly discouraged. The Model Standards distinguish mediation from practicing law or other professions, such as therapy. Consequently, the parties are encouraged to consult with other professionals to aid them in making informed decisions.

One of the most difficult issues is the role of law in the mediation process. For most mediators, however, questions of when and how to inform ignorant parties of the law present an unusually difficult dilemma. Allowing parties to make decisions without knowledge of relevant legal information prevents individuals from making fully informed decisions. On the other hand, providing legal information threatens the mediator's neutrality, especially if the information favors one party over another. The problem is intensified when party attorneys, who are supposed to be knowledgeable about the law, have failed to prepare or understand their client's legal situation.

The Model Standards include little discussion of the difficult issues surrounding the role of law in mediations. The most relevant portion of the Model Standards states:

> The primary purpose of a mediator is to help the parties' voluntary agreement. This role differs substantially from other professional-client relationships. Mixing the role of a mediator and the role of a professional advising a client is problematic, and mediators must strive to distinguish between the roles. A mediator should, therefore, refrain from providing professional advice. Where appropriate, a mediator should recommend that parties seek outside professional advice, or consider resolving their dispute through arbitration, counseling, neutral evaluation, or other processes. A mediator who undertakes, at the request of the parties, an additional dispute resolution role in the same matter assumes increased responsibilities and obligations that may be governed by the standards of other professions.

Because the Model Standards discourage mediators from "providing professional advice," they may deter mediators from informing parties of legal principles that may be relevant to the dispute. The Model Standards, however, do not forbid such action; instead, they simply state that if mediators assume an additional "professional role," they must observe the rules of conduct of that profession. This comment does not provide mediators with any guidance as to when to assume this secondary role.

In addition, the Model Standards do not give the parties or the mediator any practical guidance on the gray line that exists between offering information and offering professional advice. It is at this intersection that the debate over facilitative versus evaluative mediation is waged (Imperati, 1997). A facilitative mediator will be reluctant to give any advice, whether legal, financial, psychological, or religious, while an evaluative mediator will offer advice, albeit cloaked as information. Given the diversity of the mediation profession and the variety of interest groups that it serves, is it even possible to have one universal definition of when mediator information becomes "legal advice," "financial advice," "psychological advice," or "religious advice?" Do the Model Standards obligate mediators to use collaborative processes to explore with the parties the underlying process needs surrounding their dispute?

Within the context of mediation, the mediator's acknowledging a "substantial legal issue" without the parties' informed consent may destroy at least one party's view of the mediator's impartiality. This likely will subvert the process of mediation because disclosure of a "substantial legal issue" usually empowers one party over another. Parties seeking a mediator may select one who will not derail the resolution of the dispute by raising uncovered legal issues.

The only practical solution is to rely on the parties' right to self-determination and informed consent. Specifically, the mediator and the parties should agree on how the mediator should act if he or she spots a substantial legal issue. Just because a mediator has a law degree does not mean that he or she will give accurate legal advice, prediction, or evaluation. Therefore, the issue can be resolved by allowing the parties to determine whether, and under what circumstances, the mediator will raise legal issues. The mediator's impartiality is less likely to be questioned and the parties will more readily accept the practical ramifications of this form of mediation intervention.

Standard 7: Advertising and soliciting. The Model Standards state that all advertising or communication regarding mediation services or qualifications must be truthful. The comments provide that a mediator may refer to meeting a specific public or private entity's qualifications only if there is a procedure for such certification.

Most mediators do not advertise their style, forcing parties to speculate. If a mediator advertises her style, as "flexible" or "variable," does that violate the standard? These terms fail to describe a particular mediation style and, in fact, are designed not to put off potential clients

Standard 8: Fees. Under the Model Standards, a mediator must "fully disclose and explain the basis of compensation, fees, and charges," and the fees must be "reasonable." The comments further state that no fee can be contingent on the result or amount of settlement. This bar on contingent fees ties in philosophically with the tenets of mediator impartiality and conflicts of interest. The comments also address the sharing of fees by co-mediators (reasonable allocation) and fees for referral (which should not be accepted).

Mediators should disclose factors about mediation style that may affect the fee charged. For example, a mediator may need to point out that, in general, a facilitative mediation takes longer than an evaluative mediation.

Standard 9: Obligation to the mediation process. The Model Standards impose a duty on the mediator to actively improve the practice of mediation by educating the public, making mediation accessible, correcting abuses, and improving his or her own skills. In addition, Standard 6 imposes an affirmative duty on the mediator to recommend other options, such as arbitration, counseling, neutral evaluation, and other processes. These standards certainly encourage mediators to grapple with stylistic practices that are incongruent with the emerging ethical standards of the profession.

Finally, the Model Standards do not guide mediators in screening cases that should not be mediated. Critics argue that mediation may be an inappropriate dispute resolution process when there are power imbalances between the parties. Many mediators maintain that they have the skills and tools to address most of the power imbalances that occur during mediation. There is general consensus, however, that some cases simply are not suitable for the mediation process, regardless of the mediator's skills. For example, mediators are typically wary of working with parties in cases that involve issues of sexual, physical, or mental abuse. In cases involving more subtle power imbalances, however, the ethical norms are less clear. While some mediators will mediate cases involving parties on significantly unequal footing, others contend that such difficult disputes should be left to the court system. The Model Standards are silent on this difficult ethical dilemma.

CPR-Georgetown Commission

The CPR-Georgetown Commission drafted a Proposed Model Rule of Professional Conduct for the Lawyer as Third Party Neutral ("Draft Model Rule") because lawyers serving as third-party neutrals often found themselves in the dual professional capacities of partisan legal representatives and impartial neutrals. Because these roles often conflict, ethical rules speaking directly to the cross-practice legal professional were necessary. The commission offered its Draft Model Rule as a supplement to the already existing rules of professional conduct for lawyers.

The Model Rule, designated as Model Rule of Professional Conduct Rule 4.5 for The Lawyer as Third Party Neutral, is divided into 8 sections: The Preamble, Definitions, Diligence and Competence, Confidentiality, Impartiality, Conflicts of Interest, Fees, and Fairness and Integrity of the Process. Notice that the Rule tracks the Model Standards quite closely. This is not an accident, as the drafters of the Model Rule wanted consistency between the Standards and the Rule.

The commission hoped to clarify the distinct role of the lawyer-mediator while remedying the inadequacies of the umbrella approach as well as the silence toward cross-practice issues found in the ABA Model Rules and the state ethics rules for lawyers. The Draft Model Rule follows the view of mediation described by Riskin and others. Dividing its definitional section into four main categories—"adjudicative," "evaluative," "facilitative," and "hybrid" dispute resolution processes—the commission included mediation under both the "evaluative" and "facilitative" categories, each with a similar yet different definition. Among the types of evaluative activities deemed appropriate, the commission listed: "providing legal information, helping parties and their counsel assess likely outcomes, and inquiring into the legal and factual strengths and weaknesses of the problems presented."

In addition to listing examples of appropriate forms of evaluation, the commission restricted evaluative mediation by emphasizing self-determination, impartiality, competence, and the integrity of the mediation process. Rule 4.5.1(b), for example, restricts a lawyer-neutral's conduct by stipulating that the neutral "should decline to serve in those matters in which the lawyer is not competent to serve." Following this, the rule's comment section adopts a contextual view of competence. It provides:

> In determining whether a lawyer-neutral has the requisite knowledge and skill to serve as a neutral in a particular matter and process, relevant factors may include: the parties' reasonable expectations regarding the ADR process and the lawyer-neutral's role, the procedural and substantive complexity of the matter and process, the lawyer-neutral's general ADR experience and training, legal experience, subject matter expertise, the preparation the lawyer-neutral is able to give to the matter, and the feasibility of employing experts or co-neutrals with required substantive or process expertise. In many instances, a lawyer-neutral may accept a neutral assignment where the requisite level of competence can be achieved by reasonable preparation.

The commission concludes its definition of evaluative mediation by stating: "By agreement of the parties, or applicable law, mediators may sometimes be called on to act as evaluators or special discovery masters, or to perform other third party neutral roles." The danger, not treated by the commission, is that a mediator may shift processes without considering the potential harms. There is, for example, no assurance that the parties truly understand the differences in processes. There is also the potential for information gathered in caucus being used later for purposes that were unanticipated at the time. Confidences shared with a non-decision-making mediator may be regretted should that mediator later become an evaluator or special master.

The commission clearly acknowledges the existence and role of facilitative and evaluative mediation. The Model Rule, however, does not address the risks associated with evaluation as it relates to impartiality and self-determination nor how switching roles or processes in mid-stream may affect the process. The impartiality section deals primarily with the mediator's ongoing obligations to maintain neutrality, to disclose the potential for bias, and to avoid conflicts of interest. The rule briefly addresses the right of the parties to formulate their own solutions, though it provides little guidance as to how predictions by the mediator may interfere with the parties' self-determination. The rule also fails to adequately define or differentiate between legal information and legal advice.

Special Ethical Considerations

Confidentiality

Successful mediation requires that parties freely disclose information relating to the dispute. Consequently, confidentiality lies at the heart of the mediation process. Mediation would not be nearly as effective if the parties were not assured their discussions would remain private. Parties would be hesitant to bare their souls to the mediator if the mediator could later be called as a witness against them. Thus, confidentiality serves the crucial purpose of allowing the mediator to be seen by the parties as a neutral, unbiased third party.

Beyond its trust-facilitating function, the existence of confidentiality in mediation also lures parties to choose mediation over litigation. Parties often prefer to "keep their dispute out of the public eye." In many cases, the threat of media coverage and bad public relations can be a major concern. Confidentiality, especially of any settlement agreement, can be a powerful mechanism to address the "slippery slope" fears of oft-sued defendants such as the media and large employers. Without confidentiality, these defendants may opt to avoid settling cases for fear that a landslide of additional lawsuits will follow.

Various mechanisms exist to maintain confidentiality in a mediation session. Parties often find themselves arguing for confidentiality in situations where the mediation session has terminated and one party is seeking disclosure of information discussed during the session.

Federal Rule of Evidence 501 allows courts to create a common law privilege to cover certain relationships. The rule states in relevant part:

> Except as otherwise required by the Constitution of the United States or provided by Act of Congress or in rules prescribed by the Supreme Court pursuant to statutory authority, the privilege of a witness, person, government, State, or political subdivision thereof shall be governed by the principles of the common law as they may be interpreted by the courts of the United States in the light of reason and experience.

Examples of traditional common-law-created privileges include the attorney-client privilege, doctor-patient privilege, and priest-penitent privilege. Traditionally, when determining a claim of privilege, the courts have used the four-part Wigmore balancing test:

[The] communications must originate in confidence that they will not be disclosed; (2) this element of confidentiality must be essential to the full and satisfactory maintenance of the relations between the parties; (3) the relation must be one which, in the opinion of the community, ought to be sedulously fostered; and (4) the injury that would inure to the relation by the disclosure of the communications must be greater than the benefit thereby gained for the correct disposal of litigation.

In the context of a mediation privilege, courts would likely apply this same four-part test. The essence of finding a mediation privilege can be characterized as "the search for truth versus the nurturing of mediation as an attractive and effective alternative to litigation."

Federal Rule of Evidence 501 also states that privilege shall be determined in accordance with state law. Some jurisdictions have chosen to create a mediation privilege via statute. For example, the North Carolina statute allowing for mediation in divorce, alimony, and child support cases has specific language creating a privilege. The statute states that "all verbal or written communications from either or both parties to the mediator or between the parties in the presence of the mediator made in a proceeding pursuant to this section are absolutely privileged and inadmissible in court." Statutorily created privileges vary widely from state to state as to the scope of information to be protected and who in the mediation relationship is protected by the privilege. Legislatively created mediation privileges, such as the North Carolina statute, provide comprehensive confidentiality protection to the mediation process. Courts have generally upheld such statutes in litigation.

Federal Rule of Evidence 408 provides an evidentiary exclusion for conduct and statements made during settlement discussions. This rule can apply to the mediation process since mediation often involves compromise negotiations.

However, Rule 408 has many exceptions, many of which raise serious concerns as to whether essential portions of the mediation process would be deemed confidential. Under Rule 408, statements are excluded only if their intended use is to prove the validity of a claim or an amount of a civil claim. Mediation sessions, by their very nature, often include a discussion of a multitude of issues aside from the validity or amount of a claim. Furthermore, under Rule 408, statements can be admitted if they are offered "for another purpose" such as proving bias or prejudice of a witness, negating an accusation of undue delay, or proving an attempt to obstruct a criminal investigation. The "another purpose" exception in Rule 408 in the hands of creative counsel would leave much of the mediation session subject to disclosure. In addition, Rule 408 will not protect the confidentiality of the final mediated agreement.

Thus, Rule 408 has limited application, and cannot be relied upon to cover all mediation discussions. However, the trend is to extend Rule 408's protection to all statements during a compromise negotiation.

In an attempt to remedy these problems, some states have enacted a broader evidentiary exclusion that applies specifically to mediation. California, for example, has created a strong evidentiary protection for premediation consultations. Evidence Code sections 1115 to 1128 protect the confidentiality of the mediation process from premediation consultation forward. No statements made in mediation or premediation consultation can be used as evidence. The mediator is barred from reporting any aspect of the mediation to any adjudicative body or court, except as the parties agree or as otherwise required by law (e.g., child abuse reporting). The mediator cannot be compelled to testify or produce any notes at a later hearing or trial. Finally, referring to the fact of mediation at trial provides grounds for a mistrial if the reference materially affects the rights of a party.

Some parties have entered into private, premediation contracts providing for the confidentiality of all communications made during the mediation session. Parties fashion the terms in these agreements to fit their particular circumstances. Typical terms include agreements "not to disclose, subpoena, or offer into evidence information conveyed during a mediation proceeding."

There are several dangers in entering into a private contract. Private parties may breach the contract, forcing the other party to initiate litigation after the confidentiality has already been compromised. Private mediation contracts are not binding on third parties. Thus, if a nonparty were to bring subsequent litigation, communications made during the mediation could be allowed as evidence. In addition, some courts strike down private confidentiality contracts, finding the agreement is deliberately designed to cover evidence and thus a violation of public policy.

Courts have the power to order parties to keep mediation proceedings confidential through a protective order. In cases where the court does not grant a protective order *sua sponte*, parties may agree that confidentiality is desirable and jointly seek a protective order from the court. Federal Rule of Civil Procedure 26(c) allows the court to issue "any order which justice requires to protect a party or person from annoyance, embarrassment, oppression, or undue burden or expense."

Another potential basis to argue confidentiality in a mediation session is the common law "relevancy rule," which is recognized by most states. The relevancy rule allows the court to exclude evidence of a proposed compromise under the assumption that this information is not reliable evidence of the truth of the party making the offer's claim. As such, under the relevancy rule, "only the actual offer of settlement" in a mediation proceeding could be protected from disclosure. Conduct and independent statements of fact made during the mediation, and even the offer of settlement itself, would be admissible if a party could successfully argue it was being introduced into evidence to prove something other than liability, such as for impeachment purposes or to prove an agency relationship.

Many states have enacted statutes that provide varying degrees of confidentiality in mediation programs. Some statutes create a full mediation privilege with no exceptions, while others create more limited protection with specific exceptions to the confidentiality guarantee. To lend further confusion to the matter, many states have more than one statute, each granting a different degree of confidentiality protection to different mediation programs within the same state.

Comparison to the attorney-client privilege. The duty of confidentiality in mediation is different than the attorney-client privilege. First, the duty of confidentiality in mediation does not arise from an attorney-client relationship. Second, an attorney-client communication is deemed confidential as long as the information remains private between injury and the client. The attorney-client privilege is defeated if the parties reveal confidential attorney-client information to each other in the presence of the mediator. Unlike the attorney-client privilege, the duty of confidentiality in mediation protects all communications, either in joint session or in caucus. In addition, in states like California, any communication with the mediation in the nature of a premediation consultation is also privileged as confidential.

In some respects, the mediator's duty of confidentiality is broader than the attorney-client privilege. For example, lawyers within a law firm may divulge client confidences with firm colleagues to help client representation. A lawyer-mediator, on the other hand, must scrupulously avoid any discussion of confidential information learned in an assignment, even to lawyers within her firm.

Judicial protection of confidentiality. *National Labor Relations Board v. Macaluso, Inc.* was a test case involving mediation confidentiality in a labor relations setting. Following a mediated collective bargaining agreement, a factual dispute arose between the parties. Macaluso subpoenaed the mediator to resolve the issue by offering testimony concerning the mediation discussions. The NLRB revoked the subpoena on the grounds that revocation was necessary to preserve the neutrality and effectiveness of the mediator by not requiring a mediator to testify. Thus, the trial court was asked to weigh the need for relevant evidence against the need for confidentiality in the mediation process. The court ruled that the public interest in maintaining mediation confidentiality outweighed benefit of the mediator's testimony. In effect, the court created a mediator privilege based on a statutory provision.

This case has been followed by other cases. In *United States v. Gullo*, a federal court acknowledged a privilege on the basis of the New York Judiciary Law, which established the Community Dispute Resolution Centers Program. Part of the Act created a privilege of confidentiality for mediation and arbitration proceedings and decisions.

In *Foxgate Homeowners' Ass'n v. Bramalea California Inc.*, the mediator submitted a report to the court recommending that the defendant be sanctioned for "obstructive bad faith" tactics at the mediation. This action violated a California statute that absolutely prohibits mediators from reporting on mediation outcomes, other than to state that agreement had been reached. The California Supreme Court, in a unanimous decision, ruled that the statutory protections created in California Evidence Code section 731.6 and Code of Civil Procedure section 1121 were absolute. Therefore, no judicial exception for violating mediation confidentiality could be created, even if the parties acted in bad faith. This decision, which came after *Olam*, discussed below, establishes that mediators must hold anything said or done during mediations in absolute confidence. Mediators may only report to the court that a case has settled or not. The only exception is for certain family law matters that permit or require mediator reports to the court.

Judicial incursions on confidentiality. Mediator confidentiality, even when protected by extremely strong statutory language such as found in California, can be threatened by judicial action.

In *Olam v. Congress Mortgage Co.* 68 F.Supp.2d 1110 (1999), a California federal court construed California law to require a mediator to testify to events occurring during a mediation. This decision was made notwithstanding clear statutory language making the mediator incompetent to testify. Furthermore, the court ignored the statutory right of the mediator to resist compulsion to testify. This decision has left mediators and scholars scratching their heads because it was so obviously a wrong result. One explanation, which should be of grave concern to mediators and peacemakers, is that the court felt that mediation, if not brought under firm judicial control, would soon be the tail wagging the dog. Thus, *Olam* can be understood as an attack on mediation confidentiality for the express purpose of asserting judicial superiority over the mediation process. The irony is that the trial judge is a well-respected advocate of mediation.

With the California Supreme Court's ruling in *Foxgate*, *Olam* is now limited to situations in which the parties waive confidentiality and the court believes that the best source of information about what transpired at the mediation would come from the mediator. However, considering the strong language the California Supreme Court used in describing the absolute bar against mediator testimony in Evidence Code section 731.6, if the facts of *Olam* came before the federal court, it would most likely reach a different result. Therefore, barring statutory change, mediation confidentiality appears well-protected in California.

Situations of Extreme Power Imbalance

Few issues in relation to mediation have been as hotly debated in recent years as the interaction between the fairness of the mediation process and the existence of a power imbalance between the parties. As will be taken up in the next chapter, critics argue that the resolution of disputes with a legal content, outside the procedural safeguards of the court process, risks leading to the exploitation of parties who are not equipped to bargain as equals with the powerful.

What, for example, should the mediator do in a situation where one party appears to be using a gross inequality of power to extract consent to an outcome that is not consistent with the mediator's view of the likely judgment of a court? The presence of counsel on both sides may not alter this power dynamic, particularly if the weaker party has little in the way of financial resources to pursue the issue in court. Suppose one party does not have the resources to support a court action and the stronger party reveals to the mediator that it has deceived the other in relation to a material fact. If the stronger party cannot be persuaded to rectify the deception, are the ethical mediator's only available options to remain silent or terminate the process?

Empirical evidence demonstrates that more powerful parties appear more prone to noncooperative, manipulative, or exploitative behavior (Coyle, 1998). In light of this, many mediation practitioners advocate countering such behavior and empowering the weaker party. They recognize that the mediator's power lies in the ability to influence the outcome of negotiations. This power derives from the mediator's personal credibility and her various abilities to influence the ground rules of the process. For example she can direct the parties' exchange of views, view the parties as equally worthy of respect, and insist the parties act respectfully toward one another. She can help the parties to articulate and explore their interests and options for settlement in a principled way. She can recommend and direct the parties toward relevant professional advice when appropriate.

The problems are illustrated further in the following four hypothetical situations, set in the context of an environmental claims mediation:

(1) The chief negotiator for the polluter indicates, over a conference call involving the mediator and the landowners' negotiator, that the polluter's insurance cannot provide compensation for a particular type of loss suffered by the landowners. The mediator knows this is untrue, having been involved in previous negotiations where insurance coverage was provided.

(2) The polluter's negotiator advises the mediator in confidence that his insurance carrier and corporate governors authorized him to place several million dollars on the table over the amount previously offered. This will be used, he says, only if a settlement is otherwise impossible.

(3) The polluter's negotiator indicates in caucus to the mediator that her statement at the negotiation table, that she needs a delay of several months to reconsider the polluter's legal position, was misleading. In fact, she believes that a lengthy delay in the negotiations, which have been ongoing for several years, might help "cool" the settlement expectations of the landowners, which she says are unreasonable.

(4) The parties have not made progress in a particular mediation for several months, primarily because of a significant difference in views on the legal principles that should apply to measure the landowners' loss. The polluter's negotiator has rejected the

landowners' request that the issue be directed to a mutually accept-able neutral legal expert for a nonbinding view on the parties' legal positions. The mediation has been ongoing for several years and sig-nificant progress has occurred on other elements of the claim.

How should the mediator respond, if at all, to the potential fair-ness issues raised by each of these scenarios? How should the medi-ator reconcile knowledge of deception or "unacceptable" behavior with his or her functions as mediator (including the duty to be im-partial to both sides in the dispute) and his or her ethical framework.

What are sources of the mediator's obligations, if any, related to fairness? Can the mediator's duty of impartiality be reconciled with mediator intervention in any of these cases? If mediator intervention can be justified, how can it be take place without betraying the ex-pectations of the stronger party regarding the mediator's role as the facilitator of a process that respects both parties and their autonomy? These are questions that go to the heart of mediation practice.

In considering these questions, first ask why should a mediator care about fairness? In addition to the credibility of mediation gener-ally, there is another functional reason why it seems important for mediators to be concerned with unfairness in negotiation behavior: namely, the mediator's personal involvement in the process. The very nature of the mediation process is that it creates a triad of indi-viduals involved in the effort to resolve the dispute. Regardless of the mediator's approach, the mediator is for all purposes an integral part of the process, not a spectator. The mediator's responsibilities in fa-cilitating the parties' communications at the very least make the me-diator part of the process. In this sense, the mediator cannot help being implicated, at least at some level, in unfair behavior that the mediator becomes aware of but of which one party remains ignorant. The mediator is a moral agent involved in the process.

The mediator's first step is to recognize the limitations of media-tion. Mediation cannot assure an outcome that meets any standard of fairness independent from what the parties are ultimately able to agree upon. On the other hand, mediators have the right to withdraw from the mediation process at any time. However, this does not equip mediators with the power to determine the parties' settlement for them. Apart from the power to withdraw, the only other power is the ability to question the parties about the standards of fairness im-plicit in their positions or in a proposed settlement.

The second step is to consider the mediator's relative power. The power relationships among all three participants influence the process. Many of the standard tools of the mediator that focus on improving communications, fostering interest-based negotiations, and promoting a constructive, respectful atmosphere among the parties, may have some positive influence on the power relations at the table. These tools fit squarely within the functions of mediator objectivity, promotion of party autonomy, and enhancement of party communications. However, these tools cannot eliminate the significant differences in resources or, more importantly, of substantial variations in the strength of the alternatives to a negotiated agreement open to each party.

Finally, the mediator's power rebalancing must be reconciled with her duty of impartiality. If the stronger party engages in behavior violating procedural or substantive fairness, the mediator must consider the goals of the particular mediation and balance her conflicting duties. Although a significant power imbalance between the parties may render one party particularly vulnerable to exploitative behavior by the other, the stronger party may never resort to deceptive or unfair conduct. As such, the existence of a significant power imbalance between the parties would seem to be an important, but in the end, only a contextual factor to which the mediator should be sensitive when assessing the need to respond to fairness concerns.

Unauthorized Practice of Law

The growing concern about the unauthorized practice of law arises from reports around the country of charges filed against mediators who are not lawyers. These prosecutions-or in some cases warnings—are directed at divorce mediators who draft detailed marital settlement agreements. However, all mediators must be concerned because of the uncertainties about what constitutes the unauthorized practice of law in the context of mediation.

There are two reasons for unauthorized practice of law statutes. The first is consumer protection. Statutes ensure the competence and integrity of people who practice law. In addition, people seeking legal services gain the protection of the attorney-client privilege. The second reason is that unauthorized practices of law statutes create a monopoly over certain services. This means that prices can be maintained and competition limited.

State and local agencies enforce unauthorized practices of law statutes. Prosecutions tend to target law-related activities such as the work of accountants, real estate brokers, worker's compensation specialists, evictions service professionals, title companies, and makers of "do it yourself' divorce kits. The courts have developed five tests to distinguish the practice of law from other activities (Hoffman and Affolder, 2000). As applied to mediation, the tests are these:

The "Commonly Understood" Test. This test asks whether mediation is commonly understood to be part of a law practice in the community.

The "Client Reliance" Test. This test asks if people in mediation believe they are receiving legal services. Even if a mediator disclaims she is giving legal advice, this test is met if the parties believe they received legal advice from the mediator.

The "Relating Law to Specific Facts" Test. This test asks whether the mediator is engaged in activities that apply the law to specific facts. In other words, this test asks whether the mediation is evaluative or not. If a mediator evaluates the strengths and weaknesses of the party's case by applying legal principles to a specific fact situation, he or she is arguably engaged in the practice of law.

The "Affecting Legal Rights" Test. This test defines the practice of law as those activities affecting a person's legal rights. This test is extremely broad and would clearly encompass mediation of litigated disputes. Even in nonlitigated disputes, mediation can affect the parties' legal rights if the mediation results in a legally enforceable settlement agreement.

The "Attorney-Client Relationship" Test. This test asks whether the relationship between the mediator and the parties is substantially equivalent to an attorney-client relationship. If parties are not represented by counsel either at the mediation or in consultation before the mediation, they could view the mediator as performing the role of an attorney.

These tests illustrate that there is no definition of the practice of law in the context of mediation. In addition, courts are often interested in ancillary issues, such as the fees paid for services and the harm rendered by the services.

While a mediator does not represent individuals in a traditional attorney-client relationship, certain mediator activities require analysis to determine if they are the practice of law. The areas of a mediator's activities analyzed below include (a) mediator opinions and/or predictions regarding legal issues in dispute and (b) agreement drafting that occurs at the conclusion of successful mediation sessions. These activities are analyzed within the context of two of the three principal domains of an attorney's activity: (1) providing legal advice or counsel and (2) drafting legal documents.

Disputing parties often ask the mediator to provide either a personal opinion regarding issues in dispute or a prediction on how the dispute would be resolved by a court.

A facilitative mediator may provide general legal information, as long as the information is not particularized to a specific individual's dispute. If it were particularized, the legal information would become legal advice. Predictions and evaluations go a step beyond a mediator's offer of abstract information. They speculate how a third-party decision-maker or the mediator would apply that information.

In contrast to the facilitative mediator, the evaluative mediator does provide legal advice and make predictions on how a court may rule on a particular issue in dispute. When an evaluative mediator provides advice or makes predictions, the mediator is applying facts disclosed by the parties in the mediation session to legal principles and "delivering" an opinion.

Mediators who evaluate claims and predict court outcomes encroach upon attorneys' domain and thus engage in the practice of law. Participants in evaluative mediation sessions are likely to rely upon the determinations of the mediator.

Various courts have enjoined laymen from offering legal advice because of its inherent danger. Lawyers are specially trained to analyze facts and determine law, and laymen may not fully appreciate the consequences of a legal opinion. Clients who rely upon the advice of laymen are in danger of losing or forfeiting significant legal rights. Hence, courts prevent laymen from providing legal opinions by deeming such activity the practice of law within the principal domains of a lawyer's activity.

Drafting legal documents is another of the three areas of an attorney's domain. Thus, the agreement drafting done by mediators at the conclusion of many successful mediation sessions is another mediation process that may constitute practicing of law.

In a "true" facilitative mediation session, a mediator does not draft a contract at the end of a successful mediation session but merely memorializes the parties' own agreement. Facilitative mediators, "not being the builders of agreements but facilitators of the process of agreement, have long held themselves apart from the personal contracts that parties create." The parties themselves draft their own resolution to the dispute in a facilitative mediation session.

A facilitative mediator memorializes the parties' agreement by capturing the parties' own words as they are spoken throughout the session. At the end of the session, the mediator reads back to the parties what they have agreed upon throughout the session. If either party has questions regarding wording, those issues are negotiated between the two parties. Once the disputing parties agree upon the language, the facilitative mediator types the agreement. Thus, the facilitative mediator acts merely as a glorified secretary when memorializing the parties' agreement. A facilitative mediator does not infringe upon the principal domains of an attorney's activity when typing up the parties' agreement and, therefore, is not practicing law.

While the facilitative mediator may not be practicing law when memorializing the parties' own agreement, there is a real danger that the participants in a facilitative mediation session will rely upon the mediator to draft an enforceable agreement.

Conclusion

The ethics of mediation and peacemaking will be a source of debate among practitioners and scholars for decades to come. Ultimately, the tough ethical decisions will not be mandated by governing bodies, but will be made by caring, reflective people helping others resolve their disputes. The four basic ethical components will always be party self-determination, impartiality and neutrality, and confidentiality. Every peacemaker will be tested by these ethical principles. Ultimately, personal values, trust in the process, and integrity will determine how the difficult ethical problems are resolved. For this reason, experience, training, and seasoning may be the future necessary requisites of mediator competence.

Reflections on Chapter Fifteen

You are mediating an insurance case. The defense lawyer, in a moment of unusual candor, tells you in confidence that the insurance company is willing to settle, but wants to drag out the negotiation as long as possible to lower the plaintiff's expectations. The plaintiffs' lawyer tells you privately that her clients have to settle as soon as possible or face financial ruin. What are some of the ethical issues you face?

A mediator is facing impasse. She goes to the side that is resisting further discussion and says, "I have some information that I cannot disclose, but indicates to me that you are not properly evaluating your case." What are the ethical issues raised in each of the following scenarios:

She has no information at all, but is saying this to create a sense of asymmetrical information risk.

She has information, but has been told not to disclose its existence to the other side.

CHAPTER SIXTEEN

APOLOGY
AND FORGIVENESS

Introduction

PROFESSOR JONATHAN R. COHEN starts his article on apology with the
following stories:

> Imagine that a child damages his neighbor's house. Playing
> baseball after school, Hank, age eleven, hits a ball hard but foul,
> flying from his bat toward and then through a window of his
> neighbor Mr. Cleary's house. What should Hank do? Sneak into
> Mr. Cleary's house and retrieve the ball before Mr. Cleary gets
> home from work? Hope that Mr. Cleary won't notice? In tears,
> Hank enters his own home to tell his mother what has hap-
> pened. They talk about it and decide that the right thing for
> Hank to do is to apologize and make amends. Upon seeing Mr.
> Cleary arrive home, Hank is to go directly to Mr. Cleary's house,
> say he is sorry for breaking the window, offer to pay for a new
> window, and promise that he won't play ball in a way that might
> risk damaging Mr. Cleary's house again.
>
> Imagine instead that an adult damages his neighbor's
> house. Mr. Tiller has long dreamed of converting the flat grass of
> his back lawn into an elegant rock garden accented by a small
> hill. One spring weekend, he hires a gardener to re-landscape.
> Using light machinery, the gardener digs into the lawn and piles
> soil to form a small hill. Several weeks later, a torrential rain

412

shower hits. Peering out his living room window, Mr. Tiller sees that his yard contains not only a small hill, but also a large pool of water. This pool stretches from the foot of the new hill into his neighbor Ms. Jones' lawn. It reaches up to her back porch—or what used to be her back porch! Mr. Tiller can see that one of the corner posts of that back porch has collapsed, apparently slipping at its base. Further, the pool of water covers that spot. What should he do? Mr. Tiller knows that Ms. Jones, who lives alone, has recently left for a two-week vacation. Distraught, Mr. Tiller phones his lawyer.

'Whatever you do,' says the lawyer, 'don't run over and apologize when Jones gets back from vacation. That would just make you look bad. Also, don't call your gardener to have him flatten the hill before Jones gets back. That too would just make you look bad. Who knows, maybe the post's collapsing had nothing to do with your hill. Perhaps the severity of the rain was the root cause of the damage, or maybe the wood supporting the porch was simply rotten. By the time Jones gets back from vacation, the pool may have cleared. Just wait and see what happens. Jones might not even suspect that your hill was involved with the damage to her porch, but even if she does, it's likely she won't be able to prove it.'

How different are the ways we counsel children and adults to act when they have injured others. Parents, or at least good parents, teach children to take responsibility when they have wronged another: Apologize and make amends. In contrast, lawyers typically counsel the opposite. Most lawyers focus on how to deny responsibility, including what defenses a client might have against a charge and what counterclaims. If a lawyer contemplates an apology, it may well be with a skeptical eye: Don't risk apology, it will just create liability. While the lawyer-client relationship is of course different from the parent-child relationship, the fact that parents frequently advise children to apologize, but that lawyers rarely advise clients to apologize, ought to give us pause. If apology is often in the best interest of children, could it often be in the best interest of adults? (Cohen, 1999, p. 1009)

Apology and forgiveness are concepts that seem to separate peacemaking from settlement. If we consider peacemaking to be a reconciliation of relationships, then apology and forgiveness are fundamental. In the law, however, apology and forgiveness have little place. For a variety of reasons, not the least of which is that an apology may be construed as an admission of fault or guilt, or worse, a sign of weakness, apology and forgiveness are treated as moral niceties. Many lawyers consider apology and forgiveness essentially irrelevant to the real process of resolving cases.

The litigation process fosters this irrelevancy. Denial often takes hold early in the course of litigation. Faced with a claim, a defendant's answer is typically due within twenty or thirty days. Answers almost always deny any wrongdoing. One can always admit liability later, but once admitted, liability cannot be taken back. Further, claims frequently use antagonistic language, painting the defendant in evil, heinous, or reckless terms. Accordingly, a denial-oriented mind-set develops early in legal disputes. Once begun, denial generates a momentum of its own, and apology is nowhere to be seen.

In criminal cases, apology is more than irrelevant; it is foolish. To invoke constitutional rights, a defendant must plead not guilty at arraignment, even if guilt at some level may be clear. Having denied guilt in open court and after consultations with counsel about the defense of the case, criminal defendants begin to rationalize. Denial becomes reality and apology becomes impossible.

Despite these barriers, peacemakers must understand apology and forgiveness. In many cases, an apology by a party can mean the difference between settlement and trial. This chapter therefore concerns the nature of apology and forgiveness, the structural barriers in the law and legal system preventing apology and forgiveness, and the practical issues faced when considering apology and forgiveness in the peacemaking process.

The Nature of Apology and Forgiveness

Most people assume that apology and forgiveness are a normal part of preexisting relationships. Thus, friends, spouses, co-workers, or family members hurt one another in a way that gives rise to the need for apology. Two people who know each other now face a difficulty in their relationship that may implicate breach of trust, betrayal, hurt feelings, disappointment, frustration, and anger. The relational injury may be complicated by hierarchy, need for self-respect, and power. Apology reconnects people to restore their relationship. Often, apology is necessary because compensation is inappropriate or unavailable. As will be discussed in more detail, apology levels the moral scales that have been imbalanced by an offense.

Relationships are also involuntarily created from an injury or offense. If they have never known each other, an injury or offense now joins two strangers together in the roles of offender and victim. At a minimum, the relationship's purpose is to ask if one should compensate the other and, if so, how much? The difficulty lies in the fact that the relationship is nonconsensual. The victim did not ask for this relationship, has no control over it, and has been rendered socially powerless by the offender. The offender, on the other hand, now has caused a relationship to form where one did not exist before. As with all relationships, moral and social obligations arise. The victim wishes to be extricated from the relationship and the offender has the sole power to do so. Apology can give power back to the victim, and it can connect the people to make the relationship more constructive.

An apology, no matter how sincere or effective, does not and cannot undo what has been done. And yet, in a mysterious way according to its own logic, this is precisely what apology manages to do (Augsburger,1996). Apology, therefore, speaks to something larger than any particular offense. This larger theme concerns membership in a moral community. The stability of relationships in groups is predicated upon conformity to norms. Only by acknowledging responsibility, expressing genuine sorrow and regret, and pledging to abide by the rules does one simultaneously recall that which binds. Apologies constitute a form of self-punishment that cuts deeply because the offender is obligated to re-tell, relive, and seek forgiveness for events that surrendered claims to membership in a moral community (Augsburger, 1996).

We not only apologize to someone, but for something. An apology is a remedial ritual that reaffirms allegiance to codes of behavior challenged by transgression, whether knowingly or not. An apology thus speaks to an act that cannot go unnoticed without compromising the current and future relationship of the parties, the legitimacy of the violated rule, and the well-being of the community.

Offenses also risk retaliation and escalation of conflict. Both accounts and apologies counter retaliation and escalation by settling matters, but in quite different ways. An account resides in the energy expended in explanation. On the other hand, apology is marked by scrupulous self-exposure to justifiable retribution while pleading for unconditional forgiveness (Levi, 1997).

Appeasement and Accounts

Appeasement and accounts fall short of apology and are treated as apologetic substitutes. They do not correct a moral imbalance and therefore can escalate conflicts. Appeasement and accounts are far more common than apology because they avoid the difficult task of confronting one's error.

Appeasement is any form of moving close to the other without dealing with the injury or alienation. In this sense, appeasement is a connecting action. Passive appeasement includes groveling, acquiescence, placating, and abject apologies, but without accepting personal responsibility. Active appeasement includes seduction, persuasion, or manipulation. Both of these positions avoid taking an "I-position." Appeasement is often found when inferiors in a hierarchy are dealing with superiors. Rather than risk the uncertainty of sanction from the superior, an inferior will attempt appeasement. Lorenz notes that appeasement, rather than fostering reconciliation, is intended to prevent or inhibit aggressive behavior toward the offender (Lorenz, 1966).

Most wrongdoers offer an account of what happened and why. Accounts result from self-defense, and include justification, explanation, and self-exoneration. The law provides numerous technical defenses to liability. These technical defenses have made their way into common usage such that people resort to legalistic reasoning to justify or explain their behavior. Accounts fail to correct any moral imbalance because they deny responsibility and avoid answerability. An account requests a release from consequences due to extenuating circumstances not within the control of the offender.

When people resort to excuse, explanation, or justification, they necessarily attempt to distance themselves from their actions and their unique personal identities. They deny or suspend the imperatives of responsibility and answerability. They appeal, variously, to an impaired self, or to external forces to absolve their actions and consequences. Personal accountability is derived.

There is a fine but crucial line between an apology and account despite the fact that the two may appear similar or employ the same form of speech. In its purest expression, an apology clearly announces, "I have no excuses for what I did. I am sorry and regretful. I care. Forgive me." Personal accountability is accepted.

Apology

To apologize is to declare voluntarily that one has no excuse, defense, justification, or explanation for an action that has injured another. Apologetic speech is a decisive moment in a complex process arising from an offense and culminating in remorse and reconciliation. Each stage of the process confronts the participants with moral choices that move them toward reunion or estrangement. Each phase is acutely susceptible to miscalculation, impasse, and uncertainty. The process may fail if the original transgression is considered to be beyond redemption. The apology may be defective or ill-timed. Sorrow may give way to pride, or guilt to anger. Forgiveness may be withheld, conditional, or granted without reconciliation, thus marking the end of the relationship. Finally, some kind of rapprochement may be established but without forgiveness. Apology is, therefore, fraught with danger and is never guaranteed success.

Full and complete apology requires a two-step process called the core sequence (Retzinger and Scheff, 1996). During the core sequence, two persons perform a corrective ritual to redress a moral power imbalance between them. In the first step, the offender clearly expresses her genuine shame and remorse for her actions. The offender must be in a state of perfect defenselessness. Without this defenselessness, any apology lacks sincerity. The victim immediately senses the equivocation or defensiveness and devalues the effort.

The key to defenselessness is in its voluntary relinquishment of relational power. When the offender becomes vulnerable, the victim is empowered. The offender is now giving choice back to the victim. The victim has the opportunity to consider, "How much am I willing to risk?" "What can I afford to lose?" Therefore, the victim regains control of her relationship with the offender. She can choose the level of trust she is willing to invest in the offender, and the offender has no choice in the matter.

The core sequence is completed if the victim takes at least a first step toward forgiveness. Of course, the risk for the offender is that the victim will not take that step. The psychological danger for the offender is rejection, after rendering herself utterly vulnerable. In other words, the offender risks that the victim will choose to defend rather than connect. This state is frightening because self-esteem based on acceptance faces rejection. Furthermore, the offender is placing herself in the position she faced as a child seeking approval and love from her parents. The offender has no rationales or justifications to fall back on if the victim chooses to reject the apology. Consequently, making a full apology takes enormous courage. If the apology is accepted, the offender experiences a sense of release because she has been accepted again as a person, despite the occurrence of the offense. If the apology is rejected, the offender is left hollow and empty. She must somehow reconstruct her identity without forgiveness or reconciliation.

Even though the core sequence may be brief, it is the key to reconciliation and victim satisfaction. The core sequence is completed
when the victim acknowledges the apology. At that point, she closes
the circle of performance and establishes a new moral equilibrium.

Although apology is important as symbolic reparation, it is only
a part of the peacemaking process. Apology does not repair the substantive injury nor restore the injured party to her pre-injury status.
An automobile accident victim with severe injuries may face permanent disfigurement or physical disability. From being healthy and
functional, a victim may be unable to carry on a previous life. Apology will not restore that loss.

Similarly, apology does not extricate the offender from her offending role in the conflict. By apologizing, the offender acknowledges her lower moral stature and asks for forgiveness. By apologizing, the offender acknowledges the existence and importance of the
moral register. Thus, apology helps to stabilize social relations by acknowledging a moral standard of conduct that was breached. The offender's acknowledgment of a standard of conduct allows the victim
to feel that society does have some stable norms. The offender's admission of violation allows the victim to feel that, although the offense was unwanted, an explanation for its cause exists: someone
other than the victim was morally at fault. This lifts the shadow of
self-blame and shame from the victim.

Symbolic reparation, unlike material settlement, depends entirely upon the play of emotions and social relationships. These dynamics are governed by two events. First, symbolic reparation requires management of shame in the offender and in all the other participants, including the peacemaker. Second, symbolic reparation requires management of the degree of mutual identification and understanding between the participants.

Shame plays a crucial role in normal cooperative relationships,
as well as in conflict. Shame signals a threat to the social bond and is
therefore vital in establishing where one stands in a relationship.
Similarly, pride signals a secure bond. Shame is the emotional cog-
nate of a threatened or damaged bond, just as threatened bonds are
the source of shame. This equation allows shame language to be
translated into relationship language. Goffman (1967) has argued
that normal shame and embarrassment are an almost continuous
part of all human contact. This is why the visible expression of shame
by the offender looms so large in symbolic reparation. When we see
signs of shame and embarrassment in others, we are able to recog-

nize them as human beings like ourselves, no matter what the language, cultural setting, or context.

Forgiveness

The second part of the core sequence is the process of forgiveness. Most people view forgiveness as a simple act when, in reality, it is usually a lengthy process. Forgiveness can be classified as unilateral or mutual, and as negative or positive.

Unilateral forgiveness is most common and is epitomized by the saying, "Forgive and forget." Unilateral forgiveness sets the offended person free by releasing all resentment, all claims for recognition of the injured by the offender, and all demands for repentance or restitution. Resolution of the injury from the conflict is intrapsychic rather than interpersonal. Unilateral forgiveness is the most common forgiveness and is typified by a Western orientation to individuality, privacy, and lack of communal relationships (Augsburger, 1988, 1996).

Mutual forgiveness is much less common. It is a mutual recognition that repentance is genuine and right relationships have been restored or achieved. Mutual forgiveness is a social transaction of interpersonal reconciliation. In this type of forgiveness, the conflict belongs to the community as well as the disputants and the responsibility to seek reconciliation is shared. Mutual forgiveness is focused on regaining the other as brother or sister.

Negative forgiveness stems from a request for remission of punishment and release from the consequences, anger, and resentment of another. Negative forgiveness also seeks release from one's own feeling of guilt. Positive forgiveness is based on unconditional acceptance of the offense and acceptance of the offender back into the moral community. In positive forgiveness, someone must pay, absorb the loss, bear the cost,or accept the anger. If the offender pays, we call the process justice. If the victim accepts the burden, we call the process positive forgiveness (Augsburger, 1988, 1996).

Impediments to Apology

Cultural Issues

Culture defines how and when apology is expressed. Apology is not a prevalent norm in Western culture because of the concept of repression of shame and the ideology of individualism.

Shame is a central part of personality development. It is central to the self-recognition, self-structuring, and self-regulating processes of the mature personality. Shame is also essential in mature relationships—in reparation, repentance, and reconciliation. However, shame can be dysfunctional.

Those who are overly prone to shame have suffered devastating experiences of shame during formative periods of life. These people lack empathy, hold a wish to blot out the offense against the grandiose self, and have an unforgiving fury that is out of proportion to minor irritants. The defense against this shame combines rage, power, and righteousness into a personality that represses shame so as not to relive early memories. The no-holds-barred defense of a fragile self does not allow for vulnerability, for risking reconciliation, for repentance, or the admission of failure. These rigid defenses protect the self from further injury. Consequently, empathy with another's pain or understanding their offer of reconciliation is virtually impossible. In addition, rigid defenses distort relationships with others. As a result, failure after failure follows failure in communication and trust formation, and reconciliation becomes impossible (Augsburger, 1996).

Another cultural impediment to apology is the strong sense of individuality. In American culture, where autonomy is an important component of self-image, the dependency and emotionality implicit in apology are risks to self-image that few parties are likely to take.

In American culture, children are expected to repress their dependent needs early to become autonomous individuals. Adult Americans view dependence as a one-way affair, usually somewhat parasitic and weak. Americans strive for independence to establish strength and power in relationship to others. Apology runs completely contrary to these cultural biases. Apology creates a state of dependency and the possibility of exploitation. Therefore, apology is not automatically considered as a means of resolution, transformation, or reconciliation. In a culture based on a sense of competition, few people have the strength of character to face the potential of loss from apology.

Structural Legal Issues

In addition to cultural impediments, the Western legal tradition has prevented apology from becoming commonplace in serious disputes. In a pluralistic, liberal society, rights dominate relationships. Consequently, people are loath to make statements that may infringe on their rights. In a competitive, rights-based society, the attitude is, "You prove that I injured you!" rather than acceptance of responsibility. The law fosters this attitude in the rules of evidence, burdens of proof, and substantive law.

The central legal tension over apology is evidentiary. On the one hand, courts want to admit all relevant evidence tending to prove a case. This is called probative evidence. What could be more convincing than a party's admission of fault? On the other hand, courts want to encourage private settlement, and what could be a greater impediment to private settlement than the fear that if one offers words of apology they will be turned against one to prove one's guilt? As Wagatsuma and Rosett (1986) explain:

> The law of evidence in America is torn between the pull to encourage compromise settlement of disputes by a process that is likely to include an apology and the countervailing attraction to a common lawyer of an admission, that 'queen of proof,' which can be used to prove the claim despite the hearsay rule and other artificial strictures that make proof at common law so complex. (p. 479)

In civil cases, while apology might perform important healing work, the risk of losing compensation often overwhelms interest in emotional healing. Even a truly remorseful defendant is unlikely to brave the perceived risk of increased liability. Furthermore, in commercial mediation, apologetic ritual seems out of place between business people apparently negotiating over contract breaches, trademark or patent infringements, business torts and the like. This is because under economic theory, the single goal of a business is to maximize profit. Therefore, apology appears to be irrelevant, or worse yet, dangerous.

In addition, the civil legal system's basic remedial principle is to place the injured party as much as possible back in her rightful position. This is accomplished through a compensation system. Significantly, American law does not recognize rightful position in terms of symbolic reparation.

In civil remedies, the rightful position is measured by the value of the thing lost or injured. This concept is divided into compensation, restitution, and retribution. In compensation, although the damage cannot be repaired, the victim's needs are addressed through payment in money, goods, or services. In restitution, the wrongdoer disgorges the value of anything wrongfully obtained. In retribution, such as through punitive damages and civil fines, the wrongdoer suffers for transgression by paying extra as punishment for the intentionality of the wrong.

In compensation, restitution, and retribution, the wrongdoer pays the injured party. In reconciliation, the victim cancels the wrongdoer's debt with or without an apology, although the wrong-doer may still pay compensation or restitution. From a civil law perspective, this result is antagonistic to the entire rights-based structure of society. If the law were to incorporate reconciliation as a potential remedy, the rights of the less powerful might be jeopardized by the more powerful. Thus, the civil law sees itself as a strong corrective against power imbalances within society.

Apology as an Admission of Fault/Liability

Hearsay evidence involves a statement made out of court and offered to prove the truth of a matter stated. Hearsay evidence is inadmissible unless it falls within an established exception to the hearsay rule. Reasons for excluding hearsay evidence are (a) the statements are not made under oath; (b) the adverse party has no opportunity to cross-examine the person who made them; and (c) the jury cannot observe the witness's demeanor while making them. The emphasis today, both as a justification for the rule and as a test for its application, is on the absence of cross-examination to expose dishonesty and faulty perception or memory. The essence of the hearsay rule is that since the witness is not in court and subject to cross-examination, the jury cannot judge credibility. Normally, the hearsay rule would prevent apologies from being admitted into evidence at trial. Good lawyers, however, can always find a way around the hearsay rule.

First, the out of court statement may not be offered as a hearsay statement. If the statement is not being offered for the truth of the matter asserted, the statement is not hearsay. For example, an apology might be offered to establish the state of mind of the witness. If state of mind were relevant in the action, the statement would be admissible notwithstanding the hearsay rule.

One major exception to the hearsay rule is that admissions of parties are admissible even if they are hearsay. An admission consists of a statement or conduct of the party to the action that is offered against him at trial. Although admissions are made out of court and not subject to oath or cross-examination, they are not excluded. The party making the statement has the right to explain or contradict it.

Admissions may be express statements or may arise from conduct. Express admissions may be oral or written. Written admissions are found in many types of informal and formal documents. Admissions may be personal, such as statements of the party himself; vicarious, such as statements of another admissible against the party; or adoptive, such as statements of another adopted as the party's own statement. Any earlier statement of a party may be offered against him or her, even though it may not have been made against his or her interest, or even may have been self-serving when mad

A statement may be received as an admission even though it contains inadmissible matter. Thus, when the defendant makes a statement acknowledging responsibility for an accident, it may be introduced in evidence, notwithstanding the fact that he mentions insurance coverage. For example, "Gee, I'm sorry I ran into you. I was on my cell phone and not paying attention. Don't worry, my insurance company will handle it," is an admission. Under the admissions exception to the hearsay rule, any apology made by a party can be offered against that party at trial. However, admissions made in the course of settlement negotiations and in mediation are generally excluded from evidence on public policy grounds.

If a nonparty makes the apology, it may be admissible under a hearsay rule exception known as a declaration against interest. A declaration of a nonparty against her own interest is admitted on the theory that a person will not speak falsely or mistakenly where this would be prejudicial to her. Generally, the statement must be against the declarant's pecuniary or proprietary interest, must subject the declarant to the risk of civil or criminal liability, or must potentially subject the declarant to hatred, ridicule, or social disgrace in the community. For this evidence to be admissible, the declarant must be unavailable for trial.

The point of these evidentiary rules is that statements made by people involved in serious disputes, including apologies, may come back to haunt them. Thus, the law of evidence has created an exceptionally strong incentive to say nothing and admit nothing to anyone.

Apology is only an issue before liability is established because its probative value is in proving fault. One question to consider when thinking about apology is how clear the liability appears. If the liability is undisputed, an apology does not affect the defendant's rights. In fact, an apology may mitigate a jury's sense of the defendant's culpability.

An offender may feel at fault, but not be legally at fault. In this case, an apology may jeopardize the offender's legal rights. Consequently, the offender is left with the guilt and shame of having contributed somehow to an injury, but is unable to express remorse because of the fear of the legal consequences of apology.

Finally, there may be shared responsibility, embodied in the doctrine of comparative fault. Both the wrongdoer and the injured party may share responsibility for the injury. In this case, mutual apologies would seem appropriate, but because the percentage of fault between the parties must be apportioned, incentives toward silence are strong.

Apologies also can be used by third parties as proof of wrongdoing. In *Carney vs. Santa Cruz Women Against Rape*, 221 Cal. App. 3d 1009 (1990), Steven Carney sued Santa Cruz Women Against Rape (SCWAR) for libel, invasion of privacy, and intentional infliction of emotional distress after SCWAR published a story that Carney had assaulted and attempted to rape Karen W. At trial, the jury returned a verdict for Carney's of $7,500 in compensatory damages and $25,000 in punitive damages.

Procedurally, after Carney filed his case against SCWAR, Karen cross-complained against Carney for assault and battery. Carney and Karen subsequently settled their cross-claims and, pursuant to the settlement, exchanged letters of apology. Karen's letter acknowledged, "I was not raped by you or Mark Wilson on the night described in the flyer, or at any time, and I did not have sexual relations with you or Mark Wilson on that night or at any time."

The case proceeded to trial against SCWAR. At trial, Carney testified that he had been out with Karen on the night of June 23, 1984, and that they had engaged in various acts of sexual fondling, but that the acts were engaged in with Karen's consent.

SCWAR argued on appeal that admitting Karen's letter of apology into evidence violated California Evidence Code section 1152(a) that states:

> Evidence that a person has, in compromise or from humanitarian motives, furnished or offered or promised to furnish money or any other thing, act, or service to another who has sustained or will sustain or claims that he or she has sustained or will sustain loss or damage, as well as any conduct or statements made in negotiation thereof, is inadmissible to prove his or her liability for the loss or damage or any part of it.

Generally, the rule prevents parties from being deterred from making offers of settlement and helps the type of candid discussion that may lead to settlement. In this case, by contrast, the letter was not introduced to prove Karen's "liability" for any "loss or damage." The letter was admitted as evidence regarding the truth or falsity of the statements in the SCWAR newsletter. Thus, given that the plain language of the statute provides that evidence of a settlement is inadmissible to prove *liability* of the settling party, and that Karen's letter was not admitted to establish her liability, the appellate court concluded that the apology was properly admitted at trial.

The courts are mixed about apology in civil actions. Some courts have ruled that apology does not establish an element of proof in medical practice actions. In *Phinney v. Vinson* 605 A.2d 849 (1992), plaintiffs appealed from a summary judgment entered against them in a medical malpractice action. They argued that an admission by the defendant doctor was sufficient to avoid summary judgment on liability.

The doctor performed a transurethral resection of the prostate upon plaintiff Robert Phinney, but recurring pain caused the need for another operation by a different doctor. Following this operation, the defendant allegedly said that the second doctor told him that he had performed an "inadequate resection." The doctor thereafter apologized to the plaintiff "for his failure to do so." The plaintiffs argued that this statement, without more, was sufficient evidence of liability to allow the case to go to trial. The trial court ruled that the apology did not constitute, by itself, proof that the doctor's care fell beneath the standard of care of physicians in the community. Consequently, without more proof of negligence, plaintiffs failed to prove their case as a matter of law. Since the apology was not a clear admission of negligence, it was insufficient by itself to meet plaintiffs' burden of proof.

A similar result occurred in *Senesac v. Associates in Obstetrics and Gynecology* 449 A.2d 900 (1982). The plaintiff alleged that Dr. Gray negligently performed an abortion procedure and failed to inform her of the risks inherent in the operation.

The plaintiff did not offer expert medical testimony to show that Dr. Gray departed from the standard of care. At no point during the plaintiff's determined cross-examination did Dr. Gray concede that she departed from the standard of care ordinarily exercised by the average, reasonably skillful gynecologist. Moreover, the plaintiff offered no expert medical testimony of her own to show the asserted lack of requisite care and skill.

The plaintiff testified, however, that shortly after the operation Dr. Gray "admitted that she had made a mistake." The court ruled that Dr. Gray's statement that she "made a mistake, that she was sorry, and that it [the perforation of the uterus] had never happened before" does not establish medical negligence. Even if Dr. Gray believed her performance did not meet her *own* personal standards of care and skill, her statement did not prove a departure from the standards of care and skill *ordinarily* exercised by physicians in similar cases.

On the other hand, the statement "I'm sorry" was admissible in *Wiener v. Mizuta*, 6 Cal.App.2d 142 (1953). The plaintiff testified upon direct examination: "I asked Mr. Mizuta how it was that he didn't see my car parked there, and his answer to me was, 'I am sorry, I seen you too late.'"

The parties then pulled their cars over to the east side of the street and immediately continued with the conversation.

"A. . . . I told him that my wife was hurt.

Q. What did he say?

A. His reply was, 'You go get any doctor,' or 'Tell your doctor, that we are insured, and I hope the lady will be better'. . . .

Q. Do you recall any further conversation that you had at that time on the east side of the street immediately after you arrived there with Mr. Mizuta. . . .

A. He said to me, 'I am sorry. I seen you too late."

The court allowed the apology as an admission against interest, including the statement concerning insurance. Normally, statements concerning insurance are inadmissible at trial, so the apology was doubly damaging in this case.

Apology in settlement negotiations. Rules of evidence protecting statements made during settlement negotiations may exclude an apology at trial. Federal Rule of Evidence 408 illustrates many of the essential tensions. The easiest way to understand both F.R.E. 408 and its limitations is to begin with the common law rules that it superseded. Under the common law, statements made in the course of settlement negotiations were admissible in court unless they were made in hypothetical form. For example, a lawyer might say "Let's assume, solely for the sake of argument, that the defendant was to admit that he was responsible for. . . . " In addition any admission in settlement negotiations was normally preceded by the mantra "without prejudice." Thus, "Without prejudice to any of his rights, the defendant admits that his car crashed into the plaintiff's car. . . . "

Many difficulties emerged with these rules. As noted by the F.R.E. 408 Advisory Committee:

An inevitable effect [of these common law rules] is to inhibit freedom of communication with respect to compromise, even among lawyers. Another effect is the generation of controversy over whether a given statement falls within or without the protected area.... Further, [rules like those which would act] by protecting hypothetically phrased statements ... constituted a preference for the sophisticated, and a trap for the unwary.

Under the common law rules, to protect oneself from an admission, one had to invoke legal formalisms. Even then, the risk remained that the statement would be found independent of the settlement offer and hence unprotected.

F.R.E. 408 was designed to change this by reversing the rule. Thus, settlement negotiations became inadmissible, with or without such legal formalisms. F.R.E. 408 for once made the law follow human practice rather than the converse.

The rule states:

Evidence of (1) furnishing or offering or promising to furnish, or (2) accepting or offering or promising to accept, a valuable consideration in compromising or attempting to compromise a claim which was disputed as to either validity or amount, is not admissible to prove liability for or invalidity of the claim or its amount. Evidence of conduct or statements made in compromise negotiations is likewise not admissible. This rule does not require the exclusion of any evidence otherwise discoverable merely because it is presented in the course of compromise negotiations. This rule also does not require exclusion when the evidence is offered for another purpose, such as proving bias or prejudice of a witness, negating a contention of undue delay, or proving an effort to obstruct a criminal investigation or prosecution.

The purpose of F.R.E. 408 was straightforward: Create a protected space so as to encourage private settlements. As the F.R.E. 408 Advisory Committee explained, "The purpose of this rule is to encourage private settlements which would be discouraged if such evidence were admissible" (Cohen, 1999, p. 1034). However, the limitations of F.R.E. 408 are significant.

The first sentence of F.R.E. 408 states that evidence is inadmissible under the rule only when used, "to prove liability for or the invalidity of the claim or its amount." Nevertheless, the same evidence is admissible for other purposes. The last sentence says that evidence may be "offered for another purpose, such as proving bias or prejudice of a witness, negating a contention of undue delay, or proving an effort to obstruct a criminal investigation or proceeding." This loophole swallows the rule. For example, if a defendant who admitted his guilt when apologizing during settlement negotiations was later to deny his guilt at trial, the earlier admission likely could be used against him for impeachment.

Second, even if F.R.E. 408 were to bar an apology made during settlement negotiations from admission at trial, F.R.E. 408 does not preclude such evidence from pretrial discovery, nor does it prevent such evidence from being revealed to third parties. Such loopholes can be significant deterrents to making an apology. This is the rule expressed in *Carney v. Santa Cruz Women Against Rape*, discussed earlier in this chapter.

Third, F.R.E. 408 only protects conduct or statements made "in compromise negotiations," and in some cases there may be a question as to whether "compromise negotiations" have begun. Put differently, how developed must the dispute be before the protections afforded by F.R.E. 408 attach? Once a legal claim has been filed, F.R.E. 408 will clearly apply, but does it apply before a claim has been filed. Often an offender will want to apologize immediately after the injury. F.R.E. 408 may not cover such an apology.

Apology in mediation. Apology is protected somewhat better in California mediations. Two statutes govern confidentiality in mediation. California Evidence Code section 703.5 states:

> No person presiding at any judicial or quasi-judicial proceeding and no arbitrator or mediator, shall be competent to testify, in any subsequent civil proceeding as to any statement, conduct, decision, or ruling, occurring or in conjunction with the prior preceding, except as to a statement or conduct that could (a) give rise to civil or criminal content, (b) constitute a crime, (c) be the subject of investigation by the State Bar or Commission On Judicial Performance, or (d) give rise to disqualification proceedings under paragraphs (1) or (6) of subdivision (a) of section of 170.1 of the Code of Civil Procedure. However, this section does not apply to mediator with regard to any mediation under Chapter Eleven (commencing with section 3160) of Part 2 of Division 8 of the Family Code.

California Evidence Code section 1119 states that

> Except as otherwise provided in this chapter:
>   No evidence of anything said or any admission made for the

purpose of, in the course of, or pursuant to, a mediation or a mediation consultation is admissible or subject to discovery, and disclosure of the evidence shall not be compelled, in any arbitration, administrative adjudication, civil action, or other noncriminal proceeding in which, pursuant to law, testimony can be compelled to be given.

No writing, as defined in section 250, that is prepared for the purpose of, in the course of, or pursuant to, a mediation or a mediation consultation, is admissible or subject to discovery, and disclosure of the writing shall not be compelled, in any arbitration, administrative adjudication, civil action, or other noncriminal proceeding in which, pursuant to law, testimony can be compelled to be given.

All communications, negotiations, or settlement discussions by and between participants in the course of a mediation or a mediation consultation shall remain confidential.

Thus, according to the statutes, a mediator is not competent to testify about what has happened either before mediation or during mediation and all discussions of mediation are inadmissible. This all seemed clear until a federal court stepped in to muddy the waters. In *Olam v. Congress Mortgage Co.* 68 F.Supp.2d 1110 (N.D. Cal. 1999), a federal magistrate judge forced a mediator to testify despite California's categorical exclusion of evidence arising from mediation.

After a long mediation session, agreement was reached early in the morning. The plaintiff later disavowed the agreement, claiming among other things, that she was physically, intellectually, and emotionally exhausted and unable to give valid consent. She also cited earlier illness. The best evidence of the plaintiff's capacity was the mediator's perceptions of her capacity to contract during the mediation. Both parties agreed to waive their confidentiality rights for that purpose and asked the court to compel the mediator's testimony.

The court ordered the mediator to testify in a sealed proceeding to find out what he would say. Then the court balanced the benefits of hearing evidence against the burden on the mediator and the mediation process. While the court acknowledged that compelling testimony would have a chilling effect on future mediation participants and would take an economic and psychic toll on mediators, these factors did not outweigh the need for individual justice.

This case demonstrates that judges may ignore clear statutory authority in individual cases. In compelling cases, the clear mandate of statutory confidentiality in mediations will be disregarded. Therefore, apologies in mediations, while presumptively confidential, may nevertheless be disclosed publicly under appropriate circumstances.

Other efforts at protecting apology. Massachusetts has enacted an innovative statute designed to protect apologies from being used as admissions. Mass. Gen. Laws, ch. 233, 23D (1992) states:

> § 23D. Admissibility of Benevolent Gestures Related to Accident Victim or His Family; Definitions.
>
> As used in this section the following words shall, unless the context clearly requires otherwise, have the following meanings:
>
> "Accident," an occurrence resulting in injury or death to one or more persons which is not the result of willful action by a party.
>
> "Benevolent gestures," actions which convey a sense of compassion or commiseration emanating from humane impulses.
>
> "Family," the spouse, parent, grandparent, stepmother, stepfather, child, grandchild, brother, sister, half brother, half sister, adopted children of parent, or spouse's parents of an injured party.
>
> Statements, writings, or benevolent gestures expressing sympathy or a general sense of benevolence relating to the pain, suffering, or death of a person involved in an accident and made to such person or to the family of such person shall be inadmissible as evidence of an admission of liability in a civil action.

On its face, the statute seems to protect statements of compassion or commiseration, but not outright apologies. Furthermore, the protection is limited to personal injury actions arising from an accident. Finally, the statements are protected only so long as they are made to a narrow class of persons comprised of the family of the victim. Thus, while the statute protects some form of apologetic statement, it falls short of protecting a complete, positive apology.

Apology and Insurance. Apology also implicates important insurance issues. Insurance companies have divergent interests from clients when it comes to apology. If the insurance company is to pay the damages, the insurance company may have a strong interest that the insured not apologize. By contrast, knowing that she has insurance, the insured may feel much freer to apologize. Recall that in *Wiener*, discussed earlier, the driver apologized and said that his insurance would cover the loss.

Most insurance contracts impose on the insured a general duty of cooperation with the insurance company in defense of the claim.

Some insurance contracts also specifically prohibit the insured from voluntarily assuming liability, a restriction courts have taken as a condition precedent to the contract. Accordingly, two questions arise. Would the insured's apology be considered a breach of the general duty of cooperation? And, if the insurance contract specifically forbids the insured from assuming liability, would the insured's apology be a breach of (a condition precedent to) that contract?

Typically, insurance companies issue instructions to their insureds along the following lines: Don't say anything; Don't admit anything; Don't talk to anybody; and Don't apologize.

Obviously, these instructions are not conducive to harmonious reconciliation between the parties. If a person who feels morally responsible for the accident violates these instructions, has she breached her duty to her insurance company? The issue is resolved by the duty to cooperate and consent to settlement powers.

For the insurer to prevail by asserting that the insured breached the general duty of cooperation, the insurer must show that the insured acted in bad faith and that the insured's action substantially or materially prejudiced the insurer. Short of a case of collusion between the insured and the injured party, showing bad faith based on an apology seems most unlikely. Indeed, the insured may even argue that he was trying to help minimize the loss to the insurance company by apologizing. Further, if when apologizing, the insured simply tells the truth, one would think that any prejudice would be minimal. While some damage may be done to the insurance company's bargaining power, the insured is only offering information that he would likely have to admit later during discovery or at trial.

The trickier case arises when the insurance contract specifically forbids the insured from assuming liability absent the insurance company's consent. Would an apology that admits fault then void the insurance coverage? There are few cases on this, usually arising from automobile accidents, and the law is not settled.

Most courts have maintained the insured's coverage, but some have not. At root, the reasoning seems to be that to void the insured's coverage simply because she apologizes is contrary to public policy. The purpose of insurance, after all, is to pay for damages when a mishap has occurred, rather than to discourage moral behavior following the mishap.

One distinction courts draw is between statements by the insured that truthfully admit fault and statements that assume financial liability. The latter voids the insured's coverage, but the former does not. A policy provision against assuming liability does not prohibit the insured from giving the injured person a truthful explanation of the accident (Appleman and Appleman, 1981). This seems a sound approach: Don't bind the insurance company to a financial settlement to which it has not consented, but don't prevent the insured from telling the truth either. Nevertheless, a statement such as "I'm sorry, it was my fault. I wasn't paying attention," may be more than a statement of fact. As a conclusion drawn by the insured, it binds the insured legally as an admission. Therefore, the insurance company could argue that the apology violated the insurance contract. The mere possibility of a denial of defense or indemnity is chilling enough for most people to remain silent. The moral imperative for apology is outweighed by the possibility of financial disaster if no insurance is available.

Apology is noticeably absent in claims practices. Claims practices refer to the policies, procedures, and practices that insurance companies use to settle claims. Normally, insurance company employees called *adjusters* or *claims representatives* negotiate settlements. Their job is to minimize the amount the company must pay out in settlements. Therefore, as a general rule, adjusters and claims representatives have no interest in an apology given by their insured or in forgiveness extended by the injured claimant. Their sole interest is in minimizing payment on claim and getting the claim off their desk.

Adjusters view most plaintiffs with suspicion, always vigilant for malingering and false claims. Consequently, they have little sympathy for plaintiffs. Adjusters are trained to evaluate claims based on trends in jury verdicts and values established over a large number of cases. They are specifically trained to detach their emotions from their work. They also view their job as insulating and isolating the insured from having personal responsibility for the injury. Most people, in fact, turn liability matters over to insurance company for handling, expecting the company to handle it without muss or fuss or personal responsibility or accountability.

Because of insurance, people are able to shift financial responsibility to the insurance company. This marginalizes or eliminates moral responsibility to the victim. Finally, offenders are able to avoid apology by blaming the lawyers for the cost, expense, and delay of having claims resolved fairly and promptly. The insurance system is consequently a major impediment to apology in the context of injury and property damage claims.

Apology and Attorneys

A major theme of this book challenges the dominance of adversary ideology in legal thinking. Apology presents another reason why the ideology is seriously deficient. Most lawyers, when representing a defendant or potential defendant, will focus on how to deny responsibility, including defenses and counterclaims. Under the legal system, a person must deny liability to preserve the right to contest all aspects of a suit. This sets up a denial-oriented mindset in both the lawyer and the defendant. The unspoken assumption is that the client goal is to minimize exposure and risk. While clients may not initially think about this, when informed of all the possible defenses, they generate expectations of entitlement to a complete defense. This is easily transmuted into a belief in innocence, which mutates again into righteous indignation at being accused, sued, and having to defend oneself against such spurious claims or undeserving people.

Apology is not in the law curriculum. A teaching experience of Professor Kenney Hegland conveys this well (Hegland, 1982):

> In my first year Contracts class, I wished to review various doctrines we had recently studied. I put the following:
> In a long-term installment contract, seller promises buyer to deliver widgets at the rate of 1,000 a month. The first two deliveries are perfect. However, in the third month seller delivers only 990 widgets. Buyer becomes so incensed that he rejects delivery and refuses to pay for the widgets already delivered.
>
> After stating the problem, I asked, "If you were Seller, what would you say?" What I was looking for was a discussion of the various common law theories which would force the buyer to pay for the widgets delivered and those which would throw buyer into breach for canceling the remaining deliveries. In short, I wanted the class to come up with the legal doctrines which would allow Seller to crush Buyer.
>
> After asking the question, I looked around the room for a volunteer. As is so often the case with first year students, I found there were . . . [none]. There was, however, one eager face, that of an eight-year-old son of one of my students. It seems that he was suffering through Contracts due to his mother's sin of failing to find a sitter. Suddenly he raised his hand. Such behavior, even from an eight-year-old, must be rewarded.
>
> "OK," I said, "What would you say if you were the seller?"
> "I'd say, "I'm sorry.'"

Legal training separates emotion from objectivity as law students learn to abstract human conflict into rights and obligations. Law school places a premium on critical thinking, rational analysis, detachment, and competition. Since the Socratic Method uses as its grist published judicial opinions, students are fed a continuous diet of severely pathological situations that come to be seen as the norm. Litigation is taught as the noblest, most just way of dealing with conflict. As a result, most lawyers loathe "therapeutic" concepts. Apology is, therefore mentally, revolting from a lawyer's perspective.

Lawyers may fear that if they raise the topic of apology with a client, the client will think the lawyer disloyal, too sympathetic to the other party's case. No doubt many clients will feel uneasy when the subject of apology is first raised.

Discussing apology may run counter to the role expectations which both lawyers and clients bring to their relationship. "If I wanted someone to tell me to apologize," says the client, "I would have gone to my minister, not lawyer. What I want from you is to help me win." This logic can be self-fulfilling. A lawyer may think, "I don't talk with my clients about apology, because lawyers don't do that with clients," and a client may think similarly. However, there is no good reason to think that lawyers and clients, or at least some lawyers and some clients, cannot have different role expectations which would include a discussion of apology. The ABA Model Rules permit this in Rule 2.1:

RULE 2.1: ADVISOR

In representing a client, a lawyer shall exercise independent professional judgment and render candid advice. In rendering advice, a lawyer may refer not only to law but also to other considerations such as moral, economic, social, and political factors that may be relevant to the client's situation.

Comment

Scope of Advice

[1] A client is entitled to straightforward advice expressing the lawyer's honest assessment. Legal advice often involves unpleasant facts and alternatives that a client may be disinclined to confront. In presenting advice, a lawyer endeavors to sustain the client's morale and may put advice in as acceptable a form as honesty permits. However, a lawyer should not be deterred from giving candid advice by the prospect that the advice will be unpalatable to the client.

[2] Advice couched in narrowly legal terms may be of little value to a client, especially where practical considerations, such as cost or effects on other people, are predominant. Purely technical legal advice, therefore, can sometimes be inadequate. It is proper for a lawyer to refer to relevant moral and ethical considerations in giving advice. Although a lawyer is not a moral advisor as such, moral and ethical considerations impinge upon most legal questions and may decisively influence how the law will be applied.

Most lawyers are not aware of the scope of this rule and believe that moral considerations are beyond the scope of their engagement.

Finally, attorneys often provide psychological cover for clients to rationalize their behavior. "My attorney believes me, therefore I'm right not to apologize."

Loss aversion may also lead clients not to apologize. When faced with the choice between taking (1) a certain, but small, loss or (2) a gamble with a chance of a very large loss and a chance of no loss, many people choose the gamble. An apology is similar to a certain, but small, loss. It requires that the client take an immediate, humbling step. Many people would rather gamble than take a certain loss, and may therefore avoid apology. In fact the aversion to apology may lead the other party to increase a demand for compensation because responsibility is not acknowledged. As a practical matter, parties often escalate their demands when an acknowledgement of wrongdoing and apology are not forthcoming. In these cases, the identity goals of the injured party (self-esteem, regained sense of control over self) are masked by content goals in the form of large lawsuits.

The fear of committing legal malpractice may also stop some lawyers from counseling apology. From the viewpoint of legal malpractice, a worst-case scenario is when a lawyer gives a client a specific piece of legal advice, the client relies on it, the advice turns out to be wrong, and the client incurs a whopping liability. A lawyer who is thinking about counseling a client to make a "safe" apology may fear just this scenario. For example, assume that during the course of mediation a lawyer tells his client that it is "safe" to make an apology that admits fault. Based on advice of counsel, the client does so. The mediation fails and it later turns out that the client's apology is admissible in court. The lawyer will be in an awkward position indeed. Most lawyers will therefore not take the risk of advising on apology. More likely, the safest counsel is to advise against apology.

Many lawyers pride themselves on their toughness. Therefore, recommending apology may signal a sign of weakness. Furthermore, many lawyers view themselves as The Relentless Fighter rather than The Peacemaker. Many lawyers like to act "macho." "We don't apologize; we defeat our adversaries in courtroom battle." Apology runs counter to this ethos. Apology requires humility, and if one lacks the humility to admit that one made a mistake, one cannot apologize. Accordingly, to discuss apology with a client, a "macho" lawyer will need to break out of that mindset and be capable of envisioning how an apology could be made. This relates to the Myth of Redemptive Violence in chapter 1 as the Myth itself perpetuates antagonism toward apology, forgiveness, and reconciliation. Only annihilation of the opponent will restore justice and peace.

Lawyers also have their reputations to consider. A lawyer who recommends apology to clients may come to be known as a "softie," while a lawyer may benefit from having a reputation for being good at playing "hardball." Lawyers do not always realize that clients' reputational interests can be quite different. As most clients are involved in far fewer disputes than lawyers, a client may be much less afraid of gaining a reputation for being a "softie." Some clients may enjoy it. For example, a business may want its customers to feel that if they have any complaints, the business will respond sensitively.

Divergent interests between lawyers and clients, frequently given the economic label of "principal-agent" problems, may also play an important part in lawyers' neglect of apology. Consider a plaintiff's lawyer hired on a one-third, contingency-fee basis. A million-dollar settlement or jury award earns such a lawyer a fee of over three hundred thousand dollars. An apology, which could be worth just as much to the client, may earn the same lawyer nothing. Indeed, to the extent that the apology reduces the level of the financial settlement, plaintiffs' lawyers may have an incentive to avoid it.

Lawyers also derive income from creating and maintaining litigation. Lawyers generally benefit when disputes escalate. Apologies help bring disputes to an end, and in so doing limit the lawyers' fees. A defendant's lawyer might fail to counsel a client to apologize, for, if an apology occurred, that attorney's hourly fees could end. Some lawyers may, consistent with their self-interest, passively neglect to discuss that option.

The problem with this economic argument is that it fails to recognize the market opportunity in peacemaking. If only 20 percent of all business conflicts make their way to lawyers, imagine what the demand for services would be if the percentage doubled to 40 percent? In other words, lawyers are missing an enormous opportunity to expand their services into areas of conflict they have traditionally eschewed.

To Propose or Not Propose Apology

Apology and forgiveness presents a host of issues for the peacemaker. At the outset, forgiveness may not be the morally responsible way to respond to a particularly unjust injury. In some cases, a party is better served to resent responsibly than to forgive irresponsibly.

In general, peacemakers should avoid projecting personal judgments that may interfere with the parties' needs. Suggesting that an apology may be useful or appropriate can be counter-productive, especially when both sides are still in accusatory, higher levels of escalation. Peacemakers should refrain from issuing demands for apology absent a party initiative. Demands are likely to be seen as signs of directiveness, partiality, and lack of neutrality and must be avoided. On the other hand, peacemakers should remain alert and sensitive to tentative requests for apology or expressions of remorse. If one or both parties open the possibility to apology, one may gently and carefully follow it up.

A great danger of apology for a peacemaker is hasty peace. Hasty peace seeks to deal with the history of violence, oppression, or grave injustice by suppressing the memory, denying injury, and rewriting reality. Such a peace trivializes and ignores an oppressive situation by ignoring its causes. This is one of the central causes of dissatisfaction with the legal system. The legal system forces decisions based on apparent rationality. The underlying causes of the conflict are ignored as too messy or difficult to deal with. When reconciliation is confused with conflict mediation, the balancing, negotiating, need-meeting process becomes a way of managing the differences without a true resolution of the conflict. Reconciliation, rather than being a gift discovered, is seen as a technological common scientific process. Thus, reconciliation becomes devalued.

Conclusion

This chapter on apology and forgiveness ends with Professor David Augsburger's Corollaries of Reconciliation (Augsburger, 1996):

Reconciliation must begin with the victim.

Reconciliation comes from the victim.

While reconciliation begins with the victim, both parties are victims and have been wronged.

Reconciliation is not something we do; it is something we discover.

Forgiveness is not enacted generosity or superiority, but the discovery of similarity.

To this list we can add corollaries of apology:

Apology must begin with the wrongdoer or offender.

Apology comes from the wrongdoer or offender.

True apology requires symbolic submission and vulnerability by the wrongdoer or offender

Apology is not something we do; it is something we experience.

Apology is remorse for wrongdoing and a request to be recognized again as a moral being.

The greatest gift of peacemaking is to allow parties the experience of reconciliation. The greatest gift to the peacemaker is to have been present when reconciliation has occurred. No verdict, no victory, no win in the courtroom will ever be as satisfying as watching the reconciliation process unfold before you.

Reflections on Chapter Sixteen

Discuss how the assumptions underlying the adversary ideology prohibit the use of apology and forgiveness.

List some of the factors that inhibit lawyers from counseling their clients to offer apologies. Assume that evidentiary admissions are not at issue.

Does legal education inhibit the use of apology and forgiveness? Why or why not?

How do identity theory and apology relate?

How do justice and apology relate?

CHAPTER SEVENTEEN

PRINCIPLES OF PEACEMAKING

Introduction

PEACEMAKING IS SUCCESSFUL WHEN three fundamental steps have occurred. First, the disputants' interpretations of each other's motives and needs must be transformed from rejection of each other to recognition of each other. Second, shared interests must be developed among the disputants. Finally, the disputants must be given a sense of control over the process and the solutions it produces.

To achieve these steps requires substantial skill. First, the challenge presented by the conflict—the gap between aspirations and reality—must be identified and attention focused on specific issues created by that gap. Second, a plan for managing the parties' problem solving must be developed. Third, the level of distress caused by confronting the issues must be managed by pacing the rate of challenge and by giving structure to the process. This is not just a matter of planning and implementation, but is a continuous act of improvisation as each action generates information about the capacity of people to engage the issues and learn from them.

The peacemaker, as leader of a problem-solving group, commands and directs attention. The parties look to the peacemaker for a diagnosis of the problem and a plan for addressing it. Typically, the peacemaker acts indirectly, rather than directly, to allow the parties to discover for themselves the causes and solutions to the conflict.

Before people can work on solutions, they must broaden their understanding of the situation. The peacemaker establishes processes that permit each party to understand the other's point of view even if they vehemently disagree with it. When people begin to sense the needs, interests, emotions, limitations, and capabilities of each other, they begin to see themselves as persons with a shared problem rather than as opponents.

Because the peacemaker is expected to make decisions on direction, the peacemaker is given access to information. This information, often confidential, provides a perspective from which to assess the conflict wholistically. Since the parties are usually unable to create such a perspective for themselves, they are guided toward a broader perspective through careful and thoughtful application of processes. Because the parties must each change their own perspectives to see the complete picture, the rate of change must be paced to the parties' ability to accept change.

The peacemaker has control over the flow of information. The peacemaker can sequence facts about the conflict based on his or her assessment of the parties' resilience. Attention and access to information also brings the peacemaker the power to frame issues—to influence the terms of discussion between the parties. Oftentimes, parties will present the conflict in terms of individual positions. As this occurs, the peacemaker helps the parties shift their perspectives from positions to interests.

To maintain order and contain disorder, the peacemaker is given numerous means to orchestrate the process. As a corollary to containing disorder, the parties implicitly confer power on the peacemaker to choose the decision-making process itself, be it evaluative, facilitative, transformative, or narrative, or some variation.

People come to conflict with a narrow range of options and choices. The peacemaker designs and implements processes that expand the options and choices, permit the parties to construct agreements from the expanded list of options, and empower the parties to make joint choices on how the conflict should be dealt with.

Each of these factors and powers permits the peacemaker to help the parties do what they believe they cannot do for themselves. The process allows parties to confront the difficult and hurtful issues that divide them in an orderly, controlled, and safe fashion.

The Peacemaker as a Leader

Imagine two hikers lost in a dark forest on the side of a mountain and now at a fork in the trail. The trail signs were knocked down by the snows of the past winter and no landmarks are visible. They begin to argue over which fork to take. As their voices rise, a mountain guide appears in sight. She asks them if they need help, and they explain their predicament. After a few questions about where they are going and what their intentions are, she suggests a few alternatives for them. With the choices clearly presented to the hikers, they quickly agree on one and gratefully accept the guide's invitation to walk them out of the woods to their destination.

This story is a good analogy to the role of the peacemaker. The peacemaker, like the guide, is a leader. And, like the guide, the peacemaker does not force her ideas or goals on the parties, but listens for what they value as important. Then, using the power conferred on her by the parties, the peacemaker leads the parties through the conflict to a resolution. The peacemaker doesn't carry the parties or do the hard work for them, but acts as a guide and friend, walking with them shoulder to shoulder until the job is done.

The peacemaking process is, in essence, a group decision-making process. The group comes together voluntarily to face a joint problem—some conflict or dispute serious enough to warrant the assistance of a trained, competent, and experienced outsider. Parties in conflict look to the peacemaker for direction, protection, and order. These are critical psychological services provided by the peacemaker and provide the basis for all of the peacemaker's work.

Direction may take the form of vision, goals, strategy, and technique, but on some preconscious level, it may simply mean "finding the food site." Like the guide in the forest, the peacemaker provides process expertise on how to achieve the goals of the parties. If a crisis ensues, the group turns more of its attention to the peacemaker, expecting her to solve the problem by coming up with a technique, idea, or process to break the impasse.

The authority structure of a peacemaking session establishes places and roles for group members, including the role of the peacemaker, and by so doing creates a coordinating and problem-solving mechanism. When members know whom to turn to, they feel calmed. As part of her authority, the peacemaker must maintain an aura of hope and cautious confidence, even in the face of highly escalated conflict. This confidence allows the parties to have a sense that there is control of a situation that up to now seemed out of control.

Protection at a primal, preconscious level connotes scanning the environment for threats and mobilizing a response. In peacemaking, it means protecting the parties from disruptions in the process—such as rudeness, disrespect, and overt displays of hostility—and preventing face-damaging events. People fear peacemaking. They fear the uncertainty of the outcome. They doubt their own abilities to make peace. They often doubt the competency of the peacemaker. They have high levels of anxiety because everything seems confused and chaotic. In addition, their preconscious brain is signaling danger and invoking freeze, flee, or fight responses. This is normal and expected behavior at the beginning of peacemaking. Nevertheless, the peacemaker must not be caught up in the swirling emotions of the parties. The best and only strategy is to maintain a "non-anxious" presence (Friedman, 1985).

The capacity of a peacemaker to maintain a non-anxious presence may be one of her most significant capabilities. Not only can this capacity enable peacemakers to be more clearheaded about solutions and more adroit in difficult situations, but also a non-anxious presence will modify anxiety throughout the entire group. This aspect of leadership can sometimes do more to resolve issues than the ability to come up with good solutions.

Peacemakers are like transformers in an electrical circuit. To the extent that they are anxious themselves, when anxiety in the peacemaking session permeates their being, it flows back into the session at a higher voltage. To the extent that peacemakers can recognize and contain their anxiety, they function as step-down transformers or perhaps as circuit breakers. In this case, the peacemaker's presence, far from escalating conflict, actually serves to diminish its destructive effect.

Order consists of orienting people to their places and roles and establishing and maintaining norms. In a peacemaking session, people are oriented to their places by the preexisting conflict. However, their roles within peacemaking change in a subtle, yet powerful, way. Within the peacemaking group, new roles outside of the conflict are being created and defined. The conflict is still present, but the parties, no longer in direct relationship, are mediated by the peacemaker. Thus, they have a new role to assume. The peacemaker establishes and maintains norms through the use of ground rules that set forth expectations of behaviors and attitudes during the process. In addition, the peacemaker chooses the processes, decides when to move from phase to phase, and controls through artful interventions.

Once settled into the process, the parties seem to find their places and roles. The level of tension within the group diminishes dramatically. At the same time, cohesion increases. The peacemaker's authority provides orientation, which in turn diminishes stress and provides a hub of bonding as each member develops some tie with the peacemaker. A competent peacemaker will build these bonds slowly and carefully. The capital, in the form of cohesion and trust, acquired in early phases of the peacemaking process will usually be called upon in later phases when the more difficult problems are faced.

The Momentum of Agreement

The peacemaking process begins the moment the peacemaker is consulted about possible intervention or participation in a conflict. Typically, the parties and their counsel are agreeing on very little. In highly escalated conflicts, not even the most obvious facts can be agreed upon. One of the keys of successful peacemaking is developing the momentum of agreement.

Momentum of agreement refers to the process of reaching very small, incrementally significant agreements. These agreements will accumulate over the peacemaking process until a new reality is created in which the parties and counsel see that mutual agreements are possible. The momentum starts with the agreement to enter into the peacemaking process. The mere fact that each party has committed to the process sometimes sends a tangible signal to the others that there is some interest in resolution. This gives a slight ray of hope that can be leveraged by the peacemaker.

Initial commitments will be oral, but once commitments from all have been secured, the peacemaker must confirm the arrangements in writing. A typical engagement letter will confirm the parties, their representatives, the date, time, place, and length of sessions, the peacemaker's fee and how it is to be divided between the parties, and any other arrangements necessary to the process. The momentum of agreement is accelerated as the first positive step toward peace is created for all to see: the agreement to convene.

The second agreement should be a written confidentiality agreement signed by the parties and their representatives. The confidentiality agreement serves the direct purpose of reminding the parties that the proceedings are privileged from disclosure to outsiders and is confidential. By its very nature, the confidentiality agreement creates a new, consensual relationship between the parties. Furthermore, the parties have strong mutual interest in maintaining confidentiality. More subtly, the momentum of agreement is accelerated as another innocuous agreement is reached.

The third agreement is made when ground rules are stated and agreed upon. When every person in the meeting verbally states that he or she agrees to abide by the ground rules, everyone knows that a level playing field has been created. The mere fact that people in escalated conflict have agreed how the new game will be played undermines the old conflict behaviors. Furthermore, the parties are subtly indicating to each other that they are agreeing to work toward resolution, even if very tentatively.

The fourth agreement comes when the parties are asked to commit to being constructive and cooperative. The commitment to cooperation is a difficult, challenging agreement to obtain and to keep.

The Commitment to Cooperation

Peacemakers have many types of power, but the one power they do not have is the ability to coerce parties to be cooperative. The commitment to be cooperative must be sincere and freely given. Furthermore, the commitment must be reinforced and strengthened early in the process. When the discussions begin on the difficult issues, the parties will too easily slide back into a competitive, adversarial mode if they have not been conditioned to their commitment early on. As the Prisoner's Dilemma proves, competitive situations often preclude cooperative behavior.

The commitment to cooperation is simply an agreement that on important issues, each party will be as concerned about the other person's goals as he or she is about his or her own goals. On the Blake and Mouton Conflict Management grid, the parties are committing to locate their attitudes toward each other in the high upper right hand side. There are two aspects of this commitment that pose challenges. The first is whether the commitment can be secured at all. In some cases, the parties are so highly escalated that they cannot conceive of considering any interests other than their own. Thus, if they are honest, they will simply decline to make the commitment. Alternatively, they will simply make a conditional commitment such as, "I will if the other side will." When the commitment cannot be made or is conditional, some time has to be invested in finding out why the commitment cannot be made and discovering what must occur or change for the commitment to be unconditional. The second challenge is more common and occurs when the commitment is made, but is not truly a commitment. In other words, people make the commitment in words, but their attitudes remain distributive. The best that can be hoped for is that the superficial, oral commitment is a starting point for trust-building. With adversarial lawyers present, moving beyond a superficial commitment is very difficult. Lawyers steeped in adversary ideology are naturally distributive in orientation and view cooperative problem solving with mistrust if not outright hostility.

Nevertheless, parties wishing to be cooperative have three basic strategies of cooperation when faced with a competitive opponent: unconditional cooperation, conditional cooperation, and non-cooperation. In unconditional cooperation, a party responds to attacks or threats by exhibiting altruistic or cooperative behavior. Thus, in all situations, the cooperating party looks for the best and does not retaliate against distributive, noncooperative behavior. In conditional cooperation, a party reacts defensively for self-protection, but otherwise is cooperative. The Tit for Tat strategy discussed in game theory is a form of conditional cooperation. A party cooperates until the other side competes, then the party also competes. If the other side returns to cooperation, so does the party. In noncooperative strategy, a party responds competitively to any noncooperative acts and counterattacks when attacked. Otherwise, the party responds to cooperation with cooperation.

These basic strategies represent three widely held positions regarding cooperation. Unconditional cooperation seeks to elicit cooperation by appealing to the social conscience and good will of the subject. Noncooperation tends to elicit cooperation by use of the carrot and the stick; i.e., rewarding cooperation and punishing non-cooperation. This strategy appeals the economic motives by increasing the costs of noncooperative behavior and is based on utilitarian principles. The conditional cooperative strategy rewards cooperation and neutralizes aggression. It appeals to the self-interests of the subject through positive rather than negative incentives. It thus attempts to avoid misunderstanding and hostility resulting from punishment or coercion.

The peacemaker's task is to establish cooperation as a norm of behavior between the parties. This norm should be established in a number of ways. First, the parties should explicitly state that they are unconditionally committed to cooperation. This commitment means that they must consider the interests of the other just as much as they consider their own interests. Most people will give this commitment, but will not truly embrace it. Thus, a second process should occur. The parties should be gently challenged whenever they deviate from their unconditional commitment. Questions challenging a competitive or aggressive statement might be: "How might Other's interests be furthered by what you said?" "How might your commitment to unconditional cooperation cause you to rephrase what you said?"

These questions will sometimes provoke a hostile reaction as people resist acknowledging others. The peacemaker may deal with this hostility by caucusing individually and exploring the reasons for the anger.

A third process involves an important principle from social psychology called "social proof." Social proof bases decisions about what is correct behavior on what other people are doing around us. The actions of those around us serve several functions. First, they provide information about the boldness levels of others and about the vengefulness of the group. Hence, we can infer something about whether it pays for us to be bold or not. Second, the actions of others might contain clues about what is the best course of action even if there is no vengefulness. For example, people may be driving slowly on a certain stretch of highway, not because there is a speed trap, but because the road is poorly paved. Either way, the actions of others can provide information about how the population has been adapting to a particular environment. If we are new to the environment, this is valuable information about what our behavior should be. The actions of others provide information about what is proper for us, even if we do not know the reasons. Finally, in many cases, by conforming to the actions of those around us, we fulfill a psychological need to be part of a group. Our propensity to act on the principle of social proof is consequently a major mechanism in the support of norms.

In cases where other people are different in important ways, the principle of social proof tends to apply to those most like us. Thus, teenage girls look only to other teenage girls when selecting a new strategy, while teenage boys look only to teenage boys. This makes good sense because a strategy that is successful for a girl might be disastrous if employed by a boy.

The power of social proof can be used to establish cooperative norms in peacemaking. For example, by establishing and enforcing ground rules, processes, and attitudes that foster cooperation, participants can infer proper strategies for themselves. Similarly, if the physical environment provides clues about proper behavior, the power of social proof can be used to engender cooperation. A meeting place that resembles a church sanctuary or other place associated with peace can, by itself, provide the social proof for cooperative behavior. The peacemaker's attitude and behavior is also a guide and social proof for participants. If the peacemaker demonstrates cooperative behavior in the face of contention and competition, she will model appropriate conduct for the parties. The clues the peacemaker gives to the parties are, therefore, powerful aspects of social proof.

Managing Information

The peacemaking process gives the peacemaker unique access to information. Not only does she hear all sides of the story. She is frequently privy to confidential information that, when placed in a larger perspective, sheds light on the conflict. Part of the peacemaking process is providing for a safe exchange of information. The parties have probably failed to exchange information because of their fear of exploitation or fear of retaliation. If Sam reveals his true interests to Sally, Sally may use that information against Sam. Consequently, Sam is justifiably afraid that he will be exploited by his honest and open communications. Sally no doubt feels the same way about Sam. As a result, information that could lead Sam and Sally to a better understanding of their situation remains hidden. Thus, a central role of peacemaking is to provide a channel for information to be exchanged between the parties.

Maintaining Safety, Order, and Security

Almost every how-to book, mediator handbook, and basic mediation training manual tells mediators to establish ground rules at the beginning of the process. The ground rules establish the social power of the peacemaker as leader of the group, provide a set of behavioral norms during the process, and provide another opportunity for accelerating the momentum of agreement. A typical list of ground rules might be as follows:

- You all agree that I will lead the process.
- One person speaks at a time.
- You agree to summarize what the other person has said if I ask you to do so.
- You promise to speak the truth as you understand it.
- Everyone will remain civil and respectful.
- The process must be fair to all at all times.

Most ground rules arise from a tradition of efficiency and individuality. Ground rules may, however, ignore the realities of ethnic, cultural, and gender differences. In so doing, the rules may reinforce hierarchy and dominance. By their nature, ground rules impose standards to prevent disorder, unfairness, or harm, and, as such, are prohibitive, telling people what not to do.

Ground rules can be more dynamic if the peacemaker wishes to push the parties to adaptive work early in the process. For example, the common ground rules might be rephrased as follows:

- Communicate authentically. A person should say what she thinks and feels.
- Share, rather than conceal, differences of opinion.
- Help others to understand you and work to understand others.
- Validate whenever possible the worth of the other people here.
- Expect the best possible outcome for yourself and the others.
- Place a high premium on the potential creativity and imagination in this room.
- Before making a criticism of someone, make a positive statement about him or her.
- Affirm that we all have the same need for self-respect, autonomy, and pride.

In some cases, given enough time, the peacemaker should consider an elicitive approach to ground rules. In this process, the group creates shared expectations about the process, their roles, the peacemaker's role, and the type of outcome sought. The peacemaker encourages discussion of shared expectations by asking questions, taking notes using a flip chart, and keeping the group focused on defining its own ground rules. This process has the added advantage of increasing the momentum of agreement by providing an exercise in cooperative problem solving. The drawback to elicitive process is that it can be time-consuming and appear relatively unstructured.

While ground rules provide the social power for controlling communication, they alone are not enough to create safety and security within the peacemaking environment. The stress level is very high and the stresses must be managed effectively by creating a holding environment.

The term "holding environment" originated in psychoanalysis to describe the therapist-patient relationship (Heifetz, 1994). The therapist is said to "hold" the patient in a process of developmental learning in a way that a mother and father hold their newborn and maturing children. For the child, the holding environment serves as a containing vessel for the developmental steps, problems, crises, and stresses of growing up. Within the parental hold, the child's growth can be protected and guided. For the patient in psychotherapy, the therapist's relationship is a place to examine and make progress on hard problems. To be effective, therapists have to empathize and understand their patients' struggles so that the patients can begin to see more clearly the nature of their problems. That requires both technical knowledge and process expertise.

The holding environment provides the foundation for everything the peacemaker does. Because the parties are enmeshed in the conflict, they are unable to contain their anxiety, uncertainty, and fear of exploitation. The parties are grateful when the peacemaker can hold these emotions and fears within a safe environment.

Transforming conflicts becomes possible because the holding environment contains and regulates the stresses that the work generates. People cannot learn new ways when fear and anxiety overwhelm them. But eliminating the stress altogether eliminates the impetus for working on the conflict. The strategic task is to maintain a level of tension that mobilizes people. This is performed through intervention timing, issue control, and phase use.

Intervention timing. Timing is a central and complex issue in peacemaking. Should the peacemaker establish a policy of interrupting when the parties are caught in a very heated, emotional exchange? Should the peacemaker wait until they calm down? Or does it really make a difference when the peacemaker interrupts? Early intervention may prevent the parties from experiencing sufficient tension to motivate them to work on their problem. On the other hand, waiting too long may intensify the conflict to the point of polarization and intransigence.

Research studies show that deadlock occurs when peacemakers tend toward extremes in allowing parties very extensive or very limited freedom in exchanging information (Canary and Spitzberg, 1989). In contrast, agreement is more likely reached when peacemakers adhered to more moderate intervention timing by allowing parties to communicate among themselves. These peacemakers allowed parties to talk with each other long enough to exchange information, but not so long as to permit polarization of positions. In addition, they chose to intervene more frequently during periods of increased conflict intensity, and less frequently during periods of decreased conflict intensity.

In contrast, peacemakers who intervened randomly more often faced deadlock. The research suggests that unsuccessful peacemakers may be experiencing some difficulty implementing a consistent intervention plan to decrease conflict intensity. They intervened either too frequently or too infrequently. When they did intervene, the interventions did not appear to be timed to move the interaction in a more productive direction. Thus, intervention appears to play a critical role in maintaining a holding environment.

Issue control. Managing the holding environment is also a performance problem. Performance relates to what issues to direct the parties to discuss.

Research relating to family law mediations revealed that agreements were most frequently reached when facts and interests were discussed most, with relational issues third, and value issues last (Canary and Spitzberg, 1989). When parties deadlocked, relational issues dominated, with factual issues second, interest issues third, and value issues again last. Successful mediators focused twice as much on interests as on facts, with very little discussion of values or relational issues. In deadlock situations, the mediators split evenly between fact and interest directives, with little time spent on values or relational issues.

The deadlock transcripts revealed that couples often used factual disputes to disguise relational disputes. The deadlocked mediators often chose to become involved in these disputes at the factual level without probing the relational problems beneath them. The dominance of relational issues, combined with the mediator's unwillingness to intervene after these attacks, suggested that the mediations simply spun out of control.

This research suggests that maintenance of the holding environment requires persistent focus on facts and interests. However, if the peacemaker senses that facts and interests are acting as symbols for relational issues, the relational issues must be addressed. Typically, this can be accomplished through the process of reconciliation of injustices.

To recapitulate, reconciling of injustices involves a three-step process. The first step is the typical perspective sharing, except that the parties are asked to describe the injustices they have experienced. The listening party is asked to summarize back the injustices. This step repeats until all parties have expressed all of their injustices and feel that they have been adequately heard. The second step involves a request by peacemaker for the parties to consider how the injustices might be made right. The peacemaker will usually point out that injustices cannot be undone and cannot by their nature be remedied fully by compensation. Typically, some process of apology and forgiveness commences, although usually in a limited, equivocal way. The third step involves future intentions—how, asks the peacemaker, do we prevent these injustices from occurring in the future?

Phase use. Most mediations and peacemaking sessions fall into a four-phase model. Phase one concerns orientation, in which the parties are given ground rules, procedures, and a description of the mediator's role. Phase two concerns information gathering and sharing of perspectives or stories. This process develops the information foundation for the dispute. Phase three concerns identification of key issues, including those issues that can block cooperative interaction. Phase four concerns developing proposals, creating options, gaining accommodations, or negotiating a settlement.

Research reveals that successful versus deadlocked mediators differed significantly in their allocation of issue-processing and proposal-making interventions. (Canary and Spitzberg, 1989). Agreement mediators concentrated on identifying key issues much earlier in the dispute than deadlock mediators. Agreement mediators pursued both information development and identification of key issues early in the mediation. Agreement mediators also solicited and processed proposals toward the beginning and middle periods of the mediation, while deadlock mediators waited for later periods in the process. The research suggests that agreement mediators sought a more flexible course than deadlock mediators. Agreement mediators went along with the parties' needs as they arose instead of walking the parties through a rigid set of prescribed phases.

This research suggests that another important aspect of creating a holding environment is enabling the parties to begin adaptive work as early in the process as they are able. The precise timing will vary from conflict to conflict and from party to party, but the research seems to corroborate the principle that not feeding people enough challenge early on will defeat the likelihood of resolution.

Empathic Communication

As we now know, as conflict escalates, empathic ability decreases. At very high stages of escalation, people are absolutely incapable of recognizing each other's existence. This makes communication, understanding of perspectives, and development of shared interests almost impossible. Thus, reestablishing empathy is a central principle in peacemaking.

Empathic ability is the inferential skill that enables people to achieve some measure of insight into the thoughts and feelings of others (Ickes, Marangoni, and Garcia, 1997). It involves a biologically based, spontaneous communication process fundamental to all living things and includes innate sending and receiving mechanisms (Buck and Ginsburg, 1997). Higher order social animals must learn how to use these innate empathic mechanisms in social contexts. The ability is not magical or paranormal, but is remarkable for its ability to extend one persons' understanding of another beyond the surface meaning of words and actions. Empathic ability is composed of empathic understanding and empathic expression.

Empathic understanding is the inferential process of assessing how people actually are feeling in the moment. Empathic understanding requires an ability to enter the private perceptual world of the other and become thoroughly at home in it (Rogers, 1980). It involves being sensitive, moment by moment, to the changing feelings which flow in another person. It means temporarily living in the other's life, moving about it delicately without making judgments. It means sensing meanings of which he or she is scarcely aware, but not trying to uncover totally unconscious feelings, since this would be too threatening.

Empathic expression is the communication of one's understanding of the other person's world. It requires frequent checking with the person as to the accuracy of understanding, and a willingness to be guided by the responses received. Being empathic is a complex, demanding, and subtle way of being.

Sometimes, empathy just happens as we take another person's viewpoint and experience her world without trying at all. This is a fast, involuntary, and seemingly effortless empathy. In conflict, however, we find it very difficult to appreciate the other person's situation. We struggle against making judgments about what a fool the other person is or we wrack our brains trying to understand what is compelling in the other person's situation. These two different aspects of empathy represent what is known as automatic empathy and controlled empathy.

Automatic empathy is a specific application of the principles of automaticity discussed in chapter 6. Unconsciously registered environmental clues can prompt automatic empathy. For example, in movies, scenes are set to give viewers a certain perspective on characters. Moviegoers unconsciously relate to or empathize with those characters based on the cues provided by the scene. The viewers' initial perspective is so robust that viewers who have locked into one character are not inclined to switch perspectives when they later see information about other characters. In addition, the perspective taken in a situation is stronger and more enduring than later perspectives. Even if people allow themselves to see things quite differently later, they will still be influenced by their first perspective. Thus, the automaticity of empathy is not only fast and subtle, but can also produce states of mind that seem to preclude the adoption of alternative states.

Significantly, empathy can be automatically undermined as well. The tendency to adopt another person's perspective will be obstructed by anything that makes the person be seen or treated as an object. Thus, the automatic ability to empathize will be blocked whenever a person thinks about another's personality traits or other characteristics. This explains why, in conflict, automatic empathy disappears. As people in conflict begin to consider each other as belligerent or stubborn, their automatic empathy decreases. As the perceptions move from stubbornness to mistrust to evilness, automatic empathy evaporates.

While automatic empathy is much like tumbling down a hillside, controlled empathy is like mountain climbing. The mountain climbing analogy is useful in several ways. First, if the summit is reached, a new, broader perspective is gained. To arrive at the summit, climbers must use hand and foot holds and trails that will help them up. The steeper the climb, the more difficult and technical is the work. Controlled empathy works the same way. The more divergent the perspectives, the more difficult and technical the job of invoking controlled empathy. Just as climbing requires finding and moving to enough hand- and foot-holds to reach the summit, controlled empathy requires finding sufficient cues to the experience of others to induce an empathic state of mind. Since conflict leads to avoidance or contentiousness, the cues necessary for controlled empathy quickly become scarce. In the place of controlled empathy, people draw negative inferences of motive and intent.

Controlled empathy depends upon the production of perspectives. To produce perspectives requires people to consider and attend to the goals of another. Thus, the more relevant and accurate information available for any given perspective, the more likely that perspective can be achieved. Generally, the more experience people share with each other, the more empathic people can be. This is because the shared experiences provide so much information for people to consider.

Even if the information is sufficient for the production of perspectives, another barrier must be overcome. Controlled empathy, like any other cognitive process, requires intense mental effort. From a neuropsychological perspective, controlled empathy is resource intensive because it requires a continuous apprehension, comprehension, and evaluation of environmental cues. Empathy demands far more cognitive capacity and cognitive endurance than does impression formation or memory recall.

Going back to the climbing analogy, even if the route is an easy one, the climber still has to be in good enough physical condition to make the moves. Similarly, people must have sufficient cognitive capacity and endurance to engage in controlled empathy.

In conflict, people are usually under a high cognitive load. They are anxious, stressed, and fearful. These conditions debilitate the ability to think and process complex and subtle cues about another's perspective. Hence, conflict itself is a major contributor to one's inability to control empathy.

Yet a third barrier to controlled empathy exists. Taking another person's perspective often requires suppressing one's own perspective. Suppressing one's one point of view is not easy, especially in conflict. The concept is akin to the Zen student's attempt to empty her mind of thoughts. Eliminating extraneous thoughts is very difficult without extreme concentration over a long period of practice. Similarly, abandoning one's own perspective to take on the perspective of another is asking a lot of people, especially when they are in conflict.

The combination of uncontrolled and controlled empathy leads to an ironic, but too typical situation. If people attempt to engage in controlled empathy without adequate mental capacity, the effort unleashes a failure-producing monitoring process. The effect is to promote a state of mind opposite of what is being sought. The attempt to produce another's perspective, under mental load, makes the perceiver lose that very perspective. Conversely, the attempt to suppress another's perspective under mental load will make the perceiver ironically adopt the other's perspective.

This result is based on an ironic process theory that proposes that every act of mental control invokes two cognitive search processes (Hodges and Wegner, 1997). The first process consciously searches for thoughts that will produce the intended state of mind. The second process seeks thoughts that indicate failure of the state of mind. In essence, part of the mind exerts control and part of the mind tests the effectiveness of that control. Normally, the conscious operating process keeps the mind filled with whatever has been intended to put in it. During the process, the monitor occasionally notes failures of intended thought and reinstates the operating process.

When people produce a perspective, the ironic process theory says that they are searching for information that will bring them an empathic state of mind. At the same time, the monitoring process is looking for failures to assume the empathic state. If a person lacks sufficient cognitive capacity because of a conflict situation to produce a perspective, the ironic monitor overwhelms the conscious process and induces the opposite state being sought. In summary, controlled empathy can, in conflict situations, produce an opposing automatic effect. Consequently, when one is actually trying to take another's perspective, the mental load can lead him to be particularly insensitive and contentious.

Empathy is clearly related to conflict transformation. First, empathy dissolves alienation. For the moment, a party finds himself or herself a connected part of humanity. Second, a party feels valued, cared for, accepted as the person that he or she is. Third, the empathic understanding is nonjudgmental because accurate understanding of another's inner world is impossible if one has an evaluative opinion of that person. True empathy is always free of any evaluative or diagnostic quality. A finely tuned understanding by another individual gives the recipient a sense of personhood and identity.

Process Choice and the Escalation Stages

Conflict escalation is a gradual regression from a mature to immature level of emotional development. The psychological process develops step by step in a strikingly reciprocal way to the way we grow up. In other words, as conflicts escalate through various stages, the parties show behaviors indicating movement backward through their stages of emotional development.

As we have seen, escalation can be charted in five phases, each having its own characteristics and triggers. *Stage One* is part of normal, everyday life. Even good relationships have moments of conflict. These can only be resolved with great care and mutual empathy. In this stage, people look for objective solutions in a cooperative manner. If a solution is not found, especially because one of the parties sticks obstinately to his or her point of view, the conflict escalates.

In *Stage Two,* the parties fluctuate between cooperation and competition. They know they have common interests, but their own wishes become more important. Dealing with information becomes limited to that favoring one's own arguments. Logic and understanding are used to convince or win over the opposing side. At this stage, each party does everything possible not to show weakness. The temptation to leave the field of argument increases until the conflict escalates because of some action taken by one of the parties.

By entering *Stage Three,* the field of concrete actions, each party fears that the ground for a common solution is lost. In other words, they lose hope for a reasonable outcome. Interaction becomes hostile. All logic is focused on action, replacing fruitless and nerve-wracking discussions. Paradoxically, the parties each believe that through pressure they will change the other party. At the same time neither is prepared to yield.

At this level, stereotyping is applied as negative identification of the opponent. Power becomes important as empathy disappears.

At *Stage Four,* the parties' cognitive functioning regresses to those of six year-olds. One is aware of the other's perspectives, but is no longer capable of considering the other's thoughts, feelings, and situation. How often have we remarked that parties in conflict are acting like children. In fact, they are because of the escalation. Both sides are forced into roles from which they see no escape. If the conflict cannot be halted at this stage, the escalation undergoes a dramatic increase in intensity. Escalation results when one side commits some action that is felt by the opposite side as a loss of face.

At *Stage Five,* progressive regression appears in the form of antagonistic perspectives. By threatening and creating fear, both parties strive toward total control of the situation and thereby escalate the conflict further. To remain credible and to restrain the enemy from an act of force, the threatened party feels compelled to commit acts of force itself. This, in turn, proves to the threatening party the aggressive nature of the threatener and provokes counterforce and further escalation. This process continues until the parties reach financial or physical exhaustion, or the matter is decided in the courtroom.

De-Escalation

The process of de-escalation is not a simple matter of asking people to get along or to be reasonable. Conflict escalation implies, in ob-

Escalation Stage	Appropriate Process
Stage 1 Parties are cooperative and can communicate their respective needs and interests.	Helped Bargaining—the peacemaker acts as an honest broker helping people negotiate an agreement. Evaluative Mediation—the peacemaker offers opinions on the strengths and weaknesses of each side and may or may not predict a range of outcomes.
Stage 2 Parties become somewhat competitive. They rely on persuasion and rational argument to convince the other to change.	Evaluative Mediation at low levels of Stage 2 escalations. Facilitative Mediation focusing on interest-based negotiation.
Stage 3 Parties are highly competitive. The object is not to show weakness in any way. Preserving face becomes increasingly important.	Facilitative Mediation at low levels of Stage 3 escalations. Transformative Mediation—working on empowerment and recognition.
Stage 4 Parties are highly suspicious of each other. Any sign of reconciliation or offer to talk are viewed with disdain, as either a trick or a manipulation. The other's perspective is viewed as wrong or fraudulent or frivolous. Neither side can engage in constructive communication as each contact devolves into ad hominem attacks.	Transformative Mediation at low levels of Stage 4. Narrative Mediation—deconstructing the conflict story and reconstructing it.
Stage 5 Parties view each other as the enemy. The other is seen as evil incarnate, having no redeeming value. Worse, the other's goal is to destroy parity. Therefore, the only true solution to the conflict is annihilation of the other. Violence at all levels (intellectual through physical) erupts.	Narrative Mediation—deconstructing the conflict story and reconstructing it.

ject relations theory at least, a psychological regression in emotional development. Thus, de-escalation implies the opposite. Successful conflict de-escalation must provide for growth from the regressed state to a fully integrative state. Consequently, jumping over the sequential stages of escalation will not lead to de-escalation. Instead, the steps of escalation must be worked through patiently.

The process becomes complicated when the parties are not at the same level of escalation. Even if they are at the same level of escalation, they may progress forward at different rates. Complicating the matter even further are the presence of lawyers, who may or may not be escalated between themselves and who are loath to give control of the peacemaking process over to the peacemaker and the parties.

Processes for De-Escalation

Conflict escalation theory provides a useful way of looking at mediation orientations. Generally speaking, the lower the level of escalation, the more likely evaluative processes will work. Conversely, the higher the escalation, the less likely evaluative processes will work. Similarly, a purely facilitative approach, if not sufficiently interventional, will also fail in highly escalated conflicts. Too often, facilitative mediators are viewed as "too soft" or "unrealistic" in their approaches to highly escalated conflicts.

Since conflict escalation is based on an increasingly reduced ability to acknowledge, respect, and recognize the other, de-escalation must focus on processes that improve these abilities. The chart on the previous page shows how the various forms of mediation apply at different levels of conflict escalation.

In this model, the process becomes more focused on the interactional aspects of the conflict as the escalation level increases. This corresponds to the decreased ability of the parties to interact at higher escalation levels. Thus, at Stage 3, a transformative approach would be effective because the parties can still talk about the conflict, although in highly competitive terms. By focusing on empowerment and recognition, transformative mediation shifts attention away from winning or losing to understanding. If understanding is achieved, the conflict has been de-escalated to Stage 2.

One implication of this model concerns competency. For a peacemaker to handle all levels of conflict escalation, she must be skilled in a variety of processes. The evaluative mediator will not be successful in securing peace (or even an uneasy truce) at Stage 3, 4, or 5 if all she can do is evaluate and opine on outcome. This is because at the higher escalation levels, the parties are rationally and emotionally regressed. The mere presence or thought of the other may trigger the amygdala to immediately defend by freezing, fleeing, or fighting. If the reaction is severe enough, the signals from amygdala will overwhelm the neo-cortex, making rational thinking very difficult, if not impossible. Since evaluative mediation assumes rational self-interest, evaluative processes will not work when people are not acting rationally.

Similarly, if people are already in a cooperative place at Stage 1, they probably do not need interactional processes. More importantly, they probably view interactional processes as ineffective, soft, and a complete waste of time. What they need and want is someone to help their negotiation by enhancing information exchange and protecting bargaining positions. Thus, a transformative or narrative process is less appropriate at Stage 1 and lower levels of Stage 2 escalations.

Conclusion

The peacemaking process is far more than just following a formulaic process learned in a basic mediation training or class. The role of the peacemaker; the concept of adaptive change and adaptive work; the holding environment and framing—are all aspects of peacemaking rarely considered by even the most skilled mediators. The context of peacemaking, including generation of the momentum of agreement, the decision-making process, ground rules and inducing cooperation from competitive people in competitive situations are also topics of deep concern to peacemakers, but generally ignored in mediation training. This chapter has barely touched on the subtleties of the peacemaking process. For example, the entire concept of empathic communication is critical to successful peacemaking. The thrust of this chapter therefore has not been to build skills, but to introduce the idea that peacemaking is an extremely complex practice. If the reader comes away somewhat dazed by the various concepts presented, then she is open to the idea that many skills require mastery before one is truly a gifted peacemaker.

Reflections on Chapter Seventeen

What are some conferred social powers held by peacemakers?
What are strengths and weaknesses of each power you listed?

List the five most important conditions you think should be present for an optimal peacemaking assignment?

List the five worst conditions you think you would face in a peacemaking assignment?

Having now completed the book and the course, reflect on your view of the role of lawyers in twenty-first century. Where does the adversary ideology fit into this view?

FINAL WORD

*T*HE CONCEPT OF LAWYERS AS peacemakers should not seem so strange now. As you have learned, working with human conflict as a peacemaker requires a significant, multidisciplinary knowledge going well beyond the traditional knowledge base of lawyers. In the first two chapters, we presented a case for lawyers as peacemakers and framed the concept of peacemaking as an orientation to serious human conflicts. In chapters 3 and 4, we examined conflict resolution systems and mediation orientations. In chapter 5, we stepped back to survey philosophic and early psychological thinking about human nature. This oriented us to why people might behave the way they do and set up the essential dilemma of self-interest versus self-denial inherent in human endeavors. Chapter 6 brought us back to current times with a sketch of neuropsychology and automaticity. We learned that we humans are far more emotional than rational and that we are programmed for many behaviors, including conflict.

Chapters 7, 8, 9, and 10 delved into the specifics of identity, religion, culture, and justice demonstrating how they are involved in creating, suppressing, and transforming conflict. Chapters 11, 12, 13, and 14 considered conflict behavior, conflict theory, game theory, and conflict analysis as elements of a disciplined understanding of conflict situations. Finally, chapters 15, 16, and 17, addressing ethics, apology and forgiveness, and principles of peacemaking, looked at some of the important practical issues for lawyers as peacemakers. This has been an ambitious undertaking for you as a reader, and you are commended for taking the time to work through the issues and disciplines of peacemaking.

So, where does one go from here? First, gain experience as a peacemaker. As a law student, you may have clinical opportunities for acting as a mediator within your law school. If not, or if you are not a law student, see if your community has a Victim Offender Rec-

461

onciliation Program, and become a community mediator. Some communities with Better Business Bureaus also sponsor dispute resolution centers and look for community mediators. The opportunities for experience as a volunteer are there if you look for them. You may also wish to consider more formal mediation training classes. These are offered throughout the country by a number of universities and professional organizations. The breadth and scope of the courses is becoming broad, so skills-building classes should not be hard to find. Third, consider joining professional mediation groups such as the Association for Conflict Resolution. These organizations provide training and resources for professionals dedicated to mediation and dispute resolution. Finally, if you are one of those students intrigued by this material, consider obtaining a graduate degree in conflict resolution or in peace and conflict studies. The offerings are expanding across the United States and a Web search will quickly reveal the universities in your area. Most masters programs are highly flexible, and the material is much different than the law curriculum.

As an educator and practitioner, I personally thank you for taking this journey with me. I hope that you will use this knowledge to improve your community and your world. Go in peace, and help us transform the legal profession.

Notes

1. The Joint Standards are reprinted in John D. Feerick, *Toward Uniform Standards of Conduct for Mediators*, 38 S. Tex. L. Rev. 455, 460.

2. See chapter 11 for a further discussion of the stages of conflict escalation.

3. See chapter 11 for a further discussion of identity and relationship goals.

4. As it turns out, we cannot choose our emotions; see chapter 6. Sartre was therefore fundamentally wrong about the power to choose emotions. Perhaps he would be more correct to say that we might have some limited control over our exposure to those events that trigger unconscious emotional reactions.

5. This theory is now being accepted by neuropsychologists, who see the "mind" as a highly subjective event within the brain. Thus, reality differs for each person. Symbolic interaction provides a shared meaning sufficient that our separate, individual realities can work together.

6. Apologies to Jonathan Swift, who was an early, astute observer and commentator on cultural conflicts.

REFERENCES

ABA Address (1923). Addresses on conciliation. *American Bar Association Journal, 1923,* 746-751.

Abel, R. (1980). Delegatizion. In Von Erhard, Blankenburg, Klause, and Rottleuthner (Eds.) *Alternative Rechtsformen und Alternative zum Recht. Jarhbuch fur Rechtsoziologie und Rechtsthearie* 27, 40.

Abel, R. (1981). Conservative conflict and the reproduction of capitalism: The role of informal justice. *International Journal of Society and Law* 9:245, 256

———. (1982). The contradiction of informal justice. In R. Abel (Ed.), *1 The Politics of Informal Justice.* London, UK: Academic Press.

Adler, J., Hensler, D., and Nelson, C. (1983). *Simple Justice: How Litigants Fare in the Pittsburgh Arbitration Program.* Santa Monica, Calif.: RAND Corp.

Alfini, J. (1991). Trashing, bashing, and hashing it out: Is this the end of good mediation. *Florida State University Law Review* 19: 47.

Alinsky, S. (1971). *Rules for Radicals.* New York: Vintage Books.

Allman, J. (1998). *Evolving Brains.* New York: Scientific American Library.

American Bar Association (1999). *Annotated Model Rules of Professional Conduct* (4th ed.). Chicago: American Bar Association.

Appleman, J. and Appleman J. (1981). *8 Insurance Law and Practice.* New York: Clark Boardman.

Augsburger, D. (1988). *The Freedom of Forgiveness.* Chicago: Moody Press.

———. (1996). *Helping People Forgive.* Louisville, Ky.: Westminster John Knox Press.

Avruch, K. (1998). *Culture and Conflict Resolution.* Washington, D.C.: United States Institute of Peace Press.

Axelrod, R. (1997). *The Complexity of Cooperation: Agent-Based Models of Competition and Collaboration.* Princeton, N.J.: Princeton University Press.

———. (1984). *The Evolution of Cooperation.* New York, N.Y.: Basic Books.

Bader, R. (2000). ADR is fine, but not always welcome as alternative to battle in court. *Dispute Resolution Magazine* 6(3):21.

Bargh, J. (1997). The automaticity of everyday life. In R. Wyer, Jr. (Ed.), *The Automaticity of Everyday Life* (pp. 1-62). Mahwah, N.J.: Lawrence Erlbaum.

Bellah, R., Madsen, R., Sullivan, W., Swidler, A., and Tipton, S. (1996). *Habits of the Heart*. Berkeley: University of California Press.

Bennett-Goleman, T. (2001). *Emotional Alchemy*. New York: Harmony Books.

Berman, H. (1983). *Law and Revolution: The Formation of the Western Legal Tradition*. Cambridge, Mass.: Harvard University Press.

Bianchi, H. (1991). *Justice as Sanctuary*. Evansville, Ind.: Indiana University Press.

Bird, O. (1967). *The Idea of Justice*. New York: Praeger.

Blake, R. R., and Mouton, J. S. (1964). *The Managerial Grid*. Houston: Gulf.

Bozemand, D., and Kacmar, M. (1997). A cybernetic model of impression management processes in organizations. *Organizational Behavior and Human Decision Processes* 68:9-30.

Braithwaite, J (1989). *Crime, Shame, and Reintegration*. New York: Cambridge University Press.

Brekhus, W. (1999). "Lifestylers, Commuters, and Integrators: The Grammar and Microecology of Social Identity." Ph.D diss., Rutgers, N.J. UMI No. 9936171.

Buber, M. (1958). *I and Thou* (2nd. ed.). New York: Charles Scribners' Sons.

Buck, R., and Ginsburg, B. (1997). Communicative genes and the evolution of empathy. In W. Ickes (Ed.), *Empathic Accuracy* (pp. 17-43). New York: Guilford Press.

Burger, W. E. (1982). Remarks at the Arthur T. Vanderbilt Dinner, New York University. U.S. Supreme Court Public Information Office, Nov. 18, 1982.

Burkholder, J.R. (1988, August). *Mennonites in Ecumenical Dialogue on Peace and Justice*. Retrieved July 29, 2001, from the World Wide Web: http://www.mcc.org/respub/occasional/7.html

Burton, J. W. and Sandole, D (1986). Generic theory: The basis of conflict resolution. *Negotiation Journal, Oct. 1986,* 333-344.

Bush, R., and Folger, J. (1994). *The Promise of Mediation*. San Francisco: Jossey-Bass.

————. (1996). Transformative mediation and third-party intervention: Ten hallmarks of a transformative approach to practice. *Mediation Quarterly* 13:263.

Canary, D., and Spitzberg, B. (1989). A model of the perceived competence of mediators. *Human Communication Research* 15:630-649.

Carnevale, P. (1986). Strategic choice in mediation. *Negotiation Journal* 2:41.

Cary, J. (1996). Rambo depositions: Controlling an ethical cancer in civil litigation. *Hofstra Law Review* 25:561.

Claassen, R., Kader, P., Tilkes, C., and Noll, D. (2000). *Restorative Justice: A Framework for Fresno.* Retrieved March 20, 2001 from the World Wide Web: http://www.fresno.edu/dept/pacs/docs/rjrframe.doc

Coccarro, E., and Kavoussi, R. (1996). Neurotransmitter correlates of impulsive aggression. In D. Stoff and R. Cairns (Eds.), *Aggression and Violence: Genetic, Neurobiological, and Biosocial Perspectives* (pp. 67-86). Mahwah, N.J.: Lawrence Erlbaum.

Cohen, D. (1997). Ifs and thens in cultural psychology. In R. Wyer, Jr. (Ed.), *The Automaticity of Everyday life* (pp. 121-132). Mahwah, N.J.: Lawrence Erlbaum.

Cohen, J. (1999). Advising clients to apologize. *Southern California Law Review*72:1009, 1034.Collins, R. (1994). *Four sociological traditions.* New York: Oxford University Press.

Condlin, R. (1992). Bargaining in the dark: The normative incoherence of lawyer dispute bargaining roles. *Maryland Law Review* 1.

Conlon, D. E., Lind, A. E., and Lisak, L.(1989). Nonlinear and nonmonotonic effects of outcome on procedural and distributive fairness judgments. *Journal of Applied Social Psychology* 19:1085-99.

Coyle, M. (1998). Defending the weak and fighting unfairness: Can mediators respond to the challenge? *Osgoode Hall Law Journal* 36:625.

Croft, C. (1992). Reconceptualizing American legal professionalism: A proposal for deliberative moral community. *New York University Law Review* 67:1256.

d'Aquili, E., and Newberg, A. (1999). *The Mystical Mind: Probing the Biology of Religious Experience.* Minneapolis, Minn.: Fortress Press.

Damasio, A. (1999). *The feeling of what happens: Body and emotion in the making of consciousness.* New York: Harcourt Brace.

Delgado, R., Dunn, C., Brown, P., Lee, H., and Hubbert, D. (1985). Fairness and formality: Minimizing the risk of prejudice in alternative dispute resolution. *Wisconsin Law Review* 985:1359.

Deutsch, M. (1973). *The Resolution of Conflict: Constructive and Destructive Processes.* New Haven, Conn.: Yale University Press.

———. (1975). Equity, equality, and need: What determines which value will be used as the basis of distributive justice? *Journal of Social Issues* 31:137-149.

Duncan, H. (1960). *Communication and Social Order.* New York: Bedminster Press.

Esau, A. (1988). *Lawyers as Peacemakers.* Retrieved March 10, 2001 from the World Wide Web: http://www.umanitoba.ca/faculties/law/ Courses/esau/lr/lr_peace.html

Euwema, M., and van de Vliert, E. (1994). The influence of sex on managers' reactions in conflict with their subordinates. In A. Taylor and J. Bernstein Miller (Eds.), *Conflict and Gender* (pp. 119-140). Cresskill, N.J.: Hampton Press.

Farber, D., and Sherry, S. (1997). *Beyond All Reason: The Radical Assault on Truth in American Law.* New York: Oxford University Press.

Fisher, R., Ury, W., and Patton, W. (1981). *Getting to Yes: Negotiating Agreement Without Giving In* (2nd. ed.). New York: Penguin.

Fiss, O. (1984). Against settlement. *Yale Law Journal* 93:1073.

Folger, J., Poole, M., and Stutzman, R. (2000) *Working Through Conflict* (4th. ed.). New York: Addison Wesley Longman.

Friedman, E. (1985). *Generation to Generation: Family Process in Church and Synagogue.* New York: Guilford Press.

Galanter, M. (1974). Why the "haves" come out ahead: Speculations on the limits of legal change. *Law and Society Review* 9:95.

Gay, P. (1998). *Freud: A Man for Our Time.* New York: W. W. Norton and Co.

Gazzaniga, M. (1998). *The Mind's Past.* Berkeley: University of California Press.

Gillers, S. (1989). Popular legal culture: Taking L.A. Law more seriously. *Yale Law Journal* 98:1607.

Girard, R. (1977). *Violence and the Sacred.* Baltimore: Johns Hopkins University Press.

Glendon, M. (1994). *A Nation Under Lawyers.* Cambridge, Mass.: Harvard University Press.

Goffman, E. (1967). *Interaction Ritual.* New York: Anchor Press.

———. (1973). *The Presentation of Self in Everyday Life.* Woodstock, N.Y.: The Overlook Press.

Greenberg, J., and Mitchell, S. (1998). *Object Relations in Psychoanalytic Theory.* Cambridge, Mass.: Harvard University Press.

Hall, J. D. (1988). The theology of the cross and covenanting for world peace. *Baptist Peacemaker* 8(1), 6.

Hange, R. (1998, August). *Curtains of fire: Religious identity and emerging conflicts.* Retrieved July 29, 2001 from the World Wide Web: http://www.mcc.org/respub/occasional/24.html

Hanifi, M.A. (1988). *Survey of Muslim Institutions and Culture.* Delhi, India: Afif Book Depot.

Hart, H. (1958). Positivism and the separation of law and morals. *Harvard Law Review* 71:593.

Hegland, K. (1982). Why teach trial advocacy: An essay on never ask why. In E. Dvorkin, H. Lesnick, and J. Himmelstein (Eds.), *Becoming a Lawyer: A Humanistic Perspective on Legal Education and Professionalism.* Minneapolis, Minn.: West.

Heifetz, R. (1994). *Leadership Without Easy Answers.* Cambridge, Mass.: Harvard University Press.

Henricks, R. (1989). *Lao-Tzu Te Tao Ching.* New York: Ballentine Books.

Hobbes, T. (1651). *Leviathan; or the Matter, Forme and Power of a Common-Wealth Ecclesiasticall and Civill.* London. Publisher unknown.

Hodges, S., and Wegner, D. (1997). Automatic and controlled empathy. In W. Ickes (Ed.), *Empathic Accuracy* (pp. 311-340). New York: Guilford Press.

Hoffman, D., and Affolder, N. (2000). Mediation and UPL: Do mediators have a well-founded fear of prosecution?. *Dispute Resolution Magazine* 6:20.

Horowitz, M. J. (1998). *Cognitive Psychodynamics: From Conflict to Character.* New York: John Wiley and Sons.

— — —. (Ed.) (1991). *Person Schemas and Maladaptive Interpersonal Patterns.* Chicago: University of Chicago Press.

Hume, D. (1751). *An Enquiry Concerning the Principles of Morals.* London. Publisher unknown.

Hutchison, J. (1991). *Paths of Faith* (4th ed.). New York: McGraw Hill.

Ickes, W., Marangoni, C., and Garcia, S. (1997). Studying empathic accuracy in a clinically relevant context. In W. Ickes (Ed.), *Empathic Accuracy* (pp. 282-310). New York: Guilford Press.

Imperati, S. (1997). Mediator practice models: The intersection of ethics and stylistic practices in mediation. *Willamette Law Review* 33:703.

Johnson, D.W., and Johnson, R.T. (1989). *Cooperation and Competition: Theory and Research.* Edina, Minn.: Interaction.

Kanner, G. (1991). Welcome home, Rambo: High-minded ethics and low-down tactics in the courts. *Loyola of Los Angeles Law Review* 25:81.

Keashly, L. (1994). *Gender and Conflict: What Does Psychological Research Tell Us?* pp. 167-190). Cresskill, N.J.: Hampton Press.

Khuri, F. I. (1990). *Imams and Emirs: State, Religion, and Sections in Islam.* London: Saqi Books.

Kohn, A. (1992). *No Contest: The Case Against Competition.* New York: Houghton Mifflin.

Kovach, K., and Love, L. (1996). Evaluative mediation is an oxymoron. *Alternatives to High Cost of Litigation* 14:31.

Kovach, K., and Love, L. (1998). Mapping mediation: The risks of Riskin's grid. *Harvard Negotiation Law Review* 3:71.

Kraybill, D. B., and Hostetter, C. N. (2001). *Anabaptist World USA.* Scottdale, Pa.: Herald Press.

Kuhn, T. (1970). *The Structure of Scientific Revolutions.* Chicago: University of Chicago Press.

Lau, D. C. (1979). *Confucius: The Analects.* London, UK: Penguin.

Lederach, J (1995). *Preparing for Peace.* Syracuse, N.Y.: Syracuse University Press.

LeDoux, J. (1995). Emotion: Clues from the brain. *Annual Review of Psychology* 46:209.

———. (1996). *The Emotional Brain: The Mysterious Underpinnings of Emotional Life*. New York: Simon and Schuster.

LeFevre, P. (1966). *Understandings of Man*. Philadelphia: Westminster Press.

Lerner, M. (1986). *Surplus Powerlessness*. Oakland: Institute for Labor and Mental Health.

Levi, D. (1997). The role of apology in mediation. *New York University Law Review* 72:1165.

Levin, I., Schneider, S., and Gaeth, G. (1998). All frames are not created equal: A typology and critical analysis of framing effects. *Organizational Behavior and Human Decision Processes* 78:149-188.

Lind, M. (1980). *Yahweh Is a Warrior*. Scottdale, Pa.: Herald Press.

Lind, E. A., Lisak, R., and Conlon, D. (1983). Decision control and process control effects on procedural fairness judgments. *Journal of Applied Social Psychology* 4:338-350.

Linowitz, S. (1994). *The Betrayed Profession*. Baltimore: Johns Hopkins University Press.

Lorenz, K. (1966). *On Aggression*. New York: MJF Books.

Love, L. (1997). The top ten reasons why mediators should not help. *Florida State University Law Review* 24:937.

Lowery, R. (2000). To evaluate or not: That is not the question! *Family and Conciliation Courts Review* 38:48.

Luria, A. (1973). *The working brain: An introduction to neuropsychology*. New York: Penguin.

MacDonald, M.R. (1992). *Peace Tales: World Folktales to Talk About*. Hamden, Conn.: Linnet Books.

MacLean, P. (1989). *The Triune Brain in Evolution in Paleocerebral Functions*. New York: Plenum Press.

Maslow, A. (1987). *Motivation and Personality*. New York: Harper and Row.

Miller, D.T., and Ratner, R.K. (1996). The power of the myth of self-interest. In L. Montada and M.J. Lerner (Eds.), *Current Societal Concerns About Justice* (pp. 25-48). New York: Plenum Press.

Molm, L. (1997). *Coercive Power in Social Exchange*. New York: Cambridge University Press.

Montagu, A. (1973). *Man and Aggression*. New York: Oxford University Press.

Morrell, J. (1972). *First Blood*. New York: Harper and Row.

Nader, L. (1993). When is popular justice popular? In S. Merry and N. Milner (Eds.), *The Possibility of Popular Justice* (pp. 435-454). Ann Arbor, Mich.: University of Michigan Press.

Pillutla, M., and Morrighan, J. K. (1996). Unfairness, anger, and spite: Emotional rejections of ultimatum offers. *Organizational Behavior and Human Decision Processes* 68:208-224.

Poundstone, W. (1992). *Prisoner's Dilemma*. New York: Doubleday.

Pruitt, D. G., Peirce, R. S., McGillicuddy, N. B., Welton, G. L., and Castriano, L. M. (1993). Long-term success in mediation. *Law and Human Behavior* 17:313-330.

Rackham, H. (Ed.) (1934). *Aristotle, the Nicomachean Ethics*. London: W. Heineman.

Rasmussen, E. (1994). *Games and Information* (2nd. ed.). Madden, Mass.: Blackwell.

Raven, B. (1992). A power/interaction model of interpersonal influence: French and Raven thirty years later. *Journal of Social Behavior and Personality* 7:217-244.

Retzinger, S., and Scheff, T. (1996). Strategy for community conferences: Emotions and social bonds. In B. Gallaway and J. Hudson (Eds.), *Restorative Justice: International Perspectives* (p. 315). Monsey, N.J.: Criminal Justice Press.

Riskin, L. (1994). Mediator orientations, strategies, and techniques. *Alternatives to High Cost of Litigation, 12,* 111.

————. (1996). Understanding mediators' orientations, strategies, and techniques: A grid for the perplexed. *Harvard Negotiation Law Review* 1:7.

Rogers, C.R. (1980). *A Way of Being*. New York: Houghton Mifflin.

Rogers, N., and McEwen, C. (1994). *Mediation Law, Policy, and Practice* (2nd. ed.). Deerfield, Ill.: Clark, Boardman Callahan.

Rosenau, P (1992). *Postmodernism and the Social Sciences: Insights, Inroads, and Intrusions*. Princeton, N.J.: Princeton University Press.

Ross, M. H. (1993). *The Management of Conflict: Interpretations and Interests in Comparative Perspective*. New Haven, Conn.: Yale University Press.

Roth, A. (1993). On the early history of experimental economics. *Journal of the History of Economic Thought* 15:184-209.

Rubin J., and Brown, B. (1975). *The Social Psychology of Bargaining and Negotiation*. San Diego: Academic Press.

Rubin, J., Pruitt, D., and Kim, S. (1994). *Social Conflict: Escalation, Stalemate, and Settlement* (2nd. ed.). New York: McGraw-Hill.

Rummel, R. (1991). *The Conflict Helix: Principles and Practices of Interpersonal, Social and International Conflict and Cooperation*. New Brunswick, N.J.: Transaction Publishers.

Silbey, S., and Merry, S. (1986). Mediator settlement strategies. *Law and Policy Journal* 8:7.

Skinner, B. F. (1974). *About Behaviorism*. New York: Random House.

Smart, N. (1984). *The Religious Experience of Mankind* (3rd ed.). New York: Charles Scribners' Sons.

Spillman, K., and Spillman, K. (1991). On enemy images and conflict escalation. *International Society of Social Scientists Journal* 27:57.

Stark, J. (1997). The ethics of mediation evaluation: Some troublesome questions and tentative proposals from an evaluative lawyer mediator. *South Texas Law Review* 38:769.

Stevenson, L., and Haberman, D. (1998). *Ten Theories of Human Nature.* New York: Oxford University Press.

Straub, P., and Morrighan, J. K. (1995). An experimental investigation of ultimatums, complete information, fairness, expectations and lowest acceptable offers. *Journal of Economic Behavior and Organization* 27:345-354.

Sullivan, H. (1964). *The Fusion of Psychiatry and Social Science.* New York: Norton.

———. (1972). *Personal Psychopathology.* New York: Norton.

Tavris, C (1989). *Anger—The Misunderstood Emotion.* New York: Simon and Schuster.

Taylor, A., and Bernstein Miller, J. (1994). Introduction: The necessity of seeing gender in conflict. In A. Taylor and J. Bernstein Miller (Eds.), *Conflict and Gender* (pp. 1-15). Cresskill, N.J.: Hampton Press.

Thibaut, J., and Walker, L. (1975). *Procedural Justice.* Hillsdale, N.J.: Erlbaum.

Troeltsch, E. (1931). *The Social Teaching of the Christian Churches.* New York: Harper and Row.

Tyler, T. (1987). Conditions leading to value expressive effects in judgments of procedural justice. *Political Behavior* 4:379.

Tyler, T., and Blader, S. (2000). *Cooperation in Groups: Procedural Justice, Social Identity, and Behavioral Engagement.* Philadelphia: Psychology Press.

Tyler, T., and Lind, A. E. (1992). A relational model of authority in groups. In M. Zanna (Ed.), *Advances in Experimental Social Psychology* (25th. ed., pp. 1151-1191). New York: Academic Press.

Umbreit, M. (1994). *Victim Meets Offender.* Monsey, N.Y.: Willow Tree Press.

Ury, W. L., Brett, J. M., and Goldberg, S. B. (1988). *Getting Disputes Resolved.* San Francisco: Jossey-Bass.

Van de Vliert, E. (2000). *Complex Interpersonal Conflict Behavior: Theoretical Frontiers.* East Sussex, UK: Psychology Press.

Van Ness, D. W. (1986). *Crime and Its Victims.* Downers Grove, Ill.: InterVarsity Press.

Van Ness, D., and Strong, K. (1997). *Restoring Justice.* Cincinnati: Anderson Publishing.

Wagatsuma, H., and Rosett, A. (1986). The implications of apology: Law and culture in Japan and the United States. *Law and Society Review* 20:461.

Wilmot, W., and Hocker, J. (2001). *Interpersonal Conflict* (6th ed.). Boston: McGraw Hill.

Wink, S., and Wink, W. (1993). Domination, justice, and the cult of violence. *St. Louis Law Journal* 38:341.

Wink, W. (1993). *Engaging the Powers*. Minneapolis, Minn.: Fortress Press.

Winslade, J., and Monk, G. (2000). *Narrative Mediation: A New Approach to Conflict Resolution*. San Francisco: Jossey-Bass.

Zehr, H. (1990). *Changing Lenses*. Scottdale, Pa.: Herald Press.

———. (2000). The psychological foundation for identity rests on order, autonomy, and relatedness. Paper presented at an international conference on "Just Peace? Peacemaking and peacebuilding in the new millenium," Albany, N.Y., Massey Univ.

The Author

*D*OUGLAS NOLL, BORN IN PASADENA, California, now lives outside of Clovis, California. He was admitted to practice law in California in December 1977. As a litigator, he has tried dozens of jury and bench cases across the country before state, federal, and administrative tribunals. He is admitted to practice in numerous federal courts across the country, including the United States Supreme Court. He is listed in the Registry of Preeminent Lawyers.

Noll now limits his practice to mediation, peacemaking, and conflict management. He has mediated hundreds of complex litigated and non-litigated conflicts to resolution. He has been on the panel of arbitrators and mediators with the American Arbitration Association since 1981. He is a judge pro tem for the Fresno County Superior Court, serving as a settlement conference judge and an Early Neutral Evaluator for the U.S. District Court, Eastern District of California. Noll's community peacemaking includes victim-offender reconciliation and development of Neighborhood Restorative Justice Centers. He is a co-author of the Framework for Restorative Justice, a frequent mediation trainer, and a continuing legal and professional education panelist.

As adjunct professor of law at San Joaquin College of Law, Noll teaches remedies, critical thinking, peacemaking and the law. As adjunct professor of Forensic Psychology at Alliant University/California School of Professional Psychology, he teaches forensic mediation and conflict theory to doctoral students. Noll is a second degree black belt and tai chi instructor, a Level III PSIA certified ski instructor, a whitewater river guide, an accomplished fly fisher, and an instrument-rated airplane and helicopter pilot. In his spare time, he plays Irish and traditional American fiddle.

He is married to Jan, and together with their golden retriever and a large cat, live on their central California Sierra foothill ranch.